C++ *Programming* *for Windows*

About the Enclosed Software

Disk Contents: The disk included with this book contains all of the example programs from the book, so you will not need to type any code. Also included on this disk is a C++ Class Library and an on-line Windows help file.

System Requirements: IBM PC or PC clone or a workstation with one of the following compilers installed: Borland C++ Compiler, Microsoft C++ Compiler, Zortech C++ Compiler, or another C++ compiler. A minimum of 4MB of memory is recommended in order to support the compiler and load the example programs from the disk. See the manual for your compiler for any other hardware or software requirements. When installed, the programs contained on the C++ Programming For Windows disk will take up exactly 3,674,883 bytes.

WARNING: BEFORE OPENING THE DISK PACKAGE OPPOSITE, CAREFULLY READ THE TERMS AND CONDITIONS OF THE DISK WARRANTY FOUND ON THE BACK OF THIS PAGE.

Disk Warranty

This software is protected by both United States copyright law and international copyright treaty provision. You must treat this software just like a book, except that you may copy it into a computer to be used and you may make archival copies of the software for the sole purpose of backing up our software and protecting your investment from loss.

By saying, "just like a book," Osborne/McGraw-Hill means, for example, that this software may be used by any number of people and may be freely moved from one computer location to another, so long as there is no possibility of its being used at one location or on one computer while it is being used at another. Just as a book cannot be read by two different people in two different places at the same time, neither can the software be used by two different people in two different places at the same time (unless, of course, Osborne's copyright is being violated).

Limited Warranty

Osborne/McGraw-Hill warrants the physical diskette(s) enclosed herein to be free of defects in materials and workmanship for a period of sixty days from the purchase date. If Osborne McGraw-Hill receives written notification within the warranty period of defects in materials or workmanship, and such notification is determined by Osborne McGraw-Hill to be correct, Osborne McGraw-Hill will replace the defective diskette(s).

The entire and exclusive liability and remedy for breach of this Limited Warranty shall be limited to replacement of defective diskettes(s) and shall not include or extend to any claim for or right to cover any other damages, including but not limited to, loss of profit, data, or use of the software, or special, incidental, or consequential damages or other similar claims, even if Osborne McGraw-Hill has been specifically advised of the possibility of such damages. In no event will Osborne McGraw-Hill's liability for any damages to you or any other person ever exceed the lower of the suggested list price or actual price paid for the license to use the software, regardless of any form of the claim.

OSBORNE, A DIVISION OF McGRAW-HILL, INC., SPECIFICALLY DISCLAIMS ALL OTHER WARRANTIES, EXPRESS OR IMPLIED, INCLUDING BUT NOT LIMITED TO, ANY IMPLIED WARRANTY OF MERCHANTABILITY OR FITNESS FOR A PARTICULAR PURPOSE. Specifically, Osborne McGraw-Hill makes no representation or warranty that the software is fit for any particular purpose, and any implied warranty of merchantability is limited to the sixty-day duration of the Limited Warranty covering the physical diskette(s) only (and not the software) and is otherwise expressly and specifically disclaimed.

This limited warranty gives you specific legal rights; you may have others which may vary from state to state. Some states do not allow the exclusion of incidental or consequential damages, or the limitation on how long an implied warranty lasts, so some of the above may not apply to you.

Anthony Porter

C++ Programming
for Windows

Osborne **McGraw-Hill**

Berkeley New York St. Louis San Francisco
Auckland Bogotá Hamburg London Madrid
Mexico City Milan Montreal New Delhi Panama City
Paris São Paulo Singapore Sydney
Tokyo Toronto

Osborne **McGraw-Hill**
2600 Tenth Street
Berkeley, California 94710 U.S.A.

For information on translations and book distributors outside of the U.S.A., please write to Osborne **McGraw-Hill** at the above address.

C++ Programming for Windows

  234567890 DOC 99876543

ISBN 0-07-881881-8

Publisher	**Copy Editor**
Kenna S. Wood	Kimberly Torgerson
Acquisitions Editor	**Proofreader**
William Pollock	Colleen Paretty
Associate Editor	**Indexers**
Vicki Van Ausdall	Phil Roberts
	Peggy Bieber-Roberts
Project Editor	**Computer Designer**
Nancy McLaughlin	John Erick Christgau
Technical Editor	**Illustrator**
Werner Feibel	Lance Ravella
Developmental Editor	**Cover Design**
Scott Spanbauer	Studio Silicon

Contents

Acknowledgments

Many people contributed to this book, but there are several among them to whom I am especially grateful. Scott Spanbauer and Werner Feibel did a thorough job of reviewing the book and making me see it through the reader's eyes.

At Osborne/McGraw-Hill, Bill Pollock, Vicki Van Ausdall and Nancy McLaughlin showed extraordinary patience as I grappled with the technicalities of book publishing.

I have found CompuServe to be an invaluable resource of knowledge, and I am grateful to the staff at Microsoft and at Borland who contribute to the CompuServe forums.

Finally, if it were not for the support and encouragement of my wife Myriam, I would never have finished this book.

My sincere thanks to you all.

CHAPTER

Introduction to Windows Programming in C++

*T*his book is a practical guide to developing Microsoft Windows applications in C++. It will show you, step-by-step, how and when C++ and object-oriented programming (OOP) techniques can be applied to Windows programming, and what the advantages might be. OOP is about reusable code, so the code in *C++ Programming for Windows* and on the accompanying disk will serve as a basis for your own applications. If you are new to Windows programming, you can concentrate on reusing this code in an object-oriented way. You will find that OOP comes naturally, even if you do not have much experience with C++ or Windows. If you already have some experience, you can concentrate on the implementation details.

Why OOP?

In one popular view, OOP offers deliverance from all the gremlins that haunt traditional software development. No need to hire armies of expensive programmers. No more budget overruns. No more bug-ridden systems. Just get some cheap labor in to bolt together a few standard objects.

Of course, I suspect that anyone reading this book will realize that OOP may not be the panacea that its proponents claim it to be. I am, however, surprised to find that there are people who tend to dismiss OOP as another trendy methodology, proposed by theorists who do not have to worry about getting the job done.

We would all like software development to be easier and more reliable. Programmers get tired of reinventing the same things and debugging the same bugs. Managers get tired of always straining their budgets to pay for the overrun. Marketing people get tired of saying, *the program will be ready soon.*

Programmers have tried structured design techniques and computer-aided software engineering (CASE). Although these approaches worked for some of us, they did not help most of us. The disciplines involved in these techniques often seemed ill-suited to the complex problems they were intended to solve.

OOP is a structured design technique, but it also offers the possibility of reusing components. In the past, only low-level routines could be packaged in a library and reused in other applications. Higher-level routines, such as application modules, usually had to be re-engineered to fit another application, or *hacked,* as the programmers involved would say. A routine or function library either does what you want it to, or it does not. You might be able to rewrite the routine or function library to do what you want, as shown in Figure 1-1, but then you can no longer use it for its original purpose.

If programmers apply OOP properly, they can to a certain extent build applications from available components. These components are usually bundled into object libraries, or *class libraries* in C++ terminology. A program can modify the behavior of an OOP object without having to change the original source, as shown in Figure 1-2. Programmers using a class library can finish the application more quickly. Because less re-engineering is involved, the application should be more reliable. Applied to software engineering, the saying "If it ain't broke, don't fix it" means that if a function or module operates correctly and is robust, do not try to change it. That is sound advice until the clients want additions or the competitors have something better. With OOP, you can add new functionality without compromising the solidity of the original object.

FIGURE 1-1   Enhancing a traditional module

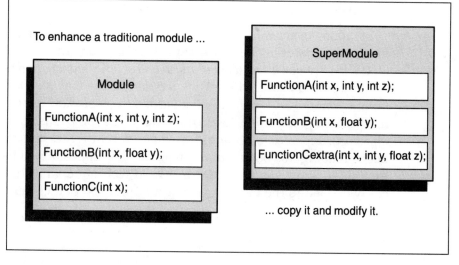

Enhancing an object

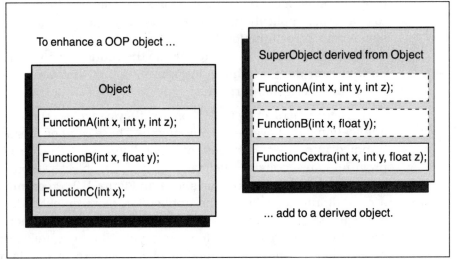

Any technique that saves development time and increases product reliability has to be an interesting technique for managers and accountants. But OOP, apparently in contrast to previous methodologies, is also an interesting technique for programmers. Once OOP relieves programmers of the burden of re-engineering and endless bug fixing, they feel that their work becomes more creative.

In talking to software professionals about OOP, I have found that they invariably answer in one of two ways. They say something along the lines of, *Oh yes, we use it and it saves us no end of time, money, and headaches.* Or they say something like, *Well, we don't have time for that right now because our project is behind schedule and the customers are complaining, and anyway, we have heard that there are problems with memory, efficiency, and understanding it.* Anyone who entirely dismisses OOP will not be reading this book, but if you are at all skeptical about its benefits, I intend to show you that OOP is a valid technique, and that it can be easily applied to the industrial projects that most of us contend with.

OOP for Windows

Windows is an ideal environment in which to apply OOP techniques. The naked Windows development environment easily rivals the complexity of mainframe operating systems of a few years back. Competent C programmers usually need 6 to 12 months to become fully productive. Of course, this is a long time to the companies that pay their salaries, especially if they have no guarantee that the programmers will stay at the end of that period.

Several libraries of C++ classes are available for Windows. Each library class wraps up a complex area of Windows programming and neatly presents the programmer with something much simpler. This book describes one such library and its implementation.

If a simple class library is available, Windows neophytes can become competent in a much shorter time. You only need to learn how to snap classes together—this book shows you how. You can leave the inner workings until later. An experienced Windows programmer will be productive after a rainy afternoon spent with this book. However, if you are planning for other people, allow around two or three months for a Windows neophyte to become productive, using the classes described here. This saves around six months.

Of course, any class library serves general programming purposes. Deriving other classes for specific uses requires more experience with Windows.

The point is that although a company will still need to employ one or more Windows experts, with OOP it is no longer necessary that all the programmers become gurus before they can do anything useful.

About This Book

I have aimed this book at programmers who are interested in both Windows and C++, and who have some experience using C or C++. If you are involved with another graphical user interface, such as the OS/2 Presentation Manager, then of course you will not be able to use the code directly; however, you might find some inspiration for designing your own classes.

If you are new to Windows programming, you might prefer to concentrate on the sections of the book that explain how to use the classes presented. You can use the classes as building blocks and impress your friends with button bars, post-modernist dialog boxes, and the rest. After you have more programming experience, you can go back and study how the classes work.

If you have some experience programming Windows in C, you might be interested in the implementation details. You may gain a better understanding of how Windows works, and you will be better equipped to implement your own classes.

This first chapter provides useful information to lead you through the rest of the book.

Chapter 2 explains the basic concepts of C++ programming and the Windows application programming interface (API). It will be easier to understand if you already have a basic knowledge of one or the other.

If you know both Windows and C++, skip Chapter 2. Go straight to Chapter 3, which covers design issues and presents an implementation for a C++ **Window** class.

Chapter 4 reviews the standard Windows controls—buttons, list boxes, scroll bars, and so on—that are the elements you will use to construct an application.

Chapter 5 expands on Chapter 4 and examines owner-draw controls that allow an application programmer to modify the appearance of the standard control. Push-buttons with icons on them represent a common type of owner-draw control. This chapter shows how an owner-draw control class can encapsulate all the functionality of these controls so that they can be used and reused as any other control. C Windows programmers will know how awkward it is to reuse individual owner-draw controls.

Chapter 6 covers dialog boxes and shows how C++ inheritance lets you create more specialized subclasses of dialog boxes.

The remaining chapters implement some of the more common Windows features. Chapter 7 reviews Windows memory management. Chapter 8 covers file input/output (I/O). Chapter 9 covers the clipboard, shows how to cope with different clipboard formats, and explains how to implement a clipboard viewer.

Chapter 10 explains the Multiple Document Interface (MDI). C++ greatly simplifies MDI applications because it provides a solution to the problem of needing separate copies of the data for each document window. This chapter also introduces other useful classes, including a timer class and a button bar class.

Chapter 11 describes Dynamic Data Exchange (DDE). It covers the DDE classes as well as the problem of maintaining and supporting DDE links within an application. The chapter features several examples of DDE, including an installation program that uses DDE commands to install application icons in a Program Manager group.

Finally, Appendix A explains how to install the supplemental diskette provided with this book, and how to get started compiling and linking the example programs.

About the Class Library

Several OOP environments and class libraries are already available for Windows. Some insulate the programmer from the Windows API almost entirely. This insulation has three advantages:

☐   The programmer does not need not to learn the API complexities. The API comprises hundreds of functions, messages, and structures, and the documentation runs to several thousand pages.

☐   The system may be portable to other environments, such as UNIX X-Windows or the Apple Macintosh.

☐   The environment may be more elegant than one that allows the rough edges of the Windows API to show through. Many environments are based on the Smalltalk model, where everything is an object. Of course, a Windows version of Smalltalk itself is available.

An OOP environment that insulates the user from the Windows API also creates some disadvantages:

❑   It is difficult to take advantage of all the facilities offered by the API, which makes it difficult to set an application apart from others.

❑   If the insulating layer is too thick, it may absorb some performance.

If the environment tries to be multiplatform, certain facilities will be omitted because a particular platform does not support them. For example, the environment may not support certain Windows features, such as Dynamic Data Exchange or Object Linking and Embedding, because they are not available under X-Windows. At the same time, the environment cannot support threads or lightweight processes, because they are not available under DOS versions of Windows. (They are available in Windows NT.) It may also be difficult to add or derive Windows-specific objects that are missing from the original library. The class library presented in this book is closer to the Windows API. The advantages and disadvantages are inverted. The objects are quite efficient in terms of memory and processing power; they are easily extendable to other Windows facilities that may be introduced in future; and they are easy to integrate with existing Windows C code. They are not, on the other hand, directly portable to other environments.

In this book, rather than packing all of the Windows elements into classes, I have concentrated on the areas that might bring the greatest increase in productivity.

Software Requirements

The code in this book and on the disk is not specific to any particular compiler or environment. You will need a C++ compiler that supports Windows, and the files and tools needed for Windows programming:

❑   Microsoft Windows version 3.0 or higher

❑   The WINDOWS.H header file

❑   A Windows-specific run-time library

❑   A Windows-compatible linker

- ☐ A resource compiler for adding Windows resources to the executable file

- ☐ A dialog box editor that lets you lay out dialog boxes interactively

- ☐ A utility for painting icons, bitmaps, and cursors

- ☐ A Windows debugger

Even if your program has no bugs, you should use a debugger to step through any new classes that you write. Then you can be sure that they are doing what you think they ought to be doing. You also can use the debugger to trigger error conditions that would normally not arise.

In the past, Windows debuggers, such as CodeView, required a second monitor. The debugger would send all its output to the second monitor while Windows and the application were visible on the primary monitor. Most debuggers, including CodeView, now run on the primary monitor, either by residing and operating in windows of their own or by switching the primary monitor mode between text and graphics.

You can still use a second monitor if you want to see the application and the debug data at the same time, but you should remember that if you have a 16-bit graphics adapter for your primary display, and you install an inexpensive 8-bit card and monitor for debugging, your primary card will be forced to operate in 8-bit mode, even when you are not debugging.

All these tools (except the second monitor) are usually supplied with the C++ compiler. If not, a Windows Software Development Kit (SDK), containing everything you need except the compiler, is available from Microsoft.

Compiling and linking uses the CPU intensively, so for development, treat yourself to a fast processor. A general Windows workstation should be homogeneous; it is not a good idea to couple a fast processor with a mediocre graphics subsystem. If you are a developer, however, this rule does not apply, and you can consider replacing the motherboard of a mediocre system with a faster one. Buy the second fastest processor on the market; the fastest one will be overpriced.

Compiler Independence

Certain compiler publishers now supply a set of base classes for Windows. You can use these base classes if you wish, but if the source is not available, or is computer-dependent, you will be committing yourself to the corresponding compiler, and you might regret this later. Since compiler developers generally try to leapfrog each other, you may wish to change to another compiler in the future. You might have to switch to another compiler for technical or political reasons. Perhaps you have a library that only supports a certain compiler, or perhaps a client or customer insists on using a certain compiler. You may find that a one compiler is quick and easy to use when you are developing a system, but that another compiler generates smaller and faster executable code. If you develop for Windows NT, you might use different compilers on different hardware platforms.

If you use more than one compiler, you may find that one or another compiler does not support certain features of C++, and so you may need to adapt your source accordingly. Usually these adaptions are relatively trivial, and it is quite feasible to have a compiler-independent source library.

The classes described in this book have been tested with the Borland, Microsoft, and Zortech C++ compilers, including the Borland Turbo C++ for Windows compiler. They should work with any other compiler that claims to support C++ for both the ANSI 2.1 standard and Windows.

Choosing a Class Library

I am not advocating my library as the best choice, since your choice should depend on your own requirements. I hope that, after reading this book, you will have a better understanding of how C++ classes can work in the Windows environment, and that you will be in a better position to make an informed decision.

If you choose to use a commercial C++ class library for Windows, such as the Microsoft Foundation Classes or Borland ObjectWindows, this book should give you plenty of ideas for developing additional classes of your own.

Object-oriented programming offers many advantages without forcing you to sacrifice the performance and flexibility of purely procedural programming. If you are not already sure of the many benefits offered by OOP, this book should convince you.

CHAPTER

Basic Concepts

*T*his chapter provides an overview of the three basic concepts used in this book:

☐   Object-oriented design

☐   C++ programming

☐   The Windows programming environment

If you are very familiar with one or more of these concepts, take a quick look at the C++ for Windows section in this chapter, which introduces how these concepts can be combined to create object-oriented C++ programming for Windows.

If you are unsure about any of the concepts listed above, this chapter should give you enough information to be able to grasp what the rest of the book is about. Other books cover these concepts individually in greater depth. To fill in any gaps in your knowledge, you may wish to consult *Windows 3.1 Programming* (by William H. Murray III and Chris H. Pappas, 1992) or *C++: The Complete Reference* (by Herbert Schildt, 1991), both published by Osborne/McGraw-Hill.

The C++ for C Programmers section in this chapter assumes that you already know C and concentrates on the additional features of C++. If you do not know C but you are familiar with another high-level language, such as Pascal, you should be able to follow along.

If you are unfamiliar with the Windows programming environment, you will find this book very useful—even if you do not understand some of the implementation details on your first reading. Try using the classes as presented to get started. As you gain more experience, you can derive new subclasses or design classes for your own ideas.

Object-Oriented Design

Object-oriented design (OOD) and object-oriented programming (OOP) are not new concepts. For example, in the mid-seventies, the SIMULA67 language provided classes very similar to those of C++. In fact, SIMULA67 was one source of inspiration for C++. Designing a system and programming it in SIMULA67 was far simpler than trying to do the same thing with FORTRAN, the major scientific language at that time. The source code was much smaller and far more elegant than with FORTRAN. Even so, there are several reasons why object-oriented techniques have been adopted slowly

First, many applications were not complex enough. There were numerical applications written in FORTRAN for solving mathematical models, especially those requiring many iterations. There were data-processing applications written in COBOL. Although these applications processed a lot of data, usually in a batch run lasting several hours, the underlying application was quite simple. Real-time applications were usually written in assembly language and had to be kept simple so that the system had time to process an event before the next one occurred.

For these early systems, the overriding concern was that the algorithms used be as efficient as possible. At the time, people did not think it worthwhile to spend very much on research into object-oriented techniques. As time went on, the basic algorithms developed in the early days became well understood, and people began to embark on more ambitious projects. The algorithms were bundled and sold as packages: database products for the commercial world, function libraries for scientists, and operating systems or kernels used in real-time applications. Having standard function libraries or subsystems was a breakthrough that greatly simplified application development. A designer could build an application from available packages instead of starting from scratch. Over time, these new ways of working have evolved into the methodologies recognized today, such as functional decomposition and data flow analysis.

These methodologies were once quite valid, and most people using them thought that although object-oriented techniques were interesting, the tools they had were good enough. However, the older methods are applied to the very complex systems being designed today, they begin to show their shortcomings and cause people to take a closer look at object-oriented techniques.

Another obstacle to the object-oriented approach was the lack of an efficient OOP language. The programming languages that were available, such as SIMULA67, were not very efficient. Although they were fine for simulations, they were not acceptable for most mainstream applications and systems. Although C++ has been around since the early eighties in the form of a preprocessor to C compilers, only in the last two or three years have integrated optimizing compilers appeared that can produce object code as efficient as that produced by "plain vanilla" C compilers. The Borland C++ and object-oriented Pascal compilers have done much to popularize OOP in the PC world, and now Microsoft has made C++ "official" with the Version 7.0 C/C++ compiler. In the UNIX world, the public domain GNU C++ compiler is converting many programmers from C. (Many UNIX programmers do not see why they have to buy anything other than UNIX itself.)

There is nothing to stop anyone from analyzing and designing a system in an object-oriented fashion, and then coding it in C or COBOL, but people do not generally work that way. New methodologies are usually applied first to programming, then to design, and finally to analysis. People like to start with something small and later move on to larger and more complex systems. Very small programs do not need much design, and larger, but well-understood systems may need design but not analysis. Traditional analysis is concerned with complex systems that have not been automated before. Typically, these are "paper-pushing" systems of the sort encountered in large organizations.

Finally, many people in the software industries are concerned about the high cost and high failure rate in software development. Many systems, when completed, prove difficult and costly to maintain. As every user knows, computer software is often unreliable. New concepts, such as a graphical user interface (GUI), increase the complexity of the system still further.

These people see object orientation as a way to provide standard, reliable components that can be reused in different systems, instead of having to start each new system design with a clean sheet of paper.

After maturing for more than 20 years, object orientation has come of age. Contemporary applications are complex enough to need it, and efficient tools are available to support it. Before examining object orientation, let's review several other methodologies in common use.

Functional decomposition and data flow analysis are the two major methodologies that have been in use since the seventies and throughout the eighties. You can be proud if you have used these proven techniques. Nevertheless, they are starting to show their limits.

Functional Decomposition

Functional decomposition is the successive division of a complex system into more simple and easily managed components, as shown in Figure 2-1. Its value comes from a principle of divide and conquer. In functional decomposition, a system is defined in terms of the high-level functions it performs. Each high-level function can, in turn, be defined in terms of lower-level functions and so on, until the functions reach the level of the functions supplied with the operating system or the database package. This principle has been applied to the code in this book. Whenever a function is relatively complex, it has been divided into several subroutines.

FIGURE 2-1 Functional decomposition

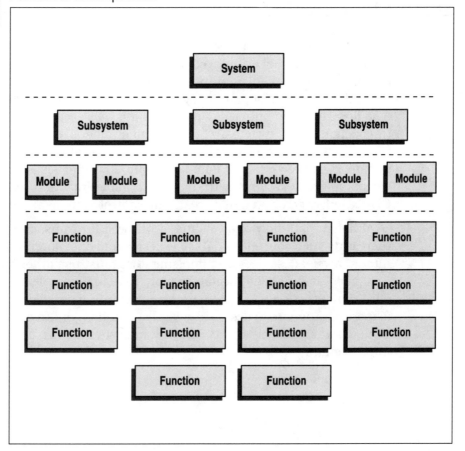

Complex systems do not always lend themselves to simple functional decomposition. The designer finds that the system can be decomposed in several ways. If the designer makes the wrong choice, a small unforeseen change to the system leads to changes in the high-level functions. These changes may, in turn, require other changes throughout the system.

Furthermore, users or clients—the people who want the system and specify it—may have trouble understanding functional decomposition. They are often used to thinking in terms of stocks and ledgers, or aircraft and tickets, but not in terms of system functions, such as inputs and updates. This cultural difference between the two groups is often a cause of misunderstanding and argument.

Data Flow Analysis

Data flow analysis considers how data moves through the system. For example, an external event becomes a piece of data. It is processed and then passed on, stored, or output. Traditionally, data flow analysts draw the system in terms of processing "bubbles," with arrows indicating the data flows between bubbles. This type of analysis seems better suited to transaction-based systems, where a small number of events gives rise to several different processes or transactions. Typically, the transactions update or add records in a database. Data flow analysis is rather weak when applied to systems with many external events, and that includes GUI-based systems as well as real-time control systems.

Although data flow analysis may work well for transaction systems, there is no such concept as data flow design and data flow programming. After analysis, designers and implementors must use other methodologies, such as functional decomposition, to actually implement the system. That in itself need not be a problem, since functional decomposition is more appropriate to design and implementation, but frequently a lack of understanding exists between the analysts and the designers and implementors.

Object Orientation

The object-oriented methodology models a system in terms of object abstractions. A system object is an abstraction because although it may not have all the attributes of the real-world object, it has all the attributes that the system needs. A system **Aircraft** object may have a flight plan, passengers, and servicing requirements, but it will probably not have control surfaces or a paint scheme, if these do not interest the system.

An object-oriented analysis and design is often easier to do than those based on traditional methodologies, such as functional decomposition and data flow analysis. It is also easier for the project team and the user to understand. Users have the opportunity to get involved up front and can spot where analysts may have misunderstood requirements.

Note   For users, object orientation means that analysis and design specifications are "what you see is what you get" (WYSIWYG). Specifications produced by older methods often turn out to be "You asked for it, you got it" (YAFIYGI), meaning that any misinterpretation of the user's requests can result in faulty program design.

The other major advantage of object orientation is the smooth progression from analysis through design to implementation, since the same methodology is used throughout the project. Many PC systems are completely developed by one or two individuals who are responsible from the entire project, from analysis to final testing. If you work that way, you still need a methodology. Without one, you can lose control of the project. Since the object-oriented approach is applicable to all project stages, it is ideal for one-person operations as well as big project teams.

Objects

Opinions arise about what an object is in terms of object orientation. To add to the confusion, object-oriented has become a marketing phrase, like Relational, Lite, and Green. As such, it is often applied to products that are not properly object-oriented.

In spite of all the discussions, there is general agreement about the basic properties of an object:

❑   An object is an abstraction of something in the system.

❑   An object has certain attributes and provides certain services.

❑   An object can occur any number of times in the system.

❑   An object can be classified, and a number of classes can all belong to a superclass (for example the **Cat**, **Dog**, and **Human** objects might belong to a **Mammal** superclass).

❑   An object may inherit attributes and services from its parents in the classification structure.

The attributes and services are exclusive to the object. Although another object may provide another service with the same name, the two services are different.

Before an object can be used, there must be an instance of it. Different instances of an object may have different values for their attributes.

Systems designed along traditional structured lines are likely to consist of several modules containing functions. Is it an object-oriented design if a system's modules correspond to real-world objects? Not exactly. A traditional module is not a true object because it cannot be designated as an instance—an occurrence of an object with its own characteristics—or classified. However, a module is a step in the right direction, because it encapsulates its data.

Much of the power of object orientation comes from classification and inheritance. When a specific object is derived from a more generic object, the new object inherits all the attributes and services of the parent, and only needs to provide the attributes and services specific to that object. For example, if a generic **Aircraft** object provides a number of services for flight-planning and air traffic control, then a specific object derived from **Aircraft**, such as **Boeing_747**, only provides specific attributes, such as range and bad weather capabilities.

General-purpose objects have a good chance of being reused. With modules, a programmer might say, *I'll take this module and change it to make it do what I want.* With objects, the programmer says, *I'll derive an object that will add the services I need.* The two approaches might appear to involve the same amount of work. The difference is that if the original module must be changed because of a bug or a modification, the traditional programmer must copy the changes to all the other modules that are based on it. If a generic object is modified, derived objects generally do not require modification—they inherit the benefits of the modification.

Objects can be reused and, as time goes on, they can be improved to increase reliability or efficiency. These improvements benefit systems that already use the objects, derived objects, and new systems. Object orientation also simplifies the task of designing system families.

C++ *for C Programmers*

For C programmers, the primary advantage of C++ over other object-oriented environments is that it is based on C. Many C++ detractors consider this its major disadvantage; however, C is probably the language most widely used by professional programmers, after COBOL. If you know C, you will not have much trouble mastering the extra facilities that C++ provides, but you might be unsure as to how to apply them correctly. You can treat C++ as C with a funny syntax, but that will not take advantage of the full power of the language.

Apart from some extra operators and a few details, two major differences between C and C++ exist in type checking and classes.

Although C++ is stricter than C, if you can compile your C code with a recent compiler without warnings, you will probably be able to compile it directly with a C++ compiler.

Type Checking

C has type checking, but it is weak. It prevents you from assigning a floating value to an address pointer directly, but there are many ways to do it indirectly. ANSI C allows function prototypes, a facility borrowed from C++ that allows you to define a function and its parameters before you use it. ANSI C, however, does not require function prototypes. Pre-ANSI versions of C did not support parameterized prototypes. In C, you can declare a function like this:

```
void func(pi, f)
  int* pi;
  float f;
{
}
```

Then you can call it somewhere else:

```
func(123.456, &i);
```

The compiler happily compiles this code, even though the float and pointer parameters have been accidently transposed, but the function does not produce the expected results when the program runs. Errors such as these are extremely hard to fix, because no matter how many times you go over the incorrect function call it still looks correct. A new-style function declaration with a prototype looks like this:

```
void func(int* pi, float f);  // prototype
...
func(123.45, &i);  //Error! does not match prototype
...

void func(int* pi, float f)  // function definition
{
...
}
```

In this example, the compiler can catch the error because the function call does not match the prototype. Another common mistake for C programmers is supplying a **short int** value when a function expects a **long int** value. If there is a function prototype, the compiler automatically converts the **short int** value to a **long int** value. If you are going to use the function in several modules, you should put the prototype in a header file, a *.H file*. When you include a header file containing the prototype in every module that uses the function, the compiler always checks that the parameters are of the correct type across all modules.

Before prototypes, a common mistake was for a programmer to change the parameters of a function, try to adapt all the calls to that function, and miss one or two. Using prototypes enables the programmer to find this type of error, provided that the new function has a different number or types of parameters than the old function.

The difference between C++ and ANSI C is that C++ insists on a prototype being present; in ANSI C, a prototype is optional in order to maintain compatibility with old pre-ANSI code. This feature of ANSI C causes a problem in cases like this:

```
void func(int i, float f);  // prototype
...
fumc(1, 123.45);  //Oops! misspelled func
...
```

An ANSI C compiler accepts this example (although some generate an optional warning,) since the compiler does not require a prototype for the misspelled function **fumc**. The linker may later generate an error unless a function called **fumc** exists elsewhere in the system, even with other parameters.

C++ requires function prototypes and introduces the concept of *type safe linking*. When a C compiler compiles a module to produce an .OBJ file for the linker, it inserts symbols corresponding to all the external functions and data items. The symbol is usually the name of the item preceded by an underscore, for example, **_func**. The linker uses these symbols to resolve references across modules.

A C++ compiler inserts symbols for data items, but for functions it adds extra characters that correspond to the type of the function and its parameters. For the function in the example, it might generate **_func__Nif**, the characters **Nif** meaning a near C++ function with **int** and **float** parameters. If the function returned a value, that would be specified as well. This process is known as "name mangling," and each compiler has its own mangling scheme. Provided that all the modules have been compiled with the same compiler, the linker ensures that functions calls are linked to functions of the same type and with the same number of parameters. The beauty of this scheme is that any standard linker will do, although it helps if the linker accepts long names of 50 characters or more. The linker simply matches symbols.

There are two advantages to type safe linking:

☐ The linker can check function and parameter types over modules.

☐ Functions can be overloaded.

Overloaded Functions

In C++, a function is said to be overloaded if two functions with different parameter specifications have the same name, for example:

```
float RaiseToPower(float a, float b){
// calculate result using logarithms
};

long RaiseToPower(int a, int b){
// calculate result using integer multiplication
};
```

Here, **RaiseToPower** is overloaded so that if it is called with two floats, the compiler applies the first version, which uses logarithms. If it is called with two **ints**, the compiler applies the second version, which uses a faster integer multiplication algorithm. Because of type safe linking, overloading will even work across different modules. To do something like this in C you would have to give the two functions different names.

To a C programmer, function overloading would seem to be of limited use. It's something that might occasionally be handy, but might not be missed, because C only provides a limited number of types. With more types, function overloading becomes useful. The **RaiseToPower** example is somewhat contrived, because what programmers really want to do is something like this:

```
float cosine(Degrees theta)
{
// return the cosine of an angle measured in degrees
}
float cosine(Radians theta)
{
// return the cosine of an angle measured in radians
}
```

In this example, the compiler can call the correct function depending on whether the angle is of type **Degrees** or **Radians**. In C, you can use **typedefs** to give the appearance of types, but appearance is all you get. Underneath the surface, **typedefs** are still **ints** and **floats**. With C++ classes, which are explained in the next section, you can create genuine new types.

Classes

Classes are the main feature that set C++ apart from C, and classes give C++ its object orientation.

A C++ class is an extension of the C **struct** that groups a number of data items. Any data item in a class is a member of that class. In addition to data items, a class can contain special functions, called *member functions*, that operate on the class data. With the extensions, a class can be considered as a typed data item, in the same way as **ints** and **floats**. Here is a C **struct** for a rectangle:

```
struct Rect {
   float top;
   float left;
   float bottom;
   float right;
};
```

A C program can now declare rectangles and use them, like this:

```
float Area( struct Rect * r)
{
   return (r->bottom - r->top) * (r->right - r->left);
}
   . . .
struct Rect rA={0.0, 0.0, 10.0, 5.0}; // Initialize rA
struct Rect rB;
   rB=rA;                             // Assign rA to rB
```

Rather than using the **struct** keyword whenever they declare an item, most C programmers declare a **typedef** for the structure:

```
typedef struct Rect {
   float top;
   float left;
   float bottom;
   float right;
} Rect;
```

With a **typedef**, rectangles can be defined directly, in this manner:

```
Rect rA={0.0, 0.0, 10.0, 5.0};
Rect rB;
```

In C++, in place of the **typedef struct** combination, a rectangle can be defined as a class like this:

```
class Rect {
public:
   float top;
   float left;
   float bottom;
   float right;
};
```

The keyword **public** indicates that the items following it can be accessed from outside the class. The **Rect** class can be used in a similar way to **structs**:

```
Rect rA;
Rect rB;
rB=rA;
```

There is no longer any need to define items such as

```
class Rect rA
```

or to use a **typedef**. Any items of the type **Rect**, such as **rA** and **rB**, are known as instances of the class **Rect**.

Member Functions

In the preceding C rectangles example, the **Area** function returns the area of a given rectangle. In a typical system written in C, several functions of this type would exist and they would need to have different names, such as **AreaRect**, **AreaCircle**, and so on.

With C++, functions of this sort can be incorporated into the class when they become class *member functions*. A member function is useful because it acts directly on the data for a class instance. An **Area** member function for the **Rect** class would be declared as:

```
class Rect {
public:
   float top;
   float left;
```

```
  float bottom;
  float right;

  float Area();
};

float Rect::Area()
{
  return (bottom - top) * (right - left);
}
```

The member function itself has a tag, **Rect::**, that tells the compiler that this member function is for the **Rect** class. The tag is needed for any data when the compiler cannot tell to which class it belongs, and so anything declared at the outermost level must be tagged.

A program cannot call a member function in isolation. A member function always needs an instance of the class, and it uses the data values for that instance, as shown in the following example:

```
Rect Rb;
  . . .
float fArea = Rb.Area();
```

Rb.Area returns the area of the rectangle **Rb**. Notice that the member function does not need a parameter, since it uses the values of the **Rb** instance directly.

If the member function is quite trivial, the code can appear directly in the class definition instead of separately outside the class:

```
class Rect {
public:
  . . .

  float Area(){return (bottom - top) * (right - left);};
};
```

Since all the items of **Rect** are public, they are always accessible. An application can access the sides of the rectangle directly, just as if they were items in a C **struct**:

```
float fTop = Rb.top;
```

As a general rule, it is better to provide member functions for accessing the data, and to give it the **protected** or **private** attribute. In doing so, you will make it much easier to improve or modify the class while keeping its external interface constant. A better designed **Rect** class might look like this:

```
class Rect {
protected:
   float top;
   float left;
   float bottom;
   float right;

public:
   float Top(){ return top;};
   float Left(){ return left;};
   float Bottom(){ return bottom;};
   float Right(){ return right;};
   float Area(){return (bottom - top) * (right - left);};
};
```

Since the data items are protected, they are only accessible to the **Rect** class or classes derived from **Rect**. The compiler generates an error if other classes try to access the items directly. Another class must use the member function to access the data, like this:

```
float fTop = Rb.Top();
```

The data has been encapsulated. This might appear to be inefficient, since a direct access must be faster than a function call. In fact, the C++ compiler can optimize the compiled code so that the item is accessed directly, as before.

Even if the code is optimized, why bother? Encapsulating the data gives you the freedom to rewrite or modify the class without changing its public interface. If the public interface does not change, you can be sure that you will not have to modify any existing code that uses the class.

As an example, profiling might reveal that a system uses the **Area** member function quite heavily. Rewriting the class to use the rectangle size can save two floating point operations in the **Area** member function:

```
class Rect {
protected:
```

```
    float top;
    float left;
    float height;
    float width;

public:
    float Top(){ return top;};
    float Left(){ return left;};
    float Bottom(){ return top + height;};
    float Right(){ return left + width;};
    float Area(){return height * width;};
};
```

In addition, since the data is not directly accessible from outside the class, you can be fairly sure that any bugs are caused by the class member functions. More often than not, simple inspection of the source code for the member functions will reveal the bug.

Constructors and Destructors

The C **struct** contains only public data. A C program can initialize the data when declaring the item, as in the **Rect** structure example. A class may contain protected data and so needs to be initialized by a member function. You could add an arbitrary member function, and call it after having declared an instance of the class, like this:

```
class Rect {
public:
    . . .

    void Set(float Top, float Left, float Bottom, float Right){
        top=Top;
        left=Left;
        bottom=Bottom;
        right=Right;
    }
};


    . . .

Rect Ra;
    Ra.Set(0.0, 0.0, 10.0 5.0);
```

There is a better way. In C++, a member function with the same name as the class is a constructor and the compiler will call it automatically whenever a program creates an instance of the class. The constructor is responsible for the class initialization. If the member function **Set** changes its name to **Rect**, a program can initialize the item while declaring it.

```
Rect Ra(0.0, 0.0, 10.0, 5.0);
```

Similarly, a member function with the same name as the class, but with a tilde added in front, as in **~Rect**, is a destructor and the compiler will call it whenever the instance is destroyed. The destructor is responsible for cleaning up. The **Rect** class does not need a destructor, since it has not allocated any additional resources, but destructors are useful for classes that use dynamic memory or other resources that must be freed when an instance is no longer needed.

Inheritance

The most interesting property of classes is that they can serve as a base class for new derived classes. If a programmer needs a class that is similar to an existing class, the programmer can derive a class with the extra facilities needed. The derived class inherits all the public and protected members of the base class. The programmer can add new members, either functions or data items, or redefine one or more of the base-class member functions.

Using inheritance is a very efficient way of working. The programmer can produce a new class at minimal cost. If anyone improves the base class in any way, the derived classes inherits the benefits when they are recompiled.

Of course, programmers can derive new classes from base classes only if suitable base classes are available. Much depends on the way classes are designed. A complex class is best implemented as a number of class layers. This approach gives the programmer a number of different levels from which to derive additional classes. For example, rather than defining

FIGURE
2-2

A hierarchy of polygons

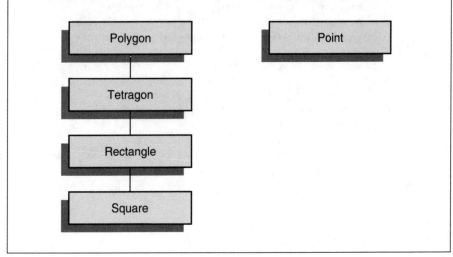

a **Rect** class directly, a programmer might define a family of classes based on a base **Polygon** class (as in Figure 2-2) like this:

```
class Point {
private:
  float x;
  float y;

public:
  // The constructor initializes the members x and y
  Point(float X, float Y){x=X; y=Y;};
  // Alternative constructor provides default initialization
  Point(){x=0; y=0;};

  // functions to access private data
  float X(){return x;};
  float Y(){return y;};
};

class Polygon {
protected:
  unsigned Sides;
  const Point * pVertices;

public:
  // The class members are tagged to distinguish
```

```
  // them from the parameters
  Polygon(unsigned Sides, const Point* pVertices){
    Polygon::Sides=Sides;
    Polygon::pVertices=pVertices;};
  Polygon(){Sides=0; pVertices=0;};

  float Area();  // left as an exercise for the reader
};

class Tetragon : public Polygon {
  public:
    // The constructor calls the base class
    // constructor with a value of 4 for the Sides
    Tetragon(const Point* pVertices):
    Polygon(4,pVertices){};
};

class Rectangle : public Tetragon {
    Point Vertices[4];
public:
  // Only two points needed to define a Rectangle
  Rectangle(Point TopLeft, Point BottomRight):
  Tetragon(Vertices){
    Vertices[0]=TopLeft;
    Vertices[1]=Point(BottomRight.X(),TopLeft.Y());
    Vertices[2]=BottomRight;
    Vertices[3]=Point(TopLeft.X(),BottomRight.Y());};
  // A simple version of Area
  float Area(){ return (Vertices[2].X()
                      - Vertices[0].X());};
};

class Square : public Rectangle {
public:
  Square(Point TopLeft, float Size):
  Rectangle(TopLeft, Point(TopLeft.X()+Size,
    TopLeft.Y()+Size)){};
};

void Test()
{
  // Declare some instances
  const Point PentagonVertices[5]={Point(0,1), Point(0,3),
               Point(2,4), Point(3,2), Point(2,0)};
  Polygon Pentagon(5,PentagonVertices);
  Rectangle(Point(3,4), Point(5,6));
```

```
        Square(Point(0,4),3);
}
```

This example contains a generic **Polygon** class. A program can define an instance of **Polygon** by specifying an array of vertices. Subclasses of **Polygon** can simplify the interface and optimize calculations for special cases. The constructor for the **Rectangle** class only needs the coordinates of the opposing corners of the rectangle, while the constructor for **Square** only needs the coordinates of one corner and the length of a side. (These classes assume that the rectangle is aligned with the coordinate system.) The **Rectangle** class also redefines the **Area** member function, since the area of a rectangle can be calculated more quickly than the area of a general polygon. Notice that the constructors of the subclasses call their parent's constructor implicitly after the **:** operator. The statement after the **:** is an initializer list and contains items (usually base classes) that should be initialized before the body of the constructor is called. If there is no base class initializer, the compiler automatically calls the default base class constructor, the one with no parameters.

Virtual Member Functions

When a member function is defined as *virtual* and is redefined in a derived class, the derived function is always used, even when the function is called through a pointer to a base class as shown in Figure 2-3.

Virtual member functions

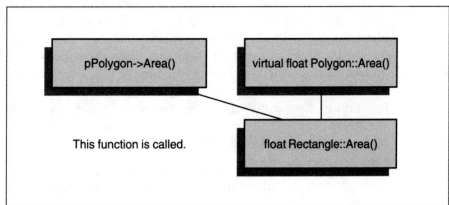

In the example, the **Rectangle** class redefines the **Area** member function. If a program declares an instance of **Rectangle** and wants its area, the compiler calls the simple **Area** member function in **Rectangle**. If the program declares an instance of **Polygon** and wants the area of that, the compiler calls the rather more complex **Area** member function declared in **Polygon**.

Of course, an instance of the **Rectangle** class is also an instance of **Polygon**, and can be treated as such. If the system also had a **Plotter** class for drawing things on paper, the class might well have a member function for drawing polygons on the plotter paper, defined like this:

```
void Draw(Polygon& Poly);   // Draws a polygon
```

Draw accepts an instance of **Polygon**, or any class derived from it. Suppose that **Draw** simply draws a line between all the vertices. If the program wants to draw a rectangle, it can just call **Draw** with an instance of **Rectangle**, like this:

```
Rectangle rA;
Plotter Plot;
Plot.Draw(rA);
```

Imagine that the **Draw** member function in **Plotter** needs to know the area of the polygon, perhaps to calculate whether there is enough ink available to fill in the polygon. When **Draw** calls **Area**, the compiler uses the **Area** member function in the **Polygon** class, since the parameter **Poly** is defined as an instance of **Polygon**, and not of the **Rectangle** class.

To have the compiler call the member function that corresponds to the instance, the base class must define the member function as with the **virtual** specifier. The compiler creates a look-up table in the base class for virtual member functions and initializes the table with the correct member function when creating the instance. If **Polygon** declares **Area** to be a virtual function, the compiler always calls the **Area** member function in **Rectangle** when the instance has been declared as a **Rectangle**, even when the instance is referred to as a **Polygon**, as in the **Draw** member function described in the preceding paragraph.

Virtual functions are so useful that you might be tempted to declare every function as virtual, just in case you might redefine it. Unfortunately there is a small overhead for each virtual function in each instance of a class, because of the virtual function table.

Other Differences

Many other differences between C and C++ exist. These are the most important ones, as far as this book is concerned:

☐ The **new** and **delete** operators

☐ Item declarations

☐ Reference variables

Rather than using **malloc** and **free**, the C library routines for allocating and freeing memory, C++ programs use **new** and **delete**. The function **new** creates an instance of a class in a dynamic memory area, and **delete** destroys the instance. The **new** and **delete** functions are redefinable. Windows programs should redefine them to use local memory in Windows. A program may also declare instances of a class as **auto** data on the stack. An instance is destroyed when the program scope passes out of the {} pair where the instance is declared.

```
Rect * func()
{
  Rect rA(0, 0, 2, 2);
  Rect * pRect;
...
  pRect = new Rect(0, 0, 5, 10);
  return pRect;
}
```

In this example, **rA** is created on the stack and is destroyed when the function returns. The function must not return a reference to **rA**, since the reference would be invalid as soon as the function returns. **pRect** is set to point to a new instance of **Rect** on the heap. This instance is not destroyed when the function returns and exists until it is explicitly destroyed with the **delete** operator.

In general, you should declare items on the stack where possible, and use **new** when you want the instance to survive the immediate scope.

In C, items must be declared at the start of a block before the other statements, like this:

```
{
  int a = 1;
  int b;
  int c;
  a = a * a;
  b = a + 2;
  a = a * a;
  c = a + b;
}
```

In C++, items can be declared anywhere in a block. In general, they should be declared just before use, like this:

```
{
  int a = 1;
  a = a * a;
  int b = a + 2;
  a = a * a;
  int c = a + b;
}
```

For small five-line functions, item declaration does not make much difference, but for fairly long functions, it is useful to have the declaration of an item near its use.

C++ programs can declare loop counters in the **for** statement:

```
for (int i=0; i<n; i++) {};
```

C++ introduces the reference type. References are for defining operations on user-defined classes and types, but they are also useful as function arguments, in place of pointers. The ampersand (**&**) operator denotes a reference, for example:

```
Rect rA;
Rect& rB = rA;
```

A reference item is effectively a pointer, in that it uses the same amount of space as a pointer, and the compiler will dereference it. The difference between a pointer and a reference is that all operations operate on the referenced data item, not on the reference itself. The reference cannot be changed and must be initialized when it is declared. Reference items are useful as function arguments.

If a function declares an argument as a reference, the compiler copies only the address of the item to the stack before calling the function, not the entire item. Inside the function, the code can refer to the argument as if it were declared locally. There is no need to dereference it all the time. For example:

```
void Plotter::Draw(Polygon& Poly)
{
  . . .
  float PArea = Poly.Area();
  . . .
}
```

Windows Basics

Since most of you have at least used Windows, this section covers Windows fundamentals from a programmer's point of view.

Windows programming might seem quite daunting at first sight. In addition to understanding tools and hundreds of functions, a Windows programmer must understand the following concepts, which are not always applicable to other programming environments:

☐ The GUI

☐ The event-driven nature of Windows programs

☐ Multitasking disciplines

It is not necessary to fully understand these concepts before starting to program for Windows, but it is important to realize that these concepts exist and that a well-designed Windows application embodies them. For many programmers, the problem is to break the habits formed while developing more traditional systems, where the application drives the user and resources are not shared.

The GUI

We all know that Windows applications have a GUI (pronounced "gooey"), but there are different degrees of graphicism (or "gooeyness").

At the lowest level are applications that are still virtually text-based. These applications may have pull-down menus and dialog boxes, but the output is presented in the form of text. It is easy to imagine how these applications would look when running under DOS in text mode. These are the main benefits of using a GUI with text-based applications:

☐ The application is not restricted to the fixed character cells of a text-mode display. The application can display more information, or it can occupy a part of the screen, leaving room for other applications.

☐ The application can use proportionally spaced text, which is generally much easier to read than fixed-space text. It also can fit more proportionally spaced text into a given area.

☐ The application can benefit from the embellishments, such as 3-D buttons, that the GUI provides.

☐ Several applications can be displayed at the same time. An application can coexist with others and perhaps share data using memory instead of files.

Text-based applications converted to GUIs used to suffer a certain sluggishness, but these days, GUIs are fast enough for most users not to notice.

On the next level up from text applications are those that use graphic elements to display information. These are the most common graphic elements:

☐ Icons or symbols used in place of text

☐ Fonts and text formatting

☐ Charts and graphs

Most Windows users have a WYSIWYG word processor that displays text in the correct font and formats it to resemble the final printed page.

Many applications use icons to represent certain conditions and to label push buttons.

Although graphic elements need more care in programming than simple text, they can be very effective. The Windows application interface (API) provides all the basic functions. Simple elements, such as icons, can be added with just a couple of lines of code.

The next level comprises applications that use graphical elements, other than simple dialog box controls, for user input. These are two examples:

- ❑ Drag-and-drop mechanisms

- ❑ Hot spots in text that do something when clicked

These elements are probably no more difficult to program than other graphic elements. The challenge lies in producing something that the user will understand. The major problem is that the user may not realize that the element can be clicked or dragged. Changing the cursor can help. Some applications change the cursor to a hand with an outstretched finger when the cursor is over an element that can be clicked.

If you are developing a one-shot application, there is nothing to be ashamed of if you make it largely text-based. On the other hand, if several applications are likely to be developed, you may find it worthwhile and rewarding to develop graphic input and output elements, provided that you are able to reuse them.

Event-Driven Applications

Many programmers have trouble adapting to the event-driven nature of a Windows application. When an application uses a dumb terminal, input/output (I/O) takes place at the command line or in question-and-answer form. In either case, the application gets some input, goes off to process it, and produces output. Then, the application either quits or asks for more input. The application is the boss, and the user acts as an intelligent database server. Menu-driven applications work in much the same way except that the user acts as a dumb database server.

Event-driven applications, in contrast, have to be able to act on events coming from a variety of sources, and not just on replies to questions or selections from simple menus. The events may come from controls that the user can activate, from other programs, or from devices such as the clock or the communications port. Event-driven applications have been around for a long time. Many major DOS applications are event driven, as are most real-time programs and operating systems. Microsoft did not invent the idea of event-driven applications, but now that it is there in Windows, programmers will not be able to dodge the issues for very much longer.

How do event-driven applications work? One way is for the application to define a routine or callback function for each event, and then to just sit back and wait. As each event occurs, the underlying system calls the function. That is the way PC systems handle interrupts. When an interrupt occurs, the system looks up the address of a subroutine in the interrupt table and calls it.

The other way, which Windows uses, is to have an event queue. Windows turns all system events into messages and sends the messages to the appropriate application. The application thens picks the messages off the queue one by one and processes them. There are some differences between the two methods:

❑   An event queue is simple and efficient and can cope with a multitude of different events. Callback functions are better suited to systems where there are a limited number of events.

❑   A callback function can be preempted if a more important event occurs while it is executing. With an event queue, the system can place important events at the front of the queue, but the application does not normally look at it until it has processed the current event. If a Windows application spends too long processing an event, the whole system will be blocked. If an application knows that the processing is likely to take some time, it must find a way of checking the event queue while processing—but that may be awkward to program. Windows NT solves the problem of an application blocking others, but messages for an individual application still arrive in the same order and the application must finish processing one before starting another.

❑   Applications that use callback functions associated with single events appear more aesthetic than those that use event queues. The code that retrieves events from the queue is often complex, since it must decide what to do with each different event.

In spite of the drawbacks, the event queue is the best choice for Windows, but programming would be easier with an additional layer on top that uses callback functions.

Multitasking

Any UNIX guru will tell you that Windows (prior to Windows NT) is not a multitasking system. UNIX, and most other major operating systems, are preemptive systems where an application can be interrupted at any time when the operating system judges that something more important needs to be done. Under a preemptive system, when an application gets stuck in a loop, other applications just carry on running. They may run more slowly than usual, since they have to share the processor with the looping application, but they run nevertheless and the user can terminate the rogue application. In contrast, a rogue Windows 3.*x* application will block the system.

That apart, Windows is effectively a multitasking system, provided that all the applications are well-behaved and hand control back to Windows frequently enough. Whenever Windows receives control, it decides which of the other applications to run. DOS applications running under Windows Enhanced mode are properly multitasked. Windows gives them timeslices, and allows them to run for a certain period before stopping them and giving control to another DOS application or to Windows.

Applications running under a multitasking system must be more sociable than applications running alone. There are some basic rules of etiquette:

❑   An application should not claim more resources than it needs, especially memory.

❑   An application must release resources when they are no longer needed, even when the application might need them again later.

□   An application should not start any lengthy operation without giving the user a chance to cancel it in an orderly manner. This rule also applies to preemptive systems; although UNIX users have the option of "killing" a lengthy process, they may well lose some work.

Device Independence

A very important advantage for developers is that Windows is largely device-independent. The device dependency is hidden away in the Windows Graphics Device Interface (GDI) and a device driver that is either bundled with the retail Windows or supplied by the device manufacturer. Back in the DOS days, developers had to decide which screen resolutions and printers to support. Usually they would support a handful of devices from Well-Known manufacturers, and hope that the devices from Less-Well-Known manufacturers would emulate one of the supported devices.

That was not ideal. In the first place marketing would always be finding clients who would buy a thousand copies of the application, provided that it would support the Tin-Pot XL69. In the second place, the Less-Well-Known manufacturers were discouraged from innovating on their interfaces, since nobody would buy an innovative device if their software would not run on it.

With Windows, developers can forget about devices. Manufacturers can produce any device they like and, provided they supply an efficient Windows driver, they can be assured of a market.

Although most Windows users realize that applications are device-independent, those new to Windows programming are often surprised to find that an application can use the same code for both drawing on the screen and for printing to the printer. The device independence extends across the type of device as well, with some minor differences. If an application is drawing to a printer, at a certain moment it must eject the page and start to draw on a new page. Otherwise, the code is the same. An application that wants to draw *Hello World*, two inches high, in italics, with a box around it, can use the same code to draw it on the screen as on a page in a printer or a sheet in a plotter. Apart from the image resolution, the result is the same in all three cases. If you have to write code to print something, you can use the same code to show a WYSIWYG display.

In early versions of Windows, the cost of this device independence was that some devices, such as Postscript printers, were not supported very well and programmers were tempted to bypass Windows and send Postscript code directly to the printer. In the current versions of Windows, the GDI is more powerful.

Elements of a Windows Application

A typical Windows application has these elements:

- A *main window* contains a title bar, a menu, and a client area. The client area serves as a canvas that the application can draw on.

- The main window of more complex applications has *child windows*. The child windows may serve to divide the client area up into different areas, or they may act as button bars or status lines.

- The application has a number of *dialog boxes* that prompt the user for information. A dialog box is a specialized child window.

- The dialog boxes contain *controls*, such as buttons and list boxes. Controls are also specialized windows.

These elements are not mandatory. Certain applications do not contain any dialog boxes at all, while others may consist of a single dialog box and little else.

If the application is going to display its output in graphic form or as formatted text, it draws the output on the client area of the main window, or a child of the main window. Applications are not obliged to display output as a graphic. If the output is simple text or a number of text fields, the programmer will find it easier to use a dialog box, and to fit it inside the client area of the window (the part inside the window frame and title), rather than trying to lay out and control the elements in the application. Dialog boxes do not need to be boxes that "pop-up" over other windows, even if they usually are.

FIGURE 2-4   The main elements of an application

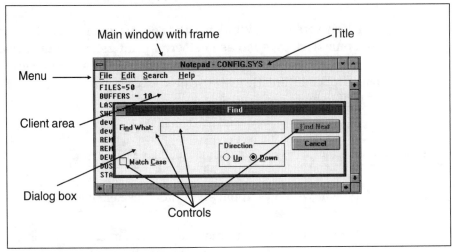

The Windows Notepad application uses the Edit control (a text window allowing simple editing) in place of the client area of its main window. The Write application, which displays text in a WYSIWYG manner, draws the text onto the client area using GDI functions.

Structure of a Windows Application

The source code of most Windows C applications looks vaguely familiar to Windows programmers. Cynics say this is because all Windows applications have been programmed by cutting and pasting from the examples delivered with the SDK or the compiler. This belief may contain more than an element of truth, but whatever the reason, most applications are structured along similar lines.

The programs in this book are structured in an object-oriented fashion, and so they differ completely from most Windows programs written in C. At times, reference is made to the classic Windows application structure for the benefit of those of you who are familiar with it.

WinMain

The root procedure **WinMain** is the entry point to the application. **WinMain** corresponds to the **main** function in all C and C++ programs written for DOS or UNIX. **WinMain** is typically used to perform the following functions:

☐ Take any necessary action if another instance of the application is running. For most applications, it does not matter if several instances are running, but if it does matter, **WinMain** can return without doing anything.

☐ Initialize any data for the application.

☐ Register with Windows the window types that the application will use. For each window type, the application must specify the procedure that will handle the window's messages and, optionally, other details, such as the color of the window background. The application program interface (API) function **RegisterClass** can do this.

☐ Create the main application window.

☐ Start a message loop.

☐ When the message loop ends, **WinMain** can return to Windows and the application is terminated.

Working with 32 Bits

Those of us who programmed for Windows 1 and 2 were taught that second and later instances of an application should reuse resources from the first instance. At the time, this was important because it saved some memory. You can still reuse items in Windows 3.*x* but the amount of memory saved is so small it is no longer worth the bother. In the 32-bit versions of Windows, the memory spaces of applications are completely separate, and an application may not even be told that other instances are running.

The Message Loop

Windows drives an application by sending it messages, but all messages are destined for individual windows in the application. The application message loop retrieves the messages and dispatches them to the corresponding window. It does this, in a loop, until the application has finished.

Why do we need a message loop? Why doesn't Windows send messages directly to the individual windows of the application? There are three reasons:

☐ Since messages sometimes arrive faster than the windows can process them, a buffer is necessary. If Windows sent messages directly to the individual windows, there would have to be a buffer for each window. With the message loop, Windows only needs to maintain a buffer for each application. Of course, the application buffer is larger than an individual window buffer would be, but a typical application has dozens of windows, and the sum of all the individual buffers is much larger than that of the application buffer.

☐ Windows keeps **WM_PAINT** messages at the back of the queue, so that an application only processes them when there is nothing else to do. The **WM_PAINT** message tells a window to repaint itself, perhaps because it has been uncovered. If Windows sent messages to individual windows, a window might start lengthy processing for a **WM_PAINT** message when there are more important messages waiting for other windows.

☐ Applications can filter keystrokes in the message loop to translate a sequence of keystrokes into some action. In fact, applications must filter keystrokes, and they must call API functions to handle accelerators and to convert sequences of keyboard actions into a character equivalent.

The third reason is not so convincing, since most applications handle the keyboard in a conventional way, and might prefer that Windows handled the standard character filtering. Windows 3.*x* provides the option of adding system hook functions for applications that need to filter messages.

Applications usually have only one message loop, but they can have more than one. If an application is going to do some lengthy operation, it can process messages every now and again while it is doing so. This allows the user to work with other functions of the application, including perhaps a function to abort or modify the lengthy operation.

The Window Procedure

Each individual window on your screen belongs to a window class. A window class, which has nothing to do with a C++ class, refers to windows having the same attributes and, in particular, the same window procedure. The API defines a few standard classes for the controls, but applications can register additional classes using the API function **RegisterClass**.

Although Windows sends messages to the application, each message contains a handle identifying the window that should receive it. The message loop dispatches messages to the window procedure for that class of window. If there are several windows of that class, the messages for all the windows go to the same procedure. The procedure uses the window handle to distinguish between them.

The window procedure usually contains little more than a huge **switch** statement. Each **case** in the switch corresponds to a message, and the procedure can ensure the appropriate response to each message.

The Windows function **DefWindowProc** carries out reasonable default actions for all the messages. For example, the default action for the **WM_PAINT** message is to paint the window with its background pattern, or brush, as defined in its window class. If a procedure is not interested in a message, it passes it on to **DefWindowProc**.

Windows literature refers to *subclassing* windows. Subclassing a window means to redefine its window procedure. An application may want to do this in order to process certain messages; afterwards, it can pass the message on to the original procedure. An application might subclass the standard edit control to make an edit control that only accepts numbers as input. The redefined procedure would only check the **WM_CHAR** message and discard it if it was a non-numeric character. It would pass numeric characters and all other messages on to the original edit window procedure.

Dialog Boxes

An application must also provide a window procedure for each dialog box that it uses. Dialog box window procedures are similar to those of ordinary application windows, but they receive one or two additional messages, such as **WM_INITDIALOG**, which ordinary windows do not receive. There is also no need to call **DefWindowProc** for a dialog box procedure. Windows carries out the default message processing by default.

An application does not need to register window classes for dialog boxes, since they use a predefined class, but a dialog box does need a template, defining the layout of the controls within the box. The template would have been created with a dialog box editor.

Controls

Controls are specialized windows that allow the user to control the application. The Windows API provides all the familiar controls—buttons, list boxes, scroll bars, and so on. An enterprising programmer can customize these controls or invent new ones. One advantage of programming Windows in C++ is that it is very easy to make reusable customized controls. Chapter 5 covers this topic in detail.

C++ for Windows

So now we have three technologies whose time has come: OOP, the C++ language, and the Windows environment. All that remains is to fit them together.

Even when programmed in C, the Windows environment is still object oriented to a certain degree. With Windows it is possible to:

☐   Classify windows and controls.

☐   Derive subclasses of existing windows or controls, and modify their behavior. A subclass does this by intercepting the parent's window procedure, processing certain messages and passing the rest back to the original window procedure.

❏   Store a limited amount of instance data in a window's private memory.

Although it is possible to program Windows in an object-oriented fashion in C, it is quite difficult and rarely do C programmers work this way. On the other hand, the object-oriented nature of Windows means that it is simple to program with an object-oriented language. C is not totally unsuited to Windows programming, but because it is difficult to work with C in an object-oriented way, program development is more time-consuming and more prone to errors. The next section addresses some of the specific problems that occur in C programming.

The Problems with C

It is difficult to subclass a window if the behavior that you want to modify is not associated with a Windows message. If you have a window that displays some items in alphabetical order, and you want a subclass that displays the items on a yellow background, that is fine. If instead, you want a subclass that just uses a different sort algorithm, it is not so easy. You can invent your own message, **WM_MY_SORT**, and have your window send it to itself so that it can be intercepted by the subclass, but you would have to be extremely dedicated to the object-oriented cause to do that.

If you want to invent some new mechanism and use it in different applications, you can define a custom control or a DLL, but you will need to define a collection of new messages to go with it. In Windows, controls and windows communicate with each other by means of messages. Messages are awkward to use, since a message has only two parameters. One parameter, **wParam**, is an unsigned int, so it is 16 bits in the DOS versions of Windows and 32 bits in the NT version. The other parameter, **lParam**, is always 32 bits. Since there are only the two parameters, you have to fit your information into them in such a way that it will still work when Windows goes 32 bits.

The Windows controls can be customized, so that you can change the color or the appearance of the controls. The control sends messages to its parent, and the parent can use the information in the message to draw or modify the control. Such controls are called Owner-Draw controls, since the controls owner, or parent draws them. The problem here is that the functionality of the control is divided between the control itself and the parent, so it is difficult to package up the control and reuse it.

The Windows messages are awkward. You need to define a big **switch** statement to handle them. The "message crackers" in Windows 3.1 help in extracting the information from the message parameters, but you still need to pack the parameters if you want to send messages to other windows.

How C++ Can Help

C++ should be able to fill in the gaps. If you have a reasonable C++ environment for Windows, you would expect it to:

☐   Largely replace messages by calls to class member functions, so that a class can define member functions for events that it wants to process, rather than processing messages in a **switch** statement. Subclasses would be able to redefine these member functions, if necessary, instead of having to subclass the window message processing function.

☐   Allow the programmer to classify more complex mechanisms that do not depend on single windows. Examples are containers, sets, and lists, and whatever your application needs, perhaps flight plans or financial transactions.

☐   Replace the message traffic between a control and its parent by extra member functions in the control class, so that the control can be fully encapsulated in its class.

You might also expect it to solve all your problems as well, but that would be asking a bit too much. While commercial class libraries provide a number of useful classes that might save you a lot of work, you or your company are only likely to be satisfied with a class library when you have developed it yourself, even if you use an existing library as a base. A company that adopts C++ is not going to make many of its programmers redundant, but it might let them have their weekends and evenings free.

Replacing Messages by Member Functions

This is something that anyone who uses C++ expects to able to do, but which is surprisingly tricky to implement. The idea is simple enough. A C program has a big switch statement to process incoming messages, but a C++ program should be able to declare a subclass of some generic **Window** class and declare member functions to handle incoming messages. The **Window** class should somehow translate messages into calls to the appropriate member function.

The simplest way to do this is for the **Window** class to have a big **switch** statement containing all possible messages and to call a virtual member function for each one. There are two problems with this approach:

☐ There are over a hundred Windows messages, so the overhead for the internal table needed for virtual member functions is quite high if the Window class supports them all.

☐ There is still the problem of user-defined messages.

The existing class libraries seem to have adopted one of two alternatives for resolving user-defined messages:

☐ Define virtual member functions for the most common messages, and let specialized subclasses convert additional messages if necessary. This is the approach taken in this book.

☐ Have each class somehow register the messages it wants to handle. This approach can be somewhat more efficient, since it needs less storage, but it is difficult to do without some help from the compiler, making the code compiler-dependent.

Whichever alternative you choose, the fact that you use member functions rather than **case** statements to process messages means that it is easier to redefine any particular function, and so there are more possibilities to derive useful subclasses from it.

Classifying More Complex Mechanisms

Although Windows allows you to classify application windows and derive subclasses from them, it is rather awkward to do, and it is rare to find a programmer who actually does it. Once you have a basic C++ class library, it is much easier to classify windows.

But C++ also enables you to classify more complex mechanisms and perhaps involve several elements. The Dynamic Data Exchange (DDE) classes, described in Chapter 11, combine windows, timers, and lists. When a class is complex, it becomes specialized and will only interest some Windows programmers, but for them it will be a powerful tool.

Anyone who has programmed Windows finds that they have to do certain tasks over and over again. Microsoft is now providing C libraries containing common dialog boxes and other useful tools, but if you cannot wait for Microsoft to solve your problems, you can build your own class. That way you only have to solve each problem once.

Encapsulating Controls

In a standard Windows application, the parent of a control has to respond to several different control notification messages. Many of these messages should be handled by the control or a derived class rather than by the parent. The most common problem is that of owner-draw controls. If you want a button to have a little icon or bitmap on it, you can declare the control as owner-draw, but then the parent window has to draw the icon onto the button. See Chapters 4 and 5 for discussion of an owner-draw subclass of button that draws the icon itself.

Summary

The combination of object orientation, Windows, and C++ promises to simplify Windows programming a great deal. Windows is already object-oriented to a certain degree, but it is difficult to take advantage of that orientation when programming in C. The C++ language should enable programmers to make full use of Windows' object orientation.

Still, there are certain technical difficulties in getting Windows and C++ to work together, especially when mapping messages onto member functions. The next chapter explains the problems in detail and shows how to solve them. Once the difficulties are out of the way, it is possible to take full advantage of the combination of these three powerful technologies.

CHAPTER

Windows

*I*t's natural to begin with a discussion of windows, because they are central to the Windows environment. Many Windows components are derived from them. Screen items such as dialog boxes, buttons, list boxes, and other controls are all specialized types of windows. Later on in this book, I will show that any unlikely component, such as a timer or a conversation between applications, can be treated as a type of invisible window.

Obviously, with a good C++ **Window** class, it would be a simple matter to derive additional C++ classes from it that correspond to all other Windows components. This chapter explains how to implement a base **Window** class and use it to create application windows. Chapters 4 and 6 explain how to derive C++ classes from the **Window** class that correspond to controls and dialog boxes.

If you are new to Windows programming or C++, you might find the Implementation section in this chapter hard going. In that case, skip the implementation details for now and concentrate on the example applications. You can return to the Implementation section when you are more comfortable with Windows and C++ programming. Try to follow the section on Design Objectives, but don't worry if you are unclear on some design issues after the first reading. They will become clearer when you have more experience with Windows.

Some Reasons Why C Is Unsuitable for Windows Programming

If you are new to Windows, and especially if you have been programming for a UNIX X11 toolkit such as Motif, you are likely to find that Windows programming is difficult, even when using a C++ class library. This may be true, but there are two consolations:

☐   It is easier programming for protected-mode and 32-bit environments than for the unprotected 16-bit real mode.

☐   It is even worse programming Windows in C.

Programmers were quick to abandon the old real mode, and most will move to 32-bit versions of Windows as soon as possible. Many programmers are reluctant, however, to make the move from C to C++, perhaps because doing so involves learning something new, while abandoning real mode and 16-bit programming involves forgetting something that is out-of-date.

To see why the basic C language is unsuitable for Windows programming when alternatives are available, recall the steps needed to create a simple application window using C:

☐   The window function must be written to handle any event that might be relevant to that window. The window may need to be redrawn, for example, or the user may be clicking the mouse in it. The function usually contains a **switch** statement, with a **case** for each event that the programmer is interested in.

☐   The window function must be exported by listing it in a definition file (a file with the .DEF suffix) so that Windows can call it when an event occurs.

☐   The window attributes, including the window function, must be registered with Windows by calling the application programming interface (API) **RegisterClass** function. Do not confuse this with a C++ class. In the Windows API, a class of windows means windows that share some basic properties. In particular, they use the same window function.
     When registering the class, the programmer specifies a class name for the window, the name of the window function, and a few other details, such as the color of the background and the shape of the cursor. The window class is typically registered in an initialization routine.

☐   To actually create a window, the programmer calls **CreateWindow**. The programmer supplies the Windows class name that has been registered previously and a few other details, such as the initial size and position of the window.

☐   Once the window has been created, Windows starts sending messages to its window function.

The C programmer faces many difficulties apart from the work needed to do these actions. The restraints imposed by C affect the whole application design—frequently the programmer must leave out features because they are too difficult to program in C within the time budgeted for the project. Here are some of the problems:

☐ In order to create a window, the programmer needs to update several different files.

☐ The window function **switch** statement that processes the messages usually becomes quite large. It is not unusual to see Windows programs containing **switch** statements several hundred lines long.
   An industrious programmer might call a separate function for each **case** of the **switch** statement, but in practice this rarely happens. Perhaps this is because the **switch** starts out small and slowly grows as the program develops.

☐ The application may have several windows with the same Windows class name, which means that they all share the same window function. Windows supplies the function with a handle to identify the window so that the program can distinguish between them. The window function may need to use some data items, perhaps to store the text or information displayed in the window. It is quite difficult for the programmer to store a copy of the data for each window. The data cannot just be declared **static**, since each window would then share it. In C programming, maintaining private copies of data for each window is accomplished with Windows API functions, which are rather cumbersome to use.

Of all the drawbacks, the third issue listed here is probably the most serious for C programmers. In the past, programmers have often been tempted to create just one window of each class and simply store the variables in **static** data. They are now discovering that in order to convert their programs to the new Multiple Document Interface (MDI), which handles multiple windows of the same type, they are obliged to more or less rewrite their programs.

It is possible that many programmers are using **static** data even now, and have simply not considered the problems of handling data when multiple copies of a window exist.

C++ offers a solution to all of these problems, and especially the last, since any data associated with a window can be stored in C++ class members for that window. If each window has its own C++ class instance, the C++ programmer can use the class members in the same way that the C programmer uses **static** variables: Just declare them and use them, and each window will have its own copy.

Design Objectives

What are the objectives for writing a C++ class for simple windows, and what can a C++ programmer expect the class to do? For a C++ **Window** class to be useful, it should provide three basic facilities:

☐ Instead of needing a message handling **switch** statement, class member functions should handle Windows events directly.

☐ There should be a one-to-one relationship between a C++ **Window** class instance and a window on the screen. The instance can keep its own copy of its data in class member variables.

☐ The window on the screen and the C++ class instance should be synchronized, so that when the instance is destroyed, the screen window is also destroyed, and vice-versa. This balance ensures that no orphaned windows or instances will remain.

Handling Windows Events

When an event occurs, such as the left mouse button being clicked or the window being resized, Windows sends a message, by means of the API **RegisterClass** function, to the correlating window function specified by the application. The **RegisterClass** function typically contains a **switch** statement for processing the message. In a typical C program, the statement looks something like this:

```
switch ( message) {
    ...
  case WM_SIZE:
    /* code to handle the Size event */
    break;
    ...
  case WM_LBUTTONDOWN:
    /* code to handle a left mouse button click */
    break;

  default:
    return DefWindowProc(hWnd, message, wParam, lParam);
}
return FALSE;
```

Any messages that do not interest the application are passed on to **DefWindowProc**, a Windows API function that performs a reasonable default action for each message. The application returns **FALSE** if it handles the message.

In a C++ **Window** class, virtual member functions can handle these events. Instead of writing a **switch** statement, the programmer derives a subclass from **Window** and provides a member function to handle each event that the window should handle. Since the member function is virtual, it will be called in place of the Window class function that it redefines. All that is needed is a mechanism to call the virtual function when an event occurs.

A Windows message has two parameters, **wParam** and **lParam**, that contain extra information relevant to the message. For many messages, **lParam** contains two 16-bit values in its low-order and high-order words. The type of information stored in these parameters depends on the message. It may be an integer notification code, or it may be a handle to a window. The application code must extract these values using the API **LOWORD** and **HIWORD** macros. If there are virtual member functions, it will be useful if these message parameters can be picked apart before the member function is called, so that the member function has meaningful parameters such as codes or handles.

Working with 32 Bits

In the 32-bit versions of Windows, **wParam** is 32 bits as well, and the information for certain messages is packed in a different way. That is another good reason for avoiding the message **switch** statement and unpacking the messages in one place. It is then a simple matter to change the unpacking code when compiling for the 32-bit version.

For example, assume that a class **ClickWin** is derived from a C++ **Window** class and needs to process size and left-button events. If virtual member functions are available, the programmer simply writes member functions for these two events. The code looks something like this:

```
BOOL ClickWin::Size(UINT Width, UINT Height, UINT Type)
{
    // Code to process size event
    return TRUE;
}

BOOL ClickWin::LButtonDown(POINT Cursor, UINT Keys)
{
    // Code to process a left button click
    return TRUE;
}
```

The **switch** statement is no longer necessary. The message parameters **wParam** and **lParam** have been picked apart and supplied to the function as relevant items—**Width**, **Type**, **Cursor**, and so on.

Of course, the code looks neater when the processing for each event is isolated in its own function, instead of being buried in a large **switch** statement. The real reason for doing things this way, which may not be immediately obvious, is that it is much easier to derive subclasses when virtual members are used.

In general, a derived class wants most events to be handled by the parent, but handles one or two specific events itself. For example, it is possible to derive a class **BeepClickWin** from **ClickWin**. Assume that **BeepClickWin** does everything that **ClickWin** does, but in addition makes a beep sound when the left button is clicked. The code for **BeepClickWin** looks something like this:

```
class BeepClickWin : public ClickWin {
  BOOL LButtonDown(POINT Cursor, UINT Keys){
    MessageBeep(0);                          // make a beep
    ClickWin::LButtonDown(Cursor, Keys); //pass to parent
    return TRUE;
  };
};
```

This function calls the API function **MessageBeep** to make the default system warning sound. Then it calls the **LButtonDown** function defined in its parent, **ClickWin**. It must use the **ClickWin::** tag to indicate the parent, otherwise it would call itself recursively.

This is the beauty of OOP. To do the same thing in C, a programmer might be sorely tempted to simply take a copy of the code for the ClickWin application and modify it. The alternative is to modify the ClickWin application in some way. If the ClickWin application is already shipping, this is generally unacceptable, and so copying is the only way.

Virtual member functions can be implemented by defining them in the base **Window** class. This class would also contain the window function to which Windows sends messages. The window function would still be a **switch** statement, and for every **case** it would call the corresponding member function with the correct parameters. This window function would still be quite messy, but once the function has been implemented and is working correctly, there is no need to look at it again. Future applications can be derived from it without having to copy the code.

The window function might look something like this:

```
LONG Window::MessageProc( HWND hWnd, UINT msg, Event& evt)
{
  switch (msg){

  // . . .

    case WM_SIZE:
```

```
      return Size(LOWORD(evt.lParam),HIWORD(evt.lParam),
                                        evt.wParam);

  // . . .

    case WM_LBUTTONDOWN:
      return LButtonDown(MAKEPOINT(evt.lParam), evt.wParam);

  // . . .

}
```

Notice how the function has picked apart the message parameters before calling the member functions.

The design problem is that there are something like 120 Windows messages defined and it is impractical to define virtual member functions for them all, since virtual member functions require storage space in every instance of the class. A compromise must be found.

In fact, for most application windows, a subset of around 20 messages is usually sufficient. Most of these messages concern user input. For simple application windows, it is enough to provide for virtual members for these messages. Occasionally, a window may want access to one of the other 100 messages. If the window function, the function that calls the virtual member functions, is itself a virtual member function, any class derived from the **Window** class can redefine it. It can then handle the messages of interest and then let the original function in the **Window** class handle the others. For example, a class that wants to process the **WM_SYSCOLORCHANGE** message will redefine the function like this:

```
LONG DerivedClass::MessageProc( HWND hWnd, UINT msg, Event& evt)
{
  switch (msg){
    case WM_SYSCOLORCHANGE :
      return SysColorChange()

  default:
    return Window::MessageProc(hWnd, msg, evt);
  }
}
```

The **MessageProc** function in **DerivedClass** calls the **Sys-ColorChange** member function if a **WM_SYSCOLORCHANGE** message arrives, but it passes all the other messages back up to the **Window** base class, which then processes them as before. This solution might seem half-baked, but in practice the other messages are usually handled by special-purpose classes in a library, and not by the application classes themselves.

Therefore, the solution is not so half-baked after all. Most windows only need the virtual member functions, but if a class ever needs to handle the other messages, it can do so.

Some C++ compilers now supply a *Message Pump* that takes Windows messages and calls virtual member functions automatically.

Borland's C++ compiler uses dynamically dispatchable member functions that are linked to Windows messages when they are declared. When a message arrives, the computer dispatches it to the function. That is a useful facility, but is particular to Borland and will not work with other compilers. The Borland computer does not pick the message parameters apart; the member function must do that itself.

The Microsoft Foundation Class (MFC) library uses a message map to link member functions with messages. Each application class must provide a message map linking all messages it is interested in with an individual function to handle each message. The MFC classes also pick the message parameters apart. The member functions are not virtual, but subclasses can redefine the message map to call their own member functions.

Both of these techniques are efficient, but both are compiler-dependent. If you are committed to using one compiler, you could convert the classes in this book to use Borland's dynamically dispatchable functions or the MFC class library.

Associating Windows with Class Instances

Since all classes derived from the base **Window** class are simply modifying the default behavior by redefining member functions, only one window function is needed. This simplifies programming, since the message **switch** statement and the message parameter analysis are centralized in the Window **MessageProc** member function.

The virtual member function **MessageProc** cannot be called by Windows directly as a window function, since Windows knows nothing about member functions and instances. Windows expects all callback functions to have the Pascal calling convention in the 16-bit API, and the C calling convention in the 32-bit API. Let's define a callback function named **CPPWinproc,** since it is the Windows procedure for the C++ environment.

When messages arrive at **CPPWinProc,** they must be dispatched to the **MessageProc** member function of the corresponding C++ class instance (see Figure 3-1). There may be several instances of the same class and so **CPPWinProc** needs to know which one to call. Since the window is referenced by its handle, there must be some way of associating window handles with C++ instances of **Window.** You could implement some sort of database containing pairs of window handles and class instances, but things would be simpler if there were a way of keeping the address of the instance in some storage area associated with the window.

The API functions **SetWindowWord** and **GetWindowWord** can be used to store data associated with a window. Windows reserves space for the

FIGURE 3-1

How messages pass from Windows to member functions

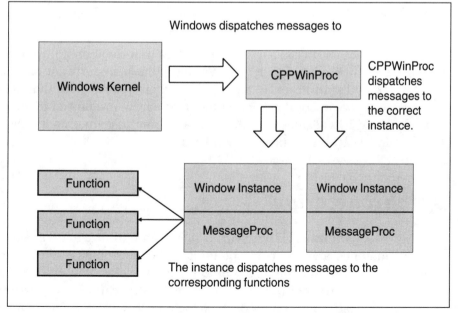

data when creating the window, according to a value supplied when the window is registered. It would be helpful to use **SetWindowWord** to store a pointer to the class instance; when a message arrived at the base window function, the pointer could be retrieved using **GetWindowWord.**

The problem here is that an application cannot reserve extra space for control windows, such as buttons, because these are pre-registered by Windows. In fact, even if it were possible to reserve extra space for controls, it would be best not to. The overhead of extra space would be carried by all the controls, even those not associated with an instance. Since most C++ applications have instances associated with controls, another solution is in order.

Fortunately, the API functions **SetProp** and **GetProp** will maintain a list of data items, or *properties*, for a window. Each property has a name that an application can use to retrieve it from the list. Since the data area is not reserved in advance, these property functions also work with pre-registered windows, such as controls. The property functions are slightly less efficient than the window data functions, but if a window does not have too many properties, the difference is negligible.

A slight problem when using properties to store instance pointers is that a property is 16 bits in the 16-bit versions of Windows. If the application is compiled using the large model, which means that all pointers are 32 bits, then two properties are needed to store the address.

Another problem with properties is that they consume space from the 64K USER data segment in Windows. Each property uses approximately 16 bytes. In practice, an application rarely has more than a few dozen windows open at any one time, and so the amount of memory used in the USER segment is still acceptably small. Again, this is only a problem in the 16-bit versions of Windows.

Synchronization

A **Window** class needs to be able to synchronize the existence of a class instance and the corresponding screen window. When an application creates an instance of a **Window** class, the class constructor must create the screen window. Similarly, when the application destroys the instance, the destructor should destroy the screen window. That is a reasonable behavior to expect, and there should be no problem in adding code to the class constructor and destructor to do it.

Screen windows also can be destroyed directly by an application or by the system. An application can destroy a window using the API function **DestroyWindow.** Whenever a window is destroyed, Windows also destroys all the child windows. A C++ **Window** class instance associated with a screen window that is being destroyed must also be destroyed, or it might be left orphaned.

Windows sends a **WM_DESTROY** message just before it destroys a window. The C++ **Window** class instance must delete itself when it receives this message.

Class Hierarchy

Before defining the **Window** class, it is useful to think about the class hierarchy. Many but not all classes will be derived from the **Window** class. Files or memory blocks will not be derived from the **Window** class. A universal class from which all other classes in the Windows environment are derived can contain members that are useful to any class.

In the class hierarchy described in this book, the universal class **WinObj** is the base of any object in the Windows environment. **WinObj** contains member functions for displaying errors and warnings, and it overloads the C++ operators **new** and **delete.**

Implementation

This section shows how the **WinObj** and **Window** classes can be implemented.

WinObj is the base class for all classes in the class library. It is empty apart from some error- and message-reporting member functions.

Window is the base class for all classes of windows. An application wishing to display a window does not declare an instance of **Window**. It defines and declares a subclass of **Window**. Member functions defined in the subclass will modify the default behavior of the base **Window** class.

The base **Window** class contains two interfaces. The first is between window handles and class instances of windows. The second is between Windows event messages and class member functions.

The first interface redirects messages to the corresponding class instance, and ensures that both the window and the class instance are deleted together. The second interface replaces the typical Windows message handling loop with calls to virtual member functions. Having a virtual member function for each event makes it practical to derive subclasses from **Window** classes.

If you are new to Windows programming, you may prefer to skip this section for now, and concentrate on using the classes. If you do skip it, try to come back to it later when you feel more comfortable with Windows concepts. It is much easier to use a class when you know how it works.

Structure of a C++ Module

Before starting with the classes themselves, let's review the structure of a C++ module. In general, a C++ class has two source files. The .HPP header file contains the class definition, and the .CPP source file contains the implementation of the class member functions. Usually there should be one class per header file.

An application that wishes to use a class includes the header file for that class by using the **include** statement. The application also needs to link with the compiled version of the .CPP file. If the application is defining a new class that uses an existing class, it should place the **include** statement for the existing class in the .HPP file for the new class. The .CPP file for the new class then only needs to include its own header file.

As the class hierarchy gets more complex, a .CPP file may indirectly include the same .HPP file several times. If a file includes header files for different classes that are all derived from the **Window** class, each of these classes would include WINDOW.HPP in its own header file.

Including a header file more than once, even indirectly, is equivalent to redefining a class, and generates a compiler error. An alternative would have been to leave out other header files in header files, and to include all the necessary header files, just once, in each .CPP file. That would be very tedious to do, since the programmer would need to know the hierarchy of each class in order to include the necessary headers.

A simpler way is to put a conditional compilation statement in each header file, so that if it is included more than once, the compiler simply skips it after the first time. The conditional compilation statements look like this:

```
#ifndef MYCLASS_INC
#define MYCLASS_INC

// include any class definitions that Myclass needs
#include "base.hpp"

// define MyClass
class MyClass : public Base {
   . . .
};
#endif // MYCLASS__INC
```

If the symbol **MYCLASS_INC** is defined, the compiler skips the subsequent source up to the **endif** statement. If the symbol is not defined, which is the case the first time that the compiler encounters this statement, the compiler examines the code up to the **endif** statement. The first thing the code does is to define the symbol so that the compiler skips this section the next time. After that, it defines the class.

There are only two things to remember when using this construction:

❑   Use the same symbol in the **ifndef** and **define** statements.

❑   Do not forget the **endif** statement.

WinObj

Here is the implementation of **WinObj**:

winobj.cpp

```
#include "winobj.hpp"

// redefine new & delete to use Windows memory
void * operator new(size_t siz)
{
  HANDLE Handle;
```

```
char str[30];
Handle = LocalAlloc( LMEM_FIXED | LMEM_ZEROINIT, siz);
if (!Handle) {
  LoadString(hInst,IDS_MEMORY,str, sizeof str);
  MessageBox(GetActiveWindow(),str,
            NULL,MB_ICONEXCLAMATION | MB_OK);
  return NULL;
}
return LocalLock(Handle);;
}
```

Any C++ program for Windows should overload the operators **new** and **delete** so that the Windows function **LocalAlloc** is used instead of the default **malloc** function from the standard C library. The **new** and **delete** operators are not member functions of **WinObj,** but since every class use **WinObj**, it is convenient to declare them here to ensure that every class will use them.

LocalAlloc allocates data on the local heap. If there is not enough memory available, **new** displays a message. The block of memory allocated is locked and left locked until it is released.

The function loads the error message from the application resource file as needed. The resource file contains all the strings, dialog box templates, icons, menus, and so on that the application needs. The resources are bound to the executable application after linking, so they can be changed without any need for rebuilding the application. As a European, I have learned to avoid including text strings in program code, because they create difficulties when converting the application to different languages. In any case, there are other advantages to having messages in the resource file. One such advantage is that a non-programmer can proofread them and, if necessary, make corrections.

The routine **new** is called whenever an instance is created using the **new** statement. Remember that an object can be declared as an automatic variable, in which case **new** is not called. Space is simply allocated on the stack.

```
void operator delete(void * obj)
{
  LocalFree( LocalHandle( (HANDLE)obj));
}
```

The **delete** frees the block of memory allocated by **new**. Here again, it is overloaded to use Windows routines.

```
int WinObj::vMessage( UINT Type, UINT Id, va_list arg_ptr)
{
  char szFmt[128];
  char sz[168]= "";
  LoadString (hInst, Id, (LPSTR)szFmt, sizeof (szFmt));
   // address of arg, not contents
  wvsprintf ((LPSTR)sz, (LPSTR)szFmt, (LPSTR)(arg_ptr));
  LoadString(hInst, IDS_APPNAME, szFmt, sizeof szFmt);
  if (!Type) Type=MB_ICONEXCLAMATION|MB_OK;
  return MessageBox (GetActiveWindow(),
          (LPSTR)sz, (LPSTR)szFmt,Type) ;

}

// Display a generic message box
int WinObj::Message( UINT Type, UINT Id, ...)
{
  va_list arg_ptr;
  va_start(arg_ptr,Id);
  return vMessage(Type,Id,arg_ptr);
}

// Display a Message Box with a Stop icon
void WinObj::Error(UINT Id, ...)
{
    va_list arg_ptr;
    va_start(arg_ptr,Id);
    vMessage(MB_ICONSTOP | MB_OK,Id,arg_ptr);
}

// Display a Message Box with an exclamation
void WinObj::Warning(UINT Id, ...)
{
    va_list arg_ptr;
    va_start(arg_ptr,Id);
    vMessage(MB_ICONEXCLAMATION | MB_OK,Id,arg_ptr);
}
```

Working with 32 Bits

UINT is a new Windows **typedef**, introduced in version 3.1 of the API. It corresponds to an unsigned **int**, so it will be 16 bits long in the 16-bit versions of Windows, and 32 bits long in the 32-bit versions of Windows. Prior to version 3.1, Windows used the **WORD typedef** to define 16-bit unsigned **ints**. **WORD** remains, but it is always 16 bits, even in the 32-bit versions of Windows. Use **UINT** for anything that will be 32 bits long in the 32-bit versions of Windows. That way, your code will be portable between the two versions of Windows.

The preceding routines can be used by any derived class to display message boxes. The message is a formatted string kept in the resource file. The parameter **Id** is the index of the string in the resource file. **Error** and **Warning** display message boxes containing a **Stop** icon and an **Exclamation Mark** icon respectively. **Message** will display any other type of message box. The parameter **Type** to **Message** specifies a combination of **MB** flags.

The reason for making these routines members of the **WinObj** class is that functions similar to these are often defined in many projects. When C++ class instances need to be mixed with existing C routines, this approach ensures there are no conflicts between the functions when the system is linked.

Here is the definition of **WinObj**:

winobj.hpp

```
#ifndef WINOBJ_INC
#define WINOBJ_INC

#include "windows.h"

#include "messages.hpp"
#include <stddef.h>
#include <stdarg.h>
```

The **define** statement is used to prevent WINOBJ.HPP from being included more than once in a compilation. Since each class is derived from **WinObj**, any module using more than one class will implicitly include WINOBJ.HPP more than once. After the first **include**, the compiler skips any following occurrences of WINOBJ.HPP.

This construction should be used in all .HPP files. Do not forget to close the **ifndef** statement with an **endif** statement at the end of the file or you will have some very puzzling compilation errors.

It's a good idea to use the version of WINDOWS.H supplied with your compiler. If you bought your compiler some time ago, you may need to upgrade to a later version of WINDOWS.H. If you use the version supplied with the Windows SDK, you may need to add some **define** statements to WINOBJ.HPP to suit your compiler. For example, if your compiler does not support huge pointers, you must redefine **huge** as **far**, like this:

```
#ifdef __ZTC__
#define _huge _far
#endif
```

MESSAGES.HPP is a file containing the indexes in the resource file of all the messages generated by the classes in this book. This file is described later in this chapter.

```
extern HANDLE hInst;
extern HANDLE hPrevInst;
extern LPSTR  CmdLine;

extern void * operator new(size_t siz);
extern void operator delete(void * obj);
```

The three variables **hInst**, **hPrevInst**, and **CmdLine** are declared in the module containing **WinMain**. **hInst** is the Windows handle to the current instance of the application, **hPrevInst** is a handle to a previous instance of the application, and **CmdLine** is a pointer to the command line for the application. They are initialized from the parameters passed by **WinMain**. Only **hInst** is used by the class library. These three variables could have been declared **static** as a member variable in **WinObj**, but almost all existing C code expects them to be declared **extern**. You will have to do the same if you are going to interface with any existing C code.

Working with 32 Bits

Remember that **hPrevInst** is becoming obsolete and, is always **NULL** in 32-bit versions of Windows. The command line will also include the application name when the application is run under 32-bit versions of Windows; under 16-bit Windows the application name is omitted. You should bear the difference in mind if you want to parse the command line.

```
class WinObj {
public:
  WinObj(){};                      // constructor

  virtual ~WinObj(){};             // virtual destructor
  virtual void Error(             // Display a message with
    UINT Id...);                   // a Stop icon

  virtual void Warning(           // Display a message with
    UINT Id...);                   // an Exclamation icon

  virtual int Message(            // Display a message box
    UINT Type,                     // Set of MessageBox flags
    UINT Id...);
private:
  int  vMessage(UINT Type,UINT Id, va_list arg_ptr);
}; // class WinObj

#endif // WINOBJ_INC
```

The class definition of **WinObj** defines the member functions. **WinObj** contains a virtual constructor and destructor which are inherited by derived classes.

Note the **endif** statement at the end!

The Window Class

Now that the base class **WinObj** is defined, a virtual **Window** class is derived from it. (See Figure 3-2.) The class is virtual because it serves as

FIGURE 3-2 The Window class hierarchy

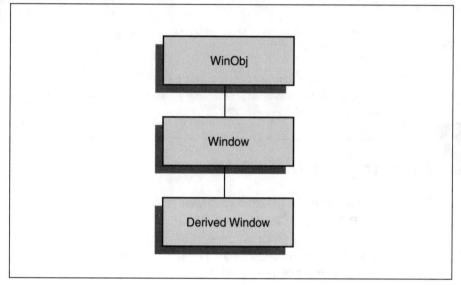

a base class from which useful classes can be derived. An application never declares an instance of **Window**; it derives a class from **Window** and declares an instance of that. **Window** itself does not display a window on the screen, but classes derived from it will. The following example explains how this works.

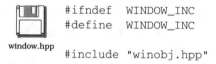

window.hpp

```
#ifndef   WINDOW_INC
#define   WINDOW_INC

#include "winobj.hpp"
```

Since **Window** will be derived from **WinObj,** the header must include the definition of **WinObj** in the WINOBJ.HPP file.

```
extern "C" {
LONG CALLBACK CPPWinProc(HWND, UINT, UINT, LONG);
}


class Event {

public:
```

```
UINT wParam;
LONG lParam;

Event(UINT w, LONG l) {wParam=w; lParam=l;};
}; // class Event
```

The **Window** class refers to **CPPWinProc**, so its prototype is needed here. **CPPWinProc** is an ordinary C function and not a CPP function, so it is declared as **extern "C"**.

Working with 32 Bits

In 16-bit versions of Windows, callback functions are declared as **FAR PASCAL**. **FAR** means that the function code is in a different code segment from Windows, and **PASCAL** means that the Pascal calling convention is used. The function is not written in Pascal, but the parameters are put on the stack from right to left, and the called function is responsible for unwinding the stack afterwards. The reason for doing this is that the Pascal calling convention uses less space on Intel 8086 processors.

The 32-bit versions of Windows do not always run on Intel processors, so there is less reason to insist on the Pascal convention. The 32-bit versions revert to the standard C left-to-right calling convention, and the **FAR** keyword is no longer necessary for 32-bit applications.

CALLBACK is defined in WINDOWS.H to the correct calling convention for the target operating system, so if you use **CALLBACK**, your code will be portable.

The **Event** class is useful for combining the two parameters of Windows messages. An instance of **Event** can be passed to member functions as a single parameter. The **wParam** part of a message will become 32 bits in future versions of Windows.

```
typedef struct {
    int RepeatCount:16,
        ScanCode:8,
        fExtended:1,
```

```
        reserved1:4,
        fAlt:1,
        fPrev:1,
        fTransition:1;
} KEYCODES;
```

The **KEYCODES** structure will be useful for accessing the codes and flags in the keyboard event messages.

```
class Window: public  WinObj, {
protected :
#ifdef WIN32
  WNDPROC DefaultHandler;
  static WNDPROC Handler;
#else
  FARPROC DefaultHandler;, // default callback
  static FARPROC Handler;, // proc instance
#endif
  void SetHandler();
  static HANDLE hAccel;
```

When the **Window** class has created a window, it replaces the message handling function with **CPPWinProc**. **DefaultHandler** is used to store the window's old message function. **Handler** is a procedure instance of the replacement C++ message function **CPPWinProc**. A procedure instance is another Windows peculiarity. You cannot simply give Windows the address of a function; you have to make a procedure instance of the function and give Windows that. Since the same function is used for all windows, only one copy of the procedure instance **Handler** is needed and it can be declared **static**. **Handler** will be initialized later on.

The **hAccel** statement is the handle to a keyboard accelerator table that the application might use. An accelerator is a short cut to an item in the menu. For example, you might want to have SHIFT-F12 as an accelerator for the menu item *File Save*. Typically, an application uses only one table, so the item is declared **static.** Note that some applications have alternative accelerator tables. This is common in applications that have been converted from DOS. The application will provide a set of accelerators complying with the IBM Common User Access (CUA) standards that Windows uses, as well as a set matching the accelerators that the old DOS application used. Users can choose whichever set they feel comfortable with. Whichever set they choose, the application uses only one accelerator table at any given time.

```
public:
  Window();                        // void constructor
  ~Window();

protected:
  void Create(                     // Create a window
    LPSTR pCaption,                // Caption
    LONG  Style,
    int x,                         // Position
    int y,
    int width,                     // Size
    int height,
    HWND hPwnd,                    // Parent handle
    HMENU hMenu=NULL);
```

Subclasses use **Create** to actually create the window on the screen.
The member **hWnd** will contain the window handle for the instance. It is
declared **public**, since there are many occasions when an API function
can be used with an class instance, provided that the window handle is
accessible.

```
public:
  HWND hWnd;                       // Window handle

  friend  LONG CALLBACK CPPWinProc(
    HWND hWnd, UINT msg, UINT wParam, LONG lParam);
```

CPPWinProc must be defined as a friend, since it needs to access the
protected members of **Window**.

```
  virtual WORD MessageLoop();
  virtual LONG MessageProc(
    HWND hWnd,
    unsigned msg,
    Event& evt);

  virtual LPSTR Register(WNDCLASS& wc);

  void Move(
    RECT *rc,                      // Move the window
    BOOL repaint=TRUE);

  BOOL Show(                       // Show or hide the window
    int nCmdShow=SW_SHOW){
    return ShowWindow(hWnd,nCmdShow);}};
```

```
    int GetText(                    // Get window text
      LPSTR pBuffer,
      int Size){
      return SendMessage(hWnd,WM_GETTEXT,Size,(LONG)pBuffer);};

    int SetText(                    // Set window text
      LPSTR pBuffer){
      return SendMessage(hWnd,WM_SETTEXT,0,(LONG)pBuffer);};
```

Move, **Show**, **GetText**, and **SetText** are general-purpose member functions that are useful for windows. These are described in more detail later in this chapter.

```
                                // Virtual event member functions
    virtual BOOL   InitMenu(HMENU hMenu)
      {return FALSE;};
    virtual BOOL   QueryClose()
      {return TRUE;};
    virtual BOOL   Size( UINT Width, UINT Height, UINT Type);
    virtual BOOL   Char(UINT Value, UINT Repeat)
      {return FALSE;};
    virtual BOOL   KeyDown(UINT VirtKey, KEYCODES KeyCodes)
      {return FALSE;};
    virtual BOOL   LButtonDown(POINT Cursor, UINT Keys)
      {return FALSE;};
    virtual BOOL   LButtonDblClk(POINT Cursor, UINT Keys)
      {return FALSE;};
    virtual BOOL   MouseMove(POINT Cursor, UINT Keys)
      {return FALSE;};
    virtual BOOL   MouseActivate(HWND hTop, UINT HitTest)
      {return FALSE;};
    virtual BOOL   LButtonUp(POINT Cursor, UINT Keys)
      {return FALSE;};
    virtual BOOL   RButtonDown(POINT Cursor, UINT Keys)
      {return FALSE;};
    virtual BOOL   RButtonUp(POINT Cursor, UINT Keys)
      {return FALSE;};
    virtual BOOL   Paint();
    virtual BOOL   SetFocus (HWND hPrev)
      {return FALSE;};
    virtual BOOL   KillFocus (HWND hNext)
      {return FALSE;};
    virtual BOOL   Command( UINT Id, UINT Code, HWND hControl);

}; // class Window
```

These are the virtual member functions for event handling. They correspond to the **WM_** messages with the same name. For example, **InitMenu** is called when the window receives a **WM_INITMENU** message. The message parameters **wParam** and **lParam** would have been pulled apart in **MessageProc** and cast into values of the correct type. Most member functions return **FALSE** to indicate to Windows that the message has not been processed. The exception is **QueryClose**, which returns **TRUE** to indicate that the application may be closed. **QueryClose** does not correspond directly to a message, but the **Window** class calls it when it receives a **WM_CLOSE** message.

Any window in a derived class can redefine these virtual member functions:

```
extern void PutWin(HWND hWnd, Window * pWin);
extern Window * GetWin(HWND hWnd);
extern Window * DelWin(HWND hWnd);
#endif // WINDOW_INC
```

These functions are used to put the class instance address in a window's property list, and extract it afterwards.

Here is the source of WINDOW.CPP:

```
#include "window.hpp"

ATOM aProp, aPropHigh;

#if defined(PTR16) || defined (WIN32)
  #define PUTPWIN(hWnd,this) \
    SetProp(hWnd,(LPSTR)MAKELONG(aProp,0),(HANDLE)this)
  #define GETPWIN(hWnd) \
    (Window *)GetProp(hWnd,(LPSTR)MAKELONG(aProp,0))
  #define DELPWIN(hWnd) \
    (Window *)RemoveProp(hWnd,(LPSTR)MAKELONG(aProp,0))
#else                          // 16-bit large model
  #define PUTPWIN(hWnd,this)\
    SetProp(hWnd,(LPSTR)MAKELONG(aProp,0),(HANDLE)this);\
    SetProp(hWnd,(LPSTR)MAKELONG(aPropHigh,0),\
    (HANDLE)((DWORD)this >>16))
  #define GETPWIN(hWnd) (Window *)\
    ((DWORD)GetProp(hWnd,(LPSTR)MAKELONG(aProp,0))|\
    ((DWORD)GetProp(hWnd,(LPSTR)MAKELONG(aPropHigh,0)) <<16))
  #define DELPWIN(hWnd) (Window *)\
```

window.cpp

```
    ((DWORD)RemoveProp(hWnd,(LPSTR)MAKELONG(aProp,0))|\
    ((DWORD)RemoveProp(hWnd,(LPSTR)MAKELONG(aPropHigh,0)) <<16))
#endif // PTR16
```

These **define** statements are used to put a pointer to a **Window** class instance into the property list of an actual window. In this way, **Window** class associates class instances with window handles. The pointer is retrieved when a message arrives from Windows, so that the class knows where to dispatch it.

Since a property is 16 bits wide, the code needs to use two properties if it has been compiled for the large model, since pointers are then 32 bits. The symbol **PTR16** indicates the medium or small model. **PTR16** should be set externally, perhaps on the compiler command line. Most compilers have a predefined symbol that indicates the size of a pointer, but the name is different for each compiler. The Microsoft compiler, for example, uses **M_I86MM** to indicate the medium model and **M_I86SM** to indicate the small model. If you wish, replace **PTR16** with whatever your compiler uses. If you forget to define **PTR16** and you use the medium or small model, the code will use 32 bits of storage, but the code will still work. Just make sure that you do not define **PTR16** if you use the large model, or all the pointers will be invalid.

The property functions use atoms, an approach that is slightly more efficient than using strings. When you create an atom, Windows stores the string in an atom table. If two atoms have the same name, they have the same atom number. It is much easier for the property functions to search through atoms, because they simply compare atom numbers and not all the characters in a string.

Working with 32 Bits

In 32-bit versions of Windows, properties are 32 bits. A 32-bit pointer to an instance fits in one property. Atoms are still 16-bits, so the **MAKELONG** macro is still necessary.

```
void PutWin(HWND hWnd, Window * pWin) { PUTPWIN(hWnd,pWin);};
Window * GetWin(HWND hWnd) {return GETPWIN(hWnd);};
Window*  DelWin(HWND hWnd) {return DELPWIN(hWnd);};
```

These functions act as wrappers around the **define** statements. The definitions are used within the **Window** class to avoid the overhead of an extra function call. This is especially important in the message loop, which calls **GETPWIN** for each message. The functions are occasionally used by other classes, but then the overhead of a function call is of no consequence.

Defined macros such as these are frowned on these days, since C++ supports **inline** functions. **PutWin** could have been defined in this manner:

```
inline void PutWinHWND hWnd, Window * pWin) {
#ifdef PTR16
  SetProp(hWnd,(LPSTR)MAKELONG(aProp,0),(HANDLE)this);
#else
 SetProp(hWnd,(LPSTR)MAKELONG(aProp,0),(HANDLE)this);
 SetProp(hWnd,(LPSTR)MAKELONG(aPropHigh,0),
        (HANDLE)((DWORD)this >>16));
#endif
}
```

The compiler then inserts the function body code inline at the place where the function is called rather than calling the function. That saves the time it takes to call the function. The snag is that most compilers do not allow inline functions to be declared **extern** as well, so the function is not accessible outside of its own module. That might seem reasonable—the compiler will not be able to insert the functions inline in other modules because it will not have the code available when it compiles them. The ideal is to have external inline functions that are treated inline in the module where they are declared, but are treated as ordinary functions elsewhere.

The alternative is to define the inline function in the header file, but I prefer to keep the header files as simple as possible.

```
#ifdef WIN32
  WNDPROC Window::Handler;
#else
  FARPROC Window::Handler;       // proc instance for CPPWinProc
#endif
HANDLE Window::hAccel;           // Current accelerator table

//  Set window message proc to CPPWinProc
void Window::SetHandler()
```

```
{
#ifdef WIN32
  DefaultHandler = (WNDPROC) GetWindowLong(hWnd,GWL_WNDPROC);
#else
  DefaultHandler = (FARPROC) GetWindowLong(hWnd,GWL_WNDPROC);
#endif
  SetWindowLong(hWnd,GWL_WNDPROC,(LONG) Handler);
PUTPWIN(hWnd,(HANDLE) this);
}
```

This function replaces the window's original function with the new message handler **CPPWinProc**. The old window function is retrieved and stored in **DefaultHandler**. The API function **SetWindowLong** needs a procedure instance. **SetHandler** should not pass it **CPPWinProc** directly. The **Window** constructor will initialize **Handler** to be a procedure instance of **CPPWinProc**.

```
// Create a window
void Window::Create(LPSTR caption, LONG style, int x, int y,
            int width, int height, HWND hPwnd, HMENU hMenu)
{

  WNDCLASS wc;

  wc.style          = 0;
  wc.lpfnWndProc    = (WNDPROC) DefWindowProc;
  wc.cbClsExtra     = 0;
  wc.cbWndExtra     = 0;
  wc.hInstance      = hInst;
  wc.hIcon          = LoadIcon(NULL,IDI_APPLICATION);
  wc.hCursor        = LoadCursor(NULL,IDC_ARROW);
  wc.hbrBackground  = (HBRUSH)(COLOR_WINDOW+1);
  wc.lpszMenuName   = 0;

  hWnd = CreateWindow(Register(wc),
                      caption,style,x,y,width,height,
                      hPwnd,hMenu,hInst,NULL);

  if (!hWnd) Error(IDS_APPLERROR, (LPSTR)"Window Creation");

  SetHandler();

}
```

Create actually produces the window that the user later sees on the screen. It is usually called from the constructor of a derived class. **Create** initializes the **WNDCLASS** structure with reasonable default values before calling the virtual member function **Register**. **Register** will be redefined by the application window class. It must supply the class name and may optionally modify the other values. For example, **Register** may set **wc.hIcon** to the icon that will be displayed when the window is minimized.

wc.Cursor is set to the default Windows arrow cursor, and **wc.hbrBackground** is set to the default color for a window. (The default color is white.)

Register must also call the API function **RegisterClass** to make the class known to Windows. An application only needs to call **RegisterClass** once, but it does not matter if **RegisterClass** is called several times for the same class. Subsequent calls are ignored and do not use any additional storage space.

The error message in the preceding example contains a text string, but this is a debugging message that should not be seen by users. If you prefer, you may replace the text "Window Creation" by an error number.

After the window has been created, **SetHandler** sets the window message handling function to the **CPPWinProc** function. From that point on, **CPPWinProc** relays messages to the **MessageProc** member function for that instance.

Note   You may wonder why we could not have specified **CPPWinProc** in **wc.lpfnWndProc** when the class was registered, instead of replacing the function after the window is created. The reason is that the lifetime of a window is slightly longer than its class instance. The window is created and receives messages before **CreateWindow** returns. It is only when **CreateWindow** returns that we know what the handle is and can start intercepting the messages. Until that time, the default function handles them. If **CPPWinProc** is specified in **wc.lpfnWndProc,** it will not know how to handle the first few messages that arrive.

In addition, **CPPWinProc** calls the default function to handle unprocessed messages. It is therefore convenient to supply the default function when the class is registered and we can be sure that the code will work with pre-registered classes, such as MDI Child windows, that have a different default message processing function.

```
Window::Window() {
  hWnd=0;
  if (!Handler) {
#ifdef WIN32
    Handler = (WNDPROC)CPPWinProc;
#else
    Handler = MakeProcInstance((FARPROC)CPPWinProc, hInst);
#endif
    aProp=AddAtom("pWindow");
    aPropHigh=AddAtom("pWindowHigh");
  }
}
```

The constructor sets member variables to zero. This example contains only one member variable, **hWnd.** All classes should initialize their members. If **new** is used to create an instance, the **GlobalAlloc** function sets the data to zero, but if a class instance is created on the stack, its data is not automatically zeroed and initially contains garbage.

If **Handler** has not yet been initialized, the **Window** constructor initializes it to a procedure instance of **CPPWinProc.** At the same time, the constructor creates the atoms used by the property list functions. Since **Handler** is in **static** memory and will be shared by all instances of **Window**, this initialization is only performed the first time a **Window**, or a subclass of **Window,** is created in an application. Procedure instances and atoms use space, so they should be created only when necessary and deleted after use. There is no need to delete **Handler** and the atoms, since once created they are used throughout the life of the application. Windows deletes them when the application terminates.

```
LPSTR Window::Register(WNDCLASS& wc) {
    Error(IDS_APPLERROR,(LPSTR)"No Register member function");
return NULL;
}
```

Classes derived from **Window** must supply a member function to register the class. If they do not, the member function here will display an error. Again, an English text string might be acceptable here, since the message is only intended to help the programmer; the user should not see it. Without this message, the programmer may not realize why a window is not being created.

```
Window::~Window()
{
  if (hWnd) {
    Show(SW_HIDE);
    //Destroy instances associated with child windows
    HWND hCwnd= GetWindow (hWnd, GW_CHILD);
    while ( hCwnd ){
       Window * pWin=(Window*) GETPWIN(hCwnd);
       do {
            hCwnd=GetWindow(hCwnd,GW_HWNDNEXT);
       } while (hCwnd  && GetParent(hCwnd)!=hWnd);
       if (pWin) delete pWin;
    }

    if (DELPWIN(hWnd) && DefaultHandler)
      SetWindowLong(hWnd,GWL_WNDPROC,(LONG) DefaultHandler);
    //if this is the top level window quit the application
    if (!GetParent(hWnd)) PostQuitMessage(0);
    DestroyWindow(hWnd);
    hWnd=0;
  }
}
```

If **hWnd** is no longer valid when the destructor is called, the destructor does nothing. Normally, **hWnd** will be valid, but subclasses may set **hWnd** to zero in their own destructors if they wish to disable the **Window** destructor.

The destructor first deletes any instances associated with any child windows. Windows maintains a list of child windows. The API function

GetWindow(hWnd, GW_CHILD);

will return the first child window in the list, and

GetWindow(hCwnd, GW_HWNDNEXT);

will return the nearest sibling of that window.

Before destroying the window, the destructor reinstates the default window procedure. That allows the window to handle the last few messages that arrive as it is being destroyed.

If this is a top-level window, having no parent, the destructor must also post a quit message to terminate the application. The parameter 0 indicates normal termination. Most applications have only one top-level window, but if for any reason a **Window** subclass needs to be a top-level window, it should provide its own destructor that does not post a quit message. The Dynamic Data Exchange (DDE) server class in Chapter 11 will do this. A DDE server must be a top-level window or Windows will not send it any **WM_INITIATE** messages.

Finally, the destructor destroys the window by calling the API function **DestroyWindow**.

```
WORD Window::MessageLoop()
{
    MSG msg;
    while (GetMessage(&msg, NULL, 0, 0)) {
      if (!hAccel ||
        !TranslateAccelerator (hWnd, hAccel, &msg)){
        TranslateMessage (&msg);
        DispatchMessage (&msg);
      }
    }
    return msg.wParam;
}
```

This is a message loop for simple applications without dialog boxes. Chapter 6 shows how to handle the keyboard interface for dialog boxes. The loop is terminated when the **WM_QUIT** message, posted by the **Window** destructor, arrives. The member function returns the parameter of the **WM_QUIT** message and the root function **WinMain** should return this value to Windows.

```
// The window message function, translates messages
// to calls to virtual functions
LONG Window::MessageProc( HWND hWnd, UINT msg, Event& evt)
{
  POINT Pt;

  switch (msg){
```

MessageProc is the virtual message handling function. The window function of most Windows applications written in C looks something like this example. The **switch** statement here acts as an interface between the message-based Windows architecture and the member function-based architecture that the C++ objects will use. For most messages, this **switch** statement simply calls the corresponding member function. A few messages, such as **WM_DESTROY**, are treated in a special way.

```
case WM_QUERYENDSESSION:
  // OK to end Windows session?
  return QueryClose();

case WM_CLOSE:
  // if OK delete this instance
  if (QueryClose ()) delete this;
  return TRUE;

case WM_DESTROY:
  if (DELPWIN(hWnd) && DefaultHandler)
    SetWindowLong(hWnd,GWL_WNDPROC,(LONG) DefaultHandler);
  Window::hWnd=0;
  delete this;
  break;
```

These messages handle the window close. **WM_QUERYENDSESSION** is sent when the user has elected to end the Windows session. **WM_CLOSE** is sent when the user closes this particular window. In both cases, the window can veto the close. This should be done if closing the window might cause the user to lose work that has not yet been saved to disk.

The two messages call the virtual member function **QueryClose**, which returns **TRUE** by default. If a derived window wishes to veto the close, it should provide a **QueryClose** member function that returns **FALSE**.

Generally, if there is work to be saved, **QueryClose** should display a message box to ask the user whether the work should be saved. The box should have three buttons, *Yes*, *No*, and *Cancel*. If *Yes* is chosen, the application should save the work and **QueryClose** returns **TRUE**, indicating that the window may be closed. If *No* is chosen, **QueryClose** returns **TRUE**, the window will be closed and the work lost. If the user chooses *Cancel*, **QueryClose** should return **FALSE** to veto the close. The old trick of unconditionally displaying an *Are you sure?* message, which used to be common in DOS applications, is not considered user friendly these days.

WM_QUERYENDSESSION simply returns the value from the **QueryClose** member function. The **WM_CLOSE** code deletes the class instance if **QueryClose** gives the OK. Deleting the instance destroys the window too, since **DestroyWindow** is called in the destructor.

The **WM_DESTROY** message arrives here if the window is destroyed by Windows while the class instance still exists. If the window is destroyed by the class destructor, this message is handled by the default window function.

In a well-structured application, windows should only be destroyed by deleting them. However, not all applications are well structured, particularly if, for one reason or another, the application must use some preexisting C code. Handling the **WM_DESTROY** message ensures that if a window is destroyed, the memory used by its class instance is released.

The following case statements simply call the member function that corresponds to each message. The message parameters **wParam** and **lParam** are converted to the correct member function parameters.

```
case WM_INITMENU:
  return InitMenu((HMENU)evt.wParam);

case WM_SIZE:
  return Size(LOWORD(evt.lParam),
             HIWORD(evt.lParam),evt.wParam);

case WM_PAINT:
  return Paint();

case WM_SETFOCUS:
  return SetFocus((HWND)evt.wParam);

case WM_KILLFOCUS:
  return KillFocus((HWND)evt.wParam);

case WM_CHAR:
  return Char(evt.wParam, LOWORD(evt.lParam));

case WM_KEYDOWN:
  if (KeyDown(evt.wParam,
     *(KEYCODES*)&evt.lParam)) return TRUE;
  return FALSE;
```

```
       case WM_LBUTTONDOWN:
         Pt.x=LOWORD(evt.lParam); Pt.y=HIWORD(evt.lParam);
         return LButtonDown(Pt, evt.wParam);

       case WM_LBUTTONUP:
         Pt.x=LOWORD(evt.lParam); Pt.y=HIWORD(evt.lParam);
         return LButtonUp(Pt, evt.wParam);

       case WM_LBUTTONDBLCLK:
         Pt.x=LOWORD(evt.lParam); Pt.y=HIWORD(evt.lParam);
         return LButtonDblClk(Pt, evt.wParam);

       case WM_RBUTTONDOWN:
         Pt.x=LOWORD(evt.lParam); Pt.y=HIWORD(evt.lParam);
         return RButtonDown(Pt, evt.wParam);

       case WM_RBUTTONUP:
         Pt.x=LOWORD(evt.lParam); Pt.y=HIWORD(evt.lParam);
         return RButtonUp(Pt, evt.wParam);

       case WM_MOUSEMOVE:
         Pt.x=LOWORD(evt.lParam); Pt.y=HIWORD(evt.lParam);
         return MouseMove(Pt, evt.wParam);

       case WM_MOUSEACTIVATE:
         MouseActivate((HWND)evt.wParam, LOWORD(evt.lParam));
         if(DefaultHandler)
         return CallWindowProc (DefaultHandler,
                hWnd, msg, evt.wParam, evt.lParam);
         else return FALSE;


       case WM_COMMAND:
       {
         WORD wNotifyCode;         // notification code
         WORD wID;                 // item, controlr ID
         HWND hWndCtl;             // handle of control

#ifdef WIN32
         wNotifyCode = HIWORD(evt.wParam);
         wID = LOWORD(evt.wParam);
         hWndCtl = (HWND) evt.lParam;
#else
         wID = (int) evt.wParam;
         hWndCtl = (HWND) LOWORD(evt.lParam);
```

```
        wNotifyCode = HIWORD(evt.lParam);
#endif
        return Command(wID,wNotifyCode, hWndCtl);
    }

    default:
      if (DefaultHandler)
      return CallWindowProc (DefaultHandler,
              hWnd, msg, evt.wParam, evt.lParam);
  } // switch
  return FALSE;
} // MessageProc
```

Notice that the default function should be called for the **WM_MOUSEACTIVATE** message, even if the class instance handles it. The default function passes the message on to the parent.

Some input messages, such as the middle mouse-button messages and the right mouse-button double-click messages, are omitted because they are rarely used in most applications. If you like to use them, you may add them to this **switch** statement.

Working with 32 Bits

Since window handles are 32 bits in 32-bit versions of Windows, the **WM_COMMAND** message needs all of the **lParam** for the handle. Consequently, the notification code is moved to the high order word of the **wParam**, which has grown to 32 bits. The code for **WM_COM-MAND** unpacks the message in one of two different ways depending on the target operating system.

```
BOOL Window::Size(UINT Width, UINT Height, UINT Type) {
  if (!DefaultHandler) return FALSE;
  return CallWindowProc (DefaultHandler,
        hWnd, WM_SIZE, Type, MAKELONG(Width, Height));
}

BOOL Window::Paint() {
  if (!DefaultHandler) return FALSE;
  return CallWindowProc (DefaultHandler, hWnd, WM_PAINT, 0,0);
}
```

```
BOOL Window::Command( UINT Id, UINT Code, HWND hControl) {
  if (!DefaultHandler) return FALSE;
#ifdef WIN32
  return CallWindowProc (DefaultHandler,
    hWnd, WM_COMMAND, MAKELONG(Id, Code), (DWORD)hControl);
#else
  return CallWindowProc (DefaultHandler,
    hWnd, WM_COMMAND, Id, MAKELONG(hControl, Code));
#endif
}
```

For the **Size**, **Paint**, and **Command** events, the default function should be called when the class instance does not handle them. The default action for the **Paint** event, for example, is to paint the window with its background brush.

Notice that there is no need to provide a member function for the **WM_CREATE** message. The class instance's constructor serves the same purpose. In any case, Windows sends **WM_CREATE** to the window before the **CreateWindow** function returns and before the **Window** instance is created. The **WM_CREATE** message never arrives here.

```
LONG CALLBACK CPPWinProc(HWND hWnd, UINT Message,
                 UINT wParam, LONG lParam)
{
  Window* pWin = GETPWIN(hWnd);
  Event evt(wParam, lParam);
  if (pWin) {
    // There is a C++ instance for the window
    return pWin->MessageProc(hWnd, Message, evt);
  }
  else return FALSE;
} // CPPWinProc
```

CPPWinProc is the function that is actually called by Windows. It extracts the pointer to the C++ class instance from the window's property list and calls the **MessageProc** member function. While **MessageProc** handles the transition from messages to member functions, **CPPWinProc** is the interface between window handles and class instances.

```
void Window::Move(RECT * rc, BOOL repaint) {
  MoveWindow (hWnd,
    rc->left,
    rc->top,
```

```
        rc->right-rc->left,
        rc->bottom-rc->top,
        repaint);
}
```

The **Move**, **Show**, **GetText**, and **SetText** member functions (the last three are defined in the .HPP file) are not strictly necessary, since all the API routines can be used with class instances of windows. Defining member functions such as these can simplify your code and give it a more object-oriented appearance.

For example, to resize a window you only need to write

```
MyWin.Move(rNewSize);
```

instead of

```
MoveWindow(MyWin.hWnd,rNewSize.left, rNewSize.top,
    rNewSize.right-rNewSize.left,
    rNewSize.bottom-rNewSize.top, TRUE);
```

Avoid the temptation of defining member functions for all the functions in the API. Otherwise, you end up with a system that is just as complex as the API and probably not so well documented as the API. In addition, you risk confusing other users of your classes. For example, you might write a member function **GetParent** to return the handle of the parent of the window in the current instance. Somebody else might think it more logical to have such a function return the class instance of the parent.

A Hello World Program

Now that the base **Window** class has been defined, you can make use of it in a simple application. Tradition has it that the first program in any new system should display *Hello World*. I do not want to break with tradition, so the first application will display the text *Hello World* centered in a window.

The first task is to derive a class from **Window** to do whatever is needed. Let's call it **MyWin**. **MyWin** needs to process the **Paint** event and to display the text whenever the window requires painting.

Since the text is centered in the window, **Paint** also needs to know the window size. The size can be found by simply calling the API function **GetClientRect**, but to make the example more interesting, **MyWin** will process the **Size** event and store the width and height of the window in two class variables.

MyWin must also register the class and create the window. Here is the class definition in the MYWIN.HPP file:

mywin.hpp

```
#ifndef MYWIN_INC
#define MYWIN_INC

#include "window.hpp"

class MyWin : public Window {
public:
    MyWin(HWND PhWnd, LPSTR Name,
        DWORD Style=WS_OVERLAPPEDWINDOW,
        int x= CW_USEDEFAULT, int y= CW_USEDEFAULT,
        int width= CW_USEDEFAULT, int height= CW_USEDEFAULT);

protected:
    int Height, Width;
    LPSTR Register(WNDCLASS& wc);
    BOOL Paint();
    BOOL Size(UINT Width, UINT Height, UINT Type);
}; // class MyWin

#endif // MYWIN_INC
```

MyWin is declared as a subclass of **Window**. Since the compiler will want to know what **Window** is, **MyWin** must include **Window**'s .HPP file. The **MyWin** constructor has parameters for the style and size, but default values are supplied so that the constructor can be called with just the parent handle and name. The constructor must be declared **public**, since it will be called from outside this class. **MyWin** uses the destructor defined in the **Window** class.

The other member functions and the class member variables **Height** and **Width** are protected. Thus, they are not accessible from other classes, but they can be used by classes derived from **MyWin**.

Since **MyWin** will redefine the **Register**, **Size**, and **Paint** member functions, it declares them here. They must be declared exactly as they are declared in the base class, although the keyword **virtual** may be omitted. If you wish, you may cut and paste the member function names from the WINDOW.HPP file.

The code for the constructor and member functions is in the .CPP file. Here is the source:

mywin.cpp

```
#include "mywin.hpp"

MyWin::MyWin(HWND PhWnd, LPSTR Name, DWORD Style,
         int x, int y,int width, int height)
{
  Create(Name,Style,x,y,width,height,PhWnd,NULL);
}
```

The constructor calls the member function **Create,** defined in the **Window** class to create the window on the screen.

```
LPSTR MyWin::Register(WNDCLASS& wc)
{
  wc.lpszClassName = "MyWin";
  wc.style = CS_HREDRAW | CS_VREDRAW;
  wc.hIcon = LoadIcon(hInst,"Hello");
  RegisterClass (&wc);
  return "MyWin";
}
```

Create calls the **Register** member function. The structure **WNDCLASS** has already been initialized with reasonable defaults, but it needs a class name. Since **MyWin** will want to keep the string "Hello World" centered in the window, it specifies the **CS_HREDRAW** and **CS_VREDRAW** styles. Windows then sends a **Paint** event whenever the size of the window changes. An alternative would have been to omit these styles, and instead invalidate the client area in the **Size** member function. With the area invalidated, Windows would send a **WM_PAINT** message to have it redrawn.

Register also specifies a little icon that is displayed when the application is minimized. If we install the application in a Program Manager group, the Windows Program Manager will also display this icon:

After registering the class, the function returns its name.

```
BOOL MyWin::Size(UINT Width, UINT Height, UINT Type)
{
  MyWin::Height =Height;
  MyWin::Width  =Width;
  return TRUE;
}
```

The **Size** member function is called whenever the size of the window changes. The parameters specify the height and width of the client area of the window. The client area is the part inside the window frame, so the actual window is a little bit larger.

The **MyWin** class members **Height** and **Width** have the same names as the parameters, so you must prefix them with the class qualifier **MyWin::**, to enable the compiler to tell them apart.

```
BOOL MyWin::Paint()
{
  PAINTSTRUCT ps;
  LPSTR pStr="Hello World";

  HDC hDC=BeginPaint(hWnd, &ps);
  SetTextAlign(hDC,TA_CENTER | TA_BASELINE);
  TextOut(hDC,Width/2,Height/2,pStr,lstrlen(pStr));
  EndPaint(hWnd,&ps);
  return TRUE;
}
```

Paint displays the text using the API function **TextOut**. The call to **SetTextAlign** means that the text will be printed with its horizontal center and baseline on the coordinates given in **TextOut**. The **hWnd** parameter to **BeginPaint** is the class variable in **Window.** It is set when the window is created. **BeginPaint** and **EndPaint** are API functions. Both the **Size** and **Paint** member functions return **TRUE** to indicate that they have processed the event.

Notice that an alternative would have been to make the two calls to **BeginPaint** and **EndPaint** in the base **Window** class, and then to define a **Paint** member function with **hDC** and **ps** as parameters. The default **Paint** member function in the **Window** class would then have to paint the window with the default background brush. This would avoid the need to call these functions in derived classes such as **MyWin**.

The choice to do this or not depends a little bit on the programming culture of the people using the classes. Those who are used to programming with the API in C may prefer that the member functions correspond to the original Windows messages, as they do here. Others might prefer that as much work as possible be done by the top-level classes.

Now that **MyWin** is written, something must create an instance of it. Another module, TEST.CPP, does that.

test.cpp

```
#include "mywin.hpp"

HANDLE hInst;
HANDLE hPrevInst;
LPSTR  CmdLine;

int PASCAL WinMain(HANDLE hInstance, HANDLE hPrevInstance,
    LPSTR lpszCmdLine, int nCmdShow)
{

    hInst = hInstance;
    char * pName = new char[80];
    LoadString(hInst,IDS_APPNAME, pName, 80);

    // Create an instance of MyWin called Win
    MyWin Win(NULL,pName);

    delete pName;

    Win.Show(nCmdShow);
    return Win.MessageLoop();

}
```

The three variables **hInst**, **hPrevInst**, and **CmdLine** are declared here. The variables are initialized from the parameters supplied with **WinMain**. Only **hInst** is used in this application.

To create the window, simply declare one. The line

MyWin Win(NULL,pName);

means "Create an item of class **MyWin**, called **Win**". The parameters are passed to the constructor in **MyWin**. Since **Win** is a top-level window, the parent window handle is **NULL**.

The application's name is stored in the resource file. The application could get it with **LoadString**, but **LoadString** would require a text buffer to load it in. **WinMain** could just declare the name as a character array on the stack, like this:

char Name[80];

but the data would then stay on the stack throughout the application's life. Of course, that would not matter for a tiny application like this example, but for real-life applications it is best to avoid leaving unused data on the stack. Here **WinMain** declares the array using the **new** operator, and removes it with **delete** once the window is created and the data is no longer needed.

A new window is invisible, and **WinMain** uses the member function **Show** to make it visible. For top-level windows, **Show** should use the parameter supplied by **WinMain,** since the system may want to display the application initially as an icon. This would be the case if the application were added to the **Load** section in the WIN.INI file, for instance. For other windows in an application, the **WS_VISIBLE** style can be used to make the window visible on creation.

Once the window has been created, **WinMain** can start the application by calling **MessageLoop. WinMain** returns the value of **MessageLoop** to Windows. This value is the Quit code and is usually zero.

A few other files are necessary. A resource file contains the icons and strings that the application uses.

test.rc

```
#include "windows.h"
#include "messages.hpp"

Hello ICON hello.ico

STRINGTABLE
BEGIN
IDS_APPNAME    "My First Object"

#include "strings.rc"

END
```

The resource file should declare the name of the application as **IDS_APPNAM**, since this identifier is used by the **WinObj** class in error messages. The resource file should also include MESSAGES.HPP and STRINGS.RC, since the classes use them for reporting error messages. STRINGS.RC should be included in the string table.

The application icon is specified here. The **Register** member function uses the icon **Hello**. In compilation, the resource file loads this icon from the file HELLO.ICO.

Here is the source of STRINGS.RC:

strings.rc

```
IDS_APPLERROR          "Application error in %s"
IDS_MEMORY             "No more memory available"
IDS_CANTOPEN           "Cannot open the file '%s'"
IDS_CANTREAD           "Cannot read the file '%s'"
IDS_CANTCREATE         "Cannot create the file '%s'"
IDS_CANTWRITE          "Cannot write the file '%s'"
IDS_ILLFNM             "Invalid filename: '%s'"
```

And here is the source of MESSAGES.HPP:

messages.hpp

```
#define IDS_APPNAME        1
#define IDS_APPLERROR    100
#define IDS_MEMORY       101
#define IDS_CANTOPEN     102
#define IDS_CANTREAD     103
#define IDS_CANTCREATE   104
#define IDS_CANTWRITE    105
#define IDS_ILLFNM       106
```

The definitions file for most C++ applications will look like this. The file is necessary, and usually you only have to change the name and the description.

test.def

```
NAME          Test

DESCRIPTION   'My first object'

EXETYPE       WINDOWS

STUB          'WINSTUB.EXE'

CODE          PRELOAD MOVEABLE DISCARDABLE
DATA          PRELOAD MOVEABLE MULTIPLE

HEAPSIZE      1024
STACKSIZE     6000
```

```
EXPORTS
    CPPWinProc      @1
```

Declare the window function as **EXPORT** so that Windows can find it when it calls it back. All windows will share the same function, so you only need to do this once. C++ programs tend to use more stack and heap space than C programs, since instances must be declared in one of these two areas. The value given for **HEAPSIZE** is only an initial value, which Windows increases automatically if necessary. The space reserved for the stack is fixed; 6000 bytes is usually enough. Complex applications may require more stack space, especially if you put instances of large and complex classes on the stack. If you run off the end of the stack, you will not see an error message, but your program will not work properly.

Hello World

After the files have been compiled and linked, you're ready to run the Hello World program. If all is proper, the result looks like Figure 3-3, with text centered even when the window is resized.

So now the **Window** class sees the light of day. The code required to write the Hello World application is slightly larger than the original C version, but more sophisticated. The program illustrates procedures for writing a **Window** subclass:

☐   Provide a constructor to create the window, and possibly create additional objects that the window might need.

 The Hello World application

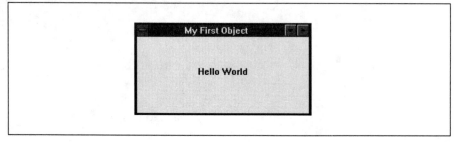

- ☐   If necessary, provide a destructor to delete the objects created.

- ☐   Define the **Register** member function to register the class.

- ☐   Define member functions for any events that the window might want to process.

- ☐   In **WinMain,** create an instance of the window and start the message loop.

An Event-Handling Program

The following **Window** subclass, which processes user input, is a little more complex. For each input type, the window displays a screen message, as in Figure 3-4. The class is similar to the Hello World program, but it processes the keyboard events and most mouse events.

The class definition specifies the extra event member functions.

evtwin.hpp

```
#ifndef EVENTWIN_INC
#define EVENTWIN_INC

#include "window.hpp"

class EventWin : public Window {
public:
  EventWin(HWND PhWnd, LPSTR Name,
    DWORD Style=WS_OVERLAPPEDWINDOW,
    int x= CW_USEDEFAULT, int y= CW_USEDEFAULT,
    int width= CW_USEDEFAULT, int height= CW_USEDEFAULT);
```

FIGURE 3-4   The event-handling program

```
protected:
  POINT Cursor;
  UINT Keys;
  UINT Value;
  char KeyName[32];

  LPSTR Register(WNDCLASS& wc);
  BOOL  Paint();
  BOOL  Char(UINT Value, UINT Repeat);
  void  MouseKeys(POINT Cursor, UINT Keys);
  BOOL  KeyDown(UINT VirtKey, KEYCODES KeyCodes);
  BOOL  LButtonDown(POINT Cursor, UINT Keys);
  BOOL  MouseMove(POINT Cursor, UINT Keys);
  BOOL  LButtonUp(POINT Cursor, UINT Keys);
  BOOL  RButtonDown(POINT Cursor, UINT Keys);
  BOOL  RButtonUp(POINT Cursor, UINT Keys);
}; // class EventWin

#endif // EVENTWIN_INC
```

The window will be updated as soon as the events arrive. The class must store certain values so that it can display the information when the window needs repainting. A window may need repainting because it has been restored from an icon or because the user has moved aside another application that was obscuring the window. These values are stored in four class members called **Cursor**, **Keys**, **Value**, and **KeyName**.

The **EventWin** class is interested in many events, so it redefines several of the virtual member functions provided in the base **Window** class. Remember that these functions must match the definitions and parameters in the **Window** class exactly.

evtwin.cpp

```
#include "evtwin.hpp"

EventWin::EventWin(HWND PhWnd, LPSTR Name, DWORD Style,
         int x, int y,int width, int height)
{
  Value= Keys=0;
  KeyName[0]=0;
  Cursor.x = Cursor.y = 0;
  Create(Name,Style,x,y,width,height,PhWnd,NULL);
}
```

The **EventWin** constructor sets the class members to zero and creates the window.

```
LPSTR EventWin::Register(WNDCLASS& wc)
{
  wc.lpszClassName = "EventWin";
  wc.hIcon = LoadIcon(hInst,"Bolt");
  RegisterClass (&wc);
  return "EventWin";
}
```

The **Register** member function gives the window an icon that looks like a bolt of lightning:

```
BOOL  EventWin::Char(UINT Value, UINT Repeat)
{
  EventWin::Value = Value;
  HDC hDC = GetDC(hWnd);
  char Str[50];
  wsprintf(Str,
           "Character <%c> entered      ",(char)Value);
  TextOut(hDC,10,10,Str,lstrlen(Str));
  ReleaseDC(hWnd,hDC);
  return TRUE;
}
```

The **Char** member function displays a string containing the character entered. The value is always an ANSI character. **Char** events are usually generated by the **TranslateMessage** function in the message loop. **TranslateMessage** combines successive **KeyDown** and **KeyUp** events into a character. For example, if the user presses the SHIFT key and then the A key, **TranslateMessage** generates a capital A.

To write to the display, **Char** needs to get a display context and write to that. The display context must be released after use. Many programmers simply invalidate the client area using the API function **InvalidateRect**, so that Windows sends a **WM_PAINT** message and the **Paint** member function (or the **WM_PAINT** code in C programs) displays the new information. This technique is slow. The **Paint** member function continually redraws the entire client area, even when only a small part has changed.

```
BOOL EventWin::KeyDown(UINT VirtKey, KEYCODES KeyCodes)
{
```

```
HDC hDC = GetDC(hWnd);
char Str[50];
GetKeyNameText(*(DWORD*)&KeyCodes,KeyName,
               sizeof(KeyName));
wsprintf(Str,"Key %10s pressed              ",
         (LPSTR)KeyName);
TextOut(hDC,10,40,Str,lstrlen(Str));
ReleaseDC(hWnd,hDC);
return TRUE;
}
```

The **KeyDown** member function displays the name of the key that was depressed. The API function **GetKeyNameText** returns the name in the local language. Any key can generate a **KeyDown** event, so the key may be a special key such as F4 or PGDN.

```
void EventWin::MouseKeys(POINT Cursor, UINT Keys)
{
  EventWin::Cursor = Cursor;
  EventWin::Keys = Keys;
  HDC hDC = GetDC(hWnd);
  char Str[80];
  wsprintf(Str,
          "Mouse buttons %c %c Position X: %d, Y: %d    ",
          (Keys&MK_LBUTTON)?'L':' ',
          (Keys&MK_RBUTTON)?'R':' ',
          Cursor.x,Cursor.y);
  TextOut(hDC,10,70,Str,lstrlen(Str));
  ReleaseDC(hWnd,hDC);
}
```

All mouse-event member functions call **MouseKeys**, which print the status of the left and right mouse keys and the cursor position. The **Keys** parameter for the mouse events contains flags indicating whether any of the mouse keys or the SHIFT and CTRL keys are pressed. The flags can be extracted with five masks:

MK_CONTROL	Set if a CTRL key is pressed
MK_SHIFT	Set if a SHIFT key is pressed
MK_LBUTTON	Set if the left mouse button is pressed
MK_MBUTTON	Set if the middle mouse button is pressed
MK_RBUTTON	Set if the right mouse button is pressed

```
BOOL  EventWin::LButtonDown(POINT Cursor, UINT Keys)
{
  MouseKeys(Cursor, Keys);
  return TRUE;
}

BOOL  EventWin::LButtonUp(POINT Cursor, UINT Keys)
{
  MouseKeys(Cursor, Keys);
  return TRUE;
}

BOOL  EventWin::RButtonDown(POINT Cursor, UINT Keys)
{
  MouseKeys(Cursor, Keys);
  return TRUE;
}

BOOL  EventWin::RButtonUp(POINT Cursor, UINT Keys)
{
  MouseKeys(Cursor, Keys);
  return TRUE;
}

BOOL  EventWin::MouseMove(POINT Cursor, UINT Keys)
{
  MouseKeys(Cursor, Keys);
  return TRUE;
}
```

All the mouse events simply call **MouseKeys**.

```
BOOL EventWin::Paint()
{
  PAINTSTRUCT ps;
  char Str[80];
  HDC hDC=BeginPaint(hWnd, &ps);
  wsprintf(Str,
          "Character <%c> entered      ",(char)Value);
  TextOut(hDC,10,10,Str,lstrlen(Str));
  wsprintf(Str,
          "Key %10s pressed           ",(LPSTR)KeyName);
  TextOut(hDC,10,40,Str,lstrlen(Str));
  wsprintf(Str,
          "Mouse buttons %c %c Position X: %d, Y: %d    ",
          (Keys&MK_LBUTTON)?'L':' ',
          (Keys&MK_RBUTTON)?'R':' ',
```

```
                Cursor.x,Cursor.y);
    TextOut(hDC,10,70,Str,lstrlen(Str));
    EndPaint(hWnd,&ps);
    return TRUE;
}
```

The **Paint** member function is called only if part of the window is revealed after having been obscured for some reason. **Paint** simply redraws the text, using the values in the class members.

The **WinMain** function is very similar to the function in the Hello World program.

testevt.cpp

```
#include "evtwin.hpp"

HANDLE hInst;
HANDLE hPrevInst;
LPSTR  CmdLine;

int PASCAL WinMain(HANDLE hInstance, HANDLE hPrevInstance,
    LPSTR lpszCmdLine, int nCmdShow)
{

    hInst = hInstance;
    char * pName = new char[80];
    LoadString(hInst,IDS_APPNAME, pName, 80);

    EventWin Win(NULL,pName);

    delete pName;

    Win.Show(nCmdShow);
    return Win.MessageLoop();

}
```

It creates an instance of **EventWin** instead of **MyWin**.

Summary

The **Window** class described in this chapter is still low-level. To use it properly, you still have to know which styles to use and how to register the class. Although member functions have replaced messages, you still need to understand that the program is event driven. On the other hand, the class is quite efficient. Extra function calls that occur in message processing do not make any noticeable difference in system performance. There is little redundant code.

The class is largely complete, but some additions will be introduced in Chapters 4, 5, and 6 to handle the demands imposed by controls and dialog boxes.

If you are used to the API, you probably prefer objects to be at this lower level. You have all the advantages of OOP without having to sacrifice any API facilities. If you are completely new to Windows programming, you might be disappointed that OOP has not solved all your problems. If so, you may need higher-level objects that are tailored to your needs. Higher-level objects can be derived quite easily from the low-level ones described here, and there may be someone available to help you do it. If not, persevere with the classes in this book. The time you spend in trying to understand the basic principles of Windows pays off when you undertake larger projects.

Remember that many applications do not need to use plain windows at all. They may be able to do all they need with dialog boxes. With the control and dialog classes described in later chapters, dialog boxes will be simple to use. Certainly, most of the applications that are implemented in text mode under DOS could be ported to Windows using dialog boxes.

The two example classes **MyWin** and **EventWin** are not likely to be reused in other applications, but with the more complex examples later in the book, you will see how it is possible to build classes that are genuinely reusable.

CHAPTER

Controls

*I*n Windows terminology, a *control* is a predefined window that has a precise function. Windows provides several controls that are available to application programs. Most users will be familiar with them:

❑ The *button* control, which includes radio buttons, check boxes, and push-buttons.

❑ The *list box* control, which may be either a single column or multiple columns.

❑ The *edit* control, which may be either a single line or multiple lines.

❑ The so-called *combo box* control, which is a single-line edit control combined with a list, or a drop-down list.

❑ The *scroll bar* control.

❑ The *static* control, which is used to display text that may not be edited.

A programmer can invent new custom controls and then use them as if they were standard Windows controls. In fact, this is not done very often, because standard controls are quite easy to customize. Custom controls are available from third-party vendors and provide a quick way of giving an application a new look. Custom controls and standard controls generally share the same interface, so most of this chapter also applies to custom controls.

Controls are important because most of the interaction with the user depends on them. An application that runs under a text-based operating system can be converted to Windows simply by using controls. Even highly graphic applications, such as paint programs or desktop publishing systems, use controls for most of the user interaction.

Why Simplify Controls?

Simplifying the use of controls is going to improve a programmer's productivity more than anything else. This chapter shows you how C++ classes for controls simplify their use without giving up any of their facilities or power. Chapter 5 shows you how to derive owner-draw classes from the basic control classes described here.

Message Handling

The standard controls already simplify things quite a bit. If you declare a push-button in a window and click on it, the button handles all its own messages. It draws itself when necessary. When you click on the button, it handles the mouse messages and redraws itself to look as if it has been pressed. When you release it, it redraws itself again, to look as if it has popped-up, and sends a message to its parent to indicate that it has been clicked.

The parent only has to handle this last message. The control does all the hard work. Still, if the parent has many controls, the parent must sort out all the messages. This results in a big **switch** statement, which has the same disadvantages that it had for simple windows, as explained in Chapter 3. A **switch** statement that grows too big becomes difficult to understand. More importantly, it becomes difficult to derive subclasses of the parent window, since one big function does most of the processing. It is always easier to derive subclasses if the base-class processing is spread over many small functions, since the subclass has more choice as to which functions it can redefine.

Callback Functions

It is simpler for the parent to give a control the address of a callback function, as shown in Figure 4-1, rather than have the control's parent handle notification messages. That way, when the control wants to notify its parent, it can just call the function back. The parent is saying, in effect, "If this button is clicked, then I want this member function executed." The program then becomes more structured, and if the callback member function is virtual, it is easy to derive subclasses that modify the parent's behavior. Most object-oriented systems use callbacks, including Widgets in the X-Windows GUI system for UNIX. A Widget corresponds more or less to a Windows control. X-Windows has the reputation of being difficult to program, even at the lowest level. Most

X-Windows programs, however, are built from standard Widgets, and then the task becomes very simple—easier in fact, than standard text-based UNIX programs.

Scroll Bar Interface

The scroll bar control is more complex than the other controls, since it sends different types of notification messages depending on which part of the bar was clicked. One of the end arrows on screen may have been clicked, or the slider moved, or the space between the slider and the arrows clicked. For some applications, it is important to differentiate between these different operations.

In a word processor, clicking on the up arrow of a scroll bar may mean "scroll the document down one line" whether the document contains 5 lines or 500,000 lines. If a scroll bar is used to scroll a window of information, clicking in the space between the end arrow and the slider should cause the contents of the window to be scrolled by almost the width or height of the window. For other applications, when the scroll bar is being used to set an arbitrary value, such as a page number within the document, it would be useful to have some default processing for the end arrows and the region outside of the slider, so that the scroll bar

FIGURE 4-1   Callback functions

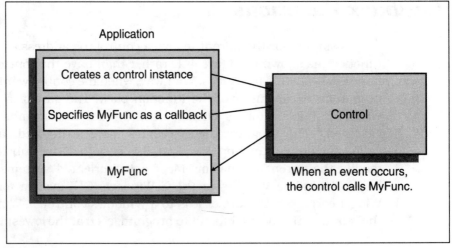

simply returns a value in its range, and sets the slider to correspond to that value.

Although scroll bar controls have a keyboard interface, it is possible to add scroll bars to a window so that the window itself is expected to handle input such as PGUP, PGDN, and the arrow keys. Some applications, such as word processors, prefer to treat this keyboard input in a different way from scroll bar input. On many word processors, using the scroll bars moves the window without moving the text cursor; only the keyboard keys move the text cursor. Many other applications prefer to have the window scroll bar intercept and process cursor-movement key strokes in order to scroll the window.

List and Combo Boxes

For the list box and combo box controls, most of the control functions require messages to be sent to the control using the API routine **SendMessage**. For example, to clear a list box and add an item to its list requires the following C code:

```
SendMessage(hList, LB_RESETCONTENT, 0, 0);
SendMessage(hList, LB_ADDSTRING, 0, (DWORD)(LPSTR)pString);
```

Although this routine is not too difficult to use, it is still awkward setting the parameters to the messages. Having simple functions for the most common operations, such as adding a string to a list box or selecting an item, is preferable.

List box controls may be created with a multiple selection attribute. The user can then select several items using the CTRL and SHIFT keys in conjunction with the mouse or arrow keys. The windows in *File Manager* work in this way. Although it is very easy to create a multiple selection list box, it is more complicated to extract the items selected. The application must:

☐   Create an integer array big enough to hold the selections.

☐   Send the list box an **LB_GETSELITEMS** message. The list box then fills the array with the indexes of the selected items.

❑   For each element in the integer array, send the list box a **LB_GETTEXT** message. The list box will then return the text of that element.

It would be useful to have a simpler mechanism that accessed the items of a multiple selection list box in one operation.

Owner-Draw Controls

The programmer can customize most controls in some way. The background and text colors can be modified, but it is also possible for the programmer's application to draw certain controls itself. These are the *owner-draw* controls. An owner-draw control has the same functionality as a standard control, but its appearance differs because it is specified by the application. You have certainly seen owner-draw controls by now. Many Windows applications use owner-draw buttons. They have little pictures on them, as well as text. If you want your push-buttons to have, for instance, an *art nouveau* look, you can achieve it with owner-draw buttons. Each button will still have the same basic properties as ordinary button: a rectangular area that generates an event when it is clicked on. If you want round buttons, you can also draw these yourself, but they will be activated if the user clicks in the rectangle that encloses the round button. If you want round buttons that ignore mouse clicks outside of the button circle, you must make custom controls.

Owner-draw controls may not be strictly necessary—they do the same job as standard controls, but not as quickly, since they take a certain amount of time to do the fancy drawing. They do, however, give an application more visual appeal and help to differentiate it from its competitors. In many cases, they make the application more intuitive, since an icon or a graphic drawing may be easier to understand than a short, cryptic text label.

A control defined as an owner-draw control sends messages to its parent indicating how it should be drawn. The messages say, in effect, "Draw me in the normal state," "Draw me to look as if I am selected," "Draw me to look as if I am disabled," and so on. The parent then draws the control as appropriate. These requests are easy to understand if there is only one control, but they become more complicated if the parent has several owner-draw child controls; the parent must remember which control has which pretty picture, and so on. In addition, it is difficult to reuse an owner-draw control, since the parent window does all the drawing. To reuse the control, a programmer must cut snippets of code out of the original parent and paste them into the new parent.

Of course, what is really needed is a simple class derived from a standard control class that draws itself the way the programmer wants. The programmer may have to program the **owner-draw** class, but only once. When programmers want to have buttons with pretty pictures, they prefer simply to specify an icon when they declare each button. All the drawing is then done by a function in the owner-draw button class. Chapter 5 explains how to accomplish this.

Advantages of C++ Over C

To summarize, C++ should alleviate the following problems that occur when programming controls in C:

☐ All communication between an application and its controls is by means of messages, when it should be by means of functions.

☐ Controls notify their parent of an event by sending a notification message, when they should instead call back a function supplied by the application.

☐ The functionality of an owner-draw control resides in the parent, when it should be encapsulated in the control itself.

☐ Some controls, especially scroll bars, could provide some default processing for some of their notification messages.

Finally, C++ programmers do not want to lose any of the power that comes with the standard controls. If they ever want to do something a little bit unusual that is not provided by a C++ class control, they still want some way of doing it, even if it means sending Windows messages to the control.

Design Problems

How can control classes be implemented? Several problem areas need attention. For all control types, extra messages need handling. In addition, the scroll bar class needs some special consideration, since it is more complex than the other controls.

Callbacks

Since a C++ **Window** class already exists, it would seem logical simply to derive a subclass for each control and have that subclass handle relevant control events. To implement a button class, for example, it is possible to create a window with the preregistered *Button* class name. The **Register** member function would simply return *Button.* It would not actually register anything. An extra member function, perhaps called **Click**, would be necessary to define the callback. The class would then redefine the **LButtonUp** member function to call the callback. The code would look something like this

```
Button::Button(HWND PhWnd, int Id, LPSTR pText, DWORD Style,
    int x, int y, int width, int height)
{
  Create(Name,Style,x,y,width,height,PhWnd,NULL);
  ClickCallback=NULL;
}

LPSTR Button::Register(WNDCLASS& wc)
{
 return "Button";
}


void Button::Click(WinObj * Inst,
    void (WinObj::*pCallback)(Button&))
{
    ClickInst = Inst;
    ClickCallback = pCallback;
}

BOOL Button::LButtonUp(POINT Cursor, WORD Keys)
```

```
{
    if (ClickCallback) (ClickInst->*ClickCallback)(*this);
    return TRUE;
}
```

When another class wants to give **Button** a callback function, it calls **Click**. Since the callback is a member function, **Button** needs to know the instance as well as the member function name. When a **LButtonUp** event occurs, **Button** calls back the member function in that instance and passes it a reference to the **Button** instance. Notice the strange syntax for member function pointers and for calling a function through a pointer. A pointer **pFunc** to a **void** function in class **Class** is defined like this:

void (Class::*pFunc)(parameter list)

and called through an instance **pClass** of **Class** like this:

(pClass->*pFunc)(parameters)

When the other class wishes to create a button control and define a callback, the code would look like this:

```
...

// Create a button
MyButton=new Button(hWnd, 100, "Beep",
        BS_PUSHBUTTON, 10,10,50,50);

// define callback
MyButton->Click(this, &MyWin::ClickHandler);
...

// this function called when button clicked
void MyWin::ClickHandler(Button& theButton)
{
    MessageBeep(0);
}
```

This code creates a push-button that is 50 pixels wide and 50 pixels high, located at 10,10 relative to the parent's client area. The button will contain the text *Beep*. The code calls the **Click** member function to define the callback, and, since the callback is a member function in the same instance, the instance is **this**. The C++ operator **this** returns a pointer to the current instance of a class. Often but not always the callback will be in the same instance.

When the button is clicked, it calls the callback. The API routine **MessageBeep** will make a beep sound.

Intercepting Messages

Intercepting a control's messages in this way is a common technique and is known as *subclassing*. The term is misleading for C++ programmers, since subclassing a control has nothing to do with C++. There are problems with intercepting and interpreting the control's messages. A button can be clicked by pressing the space bar while the button has the focus. The **Button** class would have to intercept **KeyUp** events as well. Although that might work with buttons and simple list boxes, what happens with combo boxes and scroll bars? It is impossible to know which part of the control has been clicked.

The only proper way to interface with a control is by means of notification messages sent between a control and its parent. For example, when a control is clicked, either with the mouse or by pressing the spacebar, the parent receives a **WM_COMMAND** message containing a notification code and the window handle of the control. When a button is clicked, the notification code is **BN_CLICKED**.

Other messages include **WM_HSCROLL** and **WM_VSCROLL** for scroll bars, **WM_CTLCOLOR** when the control colors may be modified, and **WM_DRAWITEM** when an owner-draw control should be drawn. The advantages of using notification messages are that all messages are officially documented. They are also easier to use, since they correspond directly to the events that the control class needs to process.

The control class should let the control handle its own internal messages and intercept the messages that are sent to the parent. These messages can be converted to a call to a member function in the control class. The parent window can bounce messages back to the control instance, translating them to a call to a member function, as illustrated in Figure 4-2.

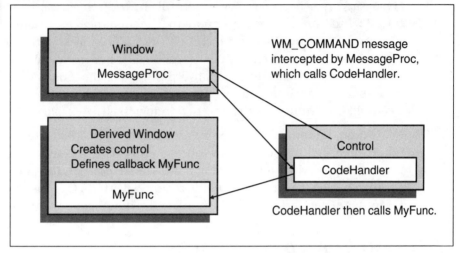

FIGURE 4-2 A control modification message is echoed to the control as a function call.

For example, if the parent received a **WM_CTLCOLOR** notification message, it could call a **CtlColor** member function in the control class. If the control class then wanted a button with red lettering, it could define the **CtlColor** member function to set the foreground color to red.

If the parent window is a window of the **Window** class, it is easy to intercept the messages. The **Window** class just needs an extension to the **switch** statement in the **MessageProc** function of the **Window** class. A **case** statement for the control messages calls the corresponding member function in the control instance. For example:

```
case WM_COMMAND:
     wID = (int) evt.wParam;
     hWndCtl = (HWND) LOWORD(evt.lParam);
     wNotifyCode = HIWORD(evt.lParam);

     if (hWndCtl) {
       // if message is from a control,
       // call the control member function
       Control * pControl =
       (Control*) (void*)GETPWIN(hWndCtl);
       if (pControl)
         return pControl->CodeHandler(wNotifyCode);
     }
     return Command(wID,wNotifyCode, hWndCtl);
```

If the window handle of a **WM_COMMAND** message is non-zero, the message has been sent by a control. In that case, the code calls the **CodeHandler** member function in the instance associated with the control. The **CodeHandler** member function handles all the notification codes. It receives each notification code as a parameter. Windows sends the notification code in the high-order word of the long parameter of the message event. If **lParam** is zero, the message refers to a menu item and should be handled by the parent window itself.

When the control instance is created, it uses **PUTPWIN** to put a pointer to its instance in the control window's property list. It leaves the control's window procedure alone. Using the instance pointer, the parent window can associate the control's window handle with its C++ instance, so that **MessageProc** can redirect the notification messages back to the instance.

Deleting Control Instances

Since the control class does not handle its own messages, it does not intercept the **WM_DESTROY** message either and cannot delete the instance when the control is destroyed. This is not a problem if the class that creates the control deletes it explicitly in its destructor; however, it is easy for a programmer to forget to add the code that does this. The best solution is for the programmer to use the **Window** class destructor deletes the instances of any child windows automatically.

The API routine **GetWindow** returns the handle of any child windows. The destructor can use this handle and check the child's property list to see whether the child has an instance associated with it. If it has, the instance can be deleted.

Window Scroll Bars

Although having the parent handle notification code works well with child controls, an anomaly exists. Windows can have scroll bars for their client areas. These bars are part of the non-client area of the window and share the same window handle as the rest of the window. They appear when a window is created with the **WS_VSCROLL** or **WS_HSCROLL** styles.

Since these scroll bars are not conventional controls, they do not work with a C++ control class, unless the class is modified. A programmer can try to simulate these scroll bars with child scroll bar controls in the correct place, so as to use a C++ control class with them, but the process is tricky. The program must give the original window three child windows—the two scroll bars and a third window representing the original client area. It must then keep these windows properly tiled. For certain complex applications, all this may be worth the effort, but in general, using the built-in scroll bars is easier.

If the scroll bar control class is modified to handle built-in window scroll bars, a parent window can create C++ scroll bar instances around these scroll bars, as long as the parent window indicates that the instance is for a built-in scroll bar, and not a control. The parent must also be responsible for deleting the scroll bar instances. The next section explains how this works.

Class Hierarchy

All controls will be derived from the **Window** class that was described in Chapter 3; however, since the different controls have some common notification functions, they will be derived from a new **Control** class, itself derived from the **Window** class. The hierarchy is shown in Figure 4-3.

Class hierarchy for controls

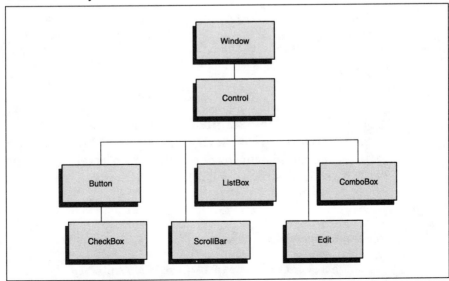

Implementation

This section shows how to implement all the control classes. First, we need to make a few minor modifications to the **Window** class described in Chapter 3.

After describing the modification, this chapter describes the base **Control** class and the individual control classes. Once again, if you find this section hard going, try looking at the examples in the following section, and come back here later.

The Window Class

The first thing to do is to modify the **Window** class to handle controls. You will find the modified WINDOW.CPP file in the CONTROLS directory on the disk that comes with this book. Here is the modified constructor.

window.cpp

```
Window::Window() {
  hWnd=0;
  HorzScrollBar=VertScrollBar=NULL;
  if (!Handler) {
#ifdef WIN32
    Handler = (WNDPROC)CPPWinProc;
#else
    Handler = MakeProcInstance((FARPROC)CPPWinProc, hInst);
#endif
    aProp=AddAtom("pWindow");
    aPropHigh=AddAtom("pWindowHigh");
  }
}
```

The new items **HorzScrollBar** and **VertScrollBar** are the instances of scroll bars associated with the window's built-in scroll bars. The constructor sets these items to zero. If the window creates instances of these scroll bars, the destructor will delete them. Here is the modified destructor:

window.cpp

```
Window: :~Window()
{
// delete the scroll bars
  if (HorzScrollBar) delete HorzScrollBar;
  if (VertScrollBar) delete VertScrollBar;
```

```
   if (hWnd) {
       Show(SW_HIDE);
       //Destroy instances associated with child windows
       HWND hCwnd= GetWindow (hWnd, GW_CHILD);
       while ( hCwnd ){
          Window * pWin=(Window*) GETPWIN(hCwnd);
          do {
                hCwnd=GetWindow(hCwnd,GW_HWNDNEXT);
          } while (hCwnd  && GetParent(hCwnd)!=hWnd);
          if (pWin) delete pWin;
       }
       if (DELPWIN(hWnd) && DefaultHandler)
         SetWindowLong(hWnd,GWL_WNDPROC,(LONG) DefaultHandler);
       //if this is the top level window quit the application
       if (!GetParent(hWnd)) PostQuitMessage(0);
       DestroyWindow(hWnd);
       hWnd=0;
       }
   }
```

The destructor also deletes any instances associated with any child windows. It uses the API function **GetWindow** to find the children and the macro **GETPWIN**, defined in WINDOW.CPP, to see if an instance is associated with them.

The message switch in **MessageProc** must handle the extra notification code for controls. It also allows the window scroll bars to handle keyboard input, if the window does not wish to handle it itself. The code for the **WM_KEYDOWN** case statement is shown here:

window.cpp

```
LONG Window::MessageProc( HWND hWnd, unsigned msg, Event& evt)
{
   switch (msg){
// existing case statements

    case WM_KEYDOWN:
       if (KeyDown(evt.wParam,
         *(KEYCODES*)&evt.lParam)) return TRUE;
       if (VertScrollBar &&
         VertScrollBar-\gKeyDown(evt.wParam,
         *(KEYCODES*)&evt.lParam)) return TRUE;
       if (HorzScrollBar &&
         HorzScrollBar->KeyDown(evt.wParam,
         *(KEYCODES*)&evt.lParam)) return TRUE;
       return FALSE;
```

If the main window does not process the **KeyDown** event, it passes it on to the **ScrollBar** instances associated with the window scroll bars. In contrast to scroll bar controls, window scroll bars do not have a keyboard interface. The window itself is expected to process events when the arrow keys or the PGUP and PGDN keys are pressed. The reason is that the application may want to separate the keyboard direction keys from the scroll bar. For example, in a word processor, using the keyboard direction keys causes the cursor (the blinking line that marks the current text entry position) to move through the document. The document is scrolled to keep the cursor in view. Clicking on the scroll bars scrolls the document, leaving the cursor where it is.

For simple windows without a cursor, users expect the keyboard direction keys to operate the scroll bars. The **ScrollBar** class will handle these keyboard events, but the code will only pass the event on to **ScrollBar** if the main window has not processed it.

The following messages are notification messages that controls send by controls to their parents. In each case, the parent calls a member function in the instance associated with the control, if one exists. The parent retrieves the control's window handle from the message and uses **GETPWIN** on the handle to find the class instance associated with the control. If a class instance exists, the parent can call the appropriate member function in the control. Extracting the control's window handle depends on the message. It may be in the low-order or high-order word of **lParam**, or it may be in a data structure pointed to by **lParam**.

Working with 32 Bits

Once again, the parameter packing for most of the notification messages will be different in 32-bit versions of Windows.

The drawn item case **WM_COMMAND** is shown here:

window.cpp

```
case WM_COMMAND:
{
  WORD wNotifyCode;          // notification code
```

```
        WORD wID;                   // item, control ID
        HWND hWndCtl;               // handle of control
// Unpack the message
#ifdef WIN32
        wNotifyCode = HIWORD(evt.wParam);
        wID = LOWORD(evt.wParam);
        hWndCtl = (HWND) evt.lParam;
#else  // 16-bit Windows
        wID = (int) evt.wParam;
        hWndCtl = (HWND) LOWORD(evt.lParam);
        wNotifyCode = HIWORD(evt.lParam);
#endif
        if (hWndCtl) {
          // if message is from a control,
          // call the control function
          Control * pControl =
            (Control*) (void*)GETPWIN(hWndCtl);
          if (pControl)
            return pControl->CodeHandler(wNotifyCode);
        }
        return Command(wID,wNotifyCode, hWndCtl);
    }
```

Controls send the **WM_COMMAND** message to their parent when user input occurs. The user may have clicked on the control, or modified the text in an edit control. Menus also send **WM_COMMAND** messages when a menu item is selected. If the message comes from a menu, the **lParam** is zero. In that case, the window should process the message itself. In the preceding example, the **Window** class calls the control member function **CodeHandler** if the message comes from a control, and the **Window** member function **Command** if it does not.

Working with 32 Bits

In 32-bit versions of Windows, the control handle is also 32 bits and occupies all of the **lParam** parameter. The notification code is moved to the high-order word of the 32-bit **wParam** parameter.

The **WM_DRAWITEM** case statement is shown here:

window.cpp

```
case WM_DRAWITEM:
{
  // Call DrawItem method in control
  Control * pControl=
    (Control*) (void*)GETPWIN((HWND)
    (((DRAWITEMSTRUCT FAR*) evt.lParam)->hwndItem));
  if (pControl)
    pControl->DrawItem((DRAWITEMSTRUCT FAR*)evt.lParam);
  break;
}
```

Owner-draw controls send the **WM_DRAWITEM** message when they need to be redrawn for any reason. The **DRAWITEMSTRUCT** data structure contains full details on how the control should be drawn. The parent sends this data structure to the control's **DrawItem** member function. This member function should be defined by any class that implements an owner-draw control. Notice that the control's window handle is embedded in the **DRAWITEMSTRUCT**; it is not packed in the **wParam** or **lParam** parameter.

The **WM_CTLCOLOR** case statement is shown here:

window.cpp

```
#Ifdef  WIN32
    case  WM_CTLCOLORMSGBOX:
    case  WM_CTLCOLOREDIT:
    case  WM_CTLCOLORLISTBOX:
    case  WM_CTLCOLORBTN:
    case  WM_CTLCOLORDLG:
    case  WM_CTLCOLORSCROLLBAR:
    case  WM_CTLCOLORSTATIC:
#else
    case  WM_CTLCOLOR:
#endif
    {
      // Call CtlColor member function in control
      Control * pControl=
        (Control*) (void*)GETPWIN((HWND)evt.lParam);
      HBRUSH Brush=NULL;
      if (pControl) Brush=pControl->CtlColor((HDC)evt.wParam);
      if (Brush) return Brush;
      if(DefaultHandler)
        return CallWindowProc (DefaultHandler,
          hWnd, msg, evt.wParam, evt.lParam);
```

```
  else return FALSE;
}
```

The **WM_CTLCOLOR** message gives a control's parent the chance to specify the brush that paints the control's background. Parents can also change the text background and foreground colors, and they can set the text mode to opaque or transparent. This message applies to all controls, and not just owner-draw controls. The control member function **CtlColor** should return a valid brush for painting the background. If the control contains text, the control should set the text background to the same color. If **CtlColor** returns **NULL**, the **Window** class calls the default window function that will return the standard background brush for that control.

Working with 32 Bits

The high-order word of **lParam** in the **WM_CTLCOLOR** message contains a code that indicates the control type. There is no room for this code in the 32-bit version of the message. Instead, **WM_CTLCOLOR** is replaced by seven different messages.

The **WM_MEASUREITEM** case statement is shown here:

window.cpp

```
case WM_MEASUREITEM:
{
  // Call MeasureItem method in control
  MEASUREITEMSTRUCT FAR * pMs=
  (MEASUREITEMSTRUCT FAR *)evt.lParam;
  Control * pControl=
    (Control*) (void*)
    GETPWIN(GetDlgItem(hWnd,pMs-\gCtlID));
  if (pControl) pControl->MeasureItem(pMs);
  else {
    pMs->itemHeight=ItemMeasurement::itemHeight;
    pMs->itemWidth=ItemMeasurement::itemWidth;
  }
  break;
}
```

An owner-draw list box or combo box will send a **WM_MEASUREITEM** message to the parent to find the size of the items. The control needs to know the size of the items to calculate which one has been clicked on. An owner-draw list box can be declared as **OWNERDRAWFIXED** or **OWNERDRAWVARIABLE**. If the list box is fixed, the items are all the same size. If the items are variable size, the message is sent for each item as the list box is filled. The **Window** class can then pass the message on to the control member function **MeasureItem** that will calculate the item's size.

If the list box contains fixed-size items, the message is sent just once when the control is created. This is awkward, since the message arrives before the constructor has had the chance to create the control instance. The parent cannot redirect the message to the control member function **MeasureItem**, and so the control cannot set the size of its items. One way around this problem would be to declare the owner-draw list box as **OWNERDRAWVARIABLE**, even if the items are actually of a fixed size. The **MeasureItem** member function would then just return the same size each time. Unfortunately, this does not work for multicolumn list boxes, which are assumed to have fixed-size items even if the attribute **OWNERDRAWVARIABLE** is specified.

This problem is resolved in Windows version 3.1. If an application is running under version 3.1, the list box class constructor can send the list box an **LB_SETITEMHEIGHT** message to set the item height after the list box has been created, but before it is displayed.

If you still have to support users running Windows version 3.0, the only solution is to use the structure **ItemMeasurement** that the control instance can initialize with the size of the list items before the control itself is actually created.

The code that handles scroll bar messages is shown here:

window.cpp

```
    case WM_HSCROLL:
    {
      HWND hCtl;
      WORD nPos;
#ifdef WIN32
      hCtl=(HWND)evt.lParam;
      nPos=HIWORD(evt.wParam);
#else
      hCtl=(HWND)HIWORD(evt.lParam);
      nPos=LOWORD(evt.lParam);
```

```
#endif
      if (hCtl){
        // a standard control
        Control * pScroll=
          (Control *)(void*)GETPWIN(hCtl);
        if (pScroll)
          pScroll->CodeHandler((WORD)evt.wParam,nPos);
      }
      else  if (HorzScrollBar){
        // a window scroll bar
        ((Control *)(void*)HorzScrollBar)
          ->CodeHandler((WORD)evt.wParam,nPos);
      }
      break;
    }

    case WM_VSCROLL:
    {
      HWND hCtl;
      WORD nPos;
#ifdef WIN32
      hCtl=(HWND)evt.lParam;
      nPos=HIWORD(evt.wParam);
#else
      hCtl=(HWND)HIWORD(evt.lParam);
      nPos=LOWORD(evt.lParam);
#endif
      if (hCtl){
        // a standard control
        Control * pScroll=
          (Control *)(void*)GETPWIN(hCtl);
        if (pScroll)
          pScroll->CodeHandler((WORD)evt.wParam,nPos);
      }
      else  if (VertScrollBar){
        // a window scroll bar
        ((Control *)(void*)VertScrollBar)
          ->CodeHandler((WORD)evt.wParam,nPos);
      }
      break;
    }
```

The messages **WM_VSCROLL** and **WM_HSCROLL** are similar. If the control window handle is non-zero, the message has been sent by a control and **Window** can call the **CodeHandler** member function in the instance associated with that control. If the handle is zero, the message refers to the built-in scroll bar in the current window. If there is a class instance associated with a built-in scroll bar, its address will be stored in either **VertScrollBar** or **HorzScrollBar**. This process is explained later in this chapter, in the section on scroll bars.

Here again the message packing depends on whether the application is compiled for 16-bit or 32-bit Windows.

```
    default:
      if (DefaultHandler)
        return CallWindowProc
          (DefaultHandler, hWnd, msg, evt.wParam, evt.lParam);
    }
  return FALSE;
}
```

Often even owner-draw list boxes contain strings of text, and it is possible for them to contain other data, such as memory handles, or indexes into a database. The **DrawItem** routine would then be responsible for representing this data in a way that is meaningful to the user, perhaps as a mix of icons and text. If you use this routine, the control also generates **WM_COMPAREITEM** messages if the list box is sorted and **WM_DELETEITEM** messages whenever an item is deleted.

A list box class will not need to handle these messages or specify the **LBS-SORT** style if it takes care in two areas: inserting new items in the correct position so that the list remains sorted, and releasing any resources when a list item is deleted.

The WINDOW.HPP file is similar to that described in Chapter 3. The following items have been added to the **Window** class:

window.hpp

```
class Window:public WinObj {
protected:
  Window * HorzScrollBar;
  Window * VertScrollBar;

public:
  int GetText(LPSTR Buffer, int Size){[return
    SendMessage(hWnd,WM_GETTEXT,Size,(LONG)Buffer);};
  int SetText(LPSTR Buffer){return
    SendMessage(hWnd,WM_SETTEXT,0,(LONG)Buffer);};
  };
```

The member functions **GetText** and **SetText** have also been added because they are very useful for handling the text of controls. They are also useful for changing the titles of ordinary windows.

The Control Class

It is now possible to start on the individual controls. Because controls share many characteristics that ordinary windows do not have, it would be best to first define a **Control** class. The extra code in the **Window** class, described in the last section, already makes use of the **Control** class.

Here is the definition:

control.hpp

```
#ifndef      CONTROL_INC
#define      CONTROL_INC

#include "window.hpp"

class Control : public  Window{
  public:
  void CreateControl(
    LPSTR ClassName,           // Windows control class
    HWND PhWnd,                // window handle of parent
    int Id,                    // Identifier for control
    LPSTR pText,               // Control text
    DWORD Style,               // Control Style
    int x= CW_USEDEFAULT,      // Position
    int y= CW_USEDEFAULT,
    int width= CW_USEDEFAULT,  // Size
    int height= CW_USEDEFAULT);

  ~Control();
  void SetFont(               // Set control font
    HFONT hFont,
    BOOL bRedraw=FALSE)
    {SendMessage(hWnd,WM_SETFONT,(UINT)hFont,bRedraw);};

  void SetRedraw(             // Allow redraws after updates
    BOOL bRedraw);

  virtual LONG CodeHandler(    // Handles command codes
    int NotifyCode,
```

```
        int Extra=0)
        {return FALSE;};

    virtual void DrawItem(        // Draws owner draw controls
        DRAWITEMSTRUCT FAR * pDs)
     {Error(IDS_APPLERROR,(LPSTR)"DrawItem");};

     virtual void MeasureItem(     // Sets owner draw control size
        MEASUREITEMSTRUCT FAR * pMs){};

     virtual HBRUSH CtlColor(       // Sets control background
     HDC hDC){return NULL;};
}; // class Control

class ItemMeasurement : public  WinObj {
public:
    static itemWidth;
    static itemHeight;
    ItemMeasurement(int Height=0, int Width=0);
    ~ItemMeasurement();
}; // class ItemMeasurement

#endif // CONTROL_INC
```

The **Control** class defines the general-purpose member functions **SetRedraw** and **SetFont**.

SetRedraw is used to temporarily suspend redrawing in a control. The function is most often used when adding or deleting items in a list or combo box, although it works with the other controls as well. If the box is visible, it would be redrawn after each item is added or deleted, and would appear to flicker. The update would also take a noticeable amount of time. To avoid this delay, the programmer can first suspend updating with **SetRedraw(FALSE)**. After all the changes have been made, they are displayed with **SetRedraw(TRUE)**.

SetFont changes the font in which the control's text or label is displayed. The font should have been created with the API **CreateFont** or a similar function. The font returned by **CreateFont** should also be deleted when it is no longer used, since it uses system resources. If the optional **bRedraw** parameter is **TRUE**, the control will be redrawn. Specify **TRUE** if you change the font in isolation while the control is displayed.

CreateControl is used to create a control of a given class. This function is preferred over **Create**, because **CreateControl** does not redefine the window message-handling procedure.

The virtual member functions for handling the different notification actions are also defined here, together with default processing. Notice that if an owner-draw control is created, a **DrawItem** member function must be defined or the control will not be drawn at all, so the default action of **DrawItem** is to generate an error message.

The **ItemMeasurement** class is also defined here. It will be explained in Chapter 5 in the section on owner-draw list boxes.

The CONTROL.CPP file is quite simple:

control.cpp

```
#include "control.hpp"


void Control::CreateControl(LPSTR ClassName,HWND PhWnd,
      int Id, LPSTR pText,DWORD Style,
      int x, int y, int width, int height)
{
  hWnd=GetDlgItem(PhWnd,Id);   //May have been created by
                               //a dialog resource
  if (!hWnd) {
    hWnd = CreateWindow(ClassName,pText,Style ,
        x,y,width,height,
        PhWnd,(HMENU)Id,hInst,NULL);
    if (!hWnd) Error(IDS_APPLERROR, ClassName);
  }
  PutWin(hWnd,this);
#ifdef WIN32
  DefaultHandler = (WNDPROC) GetWindowLong(hWnd,GWL_WNDPROC);
#else
  DefaultHandler = (FARPROC) GetWindowLong(hWnd,GWL_WNDPROC);
#endif

}

Control::~Control()
{
  DelWin(hWnd);
}
void Control::SetRedraw(BOOL bRedraw){
  SendMessage(hWnd,WM_SETREDRAW,bRedraw,0);
  if (!bRedraw) InvalidateRect(hWnd,NULL,FALSE);
```

```
}

int ItemMeasurement::itemWidth=0;
int ItemMeasurement::itemHeight=0;

ItemMeasurement::ItemMeasurement(int Height, int Width)
{
  itemWidth=Width;
  itemHeight=Height;
}

ItemMeasurement::~ItemMeasurement()
{
  itemWidth=itemHeight=0;
}
```

The member function **CreateControl** calls **CreateWindow** and puts the instance pointer in the window property list, using **PutWin**. **DefaultHandler** is set to the control's own message-handling procedure.

The destructor removes the instance pointer from the window property list. This prevents the parent window from calling the control's virtual member functions while it is being destroyed.

Chapter 6 shows the convenience of allowing the dialog box to create the controls using a template prepared with a dialog editor. With a template, the constructor does not need to create the control; it merely associates an instance with it. The first line of the **CreateControl** member function checks to see whether the control has already been created.

The Button Class

Now the way is free to start defining the controls themselves. It is best to start with push-buttons. Here is the definition:

button.hpp

```
#ifndef  BUTTON_INC
#define  BUTTON_INC

#include "control.hpp"

class Button : public Control{
protected:
  void (WinObj::*ClickCallback)(Button& );
```

```
    LONG CodeHandler(int NotifyCode, int Extra=0);
    WinObj * ClickInst;

public:
  Button(
    HWND PhWnd,                 // Window handle of parent
    int Id,                     // Identifier for control
    LPSTR pText="",             // Button text
    DWORD Style=BS_PUSHBUTTON,  // Button Style
    int x= CW_USEDEFAULT,       // Position
    int y= CW_USEDEFAULT,
    int width= CW_USEDEFAULT,   // Size
    int height= CW_USEDEFAULT);

  Button(){};

  virtual void Click(          // Sets the callback
    WinObj * Inst,             // Instance and member function
    void (WinObj::*pCallback)(Button&));
}; // class Button

typedef void(WinObj::*BUTTONCALLBACK)(Button&);

#endif  // BUTTON_INC
```

The member function **Click** is used by other objects to set the callback member function to be called when the button is clicked. The parameters are a pointer to any instance derived from **WinObj** and a member function that takes a **Button ref** as a parameter. **Click** stores these values in **ClickCallback** and **ClickInst**. **ClickCallback** is a pointer to a member function in a class derived from **WinObj**. **ClickCallback** takes a **Button ref** parameter and has no result.

Click accepts a member function in any class derived from **WinObj**, but requires an explicit cast using the **BUTTONCALLBACK typedef**. The example at the end of this chapter will explain how to do this.

Here is the definition:

button.cpp

```
#include "button.hpp"


Button::Button(HWND PhWnd, int Id, LPSTR pText, DWORD Style,
     int x, int y, int width, int height)
{
  CreateControl("Button",PhWnd, Id,pText,
```

```
      Style|WS_CHILD|WS_VISIBLE,
      x,y,width,height);
   ClickCallback=NULL;

}

void Button::Click(WinObj * Inst,
void(WinObj::*pCallback)(Button&) )
{
   ClickInst = Inst;
   ClickCallback = pCallback;
}

LONG Button::CodeHandler(int NotifyCode, int Extra)
{
   switch (NotifyCode) {

   case BN_CLICKED:
      if (ClickCallback) (ClickInst-\g*ClickCallback)(*this);
      else return FALSE;
      break;

   default:
      return FALSE;
   }
   return TRUE;
}
```

The constructor creates the control and sets the **ClickCallback** item to **NULL**. Notice that the constructor makes sure that the button has the **WS_CHILD** and **WS_VISIBLE** styles. If you want invisible buttons, you can hide them after creating them with the **Show(SW_HIDE)** member function.

The **Click** member function simply copies the parameters into the class data. The **CodeHandler** member function is only interested in one event, the button being clicked. When this happens, the callback member function is called, if it has been defined. Notice how **CodeHandler** calls the function back using the ->* operator. The parameter *this means *this instance*. The C++ keyword **this** is a pointer to the current instance, so *this is the actual instance. Since the callback takes a reference value, the compiler only passes a pointer to the instance. The compiler still requires that you specify an instance, and not a pointer.

The steps in this section are all you need to create push-buttons. Button text is usually supplied when the button is created. You can also change it with the **Window** member function **SetText**.

Check Boxes and Radio Buttons

Check boxes and radio buttons are similar classes of buttons. Radio buttons are usually grouped together to be mutually exclusive; only one button in the group may be set. Usually these controls are defined with the **AUTO** style. The check box or radio button is then toggled on or off by the control itself, and the parent simply examines the control when necessary.

It is simple to derive a check box class from **Button** like this:

checkbox.hpp

```
#ifndef CHECKBOX_INC
#define CHECKBOX_INC

#include "button.hpp"

class CheckBox : public Button{

public:
  CheckBox(
    HWND PhWnd,                 // Parent window handle of parent
    int Id,                     // Identifier for control
    LPSTR pText="",             // Text
    DWORD Style=0,              // Control style
    int x= CW_USEDEFAULT,       // Position
    int y= CW_USEDEFAULT,
    int width= CW_USEDEFAULT,   // Size
    int height= CW_USEDEFAULT)
  :Button(PhWnd,Id,pText,
      Style?Style:BS_AUTOCHECKBOX,
      x,y,width,height){};

  virtual WORD Check()          // Returns check state
    {return SendMessage(hWnd,BM_GETCHECK,0,0);};

  virtual void Check(           // Sets check state
    WORD State)
    {SendMessage(hWnd,BM_SETCHECK,State,0);};
```

```
}; // class CheckBox
#endif //  CHECKBOX_INC
```

The constructor merely passes the parameters on to the **Button** constructor, which it resembles. If **Style** is unspecified, the constructor specifies **BS_AUTOCHECKBOX** and creates an automatic check box. The C **?:** operator pair means "If the expression to the left of the ? evaluates to a non-zero value, take the expression after the ?; otherwise take the expression after the :." To create a radio button, specify the style **BS_AUTORADIOBUTTON**.

Two **Check** member functions are defined to set and return the check mark. The member functions are overloaded; they have the same name but different parameters. If a parameter is supplied, the check is set, otherwise the current check is returned.

If the check box is automatic, there is normally no need to define a callback function, you can just call **Check()** when you need to know the value. You may define a callback if you wish. Other controls may need to be disabled if a check box is set; you would disable them in the callback.

The code is so simple that the member functions are defined here in the CHECKBOX.HPP file. There is no need for a .CPP file.

The ListBox Class

List boxes are already more complex than buttons. They respond to double clicks as well as single clicks. There are several operations for manipulating the data they contain. Here is the definition:

listbox.hpp

```
#ifndef  LISTBOX_INC
#define  LISTBOX_INC

#include "control.hpp"

class ListBox : public Control{

protected:
  void (WinObj::*ClickCallback)(ListBox&);
  WinObj * ClickInst;
  void (WinObj::*DClickCallback)(ListBox&);
```

```
    WinObj * DClickInst;
    LONG CodeHandler(int NotifyCode,int Extra);

public:
  ListBox(
    HWND PhWnd,                     // Parent window handle
    int Id,                         // Child Id
    DWORD Style=0,                  // Style
    int x= CW_USEDEFAULT,           // Position
    int y= CW_USEDEFAULT,
    int width= CW_USEDEFAULT,       // Size
    int height= CW_USEDEFAULT);

  void Add(                         // Add an item
    LPSTR pstr);

  void Delete(                      // Delete an item by index
    WORD pItem);

  void Delete(                      // Delete an item by string
    LPSTR pItem);

  void ColumnWidth(                 // Set column width
    WORD Width);

  DWORD Find(                       // Find an item
    LPSTR Buf,
   int Index=-1);

  int Count();                      // Return count of items

  void Dir(                         // Fill box with dir list
    WORD Attr=0x37,
    LPSTR FileSpec="*.*");

  WORD Text(                        // Get text of an item
    int Index,
    LPSTR Buf);

  int Selection();                  // Index of current selection

  Select(                           // Select an item
    int Index);

  Select(                           // Select an item by string
    LPSTR Text,
    int Index=0);
```

```
     void Reset();                    // Remove all items

     DWORD Selection(                 // Copy selection to Buf
       LPSTR Buf);

     DWORD Selections(                // Define callback for multiple
      WinObj * Inst,                  // selections
      void (WinObj::*pCallback)(LPSTR));

     virtual void Click(              // Single click callback
       WinObj * Inst,
       void (WinObj::*pCallback)(ListBox&));

     virtual void DClick(             // Double click callback
       WinObj* Inst,
       void (WinObj::*pCallback)(ListBox&));

protected:
   DWORD DefaultStyle(DWORD  Style);
   virtual void ProcessError(int RetCode);

}; // class ListBox

typedef void (WinObj::*LISTBOXCALLBACK)(ListBox&);
typedef void (WinObj::*LPSTRCALLBACK)(LPSTR);

#endif // LISTBOX_INC
```

This example is similar to the **Button** class except for the extra member functions to handle the data, and the **DClick** member function to define a callback for double clicks. Several of the member functions, such as **Delete**, are overloaded to accept either an index of a list element, or the string corresponding to a list element.

Here is the implementation:

listbox.cpp

```
#include "listbox.hpp"

ListBox::ListBox(HWND PhWnd, int Id, DWORD Style,
     int x, int y, int width, int height)
{
   CreateControl("ListBox",PhWnd,Id,"",
       DefaultStyle(Style),
       x,y,width,height);
```

```
}

void ListBox::Click(WinObj * Inst,
     void (WinObj::*pCallback)(ListBox&))
{
  ClickInst = Inst;
  ClickCallback = pCallback;
}

void ListBox::DClick(WinObj * Inst,
     void (WinObj::*pCallback)(ListBox&))
{
  DClickInst = Inst;
  DClickCallback = pCallback;
}


DWORD ListBox::DefaultStyle(DWORD Style)
{
  if (Style | LBS_MULTICOLUMN) Style |= WS_HSCROLL;
  else Style |= WS_VSCROLL;

  Style |=  LBS_NOTIFY | WS_CHILD |WS_VISIBLE |WS_BORDER;
  return Style;
}
```

If the list box is a multicolumn box, it is best to give it a horizontal scroll bar, but you can also give it a vertical scroll bar. The scroll bars are only displayed if the box is too small to show all the items at once. Since these rules are too complex to evaluate, the inline class member function **DefaultStyle** can be used to evaluate them.

```
void ListBox::Add(LPSTR pstr)
{
    int RetVal;
    RetVal=SendMessage(hWnd, LB_ADDSTRING,0, (DWORD)pstr);
    ProcessError(RetVal);
}

void ListBox::Delete(WORD pItem)
{
  ProcessError(SendMessage(hWnd, LB_DELETESTRING,pItem,0L));
}
```

Most of these member functions simply send an equivalent message to the control and need no further explanation.

```
void ListBox::Delete(LPSTR pItem)
{
  int Index=-1;
  char String[120];
  do {
    int OldIndex = Index;
    Index=SendMessage(hWnd, LB_FINDSTRING,Index,(DWORD)pItem);
    if (Index <=OldIndex) return;
    Text(Index,String);
  } while (lstrcmp(pItem, String));
  ProcessError(SendMessage(hWnd, LB_DELETESTRING,Index,0L));
}
```

To delete a string from a list box, first find the index of the string and then delete the item with that index. **LB_FINDSTRING** finds an item that begins with the specified string; normally this will be the item that is to be deleted. However, **LB_FINDSTRING** may not find the correct item if the list box is not sorted, or if the items have mixed case. To make sure, the item found by **LB_FINDSTRING** is compared with the specified string. If they are different, **LB_FINDSTRING** continues searching until either it finds the correct item, or there are no more items.

You may wish to define a similar member function to select strings in a list, making sure that the selected string matches exactly.

```
void ListBox::ColumnWidth(WORD Param)
{
  SendMessage(hWnd, LB_SETCOLUMNWIDTH,Param,0L);
}

int ListBox::Count()
{
  return SendMessage(hWnd, LB_GETCOUNT,0,0L);
}

void ListBox::Dir(WORD Attr, LPSTR pFileSpec)
{
  SendMessage(hWnd, LB_DIR,Attr,(DWORD)pFileSpec);
}

void ListBox::ProcessError(int RetCode)
{
```

```
    if (RetCode==LB_ERR)
      Error(IDS_APPLERROR,(LPSTR)"Listbox");
    if (RetCode==LB_ERRSPACE)
      Error(IDS_MEMORY, (LPSTR)"ListBox");
}
```

ProcessError is used to examine the return code from messages. The user should not see any errors. If **ProcessError** generates an error there is something wrong in the program.

```
LONG ListBox::CodeHandler(int NotifyCode, int Extra)
{
    switch (NotifyCode) {

case LBN_DBLCLK:
    if (DClickCallback) (DClickInst->*DClickCallback)(*this);
        else return FALSE;
    break;

case LBN_SELCHANGE:
    if (ClickCallback) (ClickInst->*ClickCallback)(*this);
    else return FALSE;
    break;

default:
    return FALSE;
    }
return TRUE;
}
```

CodeHandler also processes double-click messages. Remember that a single click on a list box item does not mean that the user wants to do anything special with that item. In fact single clicks should normally be ignored. If a user runs through a list box using the keyboard arrow keys, single-click events will be generated for every item in the list.

Sometimes there is a good reason to process single clicks. For example, a static text control may exist in a status bar that shows additional information about the item currently selected. This control should be updated whenever the selection changes.

```
int ListBox::Selection()
{
    return SendMessage(hWnd, LB_GETCURSEL,0,0);
```

```
}

ListBox::Select(int Index)
{
    return SendMessage(hWnd, LB_SETCURSEL,Index,0);
}

ListBox::Select(LPSTR pText, int Index)
{
    return SendMessage(hWnd, LB_SELECTSTRING,Index,(LONG)pText);
}


DWORD ListBox::Selection(LPSTR pBuf)
{
int Index;
    Index=SendMessage(hWnd, LB_GETCURSEL,0,0);
    if (Index <0) return FALSE;
    SendMessage(hWnd, LB_GETTEXT,Index,(DWORD)pBuf);
    return TRUE;
}
```

All the above member functions translate into calls to **SendMessage**. They merely simplify the interface with the list box by replacing a cumbersome **SendMessage** call, full of codes and casts, with a call to a member function. The two **Selection** member functions are used with single-selection list boxes. The member function is overloaded. It either returns the index of the current selection, or it copies the text of the selection into a buffer. Similarly, **Select** is overloaded to select an item either by index, or by finding the first item that matches a string prefix.

For multiple-selection list boxes the following member function is used:

```
DWORD ListBox::Selections(WinObj * Inst,
        void (WinObj::*pCallback)(LPSTR))
{
  // find number of selected items
  int Items=SendMessage(hWnd, LB_GETSELCOUNT,0,0);
  if (!Items) return FALSE;

  // Allocate an array for the result
  int * SelArray = new int[Items];

  // get the indexes into the array
```

```
    DWORD retcode=
      SendMessage(hWnd, LB_GETSELITEMS,Items,(DWORD)SelArray);

    // for each item, get the text
    for (int i=0;i<Items;i++) {
      char Buffer[20];
      char * pBuf=Buffer;
      int tlen=SendMessage(hWnd, LB_GETTEXTLEN,SelArray[i],0);
      if (tlen>20) pBuf=new char[tlen];
      SendMessage(hWnd, LB_GETTEXT,SelArray[i],(DWORD)pBuf);
      // call the function back
      (Inst->*pCallback)(pBuf);
      if (tlen>20) delete pBuf;
    }
    delete SelArray;
    return retcode;
}
```

An application calls **Selections** with a callback member function as parameter. **Selections** calls the member function back for each selected item. The member function will be called with the string of the item supplied as a parameter. The example later in this chapter uses this member function.

This member function uses the **new** operator to temporarily allocate an integer array, **SelArray**. The list box fills this array with the indexes of all the items that have been selected. The **for** loop takes each item in turn. It retrieves the text of the item and passes it on to the callback. **SelArray** must be deleted before the member function returns.

```
WORD ListBox::Text(int Index, LPSTR pBuf)
{
    return SendMessage(hWnd, LB_GETTEXT,Index,(DWORD)pBuf);
}

DWORD ListBox::Find(LPSTR pBuf, int Index)
{
    return SendMessage(hWnd, LB_FINDSTRING,Index,(DWORD)pBuf);
}

void ListBox::Reset()
{
    SendMessage(hWnd, LB_RESETCONTENT,0,0);
}
```

The **ListBox** class can handle both single- and multiple-column list boxes. The boxes can be either single or multiple selection. To specify the list box type, use the **Style** parameter in the constructor. The following styles are useful:

LBS_EXTENDEDSEL	This style allows the user to select multiple items using the SHIFT and CTRL keys in conjunction with the mouse or the keyboard arrow keys. This is the preferred style for multiple-selection boxes.
LBS_MULTICOLUMN	This style specifies a multiple-column list box that can be scrolled horizontally. Use the **ColumnWidth** member function to set the width of the columns.
LBS_MULTIPLESEL	This style allows the user to select multiple items. String selection is toggled each time the user clicks on the string. This style is useful for lists containing a small number of options, because it resembles a group of check boxes in function, if not in appearance.
LBS_NOINTEGRALHEIGHT	Specifying this style creates a list box of exactly the height specified. Otherwise, the height of the box will be reduced so as to display an integral number of items. This style may be useful if you are trying to arrange controls to abut each other.
LBS_SORT	In a list box of this style, the items are sorted alphabetically.
LBS_USETABSTOPS	This style of list box recognizes TAB characters in strings. A TAB position is 32 dialog units, which is equivalent to 8 spaces in the system font.

These styles can be combined using the logical OR operator, |. For example, **LBS_MULTICOLUMN | LBS_EXTENDEDSEL | LBS_SORT** creates a sorted multiple-column list box with extended multiple select properties.

The Edit Class

The **Edit** class, in contrast, is much simpler. In general, an edit control has text. The user edits the text, if necessary, and later the text is retrieved, usually when the user clicks on an OK button in a dialog box.

It is possible to do much more with edit controls. For example, they have an undo feature, and it is possible to change the algorithm that wraps words at the end of lines. These more advanced features are not often used for simple controls, but they can be used to build a simple text editor.

The most efficient solution then, is to create a simple **Edit** class that is sufficient for controls. If the advanced functions are needed later, it is always possible to derive some sort of text editor class from **Edit**.

Here is the definition of the **Edit** class:

edit.hpp

```
#ifndef  EDIT_INC
#define  EDIT_INC

#include "control.hpp"

class Edit : public Control{
public:

  Edit(
    HWND PhWnd,                // Parent window handle
    int Id,                    // Identifier for control
    LPSTR pText="",            // Edit text
    DWORD Style=0,             // Edit Style
    int x= CW_USEDEFAULT,      // Position
    int y= CW_USEDEFAULT,
    int width= CW_USEDEFAULT,  // Size
    int height= CW_USEDEFAULT);

  void Select(                 // Select a part of text
    int First=0,
    int Last=32767);
}; // class Edit

#endif // EDIT_INC
```

This is quite simple. The only member function a control might need is **Select**, to select a part of the text. Usually, an application will want to select the entire text, so the member function has default parameters that will do this. To set and retrieve the actual text of the control, use the **Window** member function **GetText** and **SetText**.

Here is the implementation:

edit.cpp

```
#include "edit.hpp"

Edit::Edit(HWND PhWnd, int Id, LPSTR pText, DWORD Style,
    int x, int y, int width, int height)
{
  CreateControl("Edit",PhWnd, Id,pText,
    Style|WS_CHILD|WS_VISIBLE|WS_BORDER,
    x,y,width,height);
}

void Edit::Select(int First, int Last)
{
    SendMessage(hWnd, EM_SETSEL,0,MAKELONG(First,Last));
   ::SetFocus(hWnd);
}
```

When the constructor creates the edit control, it gives it a border. The **Select** member function sends a message to the control to set a selection, and then gives the control the focus. Normally, the selection is only visible when the control has the focus. Notice the **::** operator in front of **SetFocus**. This tells the compiler to take the **SetFocus** defined in the API. If this scope operator did not appear, the compiler would assume the **SetFocus** member function defined in the **Window** class.

The following styles are useful for edit controls:

ES_AUTOHSCROLL	This style automatically scrolls text horizontally. Without this style, the control will beep when the line is full.
ES_AUTOVSCROLL	This style automatically scrolls text vertically on multiple-line controls.
ES_CENTER	This style centers text.
ES_LEFT	This style aligns text to the left of the control.
ES_LOWERCASE	This style converts all characters to lowercase.
ES_MULTILINE	This style specifies a multiple-line control.

ES_NOHIDESEL	Normally, selections are only visible when the control has the input focus. With this style, they are visible all the time.
ES_OEMCONVERT	This style, which converts text to the OEM character set, is useful for controls containing file names that include European characters.
ES_PASSWORD	This style displays every character as an asterisk.
ES_RIGHT	This style aligns the text to the right of the control.
ES_UPPERCASE	This style converts all characters to upper-case.

The ComboBox Class

A combo box is a combination of a list box and an edit control. The list box can be made to drop down when an icon to the right of the edit control is pressed, or it can be displayed permanently. Combo boxes are useful as an alternative to simple list boxes, because a drop-down combo box uses less screen space. A combo box can also be used instead of a simple edit control when the contents of the edit control are frequently set to one of a small group of items. A dialog box that prompts for a name, perhaps a file name, could use an edit drop-down combo box. Whenever the user types a name into the edit control, it can be added to the drop-down list:

Since an **Edit** and a **ListBox** class exist already, it should be possible to derive the **ComboBox** class from them, using multiple inheritance. Unfortunately, this is not the case. At the level of the API, a combo box is different from both list boxes and edit controls. It uses a completely different set of messages and does not support all the features of either list boxes or edit controls. There is little choice but to treat a combo box as a separate class.

combobox.hpp

```
#ifndef  COMBOBOX_INC

#define  COMBOBOX_INC
#include "control.hpp"

class ComboBox : public Control{

protected:
  void (WinObj::*ClickCallback)(ComboBox&);
  WinObj * ClickInst;
  void (WinObj::*DClickCallback)(ComboBox&);
  WinObj * DClickInst;

public:
  ComboBox(
    HWND PhWnd,                  // Parent window handle
    int Id,                     // Child Id
    DWORD Style=0,              // Scroll bar style
    int x=CW_USEDEFAULT,        // Position
    int y=CW_USEDEFAULT,
    int width=CW_USEDEFAULT,    // Size
    int height=CW_USEDEFAULT);

  void Add(                     //Add a string to list
    LPSTR pstr);

  void Delete(                  // Delete an item
    WORD pItem);

  void Delete(                  // Delete an item
    LPSTR pItem);

  DWORD Find(                   // Find an item
    LPSTR pBuf,
    int Index=-1);

  int Count();                  // Count of items in list

  void Reset();                 // Delete all items

  void Dir(                     // Fill list with file names
    WORD Attr=0x37,
    LPSTR pFileSpec="*.*");
```

```
    WORD Text(                       // Get text of an item
      int Index,
      LPSTR pBuf);

    int Selection();                 // return current selection

    int Select(                      // Select an item
     int Index);

    int Select(                      // Select an item
     LPSTR pText,
     int Index=-1);

    DWORD Selection(                 // Get current selection
      LPSTR pBuf);

    virtual void Click(              // Callback for single clicks
      WinObj * Inst,
      void (WinObj::*pCallback)(ComboBox&));

    virtual void DClick(             // Callback for double clicks
      WinObj* Inst,
      void (WinObj::*pCallback)(ComboBox&));

protected:
  virtual void ProcessError(int RetCode);
  LONG CodeHandler(int NotifyCode, int Extra);

}; // class ComboBox

typedef void(WinObj::*COMBOBOXCALLBACK)(ComboBox&);

#endif   // COMBOBOX_INC
```

The class definition looks very much like the definition of the **ListBox** class. Most of the member functions have the same function as they had for list boxes, but the messages sent to the control are different.

combobox.cpp

```
#include "combobox.hpp"

ComboBox::ComboBox(HWND PhWnd, int Id, DWORD Style,
    int x, int y, int width, int height)
{
    CreateControl("ComboBox",PhWnd,Id,"",
      Style|WS_CHILD |WS_VISIBLE |WS_BORDER|WS_VSCROLL,
```

```
        x,y,width,height);
}
```

The constructor creates a combo box with a border and a vertical scroll bar. The scroll bar is visible only if there are too many items to be displayed in the drop-down list. The height of the combo box includes the drop-down list.

```
void ComboBox::Click(WinObj * Inst,
    void (WinObj::*pCallback)(ComboBox&))
{
    ClickInst = Inst;
    ClickCallback = pCallback;
}

void ComboBox::DClick(WinObj * Inst,
    void (WinObj::*pCallback)(ComboBox&))
{
    DClickInst = Inst;
    DClickCallback = pCallback;
}
```

The **Click** member function defines the callback for single clicks in the drop-down list. **DClick** can only be used for combo boxes that have the **CBS_SIMPLE** style, where the list is always displayed. There is no rule about this, but when you click once on a drop-down list, it disappears and you never get the chance to click a second time.

```
void ComboBox::Add(LPSTR pstr)
{
  int RetVal;
  RetVal=SendMessage(hWnd, CB_ADDSTRING,0, (DWORD)pstr);
  ProcessError(RetVal);
}

void ComboBox::Delete(WORD pItem)
{
  ProcessError(SendMessage(hWnd, CB_DELETESTRING,pItem,0));
}

void ComboBox::Delete(LPSTR pItem)
{
  int Index=-1;
  char String[120];
  do {
```

```
      int OldIndex=Index;
      Index=SendMessage(hWnd, CB_FINDSTRING,
                         Index,(DWORD)pItem);
      if (Index <=OldIndex) return;
      Text(Index,String);
   } while (lstrcmp(pItem, String));
   ProcessError(SendMessage(hWnd, CB_DELETESTRING,
                            Index,0L));
}

int ComboBox::Count()
{
   return SendMessage(hWnd, CB_GETCOUNT,0,0);
}

void ComboBox::Dir(WORD Attr, LPSTR pFileSpec)
{
   SendMessage(hWnd, CB_DIR,Attr,(DWORD)pFileSpec);
}

void ComboBox::ProcessError(int RetCode)
{
   if (RetCode==CB_ERR)
     Error(IDS_APPLERROR,(LPSTR)"Combobox");
   if (RetCode==CB_ERRSPACE)
     Error(IDS_MEMORY, (LPSTR)"ComboBox");
}

LONG ComboBox::CodeHandler(int NotifyCode,int Extra)
{
   switch (NotifyCode) {

   case CBN_DBLCLK:
     if (DClickCallback)
       (DClickInst->*DClickCallback)(*this);
     else return FALSE;
     break;

   case CBN_SELCHANGE:
     if (ClickCallback)
       (ClickInst->*ClickCallback)(*this);
     else return FALSE;
     break;

   default:
     return FALSE;
   }
```

```
  return TRUE;
}

int ComboBox::Selection()
{
  return SendMessage(hWnd, CB_GETCURSEL,0,0);
}

int ComboBox::Select(int Index)
{
  return SendMessage(hWnd, CB_SETCURSEL,Index,0);
}

int ComboBox::Select(LPSTR pText, int Index)
{
  return SendMessage(hWnd, CB_SELECTSTRING,
                     Index,(LONG)pText);
}

DWORD ComboBox::Selection(LPSTR pBuf)
{
  int Index;
  Index=SendMessage(hWnd, CB_GETCURSEL,0,0);
  if (Index <0) return FALSE;
  SendMessage(hWnd, CB_GETLBTEXT,Index,(DWORD)pBuf);
  return TRUE;
}

WORD ComboBox::Text(int Index, LPSTR pBuf)
{
  return SendMessage(hWnd, CB_GETLBTEXT,
                     Index,(DWORD)pBuf);
}

DWORD ComboBox::Find(LPSTR pBuf, int Index)
{
  return SendMessage(hWnd, CB_FINDSTRING,
                     Index,(DWORD)pBuf);
}

void ComboBox::Reset()
{
  SendMessage(hWnd, CB_RESETCONTENT,0,0);
}
```

The code too, resembles that of the **ListBox** class. Many of the messages have the same names as those of list boxes, but with a **CB** prefix instead of an **LB** prefix. Although the names are similar, the numerical values are quite different.

The following styles are useful for combo boxes:

CBS_AUTOHSCROLL

This style automatically scrolls text horizontally. Without this style, the control beeps when the line is full.

CBS_DROPDOWN

This style, which displays an edit control with a drop-down list, is useful when there are a number of common choices for the edit field.

CBS_DROPDOWNLIST

This style is similar to **CBS_DROPDOWN**, except that the edit control is replaced by a static control that displays the current selection in the list.

CBS_OEMCONVERT

This style, which converts text to the OEM character set, is useful for controls containing file names that include European characters.

CBS_SIMPLE

This style displays an edit control and a list box. The list is displayed permanently.

CBS_SORT

In a combo box of this style, the items are sorted alphabetically.

The Static Class

This is another simple class. A static control simply displays text that cannot be edited by the user, but may be changed by the application. Other than the constructor, the **Static** class has no member functions. The **Window** class member functions **GetText** and **SetText** may be used to manipulate the text in the control. The **Control** member function **SetFont** change its font.

static.hpp

```
#ifndef  STATIC_INC

#define  STATIC_INC
```

```
#include "control.hpp"

class Static : public Control{

public:

  Static(
    HWND PhWnd,                    // Parent window handle
    int Id,                        // Child Id
    LPSTR Text,                    // Static text
    DWORD Style=SS_LEFT,
    int x= CW_USEDEFAULT,          // Position
    int y= CW_USEDEFAULT,
    int width= CW_USEDEFAULT,   // Size
    int height= CW_USEDEFAULT);
}; // class Static

#endif   // STATIC_INC
```

The **Static** class can also be used to display icons and rectangles, depending on the style specified. Note that if a frame or rectangle style is specified, the text is not displayed. To display text with a frame around it, use the **WS_BORDER** style. Other useful styles are listed here:

SS_BLACKFRAME	This style draws a frame in the color currently defined for borders.
SS_BLACKRECT	This style draws a rectangle in the color currently defined for borders.
SS_CENTER	This style displays centered text.
SS_GRAYFRAME	This style draws a frame in the color currently defined for screen backgrounds.
SS_GRAYRECT	This style draws a rectangle in the color currently defined for screen backgrounds.
SS_ICON	This style displays an icon. The text specifies the name of the icon that must be in the resource file.
SS_LEFT	This style displays left-aligned text.
SS_LEFTNOWORDWRAP	This style also displays left-aligned text. If the text is too long, it is not wrapped to the next line, but simply clipped.

SS_NOPREFIX	Normally, a **&** character causes the next character to be underlined. If this style is specified, the ampersands are displayed as ampersands.
SS_RIGHT	This style displays right-aligned text.
SS_WHITEFRAME	This style draws a frame in the color currently defined for window backgrounds.
SS_WHITERECT	This style draws a rectangle in the color currently defined for window backgrounds.

The ScrollBar Class

I have been saving the best until last: Scroll bars do not contain text. They only need to have the range and thumb (or slider) position set. From that viewpoint, the interface is simple. However, what complicates the programming of scroll bars is that they generate different notification codes depending on which part of the bar has been clicked. One of the arrows may have been clicked, or the thumb dragged, or the space between the thumb and the arrows clicked.

If you need to differentiate between these events, then that is all to the good. On the other hand, scroll bars are quite often used to set some value in a range. For example, if a temperature ranges between 0 and 100 degrees Celsius, an application is not interested in which part of the bar has been operated as long as the value is changed as a result.

In the implementation described here, it is possible to define callbacks for the different scroll bar components. It is also possible to define just one general purpose callback for the whole scroll bar. In that case, the scroll bar itself changes the value appropriately depending on which part of the bar was operated. If the end arrows are clicked the value is changed in single units, and if the space between the thumb and the arrows is clicked, the value is changed by a tenth of its range.

The application does not need to specify a callback at all. It can just recover the current value of the scroll bar when it wants to; for example, when the OK button is clicked. On the other hand, if the application specified callbacks for the arrow and the space between the arrow and the thumb, it must then set the thumb position from the callbacks.

The **ScrollBar** class must also distinguish between child controls and the scroll bars built into the frame of the parent window. The class can handle both types of scroll bar, but there are differences. Child controls have their own keyboard interface. If a control has the focus, it responds to the keyboard direction keys. Window scroll bars leave the keyboard processing to the associated window. Although the window may wish to handle the direction keys itself, it usually does not. The **ScrollBar** class contains a **KeyDown** member function to handle the direction keys, but the **Window** class instance will only call it if the instance does not handle these keys itself.

scroll.hpp

```
#ifndef  SCROLLBAR_INC

#define  SCROLLBAR_INC
#include "control.hpp"


class ScrollBar : public Control{
    struct ScrollCB {                   // a structure to hold
        WinObj * Inst;                  // callback info
        void (WinObj::*Callback)(ScrollBar&, int);
    };

protected:
    // callbacks for the different events
    ScrollCB PositionCallback;
    ScrollCB LineCallback;
    ScrollCB PageCallback;
    ScrollCB TrackCallback;

    int ThumbPosition;
    int RangeMin;
    int RangeMax;
    int Type;

public:
    ScrollBar(
        HWND PhWnd,                     // Parent window handle
        int Id,                         // Child Id
        DWORD Style=0,                  // Style
        int x= CW_USEDEFAULT,           // Position
        int y= CW_USEDEFAULT,
```

```
      int width= CW_USEDEFAULT,  // Size
      int height= CW_USEDEFAULT);

   ~ScrollBar();

   virtual void Position(        // Define callback for thumb
      WinObj * Inst,
      void (WinObj::*pCallback)(ScrollBar&,int));

   virtual void Line(            // Define callback for arrows
      WinObj * Inst,
      void (WinObj::*pCallback)(ScrollBar&,int));

   virtual void Page(            // Define callback for space
      WinObj * Inst,            // between arrow and thumb
      void (WinObj::*pCallback)(ScrollBar&,int));

   virtual void Track(           // Define track
      WinObj * Inst,
      void (WinObj::*pCallback)(ScrollBar&,int));

   int SetPosition(             // Set thumb position
      int Pos,
      BOOL Redraw=TRUE);

   int GetPosition();            // Get thumb position

   void SetRange(               // Set scroll bar range
      int Min,
      int Max,
      BOOL Redraw=TRUE);

   BOOL KeyDown(                 // Process keyboard input
      WORD VirtKey,
      KEYCODES KeyCodes);

protected:
   LONG CodeHandler(int NotifyCode, int Extra);
}; // class ScrollBar

typedef void (WinObj::*SCROLLBARCALLBACK)(ScrollBar&,int);


#endif // SCROLLBAR_INC
```

So four callbacks can be defined: **Position**, **Line**, **Page**, and **Track**. If no callback is defined for either **Line** or **Page**, then the **Position** callback is called instead, if it is defined. If the thumb is dragged, the **Track** callback is called repeatedly until the thumb is released. Then, the **Position** callback is called once.

scroll.cpp

```
#include "scroll.hpp"

ScrollBar::ScrollBar(HWND PhWnd, int Id, DWORD Style,
    int x, int y, int width, int height)
{
  switch(Id) {
  case SB_HORZ:
    GetWin(PhWnd)->HorzScrollBar=this;
    Type=Id;
    hWnd=PhWnd;
    break;

  case SB_VERT:
    GetWin(PhWnd)->VertScrollBar=this;
    Type=Id;
    hWnd=PhWnd;
    break;

  default:
    CreateControl("scrollbar",PhWnd,Id,"",
      Style|WS_CHILD|WS_VISIBLE,
      x,y,width,height);
    Type=SB_CTL;
  }
 ThumbPosition=RangeMin=RangeMax=0;
 TrackCallback.Inst=NULL;
 TrackCallback.Callback=NULL;
 PositionCallback=LineCallback=PageCallback=TrackCallback;
}
```

The constructor checks the ID. If the ID is **SB_HORZ** or **SB_VERT**, the instance will be associated with the built-in scroll bar of the parent window. Otherwise, a child control is created. **SB_VERT** and **SB_HORZ** correspond to the numerical values 0 and 1, which are also reserved for the standard control IDs **IDOK** and **IDCANCEL**. The ID for a control will not accidently match **SB_HORZ** or **SB_VERT**. This means that an application can create an ordinary scroll bar control by specifying the control ID, but it can create an instance **ScrollBar** for a window scroll bar by specifying either **SB_HORZ** or **SB_VERT**.

All the class items are set to zero or **NULL**.

```
ScrollBar::~ScrollBar()
{
  Window *pWin=GetWin(hWnd);

  switch(Type) {
  case SB_HORZ:
    if (pWin) pWin->HorzScrollBar=NULL;
  break;

  case SB_VERT:
    if (pWin) pWin->VertScrollBar=NULL;
  break;

  default:
    DestroyWindow(hWnd);
  }
  hWnd=0;
}
```

The **Window** class destructor normally destroys the window having the handle **hWnd**. If the instance is based on a built-in scroll bar, **hWnd** will be the handle of the main window and should not be destroyed. The destructor destroys the control only if it is a child control, and then it sets **hWnd** to zero to prevent the **Window** class destructor from destroying the control a second time.

```
void ScrollBar::Position(WinObj * Inst,
    void (WinObj::*pCallback)(ScrollBar&,int))
{
    PositionCallback.Inst = Inst;
    PositionCallback.Callback = pCallback;
}

void ScrollBar::Page(WinObj * Inst,
    void (WinObj::*pCallback)(ScrollBar&,int))
{
    PageCallback.Inst = Inst;
    PageCallback.Callback = pCallback;
}
```

```
void ScrollBar::Line(WinObj * Inst,
      void (WinObj::*pCallback)(ScrollBar&,int))
{
    LineCallback.Inst = Inst;
    LineCallback.Callback = pCallback;
}

void ScrollBar::Track(WinObj * Inst,
      void (WinObj::*pCallback)(ScrollBar&,int))
{
    TrackCallback.Inst = Inst;
    TrackCallback.Callback = pCallback;
}
```

These are the four member functions for declaring callbacks. As there are so many of them, the class uses a structure, **ScrollCB**, to store them.

```
int ScrollBar::SetPosition(int Pos, BOOL Redraw)
{
    if (Pos<RangeMin) Pos=RangeMin;
    if (Pos>RangeMax) Pos=RangeMax;
    ThumbPosition=Pos;
    return SetScrollPos(hWnd,Type,Pos,Redraw);
}

int ScrollBar::GetPosition()
{
    return GetScrollPos(hWnd,Type);
}

void ScrollBar::SetRange(int Min, int Max, BOOL Redraw)
{
    RangeMin=Min;
    RangeMax=Max;
    ThumbPosition=min(Max,max(ThumbPosition,Min));
    SetScrollRange(hWnd,Type,Min,Max,FALSE);
    SetScrollPos(hWnd,Type,ThumbPosition,Redraw);
}
```

The **ScrollBar** class keeps track of the range and thumb position of the scroll bar. The class uses these values a lot, and keeping track of them avoids having to interrogate the control each time they are needed.

```
LONG ScrollBar::CodeHandler(int NotifyCode, int Extra)
{
  switch (NotifyCode) {
```

```
case SB_LINEUP:

  if (LineCallback.Callback){
    (LineCallback.Inst->*LineCallback.Callback)(*this,-1);
    return TRUE;
  }
  ThumbPosition—;
  break;

case SB_LINEDOWN:

  if (LineCallback.Callback){
   (LineCallback.Inst->*LineCallback.Callback)(*this,1);
   return TRUE;
  }
  ThumbPosition++;
  break;

case SB_PAGEUP:
  if (PageCallback.Callback){
    (PageCallback.Inst->*PageCallback.Callback)(*this,-1);
    return TRUE;
  }
  ThumbPosition-= (RangeMax-RangeMin)/10;
  break;

case SB_PAGEDOWN:
   if (PageCallback.Callback){
    (PageCallback.Inst->*PageCallback.Callback)(*this,1);
    return TRUE;
   }
   ThumbPosition+= (RangeMax-RangeMin)/10;
   break;

case SB_THUMBTRACK:
   if (TrackCallback.Callback){
    (TrackCallback.Inst->*TrackCallback.Callback)
       (*this,Extra);
   }
   return TRUE;


case SB_TOP:
   ThumbPosition=RangeMin;
   break;
```

```
case SB_BOTTOM:
   ThumbPosition=RangeMax;
   break;
case SB_THUMBPOSITION:
   ThumbPosition=Extra;
   break;

default:
   return FALSE;
}

   SetPosition(ThumbPosition);
   if (PositionCallback.Callback)
      (PositionCallback.Inst->*PositionCallback.Callback)
      (*this,ThumbPosition);
   return TRUE;
}
```

CodeHandler is called by the parent whenever it receives a **WM_HSCROLL** or **WM_VSCROLL** message. It does all the default processing. The **Position** and **Track** callbacks are called with the thumb position as a parameter. The **Line** and **Page** callbacks are called with either +1 or −1 to indicate a positive or negative direction. Both the **Line** and **Page** callbacks are responsible for updating the thumb position with the **SetPosition** member function. If the **Line** or **Page** callbacks have not been defined, the thumb position is adjusted by default and the **Position** callback is called instead.

```
BOOL ScrollBar::KeyDown(WORD VirtKey, KEYCODES KeyCodes)
{
   int bCTRL=GetKeyState(VK_CONTROL) &0x8000;
   if (Type==SB_CTL) return FALSE;
   switch (VirtKey) {
   case VK_UP:
      if (Type==SB_HORZ) return FALSE;
      CodeHandler(SB_LINEUP,0);
      break;

   case VK_DOWN:
      if (Type==SB_HORZ) return FALSE;
      CodeHandler(SB_LINEDOWN,0);
      break;

   case VK_LEFT:
      if (Type==SB_VERT) return FALSE;
```

```
        CodeHandler(SB_LINEUP,0);
        break;

    case VK_RIGHT:
      if (Type==SB_VERT) return FALSE;
      CodeHandler(SB_LINEDOWN,0);
      break;

    case VK_PRIOR:
      if(bCTRL && Type==SB_VERT
      || !bCTRL && Type==SB_HORZ) return FALSE;
      CodeHandler(SB_PAGEUP,0);
      break;

    case VK_NEXT:
      if(bCTRL && Type==SB_VERT
      || !bCTRL && Type==SB_HORZ) return FALSE;
      CodeHandler(SB_PAGEDOWN,0);
      break;

    case VK_HOME:
      if(bCTRL && Type==SB_VERT
      || !bCTRL && Type==SB_HORZ) return FALSE;
      CodeHandler(SB_TOP,0);
      break;

    case VK_END:
      if(bCTRL && Type==SB_VERT
      || !bCTRL && Type==SB_HORZ) return FALSE;
      CodeHandler(SB_BOTTOM,0);
      break;

    default:
      return FALSE;
  }

  return TRUE;
}
```

The **KeyDown** member function handles keyboard events for window scroll bars. The UP ARROW and DOWN ARROW keys work only with vertical scroll bars, and the LEFT ARROW and RIGHT ARROW keys work only with horizontal scroll bars. The PGUP, PGDN, HOME, and END keys affect vertical scroll bars, but if the CTRL key is pressed at the same time, the horizontal scroll bar is moved.

The member function uses the API function **GetKeyState** to see whether the control key was pressed. This function returns the state of the key at the time the current keyboard event was generated. The **GetAsynchKeyState** function returns the state at the moment the function is called. By the time the message is processed, the user may have released the key. It is important not to confuse the two functions.

If an application can update the display quick enough, it can use the same member function for **Position** and **Track**. Updating the display might be slow; for example, in a desktop publishing system with a long document. In that case, the application might only update it in the **Position** member function, and have **Track** do nothing or something that is quick to do, such as displaying the corresponding page number in a status bar.

If you look in the API reference, you will notice there are styles for defining a *size box*, which is a small gray square, as shown in Figure 4-4. Clicking and dragging the box changes the size of the parent window. It serves the same purpose as the size frame of a window. On its own, the size box is not very useful, but it is handy for filling in the little square in the bottom right-hand corner of a window that has two scroll bars along the right and bottom edges. If you use built-in scroll bars, this

FIGURE 4-4   Scroll bar components

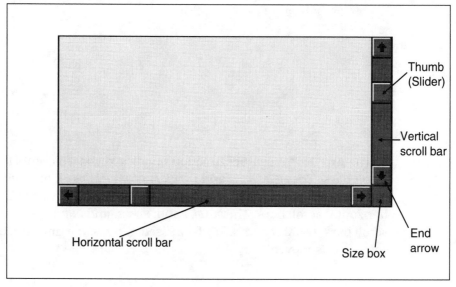

square is filled in automatically, so you normally have no need for them. A size box does not generate any messages; you simply create it. If you use the **SBS_SIZEBOX** style with the **ScrollBar** class, a size box will be created. If you think you might use more than one, you could create a **SizeBox** class. The constructor calls **CreateControl** with the **ScrollBar** class and the **SBS_SIZEBOX** style. That is all you need to create a **SizeBox** class.

Here are the other scroll bar styles:

SBS_HORZ	This style creates a horizontal scroll bar.
SBS_VERT	This style creates a vertical scroll bar.
SBS_BOTTOMALIGN	This style is used with **SBS_HORZ**. It creates a standard-width scroll bar aligned on the bottom edge of the rectangle specified in the constructor.
SBS_LEFTALIGN	This style is used with **SBS_VERT**. It creates a standard-width scroll bar aligned on the left edge of the rectangle specified in the constructor.
SBS_RIGHTALIGN	This style is also used with **SBS_VERT**. It creates a standard-width scroll bar aligned on the right edge of the rectangle specified in the constructor.
SBS_TOPALIGN	This style is used with **SBS_HORZ**. It creates a standard-width scroll bar aligned on the top edge of the rectangle specified in the constructor.

The ALIGN styles are very useful for creating a scroll bar having the same width as the system scroll bars, as shown in Figure 4-5. You usually want to do this because otherwise the scroll bars look odd. Instead of having to specify

GetSystemMetrics(SM_CXVSCROLL)

or whatever, you supply a width that is oversize, and then align the scroll bar along the top or the left with one of the align styles. The example later in this chapter does this. If you have two scroll bars side by side, you can align them on the left-hand and right-hand sides (or top and bottom) of

FIGURE
4-5
Scroll bars aligned on a rectangle

a larger rectangle. This rectangle can be positioned to line up with another feature in the window, perhaps a button. In that way you can align the scroll bars even though you do not know their width.

An Example Program

Now that all the controls are defined, let's make a serious application. The example in this section is an electronic version of an activity set for encouraging hand and eye coordination in infants. You may have seen conventional versions of these sets, with plastic boxes covered with buttons to push, knobs to twiddle, hooters to honk, things to slide up and down, and so on. With more and more home computers running Windows, the market is growing for an application like this.

The application will have a main window filled with controls, courtesy of the class **BabyWin**, which inherits from **Window**. Here is the source of **BabyWin**:

babywin.cpp

```
#include "babywin.hpp"

BabyWin::BabyWin(HWND PhWnd, LPSTR Name, DWORD Style,
          int x, int y)
{
  Create(Name,Style | WS_VSCROLL,x,y,480,180,PhWnd,NULL);

  Direct1=new ListBox(hWnd,101,
    LBS_MULTICOLUMN|LBS_SORT|LBS_EXTENDEDSEL,
    0,0,240,120);
  Direct1->Dir();
```

```
  Transfer = new Button(hWnd,102,"Transfer",
     BS_PUSHBUTTON,
     250,10,70,40);
  Transfer->Click(this,
     (BUTTONCALLBACK)&BabyWin::TransferItems);

  Direct2= new ComboBox(hWnd,103,
    CBS_DROPDOWNLIST|WS_VSCROLL,
    330,10,120,100);

  Button * Button1 = new Button(hWnd,104,"Beep",
    BS_PUSHBUTTON,
    250,60,70,40);
  Button1->Click(this,(BUTTONCALLBACK)&BabyWin::Click1);

  ScrollBar * VScroll = new ScrollBar(hWnd,SB_VERT);
  VScroll->SetRange(0,100);
  VScroll->Position(this,
     (SCROLLBARCALLBACK)&BabyWin::VScrollPos);

  VText=new Static(hWnd,105,"Vertical Scroll",0,
     330,40,120,25);

  Edit* Change = new Edit(hWnd,106,"Change Me",
    ES_AUTOHSCROLL,330,70,100,25);
  Change->Select();

  ScrollBar* HorScroll=
     new ScrollBar(hWnd,107,SBS_HORZ |SBS_TOPALIGN,
       330,100,120,20);
  HorScroll->SetRange(0,100);

  ComboCount = new Static(hWnd,108,"",0,5,120,230,22);
  TransferItems(*Transfer);

  CheckBox * Check =
     new CheckBox(hWnd,109,"Check Me",BS_AUTOCHECKBOX,
     330,120,120,22);
}

LPSTR BabyWin::Register(WNDCLASS& wc)
{
  wc.lpszClassName = "BabyWin";
  RegisterClass (&wc);
  return "BabyWin";
}
```

The constructor, which is the most complex member function in **BabyWin**, creates all the controls. In detail, the constructor performs the following activities:

- ☐ It creates the main window. This window is given an extra **WS_VSCROLL** style to generate a built-in vertical scroll bar.

- ☐ It creates a list box **Direct1** with the multiple-column and extended-selection styles. The contents of the list box will be sorted. The list box will be 240 pixels wide and 120 pixels high. After the list box has been created, the constructor fills it with the names of the files in the current directory, using the **Dir** member function.

- ☐ It creates a push-button called *Transfer*. When the infant clicks the button, the member function **TransferItems** is called, copies the names of all the selected files in **Direct2** to the combo box, and updates a static text control with the number of files copied.

- ☐ It creates a drop-down combo box called **Direct2**. There is no need to specify **WS_VSCROLL**, since the **ComboBox** constructor adds it anyway.

- ☐ It creates a button, **Button1**. When this button is clicked, member function **Click1** is called.

- ☐ A **ScrollBar** instance **VScroll** is associated with the main window's built-in vertical scroll bar. The constructor sets the range of this bar to (0,100). When the infant clicks the scroll bar, the member function **VScrollPos** will be called.

- ☐ The constructor creates a static text control called **VText**. The text is initially *Vertical Scroll*.

- ☐ It creates an edit control with the initial text *Change Me*. The text is selected.

- ☐ The constructor then creates a horizontal scroll bar control. The bar will have the width (or height, since it is horizontal) of system scroll bars, and will align along the top edge of a rectangle 120 pixels wide and 20 pixels high. The range of the scroll bar is set to (0,100).

- ☐ It creates another static control, **ComboCount**, that reports the total number of items in the combo box. The member function

TransferItems is called now, since this will initialize the text in **ComboCount**.

❏ Finally, the constructor creates a check box control containing the text *Check Me*. The box is automatic, so there is no need to handle the click events.

```
LPSTR BabyWin::Register(WNDCLASS& wc)
{
  wc.lpszClassName = "BabyWin";
  RegisterClass (&wc);
  return "BabyWin";
}


void BabyWin::Click1(Button& b)
{
  MessageBeep(0);
}
```

There is nothing special about the **Register** member function. Member function **Click1** makes a beep sound when **Button1** is clicked.

```
void BabyWin::VScrollPos(ScrollBar& Scroll, int Pos)
{
  char message[40];
  wsprintf(message,"VScroll is at %d",Pos);
  VText->SetText(message);
}
```

When the window's built-in vertical scroll bar is activated, **VScrollPos** updates the static control **VText** with a message showing the position of the scroll bar thumb.

```
void BabyWin::TransferItems(Button& B)
{
  Direct2->Reset();
  Direct1->Selections(this,
        (LPSTRCALLBACK)&BabyWin::TransferItem);
  Direct2->Select(0);
  char * str1="ComboBox contains %d items.";
  char str2[32];
  wsprintf(str2,str1,Direct2->Count());
  ComboCount->SetText(str2);
}
```

```
void BabyWin::TransferItem(LPSTR pText)
{
    Direct2->Add(pText);
}
```

The member function **TransferItems** copies the names of the files selected in the list box **Direct1** to the combo box **Direct2**. It resets the contents of **Direct2**, removing any names that are already there, copies the names, and selects the first name in the list in **Direct2**. It then updates the static text control **ComboCount** to show how many items have been copied.

Since **Direct1** is a multiple-selection list box, the member function **Selections** is used. **BabyWin** gives **Selections** a member function that will be called back for each selected item. In this case, that member function is **TransferItem**, and it adds the item's name to the combo box.

Selections does not deselect the items, so it is possible to call it more than once if necessary. You may want to display a message box of the form. The message might say *Are you sure you want to delete combo box, file2, file3?*, for example. You can call **Selections** with a member function that adds the names of the files to the string, and then call again with a member function to delete them.

```
LONG BabyWin::LButtonDown(Event& evt)
{
    ::SetFocus(hWnd);
    return TRUE;
}
```

If the mouse is clicked anywhere in the window, it is given the focus. This enables the infant to manipulate the vertical scroll bar using the keyboard direction keys.

The class definition simply declares all the controls and member functions that the class uses.

babywin.hpp

```
#ifndef BABYWIN_INC
#define BABYWIN_INC

#include "window.hpp"
#include "button.hpp"
#include "scroll.hpp"
#include "edit.hpp"
```

```
#include "static.hpp"
#include "listbox.hpp"
#include "combobox.hpp"
#include "static.hpp"
#include "checkbox.hpp"

class Babylon : public Window {
public:
    Babylon(HWND PhWnd, LPSTR Name,
        DWORD Style=WS_OVERLAPPEDWINDOW,
        int x= CW_USEDEFAULT, int y= CW_USEDEFAULT);

protected:
  Static * VText;
  ListBox * Direct1;
  ComboBox * Direct2;
  Button * Transfer;
  Static * ComboCount;

  LPSTR Register(WNDCLASS& wc);
  void Click1(Button& b);
  void VScrollPos(ScrollBar& Scroll, int Pos);
  void TransferItems(Button& B);
  void TransferItem(LPSTR pText);
  LONG LButtonDown(Event& evt);
};
#endif
```

The **WinMain** routine is similar to the one used in the Hello World
program. Here is the source:

test.cpp

```
#include "babywin.hpp"

HANDLE hInst;
HANDLE hPrevInst;
LPSTR  CmdLine;

int PASCAL WinMain(HANDLE hInstance, HANDLE hPrevInstance,
    LPSTR lpszCmdLine, int nCmdShow)
{
    hInst = hInstance;
    char * pName = new char[80];
    LoadString(hInst,IDS_APPNAME, pName, 80);

    BabyWin Win(NULL,pName);
```

```
        delete pName;

        Win.Show(nCmdShow);
        return Win.MessageLoop();
}
```

The application resource file is similar to that of the Hello Word application, except that the application name has changed.

test.rc

```
#include "windows.h"
#include "messages.hpp"

STRINGTABLE
BEGIN
IDS_APPNAME    "Baby's First Toy"

#include "strings.rc"

END
```

The definition file is also similar to that of the Hello World program, except that the name and description have changed.

test.def

```
NAME           Test

DESCRIPTION    'Baby's first toy'

EXETYPE        WINDOWS

STUB           'WINSTUB.EXE'

CODE           PRELOAD MOVEABLE DISCARDABLE
DATA           PRELOAD MOVEABLE MULTIPLE

HEAPSIZE       1024
STACKSIZE      4096

EXPORTS
    CPPWinProc     @1
```

Figure 4-6 shows how the finished application might look after Baby has been playing with it for a while. A number of items have been selected and transferred to the combo box. The scroll bar thumbs have been moved and the check box checked.

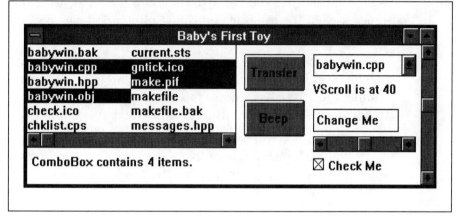

FIGURE 4-6   The Baby's First Toy application

Summary

Using C++ objects for the controls, the Baby's First Toy application is quite simple to write. The application window itself can be written in around 100 lines of code, and most of that is definitions. An equivalent program written in C would be between 300 and 500 lines of code. The hardest part of this application is working out where to place the controls. Each control is placed explicitly at a certain position. If the programmer wishes to move a control, the positions of all the others must be recalculated by hand.

An application like this would normally be implemented as a dialog box. The controls would be positioned with a dialog box editor, and the editor would produce a template which is included in the application resource file. It is then possible to rearrange the controls using the dialog editor, without having to modify the application code. In addition dialog boxes provide accelerator keys for manipulating the controls using the keyboard.

The controls described in this chapter work with dialog boxes. Creating dialog boxes with C++ will be explained in Chapter 6.

Since the window handle of the controls is accessible, it is easy to send the controls additional messages or to use API routines on them. It may be necessary to do this when you are interfacing with old C code, but it is more likely that you will use the extra messages when deriving new subclasses of the existing controls. Chapter 5 shows how specific subclasses may be derived.

These control classes have not interfered with the way Windows handles controls. The classes do everything in a completely orthodox manner. All they have done is to encapsulate the processing in the **Window** class and the control classes, where it is out of the way.

The application will be informed of asynchronous control events, such as button clicks, through callback member functions provided by the application. Using callbacks helps the programmer write a more structured application.

The scroll bar control is powerful, but time consuming to program, even if it is only required to perform a simple function. The **ScrollBar** class has the ability to handle some scroll bar functions itself. The **ScrollBar** class is simple to use in a simple situation, but the power is still there when needed.

Finally, the control classes impose virtually no extra system overhead. There is an extra function call in some places, but that will not be noticeable. In particular, the application does not intercept internal control messages. That is important, since the majority of messages flying around a typical application are likely to be control messages.

CHAPTER

Owner-Draw Controls

What a nuisance! You have written the activity program for infants, you have tested all the functions, you are pleased with the efficiency of the application, but the infants do not want to use it! Your marketing person tells you why.

The interface is too boring, the marketing person says, *no funny little icons, not much of a 3-D look, no color, the kids won't look at it!*

You try to explain how these cosmetic features do not affect the way the application functions, and how they absorb CPU execution cycles, but the marketing person is unconvinced.

I don't know about those executive bicycles, the marketing person admits, *but give me a designer look and I can shift these things by the million!*

Ah, well! Arguing aside, you will have to implement some owner-draw controls. Fortunately, the **Control** class has anticipated this possibility. This class provides virtual member functions for all of the owner-draw notification codes, so perhaps the job will not be so difficult after all.

The Controls

Since the Baby's First Toy application contains an example of every type of control, this chapter shows how to derive an owner-draw control class from each control. Some of these controls have been contrived to illustrate certain principles, so you might prefer to design your own controls rather than use these directly. The **IconButton** class is useful as it stands, since many applications use buttons containing icons.

Icon Push Buttons

To implement an owner-draw push-button, all that is necessary is to give the button the **BS_OWNERDRAW** style, and then add code to the **DrawItem** member function to draw something that looks like a button. The **DrawItem** member function receives a structure containing the device context of the rectangle that will contain the button, and some flags indicating how it should draw the button. The flags indicate whether the button is selected or not, enabled or not, has the focus, and so on.

You can draw anything you like following the scenario in this section, but your marketing person advises conventional buttons that show an icon as well as text. Learning the technique will be useful in other applications as well.

To implement an owner-draw button, create a new class **IconButton**, derived from **Button**. The constructor for this class takes an extra parameter specifying the icon. The **DrawItem** member function in **IconButton** draws something resembling a conventional button and pastes the icon and the button text into it. Once you have written this class, the only work you need to do when you want an icon button is to design the icon. Notice that **DrawItem** has to draw everything; Windows supplies owner-draw buttons with a blank rectangle instead of a plain 3-D button.

There are other ways to implement an icon button. The approach taken by both Microsoft and Borland in their class libraries is to display one of three bitmaps representing a button in the normal, selected, and focused states. The bitmaps represent the complete button, including the frame. The bitmap approach offers advantages:

❑ Drawing is faster.

❑ There is more freedom in designing the button.

There are also some disadvantages:

❑ The size of the button is fixed. If you want to change it, you must redo the bitmaps.

❑ The text label is embedded in the bitmap, so if you want a version in another language, you must redraw the three bitmaps with new text labels.

☐   The color of the button face does not change to reflect the Control Panel setting.

You will find it quite easy to adapt the **IconButton** class for bitmaps, if you prefer them.

Here is the definition of **IconButton**:

iconbutn.hpp

```
#ifndef   ICONBUTTON_INC
#define   ICONBUTTON_INC
#include "button.hpp"

class IconButton : public Button {
public:
  IconButton(
    HWND PhWnd,                  // Parent window handle
    int Id,                     // Child Id
    LPSTR Icon,                 // Name of icon
    LPSTR pText="",             // button text
    DWORD Style=0,              // Style
    int x= CW_USEDEFAULT,       // Position
    int y= CW_USEDEFAULT,
    int width= CW_USEDEFAULT,   // Size
    int height= CW_USEDEFAULT);

protected:
  HICON hIcon;                  // the icon
  BOOL bRecessed;               // TRUE if button recessed

  // the virtual function to handle DrawItem events
  void DrawItem(DRAWITEMSTRUCT FAR * pDs);

  void DrawFrame(HDC hDC, RECT& rc, BOOL Selected);
  void ChangeSelect(HDC hDC, RECT& rc,BOOL Select);
  void ChangeFocus(HDC hDC, RECT rc, BOOL Select);
  void DrawFace(HDC hDC, RECT rc, BOOL Select);
  void DrawDisabled(HDC hDC, RECT rc, BOOL Disabled);
  void DrawButton(
    DRAWITEMSTRUCT FAR * pDs,
    char * sz, HICON hIcon);
}; // class IconButton

#endif   // ICONBUTTON_INC
```

The constructor has an extra **Icon** parameter that specifies an icon's name as it appears in the application resource file. **IconButton** redefines the virtual member function **DrawItem** defined in the **Control** class. The other functions are used to draw the button. The **DrawItem** member function receives a pointer to a **DRAWITEMSTRUCT** data structure containing details of the drawing to be done. **DRAWITEMSTRUCT** is described fully in the *Structures* section of your Windows application programming interface (API) documentation, but here is a description:

```
typedef struct tagDRAWITEMSTRUCT {
    WORD    CtlType;
    WORD    CtlID;
    WORD    itemID;
    WORD    itemAction;
    WORD    itemState;
    HWND    hwndItem;
    HDC     hDC;
    RECT    rcItem;
    DWORD   itemData;
} DRAWITEMSTRUCT;

Here are the items:
```

CtlType   The control type is one of the following:

ODT_BUTTON	Owner-draw button
ODT_COMBOBOX	Owner-draw combo box
ODT_LISTBOX	Owner-draw list box
ODT_MENU	Owner-draw menu

CtlID   The control ID.

itemID   The item index. This may be −1 for an empty list.

itemAction   The drawing action. A combination of the following:

ODA_DRAWENTIRE
ODA_FOCUS
ODA_SELECT

itemState The state of the item after drawing. A combination of the following:

ODS_CHECKED
ODS_DISABLED
ODS_FOCUS
ODS_GRAYED
ODS_SELECTED

hwndItem The control's window handle.

hDC A device context in which to draw.

rcItem The bounding rectangle of the area to be drawn.

itemData The item data or a pointer to the item string.

iconbutn.cpp

```
#include "iconbutn.hpp"

IconButton::IconButton(HWND PhWnd, int Id, LPSTR Icon,
     LPSTR pText,DWORD Style,
    int x, int y, int width, int height)
:Button(PhWnd,Id,pText,Style|BS_OWNERDRAW,x,y,width,height)
{
  if (Icon)
    hIcon=LoadIcon(hInst,Icon);
  else hIcon=NULL;
  bRecessed=FALSE;
}
```

The constructor creates a button with the **BS_OWNERDRAW** style. It then loads the icon. Since the button drawing code can draw recessed buttons as well protruding buttons, the class has a flag **bRecessed**. The **IconButton** class only wants protruding buttons, so it sets the flag to **FALSE**. The flag is for the benefit of the subclasses that will be derived from **IconButton** later in this chapter.

```
void IconButton::DrawItem(DRAWITEMSTRUCT FAR* pDs)
{
  char sz[80];
  GetWindowText(pDs->hwndItem,sz,sizeof sz);
  DrawButton(pDs,sz,hIcon);
}
```

The **DrawItem** member function passes the **DRAWITEMSTRUCT**, the icon, and the button label text to the **DrawButton** member function. Again, this split is for the benefit of subclasses that may wish to modify the icon or text. They can redefine **DrawItem** and call **DrawButton** with an alternative icon or text. Several of the classes later in this chapter will do that.

```
void IconButton::DrawButton(DRAWITEMSTRUCT FAR* pDs,
                              char * sz, HICON hIcon)
{
  RECT rc=pDs->rcItem;
  switch (pDs->itemAction) {

  case ODA_FOCUS:
    ChangeFocus(pDs->hDC,rc,pDs->itemState & ODS_SELECTED);
     break;
```

This is the function that does the drawing. **itemAction** indicates the type of drawing that needs to be done. If it is **ODA_FOCUS**, only the focus has changed. The **ChangeFocus** member function will add or remove a focus rectangle to the button.

```
  case ODA_DRAWENTIRE:
  {
     SetBkMode(pDs->hDC,TRANSPARENT);
```

In this case, the member function must draw the entire button. It sets the background mode to transparent to avoid having the text overwrite details of the button or icon.

```
        int xIcon,yIcon;      // Icon position
        RECT rText=rc;        // text boundary
        WORD DrawFlags=0;
        InflateRect(&rText,-3,-3);
        if (rc.bottom-rc.top >= 35 || !hIcon){ //Icon on top
          xIcon=(rc.left+rc.right)/2-16;
          yIcon=rc.top+4;
          DrawFlags |=DT_CENTER |DT_BOTTOM;
          rText.bottom -=1;

        }
        else { //Icon to left
          xIcon=rc.left+3;
```

```
    yIcon=rc.top+3;
    DrawFlags |= DT_LEFT | DT_VCENTER;
    rText.left +=32;
}

if (pDs->itemState & ODS_SELECTED) {
  xIcon +=2;
  yIcon +=2;
  OffsetRect(&rText,2,2);
}
```

It next calculates the positions of the icon and text. If the button is large, it places the icon on top and the text beneath. Otherwise, it places the icon to the left and the text to the right. Icons always have the same size, 32 pixels square, but if you want a small icon, you just draw the detail in the upper-left corner of the icon. The background will not be visible, provided that you have drawn it in the "Screen" color. You should not fill the background of icons with a button gray color, because you cannot be sure that buttons will always be gray.

```
DrawFace(pDs->hDC, rc,pDs->itemState & ODS_SELECTED);
if (hIcon) {
  DrawIcon(pDs->hDC,xIcon,yIcon,hIcon);
}
DrawDisabled(pDs->hDC, rc,
             pDs->itemState & ODS_DISABLED);
DrawText(pDs->hDC,sz,-1,&rText,
         DrawFlags|DT_NOCLIP|DT_SINGLELINE);
DrawFrame(pDs->hDC, rc,pDs->itemState & ODS_SELECTED);
if (pDs->itemState & ODS_FOCUS)
  ChangeFocus(pDs->hDC, rc,
              pDs->itemState & ODS_SELECTED);
break;
```

Now that the code has drawn the icon and text, it can add the button frame and, if the button has the focus, the focus rectangle. If the button has been depressed, the **ODS_SELECTED** bit will be set in **itemState** (more than one bit can be set, indicating multiple states). In that case, the member function must displace the face of the button down towards the right, and change the appearance of the frame. It passes the bit on to the other member functions. If the button has been disabled, **DrawDisabled** gives the icon a washed-out look.

```
case ODA_SELECT:
  ChangeSelect(pDs->hDC, rc, pDs->itemState & ODS_SELECTED);
   break;


}
}
```

If the button has been depressed, it does not need redrawing. **ChangeSelect** displaces the face down to the right, and redraws the frame.

```
void IconButton::DrawDisabled(HDC hDC, RECT rc, BOOL Disabled)
{
  if (Disabled){
  HBRUSH brush=CreateSolidBrush(GetSysColor(COLOR_BTNFACE));
  HBRUSH Old=SelectObject(hDC, brush);
  InflateRect(&rc,-3,-3);
  BitBlt(hDC,rc.left,rc.top,
    rc.right-rc.left,rc.bottom-rc.top,
    NULL,0,0,0x00a000c9); //DPa
  SelectObject(hDC,Old);
  DeleteObject(brush);
  SetTextColor(hDC, GetSysColor(COLOR_BTNSHADOW));
  }
}
```

There are several different ways to display a disabled button. The member function shown here replaces all the bright colors of the icon with a button gray or black. In addition, it sets the text color to a dark gray. This member function does not affect monochrome icons, however. To wash out the icon, the API **BitBlt** function replaces the button face with a combination of the gray brush and replaces the existing face with the icon. The **BitBlt** (Bit Blit) function takes the bits in a specified rectangle and draws in another target rectangle, optionally modifying them at the same time. Here the target is **NULL**, so the routine modifies only the bits in place. The **AND** operation combines the color and the brush pattern with the destination, the button face. A white color will be replaced by gray. Most other colors will be replaced by gray, a dark color, or black. A brush is a Windows Graphics Device Interface (GDI) object for painting areas. A brush may have a solid color, but it may also be a bitmap or a hatched pattern.

This operation is the **ROP3 DPa** operation, which involves taking the *Destination* and the *Patterned* brush, and performing a logical AND operation. In this case, the brush has a solid pattern. The **DPa** operation effectively means "Muddy the icons' colors with some gray." To find the actual ROP3 code, 0x00a000c9, look up DPa in the Raster Operation Code table in your Windows API documentation.

If you do not want to bother with ROP3 codes, there are plenty of other ways to make the button appear disabled. One method is to paint over the button face with a fine speckled brush, where the speckles have the same color as the button face.

When the button is enabled again, Windows sends a **DRAWITEMSTRUCT** requesting that the button be redrawn.

```
void IconButton::ChangeFocus(HDC hDC, RECT rc, BOOL Select)
{
    InflateRect(&rc,-3,-3);
    if (Select)
      OffsetRect(&rc,2,2);
    DrawFocusRect(hDC,&rc);
}
```

If the button has the input focus, **ChangeFocus** draws a focus rectangle three pixels in from the edge of the button. This is one pixel in from the edge of the button face. If the button has been depressed, **ChangeFocus** must offset this rectangle down and to the right. The API function **DrawFocusRect** draws the rectangle. **InflateRect** and **OffsetRect** are also API functions. If the parameters to **InflateRect** are negative, it deflates (makes smaller) the rectangle.

```
void IconButton::DrawFace(HDC hDC, RECT rc, BOOL Select)
{
  HBRUSH brush=CreateSolidBrush(GetSysColor(COLOR_BTNFACE));
  HBRUSH Old=SelectObject(hDC, brush);
  InflateRect(&rc,-3,-3);
```

```
  if (Select)
    OffsetRect(&rc,2,2);
  FillRect(hDC,&rc,brush);
  SelectObject(hDC,Old);
  DeleteObject(brush);

}
```

This member function draws the face of the button, inside the frame. The face is just a plain gray rectangle, but the position depends on whether the button has been selected or not.

```
void IconButton::ChangeSelect(HDC hDC, RECT& rc,BOOL Select)
{
  if(Select)
    BitBlt(hDC,rc.left+5,rc.top+5,
        rc.right-rc.left-6,rc.bottom-rc.top-6,
        hDC,rc.left+3,rc.top+3,SRCCOPY);
  else
    BitBlt(hDC,rc.left+3,rc.top+3,
        rc.right-rc.left-6,rc.bottom-rc.top-6,
        hDC,rc.left+5,rc.top+5,SRCCOPY);
  DrawFrame(hDC,rc,Select);
}
```

When the user presses or releases the button, this member function moves the face 2 pixels down or up, and right or left. It then redraws the frame. It uses the API **BitBlt** function to move the image. The **SRCCOPY** operation means copy the bits without changing them.

The most awkward part of the class is drawing the frame around the face, to give the button its 3-D look.

```
void IconButton::DrawFrame(HDC hDC, RECT& rc,BOOL Selected)
{
    HBRUSH Brush;
    HBRUSH OldBrush;
    if (!bRecessed){
      Brush=CreateSolidBrush(GetSysColor(COLOR_WINDOWFRAME));
      OldBrush=SelectObject(hDC, Brush);
      FrameRect(hDC, &rc,Brush);
      InflateRect(&rc,-1,-1);
    }
```

If the button is a normal protruding button (not recessed), this member function gives it a rectangular frame in the color used for window frames, normally black. Recessed buttons look better without this frame. If it draws a frame, the rest of the button must be smaller, so it shrinks the button rectangle by one pixel all around, using **InflateRect** with negative parameters.

```
HPEN Pen1,Pen2,OldPen;
if (!Selected) {
  Pen1=CreatePen(PS_SOLID,1,RGB(255,255,255));
  Pen2=CreatePen(PS_SOLID,1,GetSysColor(COLOR_BTNSHADOW));
  if (bRecessed) {
    // Swap light and dark pens
    HPEN Temp=Pen1;
    Pen1=Pen2;
    Pen2=Temp;
  }
  OldPen=SelectObject(hDC,Pen1);
  MoveToEx(hDC,rc.right-1,rc.top,NULL);
  LineTo(hDC,rc.left,rc.top);
  LineTo(hDC,rc.left,rc.bottom-1);
  SelectObject(hDC,Pen2);
  LineTo(hDC,rc.right-1,rc.bottom-1);
  LineTo(hDC,rc.right-1,rc.top);
  SelectObject(hDC,Pen1);
  MoveToEx(hDC,rc.right-2,rc.top+1,NULL);
  LineTo(hDC,rc.left+1,rc.top+1);
  LineTo(hDC,rc.left+1,rc.bottom-2);
  SelectObject(hDC,Pen2);
  LineTo(hDC,rc.right-2,rc.bottom-2);
  LineTo(hDC,rc.right-2,rc.top+1);
}
```

All this is required just to draw a button frame. The alternative is to use the three bitmaps representing the button in its three states. At least the code only has to do it once. This function simply draws lines near the edge of the rectangle, to build up the frame. If the button is not selected, and the **bRecessed** flag is **TRUE**, it reverses the pens for the shadow and highlight, to give the impression of a recess. This function uses GDI pens to draw the frame and to draw lines. The pens here are one pixel wide and have a solid color, but they may also be wider and have one of a number of dashed styles. To draw with a pen, you must first select it with the API **SelectObject** function, and then draw lines using the API function **LineTo**. You can position it with the **MoveToEx** function.

Working with 32 Bits

Older versions of the API used the **MoveTo** function. This function returned the old position as two 16-bit values packed into one 32-bit **LONG.** That will not work in the 32-bit versions, so **MoveTo** is obsolete, and has been replaced with **MoveToEx(int *x*, int *y*, POINT * pOld)**. The old position is now put in the structure pointed to by the third parameter. Usually, you do not need the old position so the third parameter can be **NULL**. If you have an old version of the API, you can compile this code if you insert

#define MoveToEx(*x,y,p*) MoveTo(*x,y*)

in your WINOBJ.HPP file.

```
else{
   Pen1=CreatePen(PS_SOLID,1,GetSysColor(COLOR_BTNSHADOW));
   Pen2=CreatePen(PS_SOLID,1,GetSysColor(COLOR_BTNFACE));
   OldPen=SelectObject(hDC,Pen1);
   MoveToEx(hDC,rc.right-1,rc.top,NULL);
   LineTo(hDC,rc.left,rc.top);
   LineTo(hDC,rc.left,rc.bottom);
   SelectObject(hDC,Pen2);
   MoveToEx(hDC,rc.right-1,rc.top+1,NULL);
   LineTo(hDC,rc.left+1,rc.top+1);
   LineTo(hDC,rc.left+1,rc.bottom);
   MoveToEx(hDC,rc.right-1,rc.top+2,NULL);
   LineTo(hDC,rc.left+2,rc.top+2);
   LineTo(hDC,rc.left+2,rc.bottom);
   MoveToEx(hDC,rc.right-1,rc.top+3,NULL);
   LineTo(hDC,rc.left+3,rc.top+3);
   LineTo(hDC,rc.left+3,rc.bottom);
   }
SelectObject(hDC,OldPen);
```

If the button is selected, the code draws a frame with the shadow on the top and left, and the bottom and right sides in the button face color. This gives the impression that the button face is depressed to just below the surface of the window. It draws recessed buttons in the same way when they are selected, so they appear to pop out.

```
DeleteObject(Pen1);
DeleteObject(Pen2);
if (bRecessed){
  InflateRect(&rc,-2,-2);
  Brush=CreateSolidBrush(GetSysColor(COLOR_BTNFACE));
  OldBrush=SelectObject(hDC, Brush);
  FrameRect(hDC, &rc,Brush);
}
SelectObject(hDC,OldBrush);
DeleteObject(Brush);
}
```

Since the frame of recessed buttons is larger than that of protruding buttons, the member function draws an extra rectangle between the frame and the face of the button. The rectangle has the same color of the face, and serves to fill in the gap.

To use icon buttons in an application, you must follow these steps:

❑   Create an icon file with an icon editor. You can use the API paint utility, but other editors are available. Let us say that the file is called **ICON.ICO**.

❑   Add an **ICON** statement to the resource file, like this:

MyIcon ICON icon.ico

❑   Create an instance of an **IconButton**, like this:

IBut = new
IconButton(hWnd,101,"MyIcon","Text",0,10,10,60,60);

If the button is too small, the icon might be clipped, or overwritten by the text. If you want a small icon, remember to draw it in the upper-left corner of its box.

It may have been tricky writing the code to draw the button, but now it is done. The code does not need to be done again, since all the derived classes will inherit it. If you find a better way to draw the button, you can modify **DrawButton** without having to modify any of the classes that you have derived from **IconButton**. That of course is the major benefit of C++.

If you have an owner-draw button, you cannot use other API button styles with it. You cannot create an owner-draw button with the **BS_CHECKBOX** style, for example, and expect it to act like a check box. You will have to program it yourself. Luckily, it is not very difficult to derive other owner-draw button styles from the **IconButton** class.

The **IconButton** class button was difficult to draw because standard buttons have the same frame thickness regardless of the button size. If you want buttons that resemble *art nouveau* light switches, for example, you could just draw three bitmaps to represent the selected, unselected, and focused states. You can then use the API function **BitBlt** to paste them into the rectangle.

3-D Check Boxes

A standard check box is useful for indicating options. The standard box is a small square to the left or right of a line a text indicating its purpose. When the user clicks the box, a small cross appears in the box.

To implement an owner-draw check box, you must derive a class from **Button**, which is similar to deriving a class from the **IconButton** class. The **DrawItem** member function draws the background, the check icon, and the text. It alternates between the two icons each time the user clicks on the control. Draw the icons to represent the unchecked and checked states. There are a lot of possibilities for the two icons:

☐ An empty square and a square with a mark in it, similar to the standard check box.

☐ A dark circle and a brightly colored circle, emulating a button with an LED in it.

☐ A hand with the thumb up or down.

☐ A cross and a tick.

Whatever style you choose, it's a good idea to use the same style throughout the application. The class described here just refers to two icons **Checked** and **Unchecked**. In your application resource file, you can set these icons to any icon file you wish.

The check-box control described here is derived from the **IconButton** class, so it is a check -box with a 3-D look. The button resembles a normal push-button except that it displays one or the other of two icons. In the example program, it uses a white box when the item is not checked, and the same white box with a green check mark in it when the item is checked, as shown here:

As you will see, by inheriting functions from an existing class, the **IconCheck** class can be implemented very easily.

As with the standard check box, you will usually want the box to be automatic so that it checks itself when the user clicks it. In that case, you simply interrogate its status as you need to. You might want to declare a callback for the box, perhaps because you need to disable other items when the box is checked. If you declare a callback, you will set the check in the box from the callback.

IconCheckBox is derived from **IconButton**. Here is the definition:

iconchck.hpp

```
ifndef ICONCHECKBOX_INC
#define ICONCHECKBOX_INC

#include "iconbutn.hpp"

class IconCheckBox : public IconButton {
protected:
 WORD CheckState;
```

The class needs the item **CheckState** to keep track of whether or not the button is checked.

```
public:
  IconCheckBox(
    HWND PhWnd,                    // Parent window handle
    int Id,                       // Child Id
    LPSTR pText="",               // button text
    DWORD Style=0,                // Style
    int x= CW_USEDEFAULT,         // Position
    int y= CW_USEDEFAULT,
    int width= CW_USEDEFAULT,     // Size
    int height= CW_USEDEFAULT);
```

```
WORD Check(){              // Get check state
  return CheckState;
};
void Check(WORD State);    //Set check state
```

The class needs the constructor and two member functions to set and get the state of the button. The name of the member function **Check** is overloaded, since it is defined twice with two alternative parameter specifications. If it receives a parameter, the state is set, otherwise the state is returned.

```
protected:
  void DrawItem(DRAWITEMSTRUCT FAR * pDs);
  void Clicked(Button& b);

}; // class IconCheckBox

#endif // ICONCHECKBOX_INC
```

The ICONCHCK.CPP file looks like this:

iconchck.cpp

```
#include "iconchck.hpp"

IconCheckBox::IconCheckBox(HWND PhWnd, int Id, LPSTR pText,
    DWORD Style, int x, int y, int width, int height)
    :IconButton(PhWnd,Id,NULL,pText,Style|BS_OWNERDRAW,x,
    y,width,height){
  Click(this, Clicked);
  CheckState=0;
}
```

The constructor creates an **IconButton** with an undefined icon, since the class will load one of the two alternative icons in the **Check** function. **IconCheckBox** is initially automatic, and needs to know when the user has clicked the button, so it declares a callback **Clicked**. The **CheckState** item is cleared.

```
void IconCheckBox::Clicked(Button& b){
  CheckState= !CheckState;
  InvalidateRect(hWnd,NULL,NULL);
}
```

When the button has been clicked, this member function toggles the check status. It uses the API function **InvalidateRect** to cause the button to be redrawn with the correct icon. **InvalidateRect** causes Windows to send the application a Paint event saying that the specified rectangle is invalid, and needs repainting. If the second parameter is **NULL**, the entire control window needs repainting.

```
void IconCheckBox::Check(WORD State)
{
  CheckState=State;
  InvalidateRect(hWnd,NULL,NULL);
}
```

If the check status of the button is changed from outside the instance, it must again call **InvalidateRect** to cause the button to be redrawn.

```
void IconCheckBox::DrawItem(DRAWITEMSTRUCT FAR* pDs)
{
  char sz[48];
  GetText(sz, sizeof sz);
  hIcon=LoadIcon(hInst,
        (CheckState)?"Checked":"Unchecked");
  DrawButton(pDs,sz,hIcon);
}
```

The **DrawItem** member function first chooses the icon to display. It then passes the **DRAWITEMSTRUCT** data on to the member function **DrawButton**, which was defined in **IconButton**. Notice that **LoadIcon** only loads the icon if it has not already been loaded; otherwise, it returns a handle to an icon in memory. For that reason, it is better not to destroy the icon. If you do, it must be loaded again whenever it is needed.

A check-box button looks better if it is wider than it is high. If the button is less than 40 pixels high, the **DrawButton** function in the **IconButton** class positions the icon to the left of the text.

Although **IconCheckBox** declares its own callback, this does not prevent the creator of an **IconCheckBox** instance from declaring another callback if it wants to know when the button has been activated. In that case, the callback function must change the status itself using the member function **Check**.

The two icons **Checked** and **Unchecked** are defined in the resource file like this:

```
Checked ICON check.ico
Unchecked ICON uncheck.ico
```

If you want to use different icons, such as thumbs up or down, you only need to change these entries in the resource file.

As an alternative to changing the icon when the button is clicked, you can declare an icon in the constructor. as with the **IconButton** class. Just change the **bRecessed** flag defined in **IconButton** when the button is clicked. The control then looks like a standard icon button, but the button become recessed when it is "checked."

Recessed Text Controls

Sometimes graphical user interfaces (GUIs) with a 3-D look use recessed areas to display information, as shown here:

They create the illusion of a recessed area by drawing a frame with the opposite shading from that used on buttons. Buttons have the highlight on the top and left sides and the shadow on the right and bottom sides. Since people expect light sources to be above and to one side of an object, the button appears to protrude. If the shadow is above and to the left and the highlight below and to the right, the object appears to be recessed.

Since the **DrawButton** member function has a facility for drawing recessed frames, a control could use that to create a recessed static text object. It is not possible to create an owner-draw static text control, but it is possible to derive a recessed control from the **IconButton** class. The class disables the button so that nothing happens if the user should click on it.

Here is the definition of a **StaticFrame** class:

staticfm.hpp

```
#ifndef   STATICFRAME_INC
#define   STATICFRAME_INC

#include "iconbutn.hpp"

class StaticFrame :  public IconButton {

public:
  StaticFrame(
    HWND PhWnd,                    // Parent window handle
```

```
      int Id,                    // Child Id
      LPSTR Text,                // Static text
      DWORD Style=0,
      int x= CW_USEDEFAULT,      // Position
      int y= CW_USEDEFAULT,
      int width= CW_USEDEFAULT,  // Size
      int height= CW_USEDEFAULT);
protected:
  void DrawItem(DRAWITEMSTRUCT FAR *  pDs);
};  // class StaticFrame

#endif // STATICFRAME_INC
```

The class only redefines the constructor and the **DrawItem** method from the **IconButton** class.

staticfm.cpp

```
#include "staticfm.hpp"

StaticFrame::StaticFrame(HWND PhWnd, int Id,
      LPSTR pText,DWORD Style,
      int x, int y, int width, int height)
      :IconButton(PhWnd,Id,pText,NULL,Style,x,y,width,height)
{
  bRecessed=TRUE;
  EnableWindow(hWnd,FALSE);
}
```

The constructor creates an **IconButton** object without an icon. The **bRecessed** flag is set, so that **DrawButton** draws a recessed frame, and the API toolkit function **EnableWindow** with the parameter **FALSE** disables the button. When a control is disabled, it does not react to any user input.

```
void StaticFrame::DrawItem(DRAWITEMSTRUCT FAR* pDs)
{
  pDs->itemState &= ~ ODS_DISABLED;
  IconButton::DrawItem(pDs);
}
```

The **DrawItem** member function simply masks off the **ODS_DIS-ABLED** flag and passes the **DRAWITEMSTRUCT** on to the **DrawItem** member function defined in **IconButton**. The Notation **&= ~** means that the item to the left becomes the logical "AND" of itself and the logical negation of the bit pattern to the right. It has the effect of clearing the bits in the left-hand item that are set on the right-hand side. Masking off this flag prevents the button from being drawn as if it were disabled. **DrawItem** would otherwise display the text in white. This flag only affects how the button is drawn, the control itself stays disabled.

StaticFrame is best used for displaying dynamic text, such as status lines. The text may be changed using the **SetText** member function.

Be careful, because you cannot use this class with the API function **DlgDirList** or **DlgDirListComboBox**. These routines update a list box or a combo box with a directory listing, but they also update an optional static control with the name of the current directory. You can specify the static control in the parameter list. Unfortunately, they expect a proper static control, having the Windows **STATIC** window class. If you give them a control having the Windows **BUTTON** window class they give you a system error. If you want to use these functions with a recessed frame, you should create a **StaticFrame** control and place an ordinary static control inside it. You can then pass the handle of the static control to the **DlgDirList** or **DlgDirListComboBox** function.

Owner-Draw List Boxes

Things start to get more interesting with owner-draw list boxes. An owner-draw list box only allows you to draw the items within the list, and the items must be rectangular. Nevertheless, you still have a great deal of freedom with an owner-draw list box.

Owner-draw list boxes are not used very often. Sometimes they are used to display the files in a directory. An icon accompanies each file to indicate its type. The Windows File Manager does something like this. Other than that, it seems difficult to think of a use for them. If you have a database application, you could add status icons to elements of a list, perhaps to indicate that an item is inaccessible, or locked.

You might have a worthwhile use for owner-draw list boxes, but if not, you might consider using them to group owner-draw buttons. As an example, consider radio button controls. The Windows radio buttons are designed to emulate the row of buttons that radios had back in the old days. If you don't remember that far back, one button would be depressed, indicating the current station. If you pressed another button, that station would be selected, and the first button would pop out, so that there would never be more than one button depressed. The buttons were mutually exclusive.

In Windows, radio buttons are similar to check boxes. They do not need to be mutually exclusive, but when users see radio buttons, they expect them to behave in a mutually exclusive fashion.

Radio buttons are a bit tiresome to program, since you must look at each one to see which is selected, or else process click events for all the buttons so that you can keep track of the current selection.

Things are much easier with list boxes. You can put the choices in a single selection list box and just retrieve the selection when you want it. The only problem is that list boxes just do not look like radio buttons.

With an owner-draw list box, however, it is possible to have items to look like buttons. If you have three choices—FM, MW, and LW, for example—you can put them in an owner-draw list box and you have an array of three buttons. If you click on FM, it appears to be depressed; if you click on LW, FM pops out and LW appears to be depressed. They look more like real radio buttons than the standard Windows radio button controls. If the list box has the multiple-selection style, but not the extended multiple-selection style, the buttons emulate a group of check boxes. You can toggle a button in and out by clicking on it, and have more than one button depressed.

The **IconList** class described in the following example draws the items to look like buttons. In addition, the class changes the icon on the button when the user clicks on it, since this makes depressed buttons easier to see. The class is an example to show how owner-draw list boxes might be derived from the **ListBox** class. If you want to have another style of list, perhaps with file icons, you will have to derive it separately from the **ListBox** class. As you will see, it is quite simple to create specialized owner-draw listboxes.

The **IconList** class is interesting because it uses multiple inheritance. It inherits from the **ListBox** class since it remains a list box at heart. It also inherits the button-drawing routines from **IconButton**.

Here is the definition:

iconlist.hpp

```
#ifndef   ICONLIST_INC
#define   ICONLIST_INC

#include "iconbutn.hpp"
```

```
#include "listbox.hpp"

class IconList :  public ItemMeasurement,
                    public ListBox,
                  public IconButton {
```

IconList is derived from three classes, **ItemMeasurement**, **ListBox**, and **IconButton**. It uses the **ItemMeasurement** class to set the size of the items in the list, the **ListBox** class for the list box functionality, and the **IconButton** class for the button-drawing routines.

```
public:
  IconList(
    HWND PhWnd,                 // Parent window handle
    int Id,                     // Child Id
    DWORD Style=0,              // Style
    int x= CW_USEDEFAULT,       // Position
    int y= CW_USEDEFAULT,
    int width= CW_USEDEFAULT,   // Size
    int height= CW_USEDEFAULT);

  ~IconList();

protected:
  HBRUSH Brush;
  void DrawItem(DRAWITEMSTRUCT FAR * pDs);
  HBRUSH CtlColor(HDC hDC);
  LONG CodeHandler(int NotifyCode, int Extra=0){
    return ListBox::CodeHandler(NotifyCode,Extra);};
}; // class IconList

#endif // ICONLIST_INC
```

Since **CodeHandler** exists in both **ListBox** and **IconButton**, it is redefined here. **IconList** redirects calls to **CodeHandler** back to the corresponding member function in **ListBox**.

Here is the implementation:

iconlist.cpp

```
#include "iconlist.hpp"

IconList::IconList(HWND PhWnd, int Id, DWORD Style,
    int x, int y, int width, int height)
  :ItemMeasurement(20),
   ListBox(PhWnd,Id,
```

```
                    Style|LBS_OWNERDRAWFIXED|LBS_HASSTRINGS,
                    x,y,width,height),
        IconButton(PhWnd,Id,NULL)
{
  Brush=CreateSolidBrush(GetSysColor(COLOR_BTNSHADOW));
  bRecessed=FALSE;
}
```

The **IconList** constructor calls the parent constructors. By creating the instance of **ItemMeasurement**, the control sets the height of the items to 20 pixels. As I explained in Chapter 4, the **ItemMeasurement** class is part of a trick. The trick is necessary since Windows sends a **WM_MEASUREITEM** message, requesting the size of the list box items, and it sends it before the instance has been created. If you are sure that all your users are going to use Windows version 3.1 or higher, you can make use of the **LB_SETITEMHEIGHT** message, which was not available in Windows version 3.0. You can dispense with the **ItemMeasurement** class and instead send the list box a **LB_SETITEMHEIGHT** message in the constructor, like this:

SendMessage(hWnd,LB_SETITEMHEIGHT,0,20);

assuming that the item is 20 pixels high. If the list box has the **LBS_OWNERDRAWFIXED** style, sending this message sets the height of all the items.

The **IconList** list box will contain fixed-size items containing strings, so it adds the styles **LBS_OWNERDRAWFIXED** and **LBS_HASSTRINGS** to whatever is specified in the **IconList Style** parameter.

The **ListBox** constructor creates the list box control. The constructor for **IconButton** will not create a button control, since a control with the specified ID already exists; **ListBox** has just created it. The **IconButton** instance instead attaches itself to the existing control by copying the window handle into its **hWnd** member.

By default, a list box has a white background. The list items usually obscure the background, but it is visible when there are not enough items to fill the list box window. Since the items will have a button color, it would be better for the background to be dark gray. The constructor creates a brush having the color of button shadows, and the class returns it whenever the control calls the **CtlColor** member function.

Finally, the constructor sets the **bRecessed** flag to **FALSE**, indicating that the button drawing routines should draw a protruding button.

```
IconList::~IconList()
{
  DeleteObject(Brush);
}
```

The destructor deletes the gray brush. Objects use system resources, so it is important to delete them after use.

```
HBRUSH IconList::CtlColor(HDC hDC){ return Brush;};
```

The system calls the **CtlColor** member function just before the background of the control is painted. If it returns a valid brush, Windows uses it to paint the control's background.

```
void IconList::DrawItem(DRAWITEMSTRUCT FAR* pDs)
{
  char sz[48];
  Text(pDs->itemID,sz);
  hIcon=LoadIcon(hInst,
        (pDs->itemState & ODS_SELECTED)
         ?"ListSelect":"ListDeselect");
  if (pDs->itemAction & ODA_SELECT)
    pDs->itemAction = ODA_DRAWENTIRE;
  DrawButton(pDs,sz,hIcon);
}
```

The **DrawItem** member function calls **DrawButton** in **IconButton** to draw the item as if it were a button. **DrawItem** uses the **Text** member function to extract the text of the item from the list box; **itemID** provides the list box ID of the item to draw.

DrawItem sets the button icon to one or other of the two icons depending on whether the button is depressed or not. Since the icon changes when the button is selected, **DrawButton** must draw the entire button when it is selected. Normally, it just moves the button face and redraws the frame. To force a redraw, set **itemAction** to **ODA_DRAWENTIRE**. There is no need to do this if the icon does not change. An application can define the two icons **ListSelect** and **ListDeselect** in the resource file, so it can change the icons without having to change the class code. Different applications can use different icons.

Here is an example of an **IconList** object filled with file names:

This instance has been created with the **LBS_MULTICOLUMN**, **LBS_SORT**, and **LBS_EXTENDEDSEL** styles. After the object was created, but before it was filled, the column width was set to half the width of the list box, using the **ColumnWidth** member function.

The **IconList** class is useful as a general-purpose list box. Without the multiple-selection styles, the class can be used in place of a group of radio buttons. With the **LBS_MULTIPLESEL** style, it can be used in place of a group of check boxes.

It is quite easy to derive classes from **IconList** that modify its behavior, or to derive new types of owner-draw lists from **ListBox**. In a lot of cases, you only need to redefine the **DrawItem** member function. Here are some suggestions:

❑   The icon could depend on the item. If the list is intended for files, the icon could represent the file type. It would still be a good idea to have a different icon for selected buttons, even if the same icon, such as the check, were used for all selections.

❑   The item string could be an icon name. Each button would display the icon without any text. Such a class would be useful for button bars or panels. You may want a row of buttons that activate the most frequently used menu options. With such a class you might want the button to pop up when you have finished processing it. You can do that by cancelling the selection with the **Select(–1)** member function. Chapter 10 contains an example of a button bar derived from **IconList**.

If you do not want the items to look like buttons, you must replace **DrawButton** with your own function. This need not be too difficult if you simply want an icon and some text on a plain background. If you do that, remember to use the correct colors for the background and text. Use the API function **GetSysColor**. The correct indexes are **COLOR_WINDOW** and **COLOR_WINDOWTEXT** for the background and text, and **COLOR_HIGHLIGHT** and **COLOR_HIGHLIGHTTEXT** for the background and text when the item is selected. With early versions of Windows, you could get away with inverting the colors on a selected item with the **InvertRect** function, but those days are long gone.

If you want variable-height items, you must define the **MeasureItem** member function. This member function takes a reference to a **MEASUREITEMSTRUCT** item. Set the field **itemHeight** in this structure to the height of the item. The field **itemID** gives the item number. Here is the definition of **MEASUREITEMSTRUCT**:

```
typedef struct tagMEASUREITEMSTRUCT {
    WORD    CtlType;
    WORD    CtlID;
    WORD    itemID;
    WORD    itemWidth;
    WORD    itemHeight;
    DWORD   itemData
} MEASUREITEMSTRUCT;
```

Here are the items:

CtlType   The control type is one of the following:

ODT_BUTTON	Owner-draw button
ODT_COMBOBOX	Owner-draw combo box
ODT_LISTBOX	Owner-draw list box
ODT_MENU	Owner-draw menu

CtlID   The control ID.

itemID   The item index. This may be –1 for an empty list.

itemWidth   The width of an individual item.

itemHeight   The height of an individual item.

itemData   The item data or a pointer to the item string.

You must also give the list box the **LBS_OWNERVARIABLE** style. Variable-height list boxes do not work with the multiple-column style.

Again, if your users all use Windows version 3.1 or higher, you can send a **LB_SETITEMHEIGHT** message for each item instead of defining **MeasureItem**. That might be more convenient, since you can set the item height when you add it to the list box. You can also wrap **SendMessage** in a public member function, so that external classes can set the item height when they add the item.

You can define list boxes where the item is not a string, but a 32-bit value. It may be a handle to something, or an index into a database. You then draw the item as you wish. You could consult the database for the name corresponding to the item, and display that, for instance.

Windows provides facilities for sorting these non-string data types. Windows sends **WM_COMPAREITEM** messages to the parent repeatedly for pairs of items from the list, and the parent returns a code to indicate which of the two should appear first in the list. Windows also sends **WM_DELETEITEM** messages whenever an item is deleted from the list, so that the parent can delete any resources, such as memory, that it may have allocated for the item.

You could add **CompareItem** and **DeleteItem** member functions to the **Control** class, and call them from the **Window MessageProc** function, but you will find that it is unnecessary. If you have a well-written class, you can insert new items in the correct position to keep the list sorted. You can also arrange to have the **DELETE** member function and the class destructor deallocate any resources that have been allocated.

Owner-Draw Combo Boxes

It is also possible to have owner-draw combo boxes. These will be very similar to the owner-draw list boxes described in the preceding section. The list in a combo box is always single selection, and it is not possible to have multiple-column combo boxes. Since the combo box displays the item selected in the top window of the combo box, there is no longer any need to emphasize the selection with an icon. Of course, you can still use icons to differentiate between different types of items, such as file types.

Here is an example of a combo box class that draws items to look like push-buttons as in Figure 5-1, but without icons:

Here is the definition:

iconcomb.hpp

```
#ifndef   ICONCOMBO_INC
#define   ICONCOMBO_INC

#include "iconbutn.hpp"
#include "combobox.hpp"

class IconCombo :  public ItemMeasurement,
                   public ComboBox,
                   public IconButton {

public:
  IconCombo(
    HWND PhWnd,                // Parent window handle
    int Id,                    // Child Id
    DWORD Style=0,             // Style
    int x= CW_USEDEFAULT,      // Position
    int y= CW_USEDEFAULT,
    int width= CW_USEDEFAULT,  // Size
    int height= CW_USEDEFAULT);

  ~IconCombo();

protected:
  HBRUSH Brush;
  void DrawItem(DRAWITEMSTRUCT FAR * pDs);
  HBRUSH CtlColor(HDC hDC);
  LONG CodeHandler(int NotifyCode, int Extra=0){
    return ComboBox::CodeHandler(NotifyCode,Extra);};
}; // class IconCombo

#endif // ICONCOMBO_INC
```

This is similar to the definition of **IconList**. **IconCombo** inherits from **ItemMeasurement**, **ComboBox**, and **IconButton**.

iconcomb.cpp

```
#include "iconcomb.hpp"

IconCombo::IconCombo(HWND PhWnd, int Id, DWORD Style,
            int x, int y, int width, int height)
          :ItemMeasurement(20),
           ComboBox(PhWnd,Id,
             Style|CBS_OWNERDRAWFIXED|CBS_HASSTRINGS,
             x,y,width,height),
           IconButton(PhWnd,Id,NULL)
{
  Brush=CreateSolidBrush(GetSysColor(COLOR_BTNSHADOW));
  bRecessed=FALSE;
}

IconCombo::~IconCombo()
{
  DeleteObject(Brush);
}

HBRUSH IconCombo::CtlColor(HDC hDC){ return Brush;};
```

Again, the constructor, destructor, and **CtlColor** member functions are similar to those of **IconList**. The brush that **CtlColor** returns seems to affect only the background of the top window, and not the drop-down list.

```
void IconCombo::DrawItem(DRAWITEMSTRUCT FAR* pDs)
{
  char sz[48]="";
  if (pDs->itemID !=0xffff)
    Text(pDs->itemID,sz);
  hIcon=NULL;
  SetTextColor(pDs->hDC, GetSysColor(COLOR_BTNTEXT));
  DrawButton(pDs,sz,hIcon);
}
```

This **DrawItem** member function sets the icon to **NULL**. The combo box control sets the text and foreground colors of the top window when the item in that window is selected. It does this even for owner-draw combo boxes. To avoid having white lettering in the top window, **DrawItem** must set the text color to **COLOR_BTNTEXT** (normally black) before drawing the item.

Once again, it is very easy to define subclasses of **IconCombo** or **ComboBox** that draw the item in different ways. Usually, you only need to redefine **DrawItem**. If the combo box has a drop-down list, be careful that the drawing does not take too long. Drawing times that might be acceptable in a list box could be less acceptable in a combo box that is pulled down frequently.

Colored Scroll Bars

The **IconList** class changes the background color by returning a brush with the **CtlColor** member function. You may use **CtlColor** with any control, not just owner-draw controls. You can also use **CtlColor** to set the background and foreground colors for text in the control. (You can define **CtlColor** to create colored edit boxes, for example.) In fact, if the control contains text, you should set the background brush and the text background to the same color. The control will use the brush to fill in areas where there is no text. Alternatively, you may set the background mode to **TRANSPARENT**, using the API function **SetBkMode**. In transparent mode, the GDI writes the letters on whatever background is there, and normally it clears the background of each character cell.

It is interesting to use **CtlColor** to color the background of scroll bars. The background is the area between the thumb and the end arrows. Since Windows sends a **WM_CTLCOLOR** message whenever the thumb moves, it is possible to have the colors change dynamically. If you display a black background when the bar is at its minimum value, and a bright color when it is at its maximum value, the bar appears to lighten as the user advances the thumb.

Here is a class **ColorScrollBar** that does this:

colscrll.hpp

```
#ifndef  COLORSCROLLBAR_INC
#define  COLORSCROLLBAR_INC

#include "scroll.hpp"


class ColorScrollBar : public ScrollBar{

protected:
  COLORREF MinColor, MaxColor;
```

```
    HBRUSH Brush;

public:
    ColorScrollBar(
        HWND PhWnd,                 // Parent window handle
        int Id,                     // Child Id
        DWORD Style=0,              // Scroll bar style
        int x=CW_USEDEFAULT,        // Position
        int y=CW_USEDEFAULT,
        int width=CW_USEDEFAULT,    // Size
        int height=CW_USEDEFAULT);

    ~ColorScrollBar();

    void Color(                     // Specify colors
        COLORREF Min,               // at min position
        COLORREF Max);              // and max position

protected:
    HBRUSH CtlColor(HDC hDC);
}; // class ColorScrollBar


#endif   // COLORSCROLLBAR_INC
```

The **ColorScrollBar** class is derived from **ScrollBar**. It has an extra member function for defining the colors to display at the minimum and maximum of the range. If the programmer forgets to call the **Color** member function, the scroll bar simply behaves as an ordinary scroll bar.

Here is the implementation:

colscrll.cpp

```
#include "colscrll.hpp"

ColorScrollBar::ColorScrollBar(HWND PhWnd, int Id, DWORD Style,
        int x, int y, int width, int height):
            ScrollBar(PhWnd,Id,Style,x,y,width,height)
{
 MinColor=MaxColor=0;
 Brush=NULL;
}
```

The constructor creates a normal scroll bar and sets the class items to zero.

```
ColorScrollBar::~ColorScrollBar()
{
    if (Brush) DeleteObject(Brush);
}
```

The destructor deletes the brush if it exists.

```
void ColorScrollBar::Color(COLORREF Min, COLORREF Max)
{
    MinColor=Min;
    MaxColor=Max;
}
```

The **Color** member function copies the parameters to the class items **MinColor** and **MaxColor**.

```
HBRUSH ColorScrollBar::CtlColor(HDC hDC)
{
    if(!(MinColor|MaxColor)) return NULL;
    int x=ThumbPosition-RangeMin;
    int y=RangeMax-ThumbPosition;
    while (x+y > 256) {
        x >>= 1;
        y >>= 1;
    }
    DWORD Color = ((MinColor&0xff0000) *y +
                   (MaxColor&0xff0000)*x)/(x+y)&0xff0000
                  |((MinColor&0xff00) *y +
                   (MaxColor&0xff00)*x)/(x+y)&0xff00
                  |((MinColor&0xff) *y +
                   (MaxColor&0xff)*x)/(x+y)&0xff;
    if (Brush) DeleteObject(Brush);
    Brush=CreateSolidBrush(Color);
    return Brush;
}
```

The long expression in the middle is calculating the correct value for each of the three different components of the color: red, green, and blue. If the thumb is at x from the minimum, and y from the maximum, then the color of any one component is

(Color at maximum * x + Color at Minimum * y) ÷ ($x + y$)

If the scroll bar range is greater than 256, the expression will overflow. To prevent this from happening, *x* and *y* are both shifted right until the range is less than or equal to 256.

When the member function has calculated the color, it can create the brush. It must make sure that the old brush is deleted, or it will soon fill up the system with old brushes!

It is not possible to apply this technique to built-in scroll bars, since Windows does not send a **WM_CTLCOLOR** message when they are moved, although that might change in future versions. Built-in scroll bars are those that appear when a window is created with the **WS_HSCROLL** or **WS_VSCROLL** styles.

The New Toy

With all these new classes, it is now possible to create a much more attractive application. It is possible to derive a new class from **BabyWin**, but since the old application is not needed any more, it is simpler just to rewrite it.

Here is the new source file:

newwin.cpp

```
#include "newwin.hpp"

NewWin::NewWin(HWND PhWnd, LPSTR Name, DWORD Style,
          int x, int y)
{
  Create(Name,Style | WS_VSCROLL,x,y,480,180,PhWnd,NULL);
  HFONT hFont=
    CreateFont(15,0,0,0,0,0,0,0,
               ANSI_CHARSET,0,0,0,
               FF_SWISS,NULL);
```

As before, the window has a vertical scroll bar. **NewWin** sets the text of the controls to a sans-serif font. The API function **CreateFont** returns a suitable font among those available in the system. **NewWin** requests a font 15 pixels high, with the standard ANSI character set and from the *Swiss* family. *Swiss* is equivalent to sans-serif. **NewWin** sets the other parameters to zero, indicating that it will accept the default value for those parameters.

You could decide to write a font class, but unless you use fonts all the time, it is probably not worth the effort. The only disadvantage with the **CreateFont** function is putting the parameters in the right place in the parameter list.

```
Direct1=new IconList(hWnd,101,
   LBS_MULTICOLUMN|LBS_SORT|
   LBS_EXTENDEDSEL|LBS_NOINTEGRALHEIGHT,
   0,0,240,100+GetSystemMetrics(SM_CXHSCROLL));
Direct1->ColumnWidth(120);
Direct1->SetFont(hFont);
Direct1->Dir();
```

Direct1 will be an owner-draw list box. It will be multiple-column and sorted, and will have extended selection capabilities. It will be positioned at the top-left corner (0,0) of the parent's client area and will be 240 pixels wide. Normally Windows adjusts the height of a list box so that a whole number of items fit in the list window. Unfortunately, this adjustment does not take account of owner-draw items having a non-standard height. Here **NewWin** disables the automatic adjustment feature by specifying the **LBS_NOINTEGRALHEIGHT** style. Items are 20 pixels high, so it sets the height of the list box to that of five items plus the width of a horizontal scroll bar.

To avoid having the list box display a part of a column, **NewWin** sets the width of the items to half the width of the list box, as before. Finally, it sets the font for the control and fills it with a list of the files in the current directory.

```
Transfer = new IconButton(hWnd,102,"RtArrow","Transfer",
   BS_PUSHBUTTON,
   250,10,70,40);
Transfer->SetFont(hFont);
Transfer->Click(this,
   (BUTTONCALLBACK)&NewWin::TransferItems);
```

The transfer button now contains an icon, an arrow pointing right. **NewWin** sets the font of the button text to the sans-serif font. The **BS_PUSHBUTTON** style will be ignored, all owner-draw buttons have the **BS_OWNERDRAW** style.

```
Direct2= new IconCombo(hWnd,103,
  CBS_DROPDOWNLIST|WS_VSCROLL,
  330,10,120,100);
Direct2->SetFont(hFont);

Button * Button1 =
  new IconButton(hWnd,104,"GreenTick","Beep",
    BS_PUSHBUTTON,
    250,60,70,40);
Button1->SetFont(hFont);
Button1->Click(this,(BUTTONCALLBACK)&NewWin::Click1);
```

NewWin creates the combo box and the second button in a similar fashion. Note that all the icons are defined in the resource file.

```
ScrollBar * VScroll = new ScrollBar(hWnd,SB_VERT);
VScroll->SetRange(0,100);
VScroll->Position(this,
  (SCROLLBARCALLBACK)&NewWin::VScrollPos);

VText=new StaticFrame(hWnd,105,"Vertical Scroll",0,
  330,40,120,25);
VText->SetFont(hFont);
```

The vertical scroll bar that is built in to the window is the same as before, but the static control that reports its position will now have a recessed frame.

```
Edit* Change = new Edit(hWnd,106,"Change Me",
  ES_AUTOHSCROLL,330,70,100,25);
Change->Select();
Change->SetFont(hFont);
```

The edit control is standard, but it will still have the same sans-serif font as the other controls.

```
ColorScrollBar* RGScroll=
  new ColorScrollBar(hWnd,107,SBS_HORZ,
  330,100,120,GetSystemMetrics(SM_CXHSCROLL));
RGScroll->Color(RGB(255,0,0),RGB(0,255,0));
RGScroll->SetRange(0,100);
```

The scroll bar control will have a colored background that changes from red to green. The **RGB** macro defined in the API returns a color having the specified red green and blue components. The maximum value is 255. The constructor shows the alternative method of specifying a bar having the standard system height. Instead of using **SBS_TOPALIGN** and an oversize height, the API function

GetSystemMetrics(SM_CXHSCROLL)

specifies the height explicitly.

```
ComboCount = new StaticFrame(hWnd,108,"",0,5,120,230,22);
ComboCount->SetFont(hFont);
TransferItems(*Transfer);

IconCheckBox * Check =
    new IconCheckBox(hWnd,109,"Check Me",0,330,120,120,22);
Check->SetFont(hFont);
}
```

The text showing the count of the items in the combo box will have a recessed frame, and the check box will be an owner-draw check box.

```
LPSTR NewWin::Register(WNDCLASS& wc)
{
  wc.lpszClassName = "NewWin";
  wc.hbrBackground = (HBRUSH)(COLOR_BTNFACE+1);
  wc.hIcon=LoadIcon(hInst,"RtArrow");
  RegisterClass (&wc);
  return "NewWin";
}
```

The **Register** member function specifies that the window background will have the color of buttons. When you specify a system color in the **WNDCLASS** structure, you must increment it by one. **Register** sets the application icon, which **Windows** displays when the application is minimized, to the same right-arrow icon that the transfer button uses.

```
void NewWin::Click1(Button& b)
{
  MessageBeep(0);
}

void NewWin::VScrollPos(ScrollBar& Scroll, int Pos)
```

```
{
  char message[40];
  wsprintf(message,"VScroll is at %d",Pos);
  VText->SetText(message);
}

void NewWin::TransferItems(Button& B)
{
  Direct2->Reset();
  Direct1->Selections(this,
                      (LPSTRCALLBACK)&NewWin::TransferItem);
  Direct2->Select(0);
  char * str1="ComboBox contains %d items.";
  char str2[32];
  wsprintf(str2,str1,Direct2->Count());
  ComboCount->SetText(str2);
}

void NewWin::TransferItem(LPSTR Text)
{
    Direct2->Add(Text);
}

BOOL NewWin::LButtonDown(POINT Cursor, WORD Keys)
{
  ::SetFocus(hWnd);
  return TRUE;
}
```

The other member functions are identical to those in the old **BabyWin** class.

The class definition of **NewWin** is similar to **BabyWin**, but the standard classes have been replaced by the new owner-draw classes:

newwin.hpp

```
#ifndef NEWWIN_INC
#define NEWWIN_INC

#include "window.hpp"
#include "iconbutn.hpp"
#include "colscrll.hpp"
#include "edit.hpp"
#include "iconlist.hpp"
#include "iconcombo.hpp"
#include "staticfm.hpp"
#include "iconchck.hpp"
```

The **include** statements refer to the definitions of the new controls instead of those for the standard controls.

```
class NewWin : public Window {
public:
  NewWin(HWND PhWnd, LPSTR Name,
         DWORD Style=WS_OVERLAPPEDWINDOW,
         int x= CW_USEDEFAULT, int y= CW_USEDEFAULT);

protected:
  StaticFrame * VText;
  ListBox * Direct1;
  ComboBox * Direct2;
  Button * Transfer;
  StaticFrame * ComboCount;
  LPSTR Register(WNDCLASS& wc);
  void Click1(Button& b);
  void VScrollPos(ScrollBar& Scroll, int Pos);
  void TransferItems(Button& B);
  void TransferItem(LPSTR Text);
  BOOL LButtonDown(POINT Cursor, WORD Keys);
};

#endif
```

The main module, TESTNEW.CPP, is similar to TEST.CPP:

testnew.cpp

```
#include "newwin.hpp"

HANDLE hInst;
HANDLE hPrevInst;
LPSTR  CmdLine;

int PASCAL WinMain(HANDLE hInstance, HANDLE hPrevInstance,
    LPSTR lpszCmdLine, int nCmdShow)
{
    hInst = hInstance;
    char * pName = new char[80];
    LoadString(hInst,IDS_APPNAME, pName, 80);

    NewWin Win(NULL,pName);
    delete pName;

    Win.Show(nCmdShow);
    return Win.MessageLoop();
}
```

WinMain creates an instance of **NewWin** instead of an instance of **BabyWin**, otherwise it is identical. The icons are defined in TEST.RC:

test.rc

```
#include "windows.h"
#include "messages.hpp"

RtArrow ICON rtarrow.ico
GreenTick ICON gntick.ico
RedXCross ICON redcross.ico

STRINGTABLE
BEGIN
IDS_APPNAME    "Baby's First Toy"
#include "strings.rc"
END
```

The Completed Application

The completed application (Figure 5-1) has a more modern look, but on slow machines users might notice a sluggish response as the items are drawn. Some users might think that the standard controls are easier to read, especially on a low-resolution display or a laptop computer.

This chapter should have shown you that it is quite easy to derive owner-draw subclasses from controls, so go ahead and experiment. If you are developing an application, however, ensure that the appearance is consistent and that you do not have a different type of check box in each dialog box window.

FIGURE 5-1   The Owner-Draw baby's toy

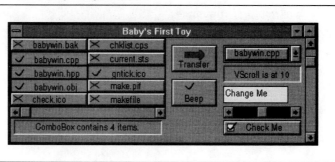

CHAPTER

Dialog Boxes

*I*n Chapter 5, the **NewWin** class implemented the infant's toy as a collection of controls arranged in a standard overlapped application window. As you probably realize, this implementation method suffers from two disadvantages:

☐ The source code states the size and position of the controls explicitly. It is a painstaking business to calculate all these values, and it will be difficult to rearrange the controls if that ever becomes necessary.

☐ There is no keyboard interface for moving the focus between the controls. The user can give a control the focus only by clicking on it with the mouse.

Occasionally, it is useful to have controls in a standard window. Sometimes you will want a single control, usually a list box or an edit control, that fills the client area of a window. If you want the controls to have fixed positions within a window, it is better to use a dialog box, which enables you to position the controls with a dialog editor. The dialog editor is an interactive Windows application that lets you lay controls out in a dialog box by clicking and dragging them into place. The dialog editor then generates a template that the application uses to position controls. Several dialog box editors are available. If you do not have one included with your compiler, you can purchase the Microsoft SDK and use the dialog editor packaged with that. It is possible to write the dialog template by hand, since it is a text file, but the task is so difficult that few attempt it.

A dialog box also provides a standard keyboard interface. The user can move the focus between controls using the TAB key, or by pressing the ALT key in combination with the underlined letter in a control's label.

Using the dialog editor, it is also easy to generate different versions of the dialog box for different languages. Not only can you write the control labels in a different language, but you can modify the size and position of the controls to accommodate labels that vary in length between languages.

Design Issues

Obviously, a dialog box class is needed to contain the controls. What issues are involved?

Modal or Modeless?

In Windows, there are two types of dialog boxes, *modal* and *modeless*. Modal dialog boxes block the application until the user closes them, but modeless dialog boxes leave the application enabled.

Applications use modal boxes to ask the user for input when the application cannot continue with the current action without the input. The *File Open* dialog box that many applications have is usually modal because the application cannot open a file without knowing the filename.

Modeless boxes are useful for displaying continuously changing information, such as the current cursor position, and for prompting the user for input that does not block the application. A paint program might display a modeless box containing a palette of colors, or a selection of brushes. The user may choose a new color or brush any time, but otherwise the application will continue with the current color and brush.

For a **Dialog** class, the ideal would be simply to state that the dialog box is modal or modeless, perhaps with a flag in the class constructor. However, there are a few obstacles to this system:

☐   Modal boxes are created with the API function **DialogBox**, and modeless boxes are created with the **CreateDialog** function.

☐   Modal boxes close themselves by calling the API function **End-Dialog**, while modeless boxes must be destroyed with the **DestroyWindow** function.

☐   The keyboard interface is built in to modal boxes, but the application must invoke the interface for modeless boxes using the API **IsDialogMessage** function in the application's message loop.

The first problem is easy to solve; just call one or the other of the two functions. You might think that you could solve the second problem in the same way, calling either **EndDialog** or **DestroyWindow**. I certainly thought so! The difference is that **EndDialog** does not destroy the dialog box immediately; it marks the box for destroying. **DestroyWindow** destroys the box immediately. You often want to close the box when the user clicks a button such as *OK* or *Cancel*. If you call **DestroyWindow** from a button callback, Windows destroys the button window immediately, which will cause an error when the callback returns. Calling **EndDialog** is safe because the system only destroys the dialog box after it has processed the current event.

For modeless dialog boxes there must be some way of postponing termination until after the current event.

The third problem is interesting. The traditional way of handling keyboard events for modeless dialog boxes is to add a line to the application's message loop, like this:

```
while (GetMessage(&msg, NULL,NULL, NULL) {
  if (hDlg == NULL || !IsDialogMessage(hDlg, &msg)) {
    TranslateMessage(&msg);
    DispatchMessage(&msg);
  }
}
```

This code assumes that the window handle of the dialog box is **hDlg**. The loop gets messages from the application message queue; the three **NULL**s mean "get any message." If the function **IsDialogMessage** recognizes the message as keyboard input and processes it, the message loop should not translate it further or dispatch it. The **TranslateMessage** function translates keyboard events into **WM_CHAR** messages, so if you press the SHIFT key and then the A key, **TranslateMessage** generates an extra **WM_CHAR** message with an uppercase A as the parameter. **DispatchMessage** sends the message to its destination window.

This is awkward, since the dialog class should be self-contained. You do not want to modify the main loop whenever you add a dialog box. In addition, if you have a complex Multiple Document Interface (MDI) application, you will not always be sure how many dialog boxes exist.

Implementing the **Dialog** class will mean finding a way to have the main message loop recognize that a message is intended for a particular modeless dialog box, and calling **IsDialogMessage** automatically.

Opening the Window and Deleting the Class

In the **Window** class, the class constructor opened the window (the window you see on the screen). If the window was destroyed, the class instance was deleted automatically. This was convenient for the **Window** class, and ensured that an application did not leave any orphaned class instances lying around in memory.

For dialog boxes, it is inconvenient to open the box in the constructor. If a constructor were to open a modal dialog box, it would only regain control when the user closed the box. Modal dialog boxes are similar to a function. When you call them, you only get control back when they are finished. Classes derived from the **Dialog** class would be unable to do anything, since they would only be constructed when the box had been closed.

It is also inconvenient to destroy the class instance when the box closes, since it will then be difficult to extract dialog box information, such as edit field contents, from the instance. The parent would have to provide a callback that the dialog instance would call before it closed.

Another inconvenience is that, for certain types of dialog boxes that are called frequently, users may prefer that the fields be initialized to the values they had the last time the box was used. For example, if an application had a dialog box for setting criteria before searching a database, users might wish to carry out several searches, varying one or two criteria each time. If the class instance were left in memory and not destroyed between calls to the dialog box, the application could leave the criteria in class items and use them to initialize the dialog box window whenever it was opened.

Finally, if modeless dialog boxes were to delete their instances when they closed, the parent window would not know whether a pointer to an instance of a modeless dialog box were valid, since the box might have deleted itself and destroyed the instance. The parent would have no safe way of closing the box explicitly or even knowing whether it were open. If the parent tried to access the instance through the pointer and the instance had been destroyed, a system error would probably occur.

For dialog boxes then, whether they are modal or modeless, it is necessary to have separate **OpenBox** and **CloseBox** member functions that open and close the window on the screen independently of the class instance.

Associating Dialog Instances with Their Windows

Another problem is mapping the dialog instance onto the window handle for the box on the screen. With standard windows, the constructor can wait until **CreateWindow** returns a handle, and then place a pointer to the instance in the window's property list. The **Dialog** class cannot do this with the **DialogBox** function, since it only returns a value when the user close the box.

The related API function **DialogBoxParm** accepts an additional parameter. Windows passes this parameter on to the dialog box in the **WM_INITDIALOG** message when it creates the dialog box. **CreateDialogParm**, for modeless dialog boxes, is a similar function.

If **Dialog** supplies the instance pointer as a parameter, there will be a way of making the association between the instance and the window handle when the **WM_INITDIALOG** message arrives. After that, **CPPWinproc** in the **Window** class can route dialog messages to **MessageProc**, which converts them to calls to member functions in the class instance.

Associating Control Instances with Dialog Box Controls

When the **BabyWin** class creates a control instance in a standard window, it creates the control itself simultaneously. When the user opens a dialog box, Windows creates all the controls straight away from information in the template. How can the dialog instance map control instances onto these controls?

The member function **CreateControl**, defined in the **Control** class, checks to see whether a control with the specified control identifier already exists. If it does exist, the function does not create the control. Instead it associates the control instance with the control window. From that point on, the control instance is connected to the control. If the control does exist, **CreateControl** ignores the text, style, size and position parameters.

If the **Dialog** class has an **InitDialog** member function, **Dialog** instances can use it to define control instances for all the control windows. For example the line

```
pOkButton = new Button(hWnd,IDOK);
```

defines a **Button** instance for the dialog control with the identifier **IDOK**. Usually this is the default **OK** button. It is then possible to set a callback for the button like this:

```
pOkButton->Click(this,(BUTTONCALLBACK)&ThisClass::OkClicked);
```

It is unnecessary to define objects for all the controls in the dialog box. It is also unnecessary to define an object for static controls, because once they are created from the template you do not need to do anything with them. If you only want to change the text of a control, you can do that with the API function **SetDlgItemText**. Similarly, you can use the API **IsDlgButtonChecked** function to determine whether a check box is checked.

So far, this is all very elegant, so it is a pity to find a fly in the ointment. The fly is the **WM_MEASUREITEM** message, sent by owner-draw list boxes and combo boxes to their parents. Windows sends all the **WM_MEASUREITEM** messages for all the owner-draw controls in the dialog box before the **WM_INITDIALOG** message. This means that the dialog instance does not get the chance to specify the sizes of items in these controls.

The proper way to get around this problem would be to have **CreateControl** destroy the control and create a new one with the same style, text, size, and position. It could recover these parameters from the old control before destroying it.

In practice, the problem only arises with multiple-column list boxes. Single-column list boxes can have the **LBS_OWNERDRAWVARIABLE** style, and Windows sends the **WM_MEASUREITEM** message before displaying each item, even if they are all the same size. Unless you want several multiple-column list boxes with different-sized items, you can get away with setting the **ItemMeasurement** class before opening the box. The examples will explain how to do this.

In Chapter 5, I pointed out that with Windows version 3.1 you can set the size of the list box items by sending the list box a **LB_SETITEMHEIGHT** message to set the height after you have created the list box. If you develop for Windows version 3.1 and above, you can remove all the **ItemMeasurement** code.

Redefining MessageProc

The **Window** member function **MessageProc** contains the **switch** statement that calls the corresponding member function for each Windows message. The **Dialog** class will need to treat some messages, such as **WM_DESTROY** and **WM_COMMAND**, in a slightly different way. **MessageProc** is a virtual member function, so the **Dialog** class can redefine it and handle these messages. Since the function is virtual, **CPPWinProc** calls the function version redefined in the **Dialog** class. The **Dialog** version of **MessageProc** passes the other messages on to the **MessageProc** in the **Window** class.

The Dialog Class in the Hierarchy

Although you might expect to put the **Dialog** class under the **Window** class in the hierarchy, it has a lot in common with the controls. In particular, Windows sends the box's parent a **WM_CTLCOLOR** message, requesting a brush with which to paint the background, just like a control. It is better then, to derive the **Dialog** class from the **Control** class as in Figure 6-1.

FIGURE
6-1

The Dialog class hierarchy

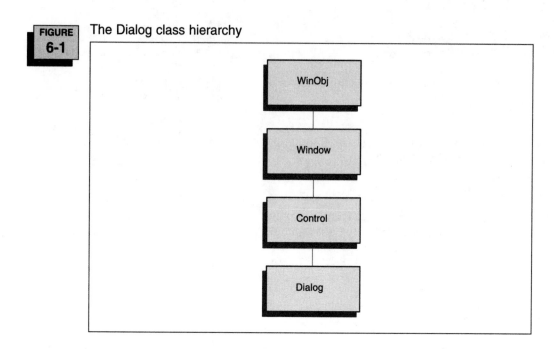

Implementation

Putting that all together, the **Dialog** class can be implemented. This implementation section is somewhat easier to understand that those of the previous chapters, so if you have skipped the other implementation sections, try following this one.

The Dialog Class

Here is the class definition for the **Dialog** class:

dialog.hpp

```
#ifndef  DIALOG_INC

#define  DIALOG_INC
#include "control.hpp"

class Dialog : public Control{
```

```
public:
  Dialog(                          // Does not open the box.
    BOOL bModal);                  // If TRUE box will be modal

  virtual int OpenBox(             // Display the box
    HWND PhWnd,                    // Parent window handle
    LPSTR Name);                   // Template name

  void CloseBox(                   // Close the box and
    int Result=0);                 // return a result.

protected:
  BOOL bModal;
  virtual void InitDialog(){};
  LONG MessageProc( HWND hWnd, unsigned msg, Event& evt);
  BOOL  DialogMessage(MSG& msg){
    return bModal?FALSE:IsDialogMessage(hWnd, &msg);};
}; // class Dialog


#endif // DIALOG_INC
```

The constructor takes a parameter indicating whether the box will be modal or not. The other public member functions open and close the box. The **OpenBox** member function takes the handle of the parent window and the name of the dialog template as parameters.

For the protected members, **InitDialog** is a new event-handling function that Windows calls when creating the box, but before it appears on the screen. The application message loop calls **DialogMessage** and gives modeless dialog boxes a chance to handle the keyboard interface. Notice that only modeless dialog boxes should call **IsDialogMessage**, so if **bModal** is **TRUE**, **DialogMessage** returns **FALSE**, indicating that the message has not been handled.

dialog.cpp

```
#include "dialog.hpp"

Dialog::Dialog(BOOL bModal)
{
  Dialog::bModal=bModal;
}
```

The constructor sets the flag **bModal** in the class definition to the parameter. The following member function redefines **MessageProc**:

```
LONG Dialog::MessageProc( HWND hWnd, unsigned msg, Event& evt)
{

  switch (msg){

  case WM_INITDIALOG:
    Dialog::hWnd=hWnd;
    ::SetFocus((HWND)evt.wParam);
    InitDialog();
    return FALSE;
```

When the **WM_INITDIALOG** message arrives, the code initializes the **hWnd** item and calls the **InitDialog** virtual member function. **CPPWinProc** in the **Window** class will have already put the instance pointer in the window property list. Derived classes will redefine **InitDialog** to set up controls and fields before the box is displayed.

The code processing the **WM_INITDIALOG** message should return **FALSE** if it sets the focus to a control. If it returns **TRUE**, Windows sets the focus to the first control in the dialog box, which is the control that the handle in **wParam** identifies. You do not want to have to keep that in mind when you use the **InitDialog** member function, so the code sets the focus to the first control explicitly and always returns **FALSE**. The **InitDialog** member function may set the focus to another control if it wants, but it does not have to return a Boolean value.

```
  case WM_QUERYENDSESSION:
    // OK to end Windows session?
    // reverse TRUE and FALSE in dialogs!
    return !QueryClose();
```

When the user wants to end the Windows session, Windows sends each top-level window the **WM_QUERYENDSESSION** message. Each Window should return **TRUE** if it has no objection, and **FALSE** if it wants to veto the close, perhaps because there is unsaved work.

A dialog box may also be a top-level window and might want to be warned about an impending session end. In a dialog box, however, the values returned by **WM_QUERYENDSESSION** should be reversed! A dialog box should return **FALSE** if it has no objection and **TRUE** if it wants to veto. The **Dialog** class handles this message in order to reverse the Boolean result of **QueryClose** with the **!** operator.

```
      case WM_COMMAND:
      {
        WORD wNotifyCode;          // notification code
        WORD wID;                  // item or control ID
        HWND hWndCtl;              // handle of control

#ifdef WIN32
        wNotifyCode = HIWORD(evt.wParam);
        wID = LOWORD(evt.wParam);
        hWndCtl = (HWND) evt.lParam;
#else
        wID = (int) evt.wParam;
        hWndCtl = (HWND) LOWORD(evt.lParam);
        wNotifyCode = HIWORD(evt.lParam);
#endif
        if (!hWndCtl) hWndCtl=GetDlgItem(hWnd,wID);
        if (hWndCtl) {
          // if message is from a control,
          // call its code hadler
          Control * pControl =
          (Control*) (void*)GetWin(hWndCtl);
          if (pControl)
            return pControl->CodeHandler(wNotifyCode);
        }
        return Command(wID,wNotifyCode, hWndCtl);
      }
```

The action for the **WM_COMMAND** message is similar to that for the **Window** class. In a dialog box, if the user presses the keyboard keys ENTER or ESC, the dialog box generates a **WM_COMMAND** message for the controls with the standard identification **IDOK** or **IDCANCEL** that are reserved for the *OK* and *Cancel* buttons. When this happens, the message does not have a control window handle, but the control ID is in the message, and the code can find the handle using the API function **GetDlgItem**. Notice again that the parameters are packed differently depending on whether the system is 16- or 32-bit Windows.

```
      case WM_CLOSE:
      {
        HWND hCancel=GetDlgItem(hWnd, IDCANCEL);
        if (hCancel) {
          Control * pCancel=(Control*)(void*)GetWin(hCancel);
          if (pCancel) {
            pCancel->CodeHandler(BN_CLICKED);
            break;
```

```
        }
      }
      if (QueryClose ()) CloseBox();
      break;
    }
```

Windows sends the **WM_CLOSE** message when the user chooses the *Close* option in the dialog box system menu. If the box has a *Cancel* button, **Dialog** will send it a **BN_CLICK** event, and that will result in the *Cancel* button callback being called.

A *Cancel* button callback should call **CloseBox** to close the dialog window, but you can also use the callback to release any extra resources that the dialog box might have needed while it was open. Remember that the **Dialog** class destructor is not called when the window closes. If the **WM_CLOSE** message simply closed the box, the programmer would have no way of releasing these resources if a user simply chose *Close* instead of clicking on *Cancel*.

If no *Cancel* button exists, **WM_CLOSE** closes the box if **QueryClose** returns **TRUE**. An application usually uses **QueryClose** to veto a close, perhaps because the user has not saved some work. A dialog box may also veto the close, but the programmer can redefine **QueryClose** to release temporary resources. This is useful as an alternative when the dialog box does not have a *Cancel* button. Modeless boxes usually have neither a *Cancel* button nor an *OK* button; the user can only close them with the system menu *Close* option.

```
case WM_DESTROY:
{
  //Destroy instances associated with child windows
  HWND hCwnd= GetWindow (hWnd, GW_CHILD);
  Window * pWin;
  while ( hCwnd ){
    pWin=GetWin(hCwnd);
    do {
     hCwnd=GetWindow(hCwnd,GW_HWNDNEXT);
    } while (hCwnd  && GetParent(hCwnd)!=hWnd);
    if (pWin && GetParent(pWin->hWnd)){
      PostMessage (GetParent(pWin->hWnd),
        WM_USER_DELETE, 0, (DWORD)pWin);
      DelWin(pWin->hWnd);
      pWin->hWnd=0;
    }
```

```
    }
    pWin=GetWin(hWnd);
    if (pWin){
      DelWin(hWnd);
      Dialog::hWnd=0;
    }
    break;
  }
```

When the dialog box is being destroyed, it must delete the control instances. It will re-create them the next time that the user opens the box. The code here is similar to that of the **Window** class. To be sure that **Dialog** does not destroy the control instances while they are active, perhaps because a dialog button callback is closing the box, it posts a **DELETE** message to the parent. When the parent receives the message, the dialog box and the controls will have been completely destroyed, and the parent can safely delete the instances.

The **WM_USER_DELETE** message is a user-defined message that will be added to the WINDOW.H file.

```
  default:
    return Window::MessageProc(hWnd, msg, evt);
  }
  return TRUE;
}
```

Dialog passes any other messages on to the **MessageProc** defined in the **Window** class.

```
int Dialog::OpenBox(HWND PhWnd, LPSTR pName)
{
  DefaultHandler=NULL;
  int Result;
  if (bModal) Result= DialogBoxParam(hInst,pName,
             PhWnd,(DLGPROC)Handler,(DWORD)this);
  else  if (hWnd) {
    ::SetFocus(hWnd);
    Result=(int)hWnd;
  }
  else Result = (int)CreateDialogParam(hInst,pName,
       PhWnd,(DLGPROC)Handler,(DWORD)this);
  if (Result==-1){
    Warning(IDS_SYSRES);
    Result=0;
```

```
  }
  return Result;
}
```

Dialog opens modal boxes with **DialogParam** and modeless boxes with **CreateDialogParam**. It is possible that a parent tries to open a modeless box twice. If the parent attempts that, **OpenBox** gives the existing dialog box the focus. There may not be enough system resources available to open the dialog box. In that case, the API functions that open the dialog boxes will return –1. **OpenBox** will display a message, and return 0 to the application, so that it can take any non-zero value as success.

The API functions will also return –1 if they cannot find the dialog box template in the resource file. If you see the *Insufficient resources* message in an application that you are developing with these classes, it is probably because you have forgotten to define the dialog box template, or that you have typed its name incorrectly.

There is no default message handler for dialog boxes. If the message function does not handle a message, it must return **FALSE** to Windows, and Windows will provide the default action.

```
void Dialog::CloseBox(int Result)
{
  if (bModal) EndDialog(hWnd,Result);
  else PostMessage(hWnd,WM_USER_DESTROY,(UINT)hWnd,0);
}
```

Dialog closes modal dialog boxes with the **EndDialog** function. Each dialog box posts a **WM_USER_DESTROY** message to itself. When the message is received, the box destroys itself. By then, the current event has been processed. This avoids having control instances destroyed while they are processing an event.

The Window Class

A few final additions to the **Window** class are necessary to accommodate dialog boxes. They concern the application message loop, the new user-defined window messages, and changes to **CPPWinProc** to handle the **WM_INITDIALOG** message. Here is the modified message loop:

window.cpp

```
// The application message loop
int Window::MessageLoop()
{
    MSG msg;
    while (GetMessage(&msg, NULL, 0, 0)) {
        if(   msg.message >=WM_KEYFIRST
           && msg.message <=WM_KEYLAST) {
            // might be intended for a modeless dialog box
            Window * pWin=GETPWIN(GetParent(msg.hwnd));
            if (pWin && pWin->DialogMessage(msg)) continue;
        }
        if (!hAccel ||
            !TranslateAccelerator (hWnd, hAccel, &msg)){
            TranslateMessage (&msg);
            DispatchMessage (&msg);
        }
    }
    return msg.wParam;
}
```

This code modifies the message-loop function so that instances of modeless dialog boxes can call **IsDialogMessage** and have their keyboard input processed. If the window has an instance associated with it, **MessageLoop** calls the virtual member function **DialogMessage**. By default, this member function returns **FALSE**, but the **Dialog** class redefines it to call **IsDialogMessage** if the box is modeless. An overhead occurs if this is done for all messages, but it is only necessary for keyboard events. **WM_KEYFIRST** and **WM_KEYLAST** are defined in WINDOWS.H; they identify the range of keyboard messages.

MessageProc has two extra **Case** statements to handle the new **WM_USER_DELETE** and **WM_USER_DESTROY** messages:

window.cpp

```
    case WM_USER_DELETE:
#ifdef PTR16
        delete (WinObj *)(WORD)evt.lParam;
#else
        delete (WinObj *)evt.lParam;
#endif
        break;

    case WM_USER_DESTROY:
        DestroyWindow((HWND)evt.wParam);
        break;
```

Finally, here is the modified **CPPWinProc** function:

window.cpp

```
LONG CALLBACK CPPWinProc(HWND hWnd, UINT Message,
                UINT wParam,LONG lParam)
{
  Window* pWin = GETPWIN(hWnd);
  Event evt(wParam,lParam);
  if (pWin) {
    // There is a C++ instance for the window
    return pWin->MessageProc(hWnd,Message,evt);
  }
  else if (Message==WM_INITDIALOG && lParam) {
      // Associate a dialog box C++ instance
      // with the window
      PUTPWIN(hWnd,lParam);
#ifdef PTR16
      return ((Window*)(WORD)lParam)
        ->MessageProc(hWnd,Message,evt);
#else
      return ((Window*)lParam)
        ->MessageProc(hWnd,Message,evt);
#endif
  }
  else if (Message== WM_MEASUREITEM) {
    // return the current owner-draw item size
    MEASUREITEMSTRUCT FAR * pMs=
      (MEASUREITEMSTRUCT  FAR *)lParam;
    pMs->itemHeight=ItemMeasurement::itemHeight;
    pMs->itemWidth=ItemMeasurement::itemWidth;
    return TRUE;
  }
  else return FALSE;
} // CPPWinProc

void Window::Move(RECT * rc, BOOL repaint) {
  MoveWindow (hWnd,
          rc->left,
          rc->top,
          rc->right-rc->left,
          rc->bottom-rc->top,
          repaint);
}
```

The **CPPWinProc** function now intercepts the **WM_INITDIALOG** and **WM_MEASUREITEM** messages. When the **WM_INITDIALOG** message arrives, it puts the instance pointer in the window property list. When the **WM_MEASUREITEM** message (the fly in the ointment) arrives, it sets the **MEASUREITEMSTRUCT** to the values in **ItemMeasurement**.

In the header file, there are two **define** statements for the new messages:

window.hpp

```
#define WM_USER_DELETE  WM_USER+0x300
#define WM_USER_DESTROY WM_USER+0x301
```

The two new messages are defined in WINDOW.HPP. New user-defined messages must have numbers starting at **WM_USER** to make sure that they do not conflict with standard messages. These messages are only sent between windows within an application, so it does not matter if another application uses the same message number for some other purpose. If you want a user message to send between applications as part of some private protocol, you should use the API function **RegisterWindowMessage** to get a unique user message number.

The header file also contains the definition of **DialogMessage**:

window.hpp

```
virtual BOOL  DialogMessage(MSG& msg){return FALSE;};
```

By default the new virtual member function **DialogMessage** returns FALSE so that standard windows do not prevent the message loop from dispatching messages.

Although a few dirty tricks were needed to get the **Dialog** class working, there is not very much extra code. Now that the class is written, it can be forgotten. An application derives actual dialog box classes from the **Dialog** class. Normally, these classes need only to redefine the **InitDialog** member function. Next we'll create a simple dialog box.

A Modal Dialog Box

The *About* box that most applications have is a simple modal dialog box. Usually it contains a few lines of text and a single *OK* button. An **About** class need only close the box when the user clicks the button.

As an aside, if a dialog box contains only one button, it is better to give it the identification **IDCANCEL** and make it the default button, even if the button has *OK* written on it. This ensures that the box will be closed if the user presses either ESC or ENTER. If the button has the identification **IDOK**, the ESC key has no effect.

Here is the definition of **About**:

about.hpp

```
#ifndef ABOUT_INC
#define ABOUT_INC

#include "dialog.hpp"
#include "button.hpp"

class About : public Dialog {
public:
  About():Dialog(TRUE){};
protected:
  void InitDialog();
  void CancelClicked(Button& b){CloseBox();};
}; // class About

#endif //ABOUT_INC
```

The constructor creates a modal **Dialog** class instance. **CancelClicked** will be set as a callback for the button and it will close the box.

about.cpp

```
#include "about.hpp"

void About::InitDialog()
{
  Button * pBut=new Button(hWnd,IDCANCEL);
  pBut->Click(this, (BUTTONCALLBACK)&About::CancelClicked);
}
```

When the box opens, it creates a button instance for the button control and sets the callback. That is all that is needed for an *About* box.

The *About* box will usually be created by the code that processes menu events, like this:

```
case IDM_ABOUT:
{
  About AboutBox;
  AboutBox.OpenBox(hWnd,"ABOUT");
```

```
        break;
    }
```

This code creates the instance of **About** locally on the stack, as an **auto** variable. The instance will be deleted automatically when the function returns. There should be a dialog box template with the name **ABOUT** in the application's resource file.

You can use the **About** class with any application provided that the box has just the single button. You define the details of the text and icons in the dialog box template, so these do not affect the processing.

When you design modal dialog boxes with a dialog editor you can give the box certain styles and attributes. How you do this depends on the dialog editor that you are using, but keep the following points in mind:

☐ Make box the box initially visible. If you do not, you will have to make it visible explicitly with the **Show** member function.

☐ Suppress idle messages. Windows sends the parent of a dialog box a **WM_ENTERIDLE** message whenever the dialog box's message queue becomes empty. You might want to make use of this message to do start some background activity, but normally the **Dialog** class does not process this message, and it carries an overhead.

☐ Give modal dialog boxes a modal frame. In the standard color scheme, this is the thick blue frame. The modal frame lets the user know that the box is, in fact, modal.

☐ Provide all pop-up dialog boxes with a caption bar and a system menu. The caption bar lets the user move the box. The system menu allows the user to close the box by double clicking the system box or by entering ALT-F4.

Owner-Draw Dialog Boxes

Any dialog box can contain owner-draw controls. For example, if you want an icon button, you specify the owner-draw style for the control with the dialog editor, and then you create an instance of **IconButton** for the control in **InitDialog**. If you create numerous owner-draw controls often, you are likely to run up against the following problems:

❑   Wanting to change the background color of the dialog box to match the controls.

❑   Wanting all controls to have the same non-system font. The dialog editor can specify a font, but it changes the size of the box and controls to match. You may find it difficult to specify fonts using the dialog editor if you use icons in your owner-draw controls, since the size of an icon may not match the text size on all displays.

❑   Wanting the background color of static controls to match the background of the dialog box, without having to define an instance of each static control. Static text controls normally have a white background; they are not transparent.

Since it is so easy to use owner-draw controls in C++, there is no reason not to create an **Owner-Draw** dialog box class straight away. The class should set the background color of all the static controls to the same color as the dialog box, and it should have a member function for setting the font of all the controls. Here is the definition of such a class:

drawdial.hpp

```
#ifndef  DRAWDIALOG_INC

#define  DRAWDIALOG_INC
#include "dialog.hpp"

class DrawDialog : public Dialog{
public:
  int OpenBox(                    // Open the box
    HWND PhWnd,                   // Parent window handle
    LPSTR Name);                  // Template name
```

```
protected:
  HBRUSH Brush;
  HFONT hFont;

  DrawDialog(BOOL bModal)
    :Dialog(bModal)
    {Brush=hFont=NULL;};

  ~DrawDialog();
  HBRUSH CtlColor(HDC hDC){return Brush;};
  LONG MessageProc( HWND hWnd, unsigned msg, Event& evt);
  void SetFonts();
}; // class DrawDialog


#endif // DRAWDIALOG_INC
```

The **DrawDialog** constructor creates an instance of the **Dialog** class and initializes the brush and font to zero. The **DrawDialog** class itself does not set these items, but classes derived from **DrawDialog** will. The **CtlColor** member function returns the brush and Windows will use it to paint the dialog box's background.

Here is the implementation:

drawdial.cpp

```
#include "drawdial.hpp"

DrawDialog::~DrawDialog()
{
  if (Brush) DeleteObject(Brush);
  if (hFont) DeleteObject(hFont);
}
```

The destructor deletes the brush and font objects if they have been set, releasing the system resources that they occupy.

```
void DrawDialog::SetFonts()
{
  if (hFont==NULL) return;
  HWND hCwnd= GetWindow (hWnd, GW_CHILD);
  while ( hCwnd ){
    SendMessage(hCwnd,WM_SETFONT,(UINT)hFont,TRUE);
    do {
        hCwnd=GetWindow(hCwnd,GW_HWNDNEXT);
```

```
        } while (hCwnd  && GetParent(hCwnd)!=hWnd);
  }
}
```

The **SetFonts** member function takes each child control in turn and sends it a **WM_SETFONT** message. The message changes the control's text font to whatever is loaded in **hFont**. This will work with all controls, even edit controls.

```
int DrawDialog::OpenBox(HWND PhWnd,LPSTR Name)
{
  ItemMeasurement::itemHeight=HIWORD(GetDialogBaseUnits())+4;
  return Dialog::OpenBox(PhWnd,Name);
}
```

OpenBox sets the height of owner-draw list elements to somewhat more than the value returned by the API function **GetDialogBaseUnits** before opening the dialog box. This is for the benefit of multiple-column, owner-draw list boxes. The extra four pixels are for the item frame.

```
LONG DrawDialog::MessageProc( HWND hWnd, unsigned msg,
                                  Event& evt)
{

  switch (msg){
  case WM_INITDIALOG:
    DrawDialog::hWnd=hWnd;
    SetFonts();
    ::SetFocus((HWND)evt.wParam);
    InitDialog();
    return FALSE;
```

This redefinition of **MessageProc** intercepts the **WM_INITDIALOG** message and calls the **SetFonts** member function:

```
#ifdef WIN32
  case WM_CTLCOLORSTATIC:
      SetBkMode((HDC)evt.wParam,TRANSPARENT);
      return (LONG)Brush;

  case WM_CTLCOLORBTN:
    if (GetWindowLong((HWND)evt.lParam,GWL_STYLE)
    & BS_GROUPBOX){
```

```
            SetBkMode((HDC)evt.wParam,TRANSPARENT);
            return (LONG)Brush;
        }
#else
    case WM_CTLCOLOR:
        if (HIWORD(evt.lParam)==CTLCOLOR_STATIC
        || HIWORD(evt.lParam)==CTLCOLOR_BTN
        && GetWindowLong((HWND)evt.lParam,GWL_STYLE)
        & BS_GROUPBOX){
            SetBkMode((HDC)evt.wParam,TRANSPARENT);
            return (LONG)Brush;
        }
#endif
        return Dialog::MessageProc(hWnd,msg,evt);

    default:
        return Dialog::MessageProc(hWnd,msg,evt);
    }
    return TRUE;
}
```

MessageProc also intercepts the **WM_CTLCOLOR** message and returns the background brush if the message refers to a static control or a group box. It sets the text mode of these controls to transparent; otherwise, the background color of the text cell would erase the brush color.

Using DrawDialog

DrawDialog on its own does not do anything useful, since it sets the background brush and font to **NULL**. The background will have the default color of dialog boxes.

Working with 32 Bits

Notice that while 16-bit Windows must look at the control type code in **lParam** to see what kind of control it has, the 32-bit version has a different message for each type of control.

To set the color or font, create a subclass of **DrawDial**, like this:

graydial.hpp

```
#ifndef  GRAYDIALOG_INC

#define  GRAYDIALOG_INC
#include "drawdial.hpp"

class GrayDialog : public DrawDialog{
protected:
  GrayDialog(
    BOOL bModal)                    // If TRUE box will be modal
  :DrawDialog(bModal){
    Brush=CreateSolidBrush(GetSysColor(COLOR_BTNFACE));
    hFont=NULL;
  };
}; // class GrayDialog


#endif // GRAYDIALOG_INC
```

GrayDial sets the brush to the color of button faces. This brush goes well with the owner-draw buttons described in the last chapter, but if you design a different set of owner-draw controls, you will want to define a different owner-draw dialog class and assign it another brush or font.

The brush can also be patterned. You create a patterned brush with the API function **CreatePatternBrush(hBitMap)**. If you want a pattern with two colors, first create a monochrome bitmap, then set the text and background colors to those that you want. You can redefine the virtual **CtlColor** member function to set these colors in addition to returning a brush. You will need to add two statements like this:

```
HBRUSH DangerDialog::CtlColor(HDC hDC){
  SetTextColor(hDC,RGB(255,0,0));   // red foreground
  SetBkColor(hDC,RGB(255,255,255)); // white background
  return Brush;
};
```

The **RGB** macro allows you to mix up any color you wish, but Windows will round the color off to the nearest color available on the display.

A Modeless Dialog Box

To create a modeless dialog box, specify **FALSE** when you call the **Dialog** constructor; everything else will be automatic. There are a few issues to keep in mind:

☐   When you define the dialog box using the dialog editor, it should not have a modal border.

☐   Usually, it is not necessary to give the box *OK* and *Cancel* buttons. The system box to the left of the title bar can be used to close the dialog box.

☐   Do not create the class instance as an **auto** item, as you would with the *About* box. Since **OpenBox** returns immediately if the box is modeless, you should return from the function and destroy the box before it has had a chance to open. Use **new** instead; then the instance will remain until you destroy it with **delete**.

☐   If you create the box when the user chooses a menu item, it is useful to have the menu item toggle the box on or off. That is, if the box does not exist, choosing the menu item creates it. If the box does exist, choosing the menu item deletes it. The menu item should have a check mark to indicate whether the box exists or not (in other words, to indicate that selecting the item again will remove the box).

☐   Use the dialog box class instance to determine whether the box exists or not. If the **hWnd** item in the instance is not zero, the box exists. You only need to delete the class instance when deleting the owner. It is not necessary to create the instance at the same time as the owner. A better way is to create the dialog box instance when the user calls it for the first time. If the user does not call it at all, you will save on local memory.

A Cursor Position Box

CursorWin is a small modeless dialog box that reports the coordinates of the mouse pointer when it is in the main window. **CursorWin** will use the **StaticFrame** recessed areas defined in Chapter 5 to display the coordinates. Since these are in fact owner-draw buttons, use buttons for these fields when you are laying out the dialog box, and give them the owner-draw style.

```
#ifndef CURSORWIN_INC
#define CURSORWIN_INC

#include "staticfm.hpp"
#include "graydial.hpp"

class CursorWin : public GrayDialog {
public:
  CursorWin():GrayDialog(FALSE){};
  void Pos(POINT Cursor);      // display cursor coordinates

protected:
  void InitDialog();
};

#endif
```

The constructor creates a non-modal instance of **GrayDialog**.

```
#include "curswin.hpp"
#include "dialog.h"

void CursorWin::InitDialog()
{
  new StaticFrame(hWnd,ID_XPOS,"");
  new StaticFrame(hWnd,ID_YPOS,"");
}

void CursorWin::Pos(POINT Cursor)
{
  SetDlgItemInt(hWnd,ID_XPOS,Cursor.x,FALSE);
  SetDlgItemInt(hWnd,ID_YPOS,Cursor.y,FALSE);
}
```

InitDialog creates the two **StaticFrame** objects and **Pos** updates them. The parent calls **Pos** whenever the cursor moves in the main window. Since the two windows will contain integers, it is easier to use the API function **SetDlgItemInt** to set the control's label to an integer, rather than converting the integer to a text string and using the **SetText** member function to write it. The only reason for declaring the two instances of **StaticFrame** is to have the **StaticFrame** class draw the recessed frame of these owner-draw controls.

The Parent Window

The parent window in this case is a test bed for the different types of dialog boxes described in this chapter. It illustrates how to use dialog box classes, as shown here.

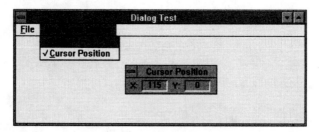

The window is an instance of **DlgWin** derived from the **Window** class. The window is a top-level application window with a menu. When a menu item is selected, the window creates an instance of a type of dialog box.

The parent window is very similar to the *Hello World* window described in Chapter 3, but this time it has a menu bar. It is very easy to add a menu bar to an application window when you do the following three things:

☐   Define the menu in the application resource file.

☐   Specify the menu in the **Register** member function.

☐   Define a **Command** member function to process menu events, such as the user selecting an item.

Optionally, you can define an **InitMenu** member function to check or "gray out" individual menu items to reflect the current application status. The **DlgWin** class will do this, too.

The menu definition in the resource file specifies the menu hierarchy and identifies each item for the **Command** member function. Here is the resource file for this application:

dlgtest.rc

```
#include "windows.h"
#include "messages.hpp"
#include "dialog.h"
#include "filedlg.h"

#include "dialog.dlg"
#include "filedlg.dlg"

AppIcon ICON dialog.ico
RtArrow ICON rtarrow.ico
GreenTick ICON gntick.ico
ListSelect ICON gntick.ico
ListDeselect ICON redcross.ico
OK ICON gntick.ico
Cancel ICON exit.ico
Checked ICON check.ico
Unchecked ICON uncheck.ico

STRINGTABLE
BEGIN
IDS_APPNAME    "Dialog Test"
#include "strings.rc"
END
```

After defining the icons and strings, the resource file defines the menu.

```
DlgMenu MENU
BEGIN
  POPUP "&File"
  BEGIN
    MENUITEM "&Open", IDM_OPEN
    MENUITEM "Save &As", IDM_SAVE
    MENUITEM "Open &Program", IDM_PROG
    MENUITEM SEPARATOR
    MENUITEM "&About Dialog Test...", IDM_ABOUT
  END
  POPUP "&Modeless Boxes"
  BEGIN
    MENUITEM "&Baby", IDM_BABY
    MENUITEM "&Cursor Position", IDM_CURSOR
  END
END
```

Here the menu is called **DlgMenu**. It has two pull-down menus (called POPUP in the API) called *File* and *Modeless Boxes*. Each pull-down menu has several items. For each item, the menu string and its identifier are specified. The **&** character in the string means that the next character will be underlined and can be used as a keyboard shortcut to select an item. The identifiers are defined in a separate file so that they are accessible to both the resource file and the application source files. Here the file is DIALOG.H:

dialog.h

```
#define  ID_BEEP          203
#define  ID_CHECKBOX      208
#define  ID_COMBOBOX      201
#define  ID_COMBOCOUNT    204
#define  ID_EDIT          207
#define  ID_HSCROLL       206
#define  ID_LISTBOX       200
#define  ID_SCOMB         101
#define  ID_SEDIT         102
#define  ID_SLIST         100
#define  ID_SSCROLL       103
#define  ID_TRANSFER      202
#define  ID_VSCROLLPOS    205
#define  ID_XPOS          220
#define  ID_YPOS          221
#define  IDM_ABOUT        1003
#define  IDM_BABY         2001
#define  IDM_CURSOR       2002
#define  IDM_OPEN         1001
#define  IDM_SAVE         1002
#define  IDM_PROG         1004
```

The last six items in this file define the menu items. The other define statements are for the dialog boxes used in the application. Your dialog editor creates and adds identifiers to this file automatically.

Here is the definition of **DlgWin**:

dlgwin.hpp

```
#ifndef DLGWIN_INC
#define DLGWIN_INC

#include "window.hpp"
#include "dialog.hpp"
```

```
#include "curswin.hpp"

class DlgWin : public Window {

public:
  DlgWin(HWND PhWnd, LPSTR Name,
    DWORD Style=WS_OVERLAPPEDWINDOW,
    int x= CW_USEDEFAULT, int y= CW_USEDEFAULT);

protected:
  Dialog * BabyBox;
  CursorWin * CursorBox;
  LPSTR Register(WNDCLASS& wc);
  // event functions
  BOOL  MouseMove(POINT Cursor, UINT Keys);
  BOOL  InitMenu(HMENU hMenu);
  BOOL  Command( UINT Id, UINT Code, HWND hControl);
};

#endif
```

BabyBox and **CursorBox** are pointers to the instances of the two modeless dialog boxes that this application can call. **BabyBox** will be a dialog box version of the Baby's First Toy application from Chapter 5 and will be described later in this chapter. **DlgWin** is interested in three events:

☐   The mouse moving, so that it can update the **CursorBox** display.

☐   The menu being pulled down, so that it can set check marks in the menu.

☐   An item being selected from the menu.

DlgWin redefines three virtual member functions from the **Window** class to handle these events. The functions are **MouseMove**, **InitMenu**, and **Command**.

dlgwin.cpp

```
#include "dlgwin.hpp"
#include "about.hpp"
#include "babywin.hpp"
#include "filedlg.hpp"
#include "dialog.h"

DlgWin::DlgWin(HWND PhWnd, LPSTR Name, DWORD Style,
```

```
              int x, int y)
{
  Create(Name,Style,x,y,480,180,PhWnd,NULL);
  BabyBox=NULL;
  CursorBox=NULL;

}
```

In addition to the **include** statements for the class .HPP header files, **DlgWin** must use some of the identifiers that are defined in DIALOG.H. In the constructor, **DlgWin** creates the main window and initializes the pointers to **NULL**. **BabyBox** is a dialog box version of the Baby's First Toy application.

```
LPSTR DlgWin::Register(WNDCLASS& wc)
{
  wc.lpszClassName = "DlgWin";
  wc.lpszMenuName = "DlgMenu";
  wc.hCursor=LoadCursor(NULL,IDC_CROSS);
  wc.hIcon=LoadIcon(hInst,"AppIcon");
  RegisterClass (&wc);
  return "DlgWin";
}
```

To use a menu, all **DlgWin** needs to do is assign its name to the **lpszMenuName** item in the **Register** member function. **DlgWin** will give the cursor a cross-hair form when it is in the window, so it specifies that as well. It will use the standard cursor **IDC_CROSS**, but it could have used a custom cursor from the resource file. **Register** would then have contained a line like this:

wc.hCursor=LoadCursor(hInst,"MyCursor");

There is an icon, **AppIcon**, for this application, so **Register** specifies that as well.

```
BOOL DlgWin::InitMenu(HMENU hMenu)
{
  CheckMenuItem(hMenu,IDM_BABY,
    (BabyBox && BabyBox->hWnd)?MF_CHECKED:MF_UNCHECKED);
  CheckMenuItem(hMenu,IDM_CURSOR,
    (CursorBox && CursorBox->hWnd)?MF_CHECKED:MF_UNCHECKED);
  return TRUE;
}
```

The system calls the **InitMenu** member function just before the user pulls the menu down, and gives the application a chance to initialize it. **CheckMenuItem** is an API function. **DlgWin** puts a check mark next to the menu item corresponding to the modeless dialog boxes if the instance exists, and if the window handle is not zero, indicating that the box is on the screen.

You will notice that I like to use the **?:** operator when parameters depend on a Boolean value. If the expression in front of the **?** operator is true, the value that appears after the **?** is used. If the expression is false, the value that appears after the **:** operator is used. Many people detest the **?:** operator. If you are among them, I will not argue with you, and time may prove you right. The alternative is to write something like this:

```
if (BabyBox && BabyBox->hWnd)
  CheckMenuItem(hMenu,IDM_BABY,MF_CHECKED);
else
  CheckMenuItem(hMenu,IDM_BABY,MF_UNCHECKED);
```

If you use the **?:** operator, remember that it has a higher precedence than the other operators, so you should enclose the three expressions in parentheses.

Trying to toggle the check mark every time the user selects an item does not work. If the user deletes the box by double clicking the system box, the application will not know about it, and the menu item will stay checked.

You should also use **InitMenu** to disable any menu items that are temporarily invalid for some reason. For example, if your application has a standard *Edit* menu, gray the *Paste* item when there is nothing in the clipboard. The example program in Chapter 10 will do this.

```
BOOL DlgWin::MouseMove(POINT Cursor, WORD Keys)
{
  if(CursorBox && CursorBox->hWnd)
    CursorBox->Pos(Cursor);
  return TRUE;
}
```

The system calls **MouseMove** whenever the cursor is moved in the main window. **Cursor** contains the X and Y coordinates of the mouse cursor. **DlgWin** passes these coordinates on to the dialog box by calling its **Pos** function, if it exists. The **if** condition first checks whether the instance has been created, and if it has, whether the window handle is valid.

```
BOOL DlgWin::Command(UINT Id, UINT Code, HWND hControl)
{
  switch (Id) {

  case IDM_ABOUT:
  {
    About AboutBox;
    AboutBox.OpenBox(hWnd,"ABOUT");
    break;
  }
```

The **Command** member function receives events from the menu. Only the **ID** parameter is significant if the event comes from a menu and it identifies the menu item. **Command** still contains a **switch** statement. *Why not a menu class?* I hear you say. In fact, it is difficult to design a useful menu class that can handle menu events. The **WM_COMMAND** window message contains the menu item identifier, but does not identify the menu, making it difficult to translate this message into a call to a function in an instance of a **Menu** class.

The first **case** statement opens the **About** box described earlier.

```
case IDM_BABY:
  if(!BabyBox) BabyBox = new BabyWin;
  if (!BabyBox->hWnd)
    BabyBox->OpenBox(hWnd,"BABYS_TOY");
  else  BabyBox->CloseBox();
  break;

case IDM_CURSOR:
  if(!CursorBox) CursorBox = new CursorWin;
  if (!CursorBox->hWnd)
    CursorBox->OpenBox(hWnd,"CURSOR_POS");
  else  CursorBox->CloseBox();
  break;
```

For the two modeless dialog boxes, if the instance does not exist, **DlgWin** creates it. The first time the user selects the menu item, the instance will not exist. If the dialog box is not open, **DlgWin** opens it, otherwise it closes it. The menu item for these dialog boxes acts as a toggle.

```
default:
    return FALSE;
}
return TRUE;
}
```

The Baby's First Toy Dialog Box

When **NewWin** implemented the infant's toy as a window, there was no keyboard interface. It was difficult to position the items on the screen. All these problems disappear when the toy is implemented as a dialog box. The previous section revealed the code in DLGWIN.CPP that calls the **BabyWin** dialog box, so it is time to look at **BabyWin** itself.

When you design the dialog box, add labels for the controls other than the buttons, as shown in Figure 6-2. The labels will have an accelerator letter, the underlined letter. Using the dialog editor's *Groups* option, you can order the controls to position the labels before the relevant control,

The Baby's First Toy application implemented as a dialog box

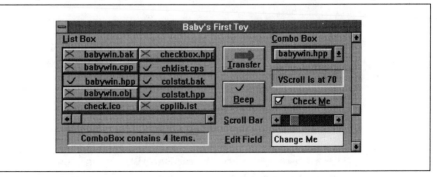

and give that control a TAB stop. If you do that, when the user enters the accelerator key, Windows gives the focus to that control. The text of a button should also have an accelerator key, which will enable the button to be activated directly.

babywin.hpp

```
#ifndef BABYWIN_INC
#define BABYWIN_INC

#include "dialog.hpp"
#include "button.hpp"
#include "iconbutn.hpp"
#include "scroll.hpp"
#include "colscrll.hpp"
#include "edit.hpp"
#include "static.hpp"
#include "iconlist.hpp"
#include "iconcomb.hpp"
#include "staticfm.hpp"
#include "iconchck.hpp"
#include "graydial.hpp"


class BabyWin :  public GrayDialog {
public:
  BabyWin():GrayDialog(FALSE){};

protected:
  StaticFrame * VText;
  ListBox * Direct1;
  ComboBox * Direct2;
  Button * Transfer;
  StaticFrame * ComboCount;
  void Click1(Button& b);
  void VScrollPos(ScrollBar& Scroll, int Pos);
  void TransferItems(Button& B);
  void TransferItem(LPSTR Text);
  void InitDialog();
};

#endif // BABYWIN_INC
```

The non-dialog version of **BabyWin** was described in Chapter 5. **BabyWin** is now derived from **GrayDialog**, instead of **Window**. The constructor creates a modeless **GrayDialog** instance and all the code that

used to be in the **BabyWin** constructor has moved to **InitDialog**. The
other member functions are unchanged.

Here is the code for **InitDialog**:

babywin.cpp

```cpp
#include "babywin.hpp"
#include "dialog.h"
#include "colstat.hpp"


void BabyWin::InitDialog()
{
  Direct1=new IconList(hWnd,ID_LISTBOX);
  RECT rc;
  GetClientRect(Direct1->hWnd,&rc);
  Direct1->ColumnWidth(rc.right/2);
  Direct1->Dir();

  Transfer = new IconButton(hWnd,ID_TRANSFER,"RtArrow");
  Transfer->Click(this,
    (BUTTONCALLBACK)&BabyWin::TransferItems);

  Direct2= new IconCombo(hWnd,ID_COMBOBOX);

  Button * Button1 =
    new IconButton(hWnd,ID_BEEP,"GreenTick");
  Button1->Click(this,
    (BUTTONCALLBACK)&BabyWin::Click1);

  ScrollBar * VScroll = new ScrollBar(hWnd,SB_VERT);
  VScroll->SetRange(0,100);
  VScroll->Position(this,
    (SCROLLBARCALLBACK)&BabyWin::VScrollPos);

  VText=
    new StaticFrame(hWnd,ID_VSCROLLPOS,"Vertical Scroll");

  Edit* Change = new Edit(hWnd,ID_EDIT);
  Change->SetText("Change Me");
  Change->Select();

  ColorScrollBar* RGScroll=
    new ColorScrollBar(hWnd,ID_HSCROLL);
  RGScroll->Color(RGB(255,0,0),RGB(0,255,0));
  RGScroll->SetRange(0,100);

  ComboCount = new StaticFrame(hWnd,ID_COMBOCOUNT);
```

```
TransferItems(*Transfer);

new IconCheckBox(hWnd,ID_CHECKBOX,"Check Me");
}
```

Other member functions have been omitted because they are identical to those described in Chapter 5. **InitDialog** is very similar to the constructor in the original **BabyWin** class. It is no longer necessary to specify the text, style, size, or position of the controls, because they are all defined in the document template. The statements to create the background window and set the fonts are also gone.

Although there is a keyboard interface for the controls, the keyboard interface for the vertical scroll bar has disappeared. The background window never has the focus; it always passes it on to a control. In fact, built-in scroll bars are not very useful in dialog boxes. It is usually better to have a scroll bar control. I intended the vertical scroll bar to be an example of scroll bars in standard windows, when they serve to scroll the contents of the window.

A File Dialog Class

Except for small utilities, most applications have file dialog boxes. They serve to open files, save them under a new filename, include files, and so on. If you have ever programmed one, you know the problems: You have to cut file specifications into pieces, add default extensions, change directories, and so on. Not only that, but every file dialog box is a little bit different from all the others. If the wording of the labels does not change, then there are extra options and check boxes. This section introduces a file dialog class, **FileDialog**.

Version 3.1 of the Windows API now provides some common dialog boxes, including a file dialog box, so you can use those if you wish. The common dialog boxes are easy to use and you can configure them in a variety of ways.

The only problem with the common dialog boxes is that they display all the text and error messages in the language of the installed version of Windows. In Europe at least, that is a problem since the language of the application is very often different from that of the Windows system that is running it. The application might be in English and the Windows system might be French. Many applications, especially those for vertical markets are multilingual, and the user can select the application language from its menu.

The problem, then, is that the application is all in one language, but when the user tries to open a file, up pops a dialog box in another language. Users invariably get knocked off their stride when this happens, even if they know the other language, and they always think that there is something wrong with the application.

To get around this problem, many European developers are avoiding the common dialog boxes and are continuing to roll their own.

Even if you prefer the API common dialog boxes, this section will show how to derive a modeless dialog box from the **Dialog** class (such as the one shown in Figure 6-3), and then how to modify it by deriving from it.

There is nothing very special about the **FileDialog** class. A file dialog box simply contains a small assortment of controls. In common with many dialog boxes, the controls interact with each other to some extent. If the user selects a file directory from the directory list box, for example, the file list box should be updated with files from that directory. The two list boxes are rather special because they contain file or directory names. Several API functions deal with list boxes of this type. It is possible to use

FIGURE
6-3

The Open File dialog box

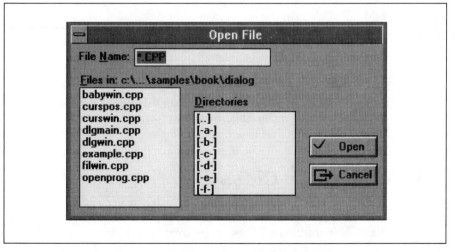

Working with 32 Bits

Windows NT will introduce the NT File System (NTFS.) NTFS promises many benefits in terms of performance and security, but the feature that concerns most programmers is the abandonment of the DOS 8.3 file-naming system. Under NTFS, file and directory names have no length restriction. That is good news for users, but makes things awkward for programmers who have set aside fixed-length buffers for paths and directories. From now on, programs will have to check that buffers are large enough for the data. That is why the **DlgDirSelect** function has been retired to make way for **DlgDirSelectEx**.

DlgDirSelectEx takes an extra parameter that specifies the length of the buffer. With the DOS 8.3 file system, this parameter was redundant,since as long as the application had a buffer of 13 bytes, there was no problem. **DlgDirSelect** is still supported in Windows 3.1 but will not be supported after that. If you want to support Windows 3.0, add a **define** statement something like this:

```
#if (WINVER < 0x030a)  // earlier than 3.1
#define DlgDirSelectEx(hWnd, pStr, nlen, Id)\
 DlgDirSelect(hWnd, pStr, Id)
#endif
```

the **ListBox** class, described in Chapter 4, and use the API functions on the **ListBox** instances, but the proper thing to do is to derive a subclass of **ListBox** to handle files and directories.

The DirListBox Class

A directory list box is just like any other list box, except that the list items are names of files, directories, or drive letters. To save you the bother of getting a list of files and adding them one by one to the list box yourself, Windows provides the API function **DlgDirList** to fill the list box for you. In addition, **DlgDirList** writes the name of the current directory path to a static text control, if you specify one. That is a useful feature, since **DlgDirList** is intelligent enough to measure the static control. If the control is too small, **DlgDirList** shortens the path by replacing the middle part with dots.

When the list has been filled with **DlgDirList**, files are shown as they are but directories are enclosed in square braces like this: [windows] and drive letters are enclosed in braces and hyphens, like this: [-a-]. Once again, to save you from having to parse these items when you extract a selection from the list, the API function **DlgDirSelectEx** extracts the directory or drive name and converts it into a conventional path specification with a backslash (\) at the end.

The only other problem when using these API functions on directory list boxes is that you must make sure that the current drive and path is the same when you select from the list box as when you fill it.

dirlist.hpp

```
#ifndef  DIRLISTBOX_INC
#define  DIRLISTBOX_INC

#include "listbox.hpp"

class DirListBox : public ListBox {
public:
  DirListBox(
    HWND PhWnd,                // Parent window handle
    int Id,                    // Child Id
    int TextId=0,              // static control for path
    LPSTR pPath=".",           // initial path
    int Attrs=0xc010,          // file attributes
    DWORD Style=0,             // control style
    int x= CW_USEDEFAULT,      // position
    int y= CW_USEDEFAULT,
    int width= CW_USEDEFAULT,  // size
    int height= CW_USEDEFAULT);

  LPSTR Path(){                // return current path
    return FilePath;};

  void Path(                   // Get current path
    LPSTR pPath)               // in a string
```

```
        {lstrcpy(pPath,FilePath);};

    BOOL DirSelection(              // Get current selection
      LPSTR pSelect,
      int nSize);

    void SetPath(                   // Set current path
      LPSTR pPath);

protected:
  int Attrs;
  HWND PhWnd;
  int TextId;
  char FilePath[300];             // NTFS ready!
};  // class DirListBox

#endif // DIRLISTBOX_INC
```

DirListBox is a **ListBox** that shows a directory listing. Extra parameters in the constructor specify the following:

TextId   The ID of an optional static control that will display the current path. It must be a proper A static control, not an owner-draw button as used by the StaticFrame class.

pPath   The initial path for the list box. The path may include a drive specifier.

Attrs   The attributes of the files to be shown. The default, 0xc010, shows only subdirectories and drives.

Attributes may be a combination of the following values:

0x0001	Read-only files
0x0002	Hidden files
0x0004	System files
0x0008	Labels
0x0010	Subdirectories
0x0020	Archives
0x4000	Drives
0x8000	Do not display normal files

These may be combined by doing a logical **OR** on them. Common combinations are listed here:

0xc010   Drives and subdirectories only

0x4011   Drives, subdirectories, and normal files, read-only or not

0x4010   Drives, subdirectories, and writeable files

0x0   Ordinary files only

The attribute values shown here are in hexadecimal. If you do not know hexadecimal, combine the values using the | operator, so **0x4000 | 0x0010 | 0x8000** is the same as **0xc010**.

The **DirListBox** class also has a member function **SetPath** to change the directory path, and a member function **Path** that returns the directory path. The **DirSelection** member returns the current selection as a path.

```
#include "dirlist.hpp"
#include <dos.h>
#include <direct.h>

DirListBox::DirListBox(HWND PhWnd, int Id,
  int TextId, LPSTR pPath,
  int Attrs, DWORD Style,
  int x, int y, int width, int height):
  ListBox(PhWnd, Id, Style, x, y, width, height)
{
  DirListBox::Attrs=Attrs;
  DirListBox::PhWnd=PhWnd;
  DirListBox::TextId=TextId;
  lstrcpy(FilePath,pPath);
  DlgDirList(PhWnd,FilePath,Id,TextId,Attrs);
  getcwd(FilePath,sizeof(FilePath));
}
```

dirlist.cpp

The constructor creates a list box and fills it with **DlgDirList**. After that, it writes the current file path to **FilePath**. The standard C function **getcwd** returns the current file path. The class can reset the current directory and drive to **FilePath** whenever it needs to modify the directory list.

```
void DirListBox::SetPath(LPSTR pPath)
{
  unsigned numdrives;
  int Id=GetDlgCTRLID(hWnd);
  chdir(FilePath);
  _chdrive(*FilePath-'A'+1);
  DlgDirList(PhWnd,pPath,Id,TextId,Attrs);
  getcwd(FilePath,sizeof(FilePath));
}
```

SetPath serves to change the directory shown in the list box. The path may be a complete specification including a drive, for example:

C:\WINDEV\INCLUDE\WINDOWS.H

but it may also be a path relative to that of the directory list, for example:

...\INCLUDE\WINDOWS.H

In case the path is relative, **SetPath** sets the current directory and drive to the contents of **FilePath** before calling **DlgDirList**. The C function **chdir** will change the current directory on a disk, but it will not change to that disk. **SetPath** must call **_chdrive** to change the drive.

```
BOOL DirListBox::DirSelection(LPSTR pSelect, int nSize)
{
  int Id=GetDlgCTRLID(hWnd);
  return DlgDirSelectEx(PhWnd,pSelect, nSize, Id);
}
```

DirSelection gets the current selection as a path string. If the selection is a directory, *[windows]* **DirSelection** returns *windows*. If the selection is a drive, *[-d-]*, **DirSelection** returns *D:*.

With **DirListBox**, there is no longer any problem in maintaining directory list boxes. The class can be used in the implementation of the generic file dialog box.

filedlg.hpp

```
#ifndef FILEDLG_INC
#define FILEDLG_INC
```

```
#include "graydial.hpp"
#include "iconbutn.hpp"
#include "edit.hpp"
#include "dirlist.hpp"
#include "listbox.hpp"

class FileDlg : public GrayDialog {
public:
  FileDlg(
    LPSTR pFileSpec,            // Initial file spec
    LPSTR pExt="");             // Default file extension

  LPSTR FilePath()             // returns file selected
    {return FileSpec;};

protected:
  char FileSpec[300];
  char DefExt[32];
  Edit * pEdit;
  DirListBox * pFileList;
  DirListBox * pDirList;
  void DirClicked(ListBox& list);
  void CancelClicked(Button& b);
  void OkClicked(Button& b);
  void FileClicked(ListBox& list);
  void DoubleClicked(ListBox& list){OkClicked(Button());};
  void ChangeDefExt(LPSTR pFileName);
  void SeparateFile(LPSTR pPath,
        LPSTR pFileName, LPSTR pFileSpec);
  void AddExt(LPSTR Name);
  void InitDialog();
}; // class FileDlg

#endif  // FILEDLG_INC
```

The constructor specifies the file specification and an optional default extension. If the extension is omitted, **FileDlg** will set it to the extension of the specified file. The other public member function **FilePath** returns the file specification. An application will generally call **FilePath** after the dialog box has closed, to get the final selected file path. The **DoubleClicked** function will be a callback for the two list boxes. It calls the OK button callback **OkClicked** directly, giving it a dummy button that **OkClicked** does not use.

Working with 32 Bits

Notice that **FileDlg** already uses large buffers in readiness for NTFS. These buffers may still be too small for Windows NT, while they are rather large for Windows 3.*x*. It might be better to define different buffer sizes for the two versions of Windows.

filedlg.cpp

```
#include "filedlg.hpp"
#include "filedlg.h"
#include <string.h>

FileDlg::FileDlg(LPSTR pFileSpec,LPSTR pExt)
:GrayDialog(TRUE)
{
  lstrcpy(FileDlg::FileSpec,pFileSpec);
  lstrcpy(DefExt,pExt);
  AnsiUpper(FileDlg::FileSpec);
  AnsiUpper(DefExt);
}
```

The constructor creates an instance of a **GrayDialog** dialog box and copies the parameters to class items.

```
#include "filedlg.hpp"
#include "filedlg.h"
#include <string.h>

FileDlg::FileDlg(LPSTR pFileSpec,LPSTR pExt)
:GrayDialog(TRUE)
{
  lstrcpy(FileDlg::FileSpec,pFileSpec);
  lstrcpy(DefExt,pExt);
  AnsiUpper(FileDlg::FileSpec);
  AnsiUpper(DefExt);
}

void FileDlg::InitDialog()
{
  char Path[300];
```

```
char FileName[60];
SeparateFile(Path, FileName,FileSpec);
if (!lstrlen(DefExt)) ChangeDefExt(FileName);
(new IconButton(hWnd,IDCANCEL,"Cancel"))
->Click(this,(BUTTONCALLBACK)&FileDlg::CancelClicked);
(new IconButton(hWnd,IDOK,"OK"))
  ->Click(this,(BUTTONCALLBACK)&FileDlg::OkClicked);
pEdit=new Edit(hWnd,ID_FILENAME);
pEdit->SetText(FileName);
pEdit->Select();
pDirList =
  new DirListBox(hWnd,ID_DIRLIST,ID_DIRECTORY,Path);
pDirList->Click(this,
  (LISTBOXCALLBACK)&FileDlg::DirClicked);
pDirList->DClick(this,
  (LISTBOXCALLBACK)&FileDlg::DoubleClicked);
lstrcpy(FileName,"*");
AddExt(FileName);
pFileList =
  new DirListBox(hWnd,ID_FILELIST,NULL,FileName,0);
pFileList->Click(this,
  (LISTBOXCALLBACK)&FileDlg::FileClicked);
pFileList->DClick(this,
  (LISTBOXCALLBACK)&FileDlg::DoubleClicked);
::SetFocus(pEdit->hWnd);
}
```

InitDialog creates the control instances. It splits the file specification into a path and a filename. The path will initialize the directory list box, and the filename will go in the edit control. A separate list box contains files in the current directory. Notice that when the button instances are created, their pointers are not stored anywhere. The button instances are not needed after the callbacks are defined; they will be destroyed when the dialog box closes.

```
void FileDlg::DirClicked(ListBox& list)
{
  char Path[300];
  char FileName[60];
  pEdit->GetText(FileSpec, sizeof FileSpec);
  if (strchr(FileSpec, '*') || strchr(FileSpec, '?')) {
      SeparateFile(Path, FileName,FileSpec);
      ChangeDefExt(FileName);
      pEdit->SetText(FileName);
      pEdit->Select();
```

```
  }
  else {
   lstrcpy(FileName,"*");
   AddExt(FileName);
  }
  pDirList->DirSelection(FileSpec, sizeof FileSpec);
  lstrcat(FileSpec,FileName);
  pEdit->SetText(FileSpec);
}
```

When the user selects an item in the directory list box, **FileDlg** adds the directory to the edit control. If the edit control already contains a file wildcard specification (one containing ***** or **?** characters), the specification is kept, otherwise **FileDlg** adds the default extension.

```
void FileDlg::FileClicked(ListBox& list)
{
  char FileName[60];
  pFileList->DirSelection(FileName, sizeof FileName);
  pEdit->SetText(FileName);
}
```

If the user has chosen a file from the list of files, **FileDlg** puts the filename in the edit box.

```
void FileDlg::CancelClicked(Button& b)
{
  lstrcpy(FileSpec,"");
  CloseBox();
}
```

If the user aborts the box, **FileDlg** sets the file specification to an empty string.

```
void FileDlg::OkClicked(Button& b)
{
  char Path[300];
  char FileName[60];
  if (!pEdit->GetText(FileSpec, sizeof FileSpec)){
    lstrcpy(FileSpec,"*");
    AddExt(FileSpec);
  }
  SeparateFile(Path, FileName,FileSpec);
  pDirList->SetPath(Path);
  pDirList->Path(FileSpec);
```

```
if (lstrlen(FileSpec)>3) lstrcat(FileSpec,"\\");
lstrcat(FileSpec,FileName);
if (strchr(FileName, '*') || strchr(FileName, '?')) {
    ChangeDefExt(FileName);
    pFileList->SetPath(FileSpec);
    pEdit->SetText(FileName);
    pEdit->Select();
    return;
}
AddExt(FileSpec);
CloseBox(TRUE);
}
```

OkClicked examines the contents of the edit control. If the control is empty, it is set to a wildcard specification of all the files with the current extension, for example *.TXT. If the control contains a wildcard specification, **OkClicked** uses it to update the list of files and does not close the box. If the control contains a file specification, **OkClicked** can close the box. Notice that it passes the file specification through the **pDirList** instance by calling **SetPath(Path)** and then **Path(FileSpec)**. That translates a possible relative file specification in **Path** (such as ...\INCLUDE) to a full file path (such as C:\WINDEV\INCLUDE) in **FileSpec**.

```
void FileDlg::ChangeDefExt(LPSTR pFileName)
{
  LPSTR pExt = pFileName;
  while (*pExt && *pExt != '.') pExt=AnsiNext(pExt);
  if (*pExt){
    LPSTR pTmp=pExt;
    while (*pTmp && *pTmp!= '*' && *pTmp!= '?')
      pTmp=AnsiNext(pTmp);
    if (!*pTmp) lstrcpy(DefExt, pExt);
  }
}
```

ChangeDefExt stores the extension of a file in **DefExt**.

```
void FileDlg::SeparateFile(LPSTR pPath, LPSTR pFileName,
                           LPSTR pFileSpec)
{
  LPSTR pTmp = pFileSpec +  lstrlen(pFileSpec);
  while (*pTmp != ':' && *pTmp != '\\' && pTmp > FileSpec)
      pTmp = AnsiPrev(pFileSpec, pTmp);
  if (*pTmp != ':' && *pTmp != '\\') {
      lstrcpy(pFileName, pFileSpec);
```

```
        pPath[0] = 0;
        return;
    }
    lstrcpy(pFileName, pTmp + 1);
    *(pTmp + 1)=0;
    lstrcpy(pPath, pFileSpec);
}

void FileDlg::AddExt(LPSTR pName)
{
  PSTR pTptr;

  LPSTR pTmp = pName;
  while (*pTmp && *pTmp != '.')
      pTmp=AnsiNext(pTmp);
  if (*pTmp != '.')
      lstrcat(pName, DefExt);
}
```

SeparateFile takes a file specification and splits it into a path component and a filename.

```
void FileDlg::AddExt(LPSTR pName)
{
  PSTR pTptr;

  LPSTR pTmp = pName;
  while (*pTmp && *pTmp != '.')
      pTmp=AnsiNext(pTmp);
  if (*pTmp != '.')
      lstrcat(pName, DefExt);
}
```

AddExt adds the default extension to a filename if that name does not already have an extension.

Using the FileDlg Class

For simple *Open* and *Save As* dialog boxes, **FileDlg** works well as it is. There is no need to derive a subclass.

The first step is to draw the dialog box. You could copy the box used for the dialog test application, but usually you will want to modify the wording in some way. You may wish to label the box *Open Document*, for example. When you create the dialog box using your dialog box editor, you should use the include file FILEDLG.H that contains **define** statements for the controls used in the box. The box must contain the following controls:

ID_DIRECTORY A static control in which the name of the current directory will appear.

ID_DIRLIST A list box that will show drives and subdirectories.

ID_FILELIST A list box that will show the files in the current directory.

ID_FILENAME An edit control which may show a default filename.

IDOK An OK button or equivalent.

IDCANCEL A cancel button.

The dialog editor will create a dialog template file that you might call, say, FILEDLG.DLG. You may create several templates or dialog boxes for this file, for example you may have an *Open* box, a *Save As* box, and an *Include File* box.

You should include FILEDLG.H and FILEDLG.DLG in the application's .RC file. You should also include the icons **OK** and **Cancel** that the **FileDlg** class uses. The dialog test application uses a green tick and an exit symbol for these two icons, but you may choose other icons.

After that, opening the dialog box is quite simple. Here is the code used by the test program DLGWIN.CPP:

dialog.cpp

```
case IDM_OPEN:
  FileDlg Open(".\\*.cpp");
  if (Open.OpenBox(hWnd,"OPEN_FILE")) {
    char * pName = new char[400];
    LoadString(hInst,IDS_APPNAME, pName, 80);
    lstrcat(pName," - ");
    lstrcat(pName,Open.FilePath());
    SetText(pName);
    delete pName;
  }
  break;
```

To open a file, create an instance **Open** of **FileDlg**. **Open** will show all the **.CPP** files in the current directory, which is the directory from which the application was run. In a real application, you might prefer to set **Open** to another directory, perhaps a default defined in a profile file.

The system displays the dialog box after the call to **OpenBox** specifying the dialog template name OPEN_FILE. Since this is a modal box, **OpenBox** returns when the user closes the box. If **OpenBox** returns **TRUE**, indicating that the user did not press *Cancel*, the code adds the name of the file to the window title. A real application would call code to read the file.

```
case IDM_SAVE:
{
  char * pName = new char[400];
  GetText(pName,400);
  while (*pName && *pName!='-') pName=(char *)AnsiNext(pName);
  if (*pName=='-') pName=(char *)AnsiNext(AnsiNext(pName));
  else lstrcpy(pName,".\\");
  FileDlg SaveAs(pName,".cpp");
  if (SaveAs.OpenBox(hWnd,"SAVE_FILE")) {
    LoadString(hInst,IDS_APPNAME, pName, 80);
    lstrcat(pName," - ");
    lstrcat(pName,SaveAs.FilePath());
    SetText(pName);
  }
  delete pName;
  break;
}
```

The *Save* case is similar to the *Open* case, except that it initializes the box to the file appearing in the window title. If there is no file in the title, the dialog box shows files in the current directory, and the edit control is initially empty.

Deriving Classes from FileDlg

Although **FileDlg** is fine for standard file dialog boxes, often you need an extra feature. In that case, you need to derive a class from **FileDlg**.

As an example, the **OpenProg** class is a special dialog box (shown in Figure 6-4) for opening program source files. It is similar to the standard dialog box, except that there is an extra combo box containing the suffixes **.CPP**, **.HPP**, **.C**, and **.H**. If the user chooses one of these suffixes, **OpenProg** fills the list box with the names of files of that type.

FIGURE
6-4

The Open Program dialog box

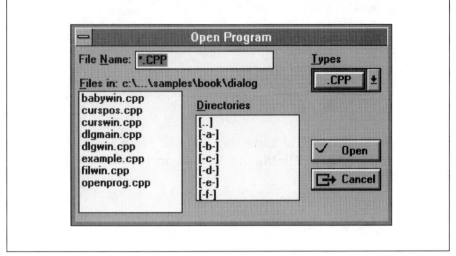

You can implement **OpenProg** like this:

openprog.hpp

```
#ifndef OPENPROG_INC
#define OPENPROG_INC

#include "filedlg.hpp"
#include "iconcomb.hpp"

class OpenProg : public FileDlg {
public:
  OpenProg(LPSTR FileSpec,LPSTR Ext="")
    :FileDlg(FileSpec,Ext){};
protected:
  void InitDialog();
  void ComboClicked(ComboBox& Suffix);
};
#endif
```

The constructor simply creates an instance of a **FileDlg**.

openprog.cpp

```
#include "openprog.hpp"

void OpenProg::InitDialog()
{
```

```
ComboBox * pSuffix=new IconCombo(hWnd,100);
pSuffix->Add(".CPP");
pSuffix->Add(".HPP");
pSuffix->Add(".C");
pSuffix->Add(".H");
pSuffix->Select(0);
pSuffix->Click(this,
  (COMBOBOXCALLBACK)&OpenProg::ComboClicked);
FileDlg::InitDialog();
}
```

InitDialog initializes the combo box with some suffixes and then calls **InitDialog** in **FileDlg** to set up the rest of the dialog box.

```
void OpenProg::ComboClicked(ComboBox& Suffix)
{
  Suffix.Selection(DefExt);
  char FileName[14];
  lstrcpy(FileName,"*");
  AddExt(FileName);
  pEdit->SetText(FileName);
  pFileList->Reset();
  pFileList->Dir(0,FileName);
}
```

When the user selects an item in the combo box, **ComboClicked** sets the default extension, and updates both the file list box and the edit control.

The class works in exactly the same way as **FileDlg**. Here is the code in DLGWIN.CPP that opens the box using its template OPEN_SOURCE:

dlgwin.cpp

```
case IDM_PROG:
  {
    OpenProg Open(".\\*.cpp");
    Open.OpenBox(hWnd,"OPEN_SOURCE");
  }
  break;
```

Summary

Using a dialog box class removes some of the difficulties associated with programming dialog boxes in C. The class treats both modal and modeless boxes in the same way, and handles the keyboard interface for modeless boxes.

The big payoff comes when an application or a series of applications has a number of dialog boxes that share some common functions, even if the boxes themselves are all different. It is then possible to create a class that implements the common features, and to derive individual classes from that.

The **Dialog** class described here uses the templates generated by the dialog editor or any other resource editor. It is easy to create alternative templates for the same dialog box, using different wording or different languages.

CHAPTER

Memory

Windows simplifies the programmer's job when it comes to handling system memory. For example, consider the following features:

❑ The old 640K barrier that DOS programmers had to deal with does not exist in the Windows environment.

❑ Windows provides virtual memory on a disk swap file, so applications can use more memory than is physically present in the system.

❑ As long as an application is written as a number of reasonably sized modules, Windows handles swapping the modules in and out of memory as required.

❑ Simple functions allocate application data memory.

If you are new to the Windows programming environment, keep in mind that Windows applications, even small ones, have to be sociable in their memory use. DOS programs often allocate all available memory, since other applications are not running. Windows applications share memory resources with other applications, and so they have to be careful not to allocate more memory than necessary, and to release it when it is no longer needed.

Remember   Although Windows has swept away system memory barriers, many users still have 286 machines with 1MB or 2MB of RAM, and can only run memory-frugal applications.

Memory management under Windows, while simpler than it is under DOS, is still more complicated than it is under UNIX, for example, where programmers use just two standard C functions— **malloc** and **free**—for all dynamic memory. Under Windows, memory management is complicated somewhat by the constraints imposed by the 16-bit segmented architecture of the Intel 8086 and 80286 processors, and the legacy of the unprotected real mode of early versions of Windows, where all applications shared the same address space in the first 640 kilobytes of memory.

Working with 32 Bits

Most of the remaining difficulties caused by the 16-bit segmented architecture when using Windows memory disappear in the 32-bit versions. Each 32-bit application has a flat memory address space of 2Gb. (It should be 4Gb, but the Windows kernel reserves 2Gb for itself.) Physical memory is always a limited resource, however, even on 32-bit systems. As a matter of course, applications should take care not to allocate more memory than necessary, and to release it after use.

If you write a 32-bit application, users can run it under Windows 3.1 as long as it does not incorporate any of the more advanced Windows NT facilities, such as process threads. Microsoft provides a Dynamic Link Library (DLL) that maps calls to the 32-bit application programming interface (API) onto calls to the 16-bit API.

Most of the discussion in this chapter concerns programming for 16-bit Windows.

Local and Global Memory

One complication of memory management is that programmers must decide whether to use local or global memory. In general, local memory is best for small blocks of memory up to a few hundred bytes in size, especially if they are allocated and released frequently. Global memory is better suited for larger blocks, especially if they will be kept for a relatively long time. In certain cases, there is no choice. For example, global memory must be used for Dynamic Data Exchange (DDE) links, and local memory must be used with edit control buffers.

This complication is not a Windows design fault. It arises out of the segmented nature of Intel 8086 and 80286 processors. With these processors, an application can access an address space of only 64 kilobytes directly. The processor uses a segment register as a base address for all memory operations. If a program wants to use another 64K of data, it must first set the segment register to point to the data. By juggling with the segment registers, a program can access all of the memory. Of course, the application itself does not have to do anything with the segment registers; the compiler sorts everything out for you. Nevertheless, the juggling is still there, and it imposes a high overhead on the performance of the system.

The 80286 processor (and higher Intel processors when running 16-bit Windows) has four segment registers: code segment (CS), stack segment (SS), data segment (DS) and extra segment (ES). CS is for program instruction code, and SS is for the procedure stack. DS is used for the most efficient data access, but ES can also be used to access data.

Rather than juggling the segment registers all the time, the most efficient thing to do is to leave DS pointing to the same 64K area (the *local segment*) and to use ES to access any data outside this segment (*far data*). This is how the compiler's medium model operates. With the medium model, any data in an application's local segment can be accessed quickly, and the application can still access far data when it needs to. Since each application has its own local segment, Windows must set the DS register to point to the application's local segment each time it calls the application. The simplest and fastest way to do this is to have the SS and DS be the same; simply copy SS into DS. This trick does not work for code in a DLL. A DLL has its own data segment but shares the application's stack. Compilers have a switch or an option for setting DS equal to SS.

To sum all that up, for efficiency in 16-bit Windows, applications have a local memory area of 64K that contains the procedure stack, all program data declared at a module level, and the local heap. Applications can also allocate extra global memory in another segment, which will be slower to access. Remember, global memory also has the 64K addressing limitation. If you allocate a global block of more than 64K, you can access it with a huge pointer, but that causes the compiler to generate even more segment-register-juggling code than before. Finally, all data allocated with the C++ **new** operator, including class instances, is placed in the local heap.

Fixed and Moveable Memory

Another complication is that Windows provides both fixed and moveable memory. Fixed memory stays in the same place until it is deallocated. If you allocate memory as moveable memory, Windows moves it when necessary, to make room for other memory allocation requests. Typically, Windows moves memory when compacting memory to coalesce a number of small free memory blocks into one large block.

Obviously, using moveable memory would appear to be more efficient in allowing Windows to satisfy other memory requests. The only problem is that the programmer can never be sure where the block will be when it is needed. Whenever the programmer needs to access the data, the block must be fixed in position with a **Lock** function. This function locks the block into place and returns the current address of the block. After the data has been accessed the **Unlock** function frees it. The programmer must be careful not to keep any references to the data, since these may not be valid the next time the block is locked.

When Windows is running in the protected mode (standard or enhanced), it can move global memory even when the block is fixed. In this mode, the system accesses data through a descriptor that maps virtual memory, as used by the programmer, onto the physical memory of the machine. Windows can then move memory by changing the descriptor. The address does not change. Windows version 3.1 no longer supports real (non-protected) mode, so as far as global memory goes, there is no difference between fixed and moveable memory.

As an aside, the 386 enhanced mode has two advantages over standard mode for Windows:

❑   DOS application windows

❑   Demand-paged virtual memory

Most DOS applications have to be run in real mode. Under standard protected mode, this means switching the processor into real mode, running the DOS application, and switching back into protected mode when it has finished or the user switches applications. While the processor is in real mode, nothing else can run while the DOS application is running. On a 386 machine in enhanced mode, the processor can provide virtual real mode sessions to an operating system running in protected mode. The processor is still running in protected mode, but each virtual session thinks it is running alone in real mode. In enhanced mode, it is possible to have several DOS sessions running at the same time, in different windows on the screen.

The other benefit, demand-paged virtual memory, means that the operating system can have more memory than is actually present on the computer. Your application can use it even though it is not really there. Virtual memory can be mapped onto a disk file so that when the processor attempts to access the missing memory, it generates an interrupt, and the interrupt handler then loads the page in and restarts the last instruction. Under standard mode, a swap file exists. Windows can swap entire segments in and out of the file as needed, but this is not nearly so efficient as demand-paged virtual memory.

From the programmer's point of view, standard and enhanced mode are the same. Both use protected mode.

 Note   Protected mode does not help with moveable local memory. If you allocate a block of local memory for any length of time, make it moveable, lock it before use, and unlock it afterwards. That lets Windows shift it aside to make room for other blocks.

Using moveable memory is not difficult. The problems arise when you forget to unlock memory after having locked it, or unlock memory that has not yet been locked. This sort of thing may occur when a function has a **return** statement in the middle of the code. The memory is locked at the beginning and unlocked at the end, but sometimes the function returns in the middle and the block is left locked.

Discardable Memory

You can also allocate discardable memory; that is, memory that Windows reuses if there is not enough free memory for other requests. It is useful to make memory discardable if its contents are not absolutely necessary, but may come in handy. Data that can be read from a file could be made discardable, for example. Windows will only start discarding global memory when the virtual memory is full. If you use demand-paged virtual memory (known as a *permanent swap file* to users), Windows pages to disk before discarding memory.

You might think that discardable memory is something obscure—something that everyday applications do not need to bother about. Many common applications, however, can benefit from using discardable memory. For example, in many database applications, users tend to repeat queries. Unless the database system is very fast or has a local memory cache of its own, it is useful to store results of queries in discardable memory in case they are needed again. If the memory has been discarded in the meantime, the application just consults the database again, as before.

If Windows has discarded the memory, the application receives a **NULL** buffer the next time it attempts to lock the memory. The application should check for this **NULL** value.

To create discardable memory, use the **GMEM_DISCARDABLE** or **LMEM_DISCARDABLE** flag. The memory must be specified as moveable as well, with the **MOVEABLE** flag, like this:

GMEM_DISCARDABLE I GMEM_MOVEABLE

Design Considerations for a Memory Class

Although Windows has greatly simplified memory management, an appropriate C++ class simplifies it even more. A C++ **Memory** class can help by:

☐   Freeing memory in its destructor.

☐   Removing some of the distinction between global and local memory.

☐   Simplifying the use of memory locks.

Deallocating in the Destructor

The most obvious benefit to be gained from a **Memory** class is that the class destructor can deallocate the memory that has been allocated in the constructor. Of course, if you have created the class instance with **new,** you must still remember to destroy it with **delete,** or the destructor will not be called. Quite often, though, you need a block of memory for a short time when executing a function. If you declare the instance locally in a function, instead of with **new,** you can be sure that the memory will be released when the function returns, even if it returns in the middle of the function.

Using Locks

It would be tempting to have the **Memory** class simply lock the block and return the address of a fixed block of memory. This would save having to lock the data and unlock it afterwards. The redefinition of **new** in the **WinObj** class does this, since class instances have to be fixed in memory. Moveable memory is much easier to use if there is a separate **Lock** class. Locks are usually only needed for a short time within a function. If the **Lock** class destructor frees the memory block, you only need to declare the locks in a function, and you can be sure that the locks will be removed when the function returns.

You could write something like this:

```
void SortData(Memory& DataMem)
{
   Lock Data(DataMem);

   // lots of code
```

```
    return;      //DataMem unlocked here

    // more code

    return;      //DataMem unlocked here
}
```

Data would lock the memory block. The **Lock** class would contain an item **Buffer** that pointed to the actual memory data. Since **Data** is not an **auto** item, the function would call its destructor when it returned, and the memory block would be unlocked.

With a **Lock** class, you only need one extra line of code to lock a block of memory and free it afterwards.

Combining Local and Global Data

In the API, different functions handle local and global data. The functions for handling local data have the prefix **Local**, **LocalFree**, **LocalLock**, **LocalSize**, and so on. The functions for handling global data are called **GlobalFree**, **GlobalLock**, **GlobalSize**, and so on. Using different functions can be a nuisance if you want to write some general function in C to handle a memory block. For example, if you wanted to write a function to sort the data in a memory block, you would have to decide to support only global memory blocks, then use **GlobalLock**, **GlobalSize**, and so on. You would not be able to use the function to sort a local block. To avoid this problem, most general C functions handle pointers to memory instead of memory handles, but then the programmer must lock the memory before calling the function and free it afterwards.

It would be useful to combine local and global memory into one class. The programmer would still have to choose between the two when the memory was allocated, but after that it would be treated as just a block of memory. The **Memory** and **Lock** classes would still have to distinguish between the two types internally, to call the appropriate API functions. Outside of these classes the two types would appear to be identical.

Once that is done, nothing prevents anyone from writing other classes that act on instances of the **Memory** class, instead of buffers. For example, you could make a **File** class to read a file into a **Memory** instance. You might also have a **Display** class to display the contents of the memory in a window, and an **Editor** class to modify it. A high-level programmer would no longer have to worry about locks and buffers at all. The **Memory** instance would just be shunted about between objects.

Sometimes you do need to distinguish between the two types of memory. As I mentioned before, DDE only works with global memory, so a **DDE** class would need some way of rejecting local memory blocks.

Memory Class Hierarchy

All that is necessary is to define a **Memory** class and to derive from it both a **GlobalMem** and a **LocalMem** class, as shown in Figure 7-1. The **Memory** class will define empty virtual member functions that can be redefined in the two derived classes to call the correct API functions. When an application needs to allocate memory, it creates an instance of either **GlobalMem** or **LocalMem**. Imagine that it created an instance of **GlobalMem**. This instance would then be treated as if it were of the **Memory** class. It could be passed to an instance of another class that did not care whether the memory were local or global. If that class wanted to know the size of the block, it could call the virtual member function

FIGURE
7-1

Memory class hierarchy

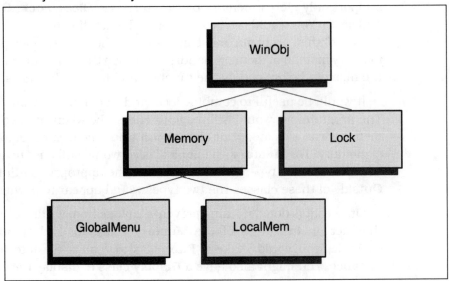

Size declared in **Memory**. Since the object would actually be an instance of **GlobalMem**, the **Size** member function in **GlobalMem** would be called, and this in turn would call the API function **GlobalSize**.

On the other hand, if a member function in a class were defined as taking a **LocalMem** parameter, the compiler would generate a type mismatch error if you tried to pass the member function an instance of **GlobalMem**.

You gain both ways. If you do not care about the type of memory, the virtual member functions sort things out. If you do care, C++ type checking catches any mistakes before they are compiled.

Implementation

The **Memory** and **Lock** classes are quite simple. The **Memory** class provides member functions to allocate and reallocate memory, and to return the size of the allocated block. It also provides functions to load the memory block from a buffer, or another instance of **Memory.**

memory.hpp

```
#ifndef   MEMORY_INC
#define   MEMORY_INC

#include "winobj.hpp"

class Memory : public WinObj {
public:
  HANDLE Handle;
  BOOL Local;
  BOOL Private;

  virtual DWORD Size()            // Size of block
    {return 0;};

  virtual void ReAlloc(           // Reallocates block
    DWORD Sz,
    WORD Flags=LMEM_MOVEABLE|LMEM_ZEROINIT){};

  void Load(                      // Copies data into block
    Memory * Mem,
    DWORD Pos=0);
```

```
    void Load(                    // Copies a buffer into block
      LPSTR Info,
      DWORD Ssrc,
      DWORD Pos=0);

    virtual void SetHandle(       // Sets memory handle
      HANDLE hMem,
      BOOL Private=TRUE){};
};  // class Memory
```

The class **Memory** declares the empty virtual member functions. There are three data items:

HANDLE Handle	A handle to the memory
BOOL Local	TRUE if the memory is allocated on the local heap
BOOL Private	TRUE if the data is private to the application

```
class LocalMem : public Memory{

public:
  LocalMem(
    WORD Size,
    WORD Flags=LMEM_MOVEABLE|LMEM_ZEROINIT);
  ~LocalMem();
  DWORD Size();
  void ReAlloc(
    WORD Sz,
    WORD Flags=LMEM_MOVEABLE|LMEM_ZEROINIT);
  void SetHandle(HANDLE hMem, BOOL Private=TRUE);

};// class LocalMem

class GlobalMem : public Memory{
public:
  GlobalMem(
    DWORD Size,
    WORD Flags=GMEM_FIXED|GMEM_ZEROINIT);
  ~GlobalMem();
  DWORD Size();
  void ReAlloc(DWORD Sz,
    WORD Flags=GMEM_FIXED|GMEM_ZEROINIT);
  void SetHandle(HANDLE hMem, BOOL Private=TRUE);
};  // class GlobalMem
```

LocalMem uses moveable memory by default, while **GlobalMem** uses fixed memory whether it is specified as moveable or not. The memory is also initialized to zero by default when it is allocated.

```
class Lock : public WinObj {
protected:
    Memory * LockedMem;
public:
    void FAR * Buffer;
    Lock(Memory * Mem);
    void Unlock();
    ~Lock();
};
#endif    // MEMORY_WC
```

The **Lock** class is also defined here, since the **Lock** and **Memory** classes are always used together. The only reason for defining **Lock** as a separate class instead of a member function in **Memory** is to have the **Lock** destructor release the lock.

memory.cpp

```
#include "memory.hpp"
extern "C" {
    #include <string.h>
    #include <dos.h>
}

#define GLOBAL_MESS " - Global Segment"
#define LOCAL_MESS " - Local Segment"
```

The **extern "C"** statement indicates that all the function prototypes in the included files are C functions, and that they should be called with the C calling convention instead of the C++ calling convention. If all the prototypes have used the **cdecl** keyword, the **extern "C"** statement may be unnecessary, but it does no harm always to use it when including prototypes for C functions.

The two **define** statements are identifiers that are added to error messages when the system runs out of memory. They are useful while a system is being developed, but they should be removed before it is shipped.

```
LocalMem::LocalMem(WORD Sz,WORD Flags)
{
```

```
        Local=TRUE;
        Private=TRUE;
        if (!Sz) {
          Handle=NULL;
          return;
        }
        Handle=LocalAlloc(Flags,Sz);
        if (!Handle)
          Error(IDS_MEMORY, (LPSTR) LOCAL_MESS);
      }

LocalMem::~LocalMem()
{
   if (Handle && Private) LocalFree(Handle);
}
```

The constructor for **LocalMem** allocates a block of local memory, and the destructor releases it. The destructor only deallocates the memory if it is private memory that has been allocated by the application. If not enough memory is available, an error message is generated.

```
GlobalMem::GlobalMem(DWORD Sz,WORD Flags)
{
  Local=FALSE;
  Private=TRUE;
  if (!Sz) {
    Handle=NULL;
    return;
  }
  Handle=GlobalAlloc(Flags,(WORD)Sz);
  if (!Handle) Error(IDS_MEMORY, (LPSTR) GLOBAL_MESS);
}

GlobalMem::~GlobalMem()
{
  if (Handle && Private) GlobalFree(Handle);
}
```

GlobalMem does something similar for global memory.

```
void LocalMem::ReAlloc(WORD Sz, WORD Flags)
{
  HANDLE h=LocalReAlloc(Handle, Sz, Flags);
  if (!h) Error(IDS_MEMORY,(LPSTR) LOCAL_MESS);
  else Handle=h;
}
```

```
void GlobalMem::ReAlloc(DWORD Sz, WORD Flags)
{
  HANDLE h=GlobalReAlloc(Handle, (WORD)Sz, Flags);
  if (!h) Error(IDS_MEMORY,(LPSTR) GLOBAL_MESS);
  else Handle=h;
}
```

The two **ReAlloc** member functions call either the **LocalReAlloc** or the **GlobalReAlloc** API functions. These functions reallocate the memory block to a different size. They can shrink the block or expand it. The reallocation functions can also change the flag setting for a memory block. It is possible, for example, to change a block from being moveable to fixed.

```
void LocalMem::SetHandle(HANDLE hMem)
{
  if (Handle && LocalMem::Private) LocalFree(Handle);
  Handle=hMem;
  LocalMem::Private=Private;
}

void GlobalMem::SetHandle(HANDLE hMem)
{
  if (Handle && GlobalMem::Private) GlobalFree(Handle);
  Handle=hMem;
  GlobalMem::Private=Private;
}
```

The **SetHandle** member function is useful for creating an instance of **Memory** when the memory handle has already been created somewhere else. It might be a handle to data in the clipboard returned by an API function. In such cases, the application sets the **Private** flag to **FALSE**, indicating that the memory is public memory and should not be deallocated by the destructors.

```
DWORD LocalMem::Size()
{
  if (!Handle) return 0;
  else return LocalSize(Handle);
}

DWORD GlobalMem::Size()
{
```

```
  if (!Handle) return 0;
  else return GlobalSize(Handle);
}
```

The **Size** member functions are simple enough. They call the API functions **LocalSize** or **GlobalSize** to get the size of the memory block. If you allocate global memory, the system might give you more memory than you asked for. Under Windows version 3.1, the system rounds global requests up to the next 16-byte boundary. The **Size** function tells you how much memory has actually been allocated.

```
void Memory::Load(Memory * Mem, DWORD Pos)
{
  Lock BufSource(Mem);
  Lock BufTarget(this);
  if (!BufSource.Buffer || !BufTarget.Buffer) return;
  DWORD MoveBytes=Size()-Pos;
  DWORD Ssrc=Mem->Size();
  if (MoveBytes>Ssrc) MoveBytes=Ssrc;
#ifdef WIN32
  memcpy((void*)((char*)BufTarget.Buffer +Pos),
  (const void*)BufSource.Buffer, MoveBytes);
#else
  movedata(FP_SEG(BufSource.Buffer),
           FP_OFF(BufSource.Buffer),
           FP_SEG(BufTarget.Buffer),
           FP_OFF(BufTarget.Buffer)+Pos,MoveBytes);
#endif
}
```

The preceding code is one of two overloaded **Load** member functions. If you call **Load** with a pointer to an instance of **Memory,** it copies the contents of the memory block into the current block at the specified position. The two blocks are locked and then the **Buffer** items in the **Lock** instances point to the data. The **movedata** function is in the C library; it is a cumbersome function to use, since it requires the addresses to be split into segments and offsets, but it is efficient.

```
void Memory::Load(LPSTR Info, DWORD Ssrc, DWORD Pos)
{
  Lock BufTarget(this);
  if (!Info || !BufTarget.Buffer) return;
  DWORD MoveBytes=Size()-Pos;
  if (MoveBytes>Ssrc) MoveBytes=Ssrc;
```

Working with 32 Bits

In the 32-bit version of Windows, juggling segments and offsets is unnecessary. The ordinary **memcpy** function will suffice. In 16-bit Windows, **memcpy** only works with near pointers.

```
#ifdef WIN32
  memcpy((void*)((char*)BufTarget.Buffer +Pos),
          (const void*)Info, MoveBytes);
#else
  movedata(FP_SEG(Info),
          FP_OFF(Info),
          FP_SEG(BufTarget.Buffer),
          FP_OFF(BufTarget.Buffer)+Pos,MoveBytes);
#endif
}
```

The second overloaded **Load** member function does something similar for pointers to a buffer. **Ssrc** is the size of the source block, and **Pos** is the offset within the current block to which the memory should be copied.

```
Lock::Lock(Memory * Mem)
{
  LockedMem=Mem;
  if (Mem->Local){
    Buffer=LocalLock(Mem->Handle);
  }
  else {
    Buffer=GlobalLock(Mem->Handle);
  }
}

void Lock::Unlock()
{
  if (LockedMem->Local) LocalUnlock(LockedMem->Handle);
  else GlobalUnlock(LockedMem->Handle);
}
```

```
Lock::~Lock()
{
  Unlock();
}
```

The member functions in **Lock** use the **Local** item to distinguish between the two types of memory. **Local** was set to **TRUE** or **FALSE** in the memory constructors.

An instance of **Lock** must remember the handle of the memory it has locked, so that it can release it afterwards.

Using the Memory and Lock Classes

To allocate a block of memory, declare an instance of either **GlobalMem** or **LocalMem.** To get a pointer to the data contained in the block, declare an instance of **Lock** on the memory. For example, to use a block of global memory, you can write something like this:

```
GlobalMem GBlock(500);     // Create a block
LPSTR pBlock =             // get the address
    (LPSTR)Lock(&GBlock).Buffer;
```

This code creates an instance of global memory called **GBlock**, which will contain 500 bytes of fixed memory. Although the block has been allocated, the address of the data is still needed. The code creates an instance of **Lock** using the memory block. The member **Buffer** in **Lock** contains the address of the data. When the function containing this code returns, it deletes the instance of **Lock**, and then **GBlock**, which means that the block is first unlocked and then freed. Because this block is fixed, whether it is locked or not is unimportant. If the block were discardable memory or moveable local memory, it would be necessary to unlock the block before freeing it.

```
// create a block and lock it in one go
pBlock = (LPSTR)Lock(&GlobalMem(500)).Buffer;
```

This code has the same effect as the previous example, except that it creates the instance of **GlobalMem** while it is calling the **Lock** constructor. This alternative is useful if you do not need to access the instance of

GlobalMem afterwards. If you do need to access it, perhaps to reallocate the block to a larger size, use the first form, and give the instance a name.

If you want the memory block to outlast a function's scope, you need to use **new** to create the instance and, eventually, **delete** to destroy it. You can still use **Lock** locally in a function to get the address of the data, and **Lock** will unlock the block in its destructor.

Deriving from the Memory Class

Although the **Memory** class is powerful on its own, you can use C++ to derive application-specific classes that are even more powerful. As an example, applications frequently need to use blocks of global memory as an array of items. Quite often, the application does not know how many items there will be when it allocates the block, and must reallocate it to a larger size later on, when it fills up. It would be useful to derive a class to handle the array of items. The following code shows a class derived from **GlobalMem** that handles arrays of complex numbers in a global memory block. A complex number is a useful mathematical concept. It extends the notion of simple or real numbers by adding an imaginary part; for example, the square root of a negative number is an imaginary number. You can represent a complex number like this:

(*real, imaginary*)

so the ordinary number −1 will be (−1,0) since it has no imaginary part, and its square root will be (0,1). Anyway, if you are unsure about that example, replace *real* and *imaginary* by *x* and *y*, and think about the example in terms of a coordinate system. The class described here is an elementary **Complex** class, because it omits many complex number operations.

complex.hpp

```
#ifndef COMPLEX_INC
#define COMPLEX_INC

// A (simple!) complex number class
class Complex {
public:
  // construct a default complex number
  Complex(){real=0.0; imaginary=0.0;};
```

```
// construct a specific complex number
Complex(float r, float i){real=r; imaginary=i;};

// the components of the number
float real;
float imaginary;
};
```

First, the **Complex** class itself must be defined. This class contains the two components of the number—real and imaginary—and two constructors to initialize it. The first constructor is a default constructor that initializes it to zero, the other initializes it to a certain value.

```
// A dynamic array for complex numbers
class ComplexGlobalMem : public GlobalMem {
public:
  // create a block large enough for initial number of elements
  ComplexGlobalMem(int nElements)
    :GlobalMem(nElements * sizeof( Complex))
    {nBound=nElements;};

  // a type conversion to an element pointer
  operator Complex FAR *(){
    return (Complex FAR *)GlobalLock(Handle);};

  // overload the subscript operator to do bound checking
  Complex FAR * operator[](UINT Subscript){
    if (Subscript>=nBound){
      ReAlloc((Subscript+1)*sizeof (Complex));
      nBound = Subscript+1;
    }
    return (Complex FAR *)
      (GlobalLock(Handle)+Subscript*sizeof (Complex));
  };
protected:
  UINT nBound;
};

#endif  //COMPLEX_INC
```

The class **ComplexGlobalMem** is derived from **GlobalMem**. The constructor creates a global block big enough for a certain number of elements, rather than a certain number of bytes.

To make this class easier to use, the constructor provides a type conversion to a **Complex FAR *** by redefining the **()** operator as another

C++ operator, the subscripting operator **[]**. Remember, one of the features of C++ is that almost all of the operators can be redefined.

The type conversion is redefined to return the address of the block as a pointer to a **Complex** array. The subscript operator also returns the address of a certain element. In addition, the operator checks the subscript against the upper bound of the array and reallocates it if necessary.

Once that is done, using the class is a simple matter.

```
ComplexGlobalMem CMem(5);     // create a block
Complex FAR * pComp=CMem;     // assign of block
ComplexGlobalMem * pCMem      // assign address of
    = &CMem                   // instance
*CMem=*pComp;                 // write into the data
*(CMem +1)=*pComp;            // do pointer arithmetic
pComp=CMem+1;
Complex A;
A=*CMem[1];                   // do array subscripting
*CMem[10]=A;                  // it gets reallocated here
A=*pComp;
```

The instance of **ComplexGlobalMem** can now be treated exactly as if it were a pointer to an array of **Complex** items. It can be dereferenced and subscripted with the additional benefit of automatic reallocation. When the function containing this code returns, the instance are deleted and the memory block freed. The first line of this code creates an array of five **Complex** elements in global memory. Since each **Complex** element occupies eight bytes (two floats of four bytes each), the block will be 40 bytes long.

Notice the distinction between the second and third lines. The second line assigns **CMem** to a **Complex FAR *** pointer. This causes the compiler to call the type conversion operator in **ComplexGlobalMem**, which returns the address of the global memory block. In the third line, the compiler simply assigns the address of the instance to **pCMem**. Remember, an instance of **Memory** does not contain the data, only a handle to the data.

When **CMem** is treated as a pointer to **Complex**, you can do pointer arithmetic on it. Therefore, ***(CMem + 1)** means a pointer to the second **Complex** element, since ***CMem** is a pointer to the first element. Pointer arithmetic, however, does not give you the benefit of automatic reallocation. I have included the pointer arithmetic example here to show that it works. You should use the subscript notation instead, as in ***CMem[1]**, which is just as efficient and much easier to understand.

If **ComplexGlobalMem** had used local memory instead of **FAR** memory, you could have written the **[]** operator like this:

```
Complex&  operator[](UINT Subscript){
  if (Subscript>=nBound){
    ReAlloc((Subscript+1)*sizeof (Complex));
    nBound = Subscript+1;
  }
  return *(Complex *)
    (LocalLock(Handle)+Subscript*sizeof (Complex));
};
```

When the operator is defined as **Complex&**, it returns a reference to the element. Then, the instance can be used as if it were an array instead of a pointer to an array, like this:

```
CMem[2]=CMem[5];
```

If you think **ComplexGlobalMem** is useful, you may want to create similar classes for all your own structures and classes. Before you copy **ComplexGlobalMem** and replace all the occurrences of **Complex** by the name of your own class, read Chapter 11, which shows you how to use templates for writing generic classes, and which presents an alternative way to define generic classes if your compiler does not support templates.

Using New and Delete

The C++ functions **new** and **delete** can allocate and deallocate memory for any kind of data, not just class instances. The **new** function allocates fixed data on the local heap, so it should only be used for small amounts of data—a few hundred bytes, for example. The example programs in previous chapters use **new** to temporarily allocate storage for loading the application's name in **WinMain.** If the data had just been declared local to a function, it would remain on the stack until **WinMain** returned, meaning that the data would stay throughout the application's lifetime, and the application would require a larger stack.

```
char * pStr = new char[200];  // allocate local fixed memory
...
delete pStr;                  // deallocates the memory
```

The only problem with **new** is that unless **delete** is called, the memory remains allocated until the application finishes. If you require a temporary block of memory in a function, you might consider using this construction:

```
char *pStr = (char*)LocalMem(200,LPTR).Handle;
... // use pStr as before;
```

LocalMem allocates the 200 bytes on the local heap as before, but this time the class destructors deallocate the memory when the instance of **LocalMem** passes out of scope. The **LPTR** flag combines the **LMEM_FIXED** and **LMEM_ZEROINIT** flags. Since the memory is fixed, the value in **Handle** is the actual address of the data and can be cast to a pointer.

If any class instance is within a compound statement of a function, its destructor will be called as soon as control passes out of that statement. A compound statement is a group of statements enclosed in a pair of braces {}. For example:

```
if (this==that) {
  LocalMem MyMem(200);  // memory allocated here
  ...
} // memory deallocated here
```

In general, this is what you want, but beware of allocating objects in loops, since the constructors and destructors are called on each pass of the loop. The result affects your application's performance.

```
for (int i=0;i<1000;i++) {
  LocalMem MyMem(200)  // memory allocated and
                          deallocated 1000 times
  ..
}
```

Summary

The **Memory** class simplifies allocating and deleting local and global data. There is no longer any distinction between fixed and moveable global memory, so memory locks have no effect on global memory, other than returning the block address, unless the memory is declared as discardable. Locks are still useful for local memory and global discardable memory.

More importantly, **Memory** allows you to design classes that process instances of the **Memory** class, whether or not the memory allocated is local or global, discardable or not. At a high level in the application, instances of **Memory** are just passed from one class to another for processing. The intricacies of locks are left to the classes that do the processing. The **File** class in Chapter 8 is an example of such a class.

CHAPTER

Files

*T*he Windows application programming interface (API) does not appear to offer many facilities for file handling; only low-level file operations are provided. Because of the multitasking nature of Windows, programmers should keep files closed when they are not being used.

With DOS, it is acceptable to open all the necessary files when the application starts and to close them when the application finishes. A simple DOS database, for example, might open the data and index files. The files would be accessed for each query and only closed if the user explicitly changed files.

Under Windows, applications should not keep files open, since other applications might be accessing the file. While it is possible for several applications to open a file at the same time there are dangers in doing so, especially when the file is on a removeable disk, such as a diskette or a compact disc. If you open a file on a removeable disk and keep it open, the user may change disks while working on another application. When the user returns to your application, the handle on the open file will no longer be valid. Files should be closed before handing control back to Windows.

Opening or closing files involves little performance overhead, since the Windows disk cache, SmartDrive, usually does the update in memory. In practice, files should be opened just before they are accessed and closed immediately afterwards. Creating a class that does this is not a very difficult task.

The Windows API functions perform unbuffered, unformatted input/output (I/O). If you read 1000 bytes, the system goes to the file and reads 1000 bytes. The data has the same format on the file as it has in memory. Thus a short integer, such as 1234, would occupy 2 bytes, one containing 4 and the other containing 210 (4*256 + 210 = 1234). You would get the exact data that existed on the file. These routines are known as unbuffered routines because they attempt to read or write the file each time you call them. Buffered file functions save data up and write a large block in one go, or else read a block and give you the data byte by byte as you need it. Even though the Windows API functions attempt to be unbuffered, SmartDrive still buffers the I/O from these functions, as it buffers the I/O for the entire system.

If you want to do unformatted I/O, it is usually not worth trying to buffer it yourself, unless you are reading or writing a few bytes at a time. Unformatted I/O is useful for reading and writing raw data. This will normally take the form of C structures or arrays. An application can use unformatted I/O to write an entire array of complex structures to a file using just one function call. Later, it can read the array back in with another function call. Unformatted I/O is the most efficient form of I/O. The only drawback is that it is not easily readable by humans.

What about formatted file I/O? In formatted I/O, the data is converted into printable characters and formatted with spaces and new lines. An integer 1234 would appear as 4 bytes (49, 50, 51 and 52), since these values represent the printable characters "1," "2," "3," and "4." Obviously, if humans are going to want to read the file, formatted I/O is the best choice. On the other hand, if the file is only going to be read by another computer, formatted I/O would seem to be a waste of time. In the PC world, it is rare to find formatted files other than those that are written or read by humans, yet in the UNIX world, many files are formatted even though they are only used by other computers. Why is that? Until recently, all PCs were 16-bit Intel processors; that is, even if they were 32-bit Intel processors, they were still treated as 16-bit processors. The entire PC universe was homogeneous. UNIX, on the other hand, has always been a heterogeneous universe. All sorts of machines run UNIX: Intel, Motorola, RISC, 16-bit, 32-bit, and 64-bit. If a UNIX machine writes unformatted data to a file, its neighbor will probably not be able to read it. There are two reasons why unformatted data might be incompatible between two machines:

☐ Word size

☐ Byte order

Word size is a problem between 16-, 32-, and 64-bit machines. A 16-bit machine writes 2 bytes when it writes an integer, while a 32-bit machine expects to read 4 bytes. Byte order is a problem between architectures. The Intel series stores the least significant byte of a value first, so the integer 1234 would be stored as a byte containing 210, followed by a byte containing 4. Some other machines, such as the DEC VAX, also follow this convention. However, such machines as the Motorola 68000 series store the high-order byte first. This difference in architecture is known as "little-endian" versus "big endian," in an allusion to the opposing factions in "Gulliver's Travels" who would open their breakfast eggs by either the little or the big end.

The word size problem can be avoided with diligent programming. The trick is to use data items with a fixed size, so a 16-bit **short int** can be used instead of an undefined **int.** Byte order is more of a problem. It is possible to reverse the bytes when reading an unformatted file, but only if the machine reading the file is sure that the program was written by a machine of the opposite polarity.

Because of these problems, it is the custom in heterogeneous computer environments such as UNIX to write files as formatted text when they are likely to be read by other machines.

In C++, there is a comprehensive specification for buffered I/O, called **iostream.** The **iostream** library is a C++ class library; it is not just a library of C routines. The two base classes in **iostream** are **ios** and **streambuf.** Classes derived from the **ios** class performs formatted I/O to an instance of **streambuf,** which is an interface to the target device. The **ios** class family is shown in Figure 8-1, and **streambuf** in Figure 8-2. The two classes that do most of the formatting work are **istream** and **ostream** for input and output. An application sends data to an instance of **ostream** and reads from an instance of **istream.** The streams read or write data items as well as strings. The library already contains formatting functions for standard types, such as **floats** or **ints,** and these are converted to and from a string of digit characters.

An application performs I/O using the **<<** and **>>** operators on a stream. If the application wishes to send some text or values to a file, it can declare an instance of **ofstream** and send the data to that instance:

```
//declare an instance of ofstream
ofstream aStream("MYFILE.TXT");

// Write some text followed by a newline
aStream << "This is the data." << endl;

// write some data
int i = 123;
aStream << "The value of i is " << i;

float f = 123.456;

aStream << f << " squared is " << f*f << endl;
```

While the standard **iostream** classes provide facilities for basic types, it is possible to overload the **<<** and **>>** operators in your own classes, so

FIGURE
8-1

The **ios** class family

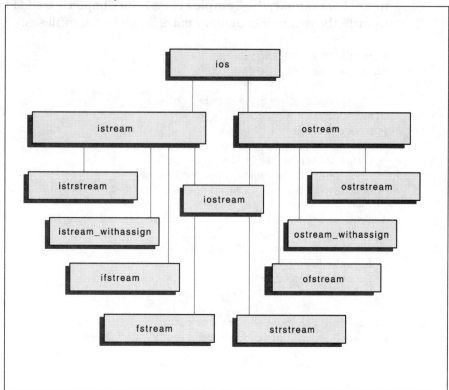

FIGURE
8-2

The **streambuf** class

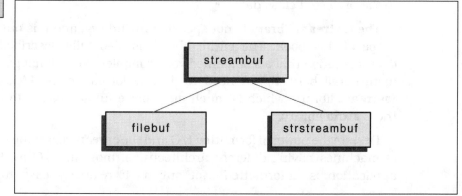

that they format themselves for output or initialize themselves from input. For example, the **Complex** class from Chapter 7 could format itself to write the real and imaginary parts between parentheses:

```
#ifndef COMPLEX_INC
#define COMPLEX_INC

// A (simple!) complex number class
class Complex {
public:
  // construct a default complex number
  Complex(){real=0.0; imaginary=0.0;};
  // construct a specific complex number
  Complex(float r, float i){real=r; imaginary=i;};

friend ostream& operator<< (ostream& ostr, Complex& cplx);
protected:
  // the components of the number
  float real;
  float imaginary;
};

// define the ostream << operator for Complex
ostream& operator<< (ostream& ostr, Complex& cplx)
{
  ostr << "(" << cplx.real << "," << cplx.imaginary << ")";
  return ostr;
}

#endif  //COMPLEX_INC
```

The operator outputs the class data items interspersed with text. The **<<** operator needs to be declared as a friend, so that it can have access to the protected class data.

The **iostream** library is not specific to Windows, and it is outside the scope of this book. The entire library is also fully described in the documentation that accompanied your compiler, so I will not go into any more detail here. If you need to do any formatted file I/O, use the **iostream** library, which is much more powerful and easier to use that the C **stdio** library.

Despite the power of formatted I/O and the caveats regarding networks of machines having different architectures, most file I/O in Windows application is unformatted. Not only is it relatively easy to load a structure, or an array of structures, directly from a file, but there are also many existing unformatted files from other applications that must be read as they are.

If the **iostream** library can handle formatted I/O, all that is needed for now is a class that handles unbuffered file I/O.

Usually, the file reads from, or writes to, some data that has been allocated by an instance of the **Memory** class. The read and write functions should accept an instance of **Memory** as an alternative to a pointer to a buffer. This can be done by overloading the functions.

Implementation

The **File** class provides the main facilities of opening and closing files, and reading and writing to files. It also adds the functions to position within the file, and to return its path and size. The following example defines the **File** class:

file.hpp

```
#ifndef FILE_INC
#define FILE_INC

#include "winobj.hpp"
#include "memory.hpp"

class File : public WinObj{
protected:
  WORD Flags;
  OFSTRUCT OfStruct;
  DWORD FileSize;
  DWORD SeekPos;
  BOOL bOpened;

public:
  File(                        // Opens a file
    LPSTR pPath,
    WORD Style=OF_READ);

  virtual DWORD Read(          // Reads file to a
    Memory * pMem,             // Memory instance
    DWORD Size);
```

```
virtual DWORD Read(          // reads file to a
   LPSTR pBuffer,            // buffer
   DWORD Size);

virtual DWORD Write(         // Writes a Memory
   Memory * pMem,            // instance to a file
   DWORD Size);

virtual DWORD Write(         // Writes a buffer
   LPSTR pBuffer,
   DWORD Size);

File& operator=(File& File2); // Copies a file

DWORD Size();                // returns file size

LPSTR Path();                // returns file path

void Seek(                   // Seeks a file relative
   DWORD Pos)                // to start
   {SeekPos=Pos;};

DWORD Tell()                 // returns seek position
   {return SeekPos;};
}; // class File

#endif // FILE_INC
```

The **File** class defines the main file operations of reading and writing. **Seek** sets the pointer within the file, and **Tell** returns the current position. Both **Seek** and **Tell** use a position relative to the beginning of the file. One option is to allow relative positioning as well:

file.cpp

```
#include "file.hpp"

extern "C" {
#include <io.h>
#include <sys\types.h>
#include <sys\stat.h>
#include <string.h>
#include <dos.h>
}
```

The **File** class uses functions from the standard C library, and the prototypes are enclosed in an **extern "C"** statement to ensure that calls to these functions will be compiled with the C calling convention instead of the C++ convention.

The constructor attempts to open the file using the API function **OpenFile**:

```
File::File(LPSTR pPath, WORD Style)
{
  struct stat FStatus;
  int Fhnd;
  WORD oStyle=Style;
  if (oStyle==OF_EXIST) oStyle=OF_READ;
  Fhnd=OpenFile((LPSTR)pPath, (LPOFSTRUCT)&OfStruct, oStyle);
  if (Fhnd==-1) {
    if(Style==OF_READ)
      Error(IDS_CANTREAD,(LPSTR)OfStruct.szPathName);
    else if(Style==OF_CREATE)
      Error(IDS_CANTCREATE,(LPSTR)OfStruct.szPathName);
    else if(Style==OF_WRITE)
      Error(IDS_CANTWRITE,(LPSTR)OfStruct.szPathName);
    else if(Style==OF_READWRITE)
      Error(IDS_CANTOPEN,(LPSTR)OfStruct.szPathName);
    FileSize=0;
    bOpened=FALSE;
  }
  else {
    FileSize=_llseek(Fhnd,0,2);    // seek to end
    _llseek(Fhnd,0,0);;            // seek back to start
    close(Fhnd);
    bOpened=TRUE;
  }
  SeekPos=0;
}
```

If the file cannot be opened, it generates an appropriate error message. It sets the flag **bOpened** if the file can be opened without error. It only opens the file to test whether it is possible to open it, and to discover the size of the file. After having opened the file, the constructor closes it again, since files must not be left open.

When writing to a file, you should usually use the **OF_CREATE** style. This style creates the file if it does not exist, and truncates it to zero length if it does exist. The **OF_WRITE** style causes the constructor to issue an error message if the file does not exist. If the file does exist, it will not be truncated. **OF_WRITE** is used for writing into existing files, perhaps to update individual records in a data file.

```
LPSTR File::Path()
{
  return (LPSTR)OfStruct.szPathName;
}
```

The member function **Path** is useful since it returns the complete file specification, including the drive. The parameter supplied to the constructor may have been an incomplete specification, such as a file in the current directory, for example. The **OpenFile** function initializes **Ofstruct** when it opens the file.

Read is an overloaded member function that accepts either a pointer to an instance of **Memory,** or a pointer to a buffer:

```
DWORD File::Read(Memory * pMem, DWORD Size)
{
  Lock MemLock(pMem);
  return Read((LPSTR)MemLock.Buffer,Size);
}

DWORD File::Read(LPSTR pBuffer, DWORD Size)
{
  int Fhnd;
  DWORD Result=0;
  if (!FileSize|| !pBuffer || !bOpened) return 0;
  Fhnd=OpenFile("",
      (LPOFSTRUCT)&OfStruct, OF_READ |OF_REOPEN);
  if (Fhnd==-1)
    Error(IDS_CANTREAD,(LPSTR)OfStruct.szPathName);
  else {
    if(_llseek(Fhnd,SeekPos,0)==-1) return 0;
    Result=_lread(Fhnd,pBuffer,Size);
    close(Fhnd);
  }
  SeekPos +=Result;
  return Result;
}
```

If the parameters are invalid, or if the file cannot be opened in the constructor, **Read** does nothing. Otherwise it opens the file, resets the pointer, reads the data, and closes the file again. The **File** class uses the API functions **_lread, _llseek,** and **_lwrite** to perform the I/O.

The read operation may still fail, even if the file had been successfully opened in the constructor. Another application may have deleted the file in the meantime, or another user on a network may be writing to it. In that case, the member function displays an error message.

The **Write** member function is similar to the **Read** member function:

```
DWORD File::Write(Memory * pMem, DWORD Size)
{
  Lock MemLock(pMem);
  return Write((LPSTR)MemLock.Buffer,Size);
}


DWORD File::Write(LPSTR pBuffer, DWORD Size)
{
  int Fhnd;
  DWORD Result=0;
  if (!Size || !pBuffer || !bOpened) return 0;
  Fhnd=OpenFile("",
        (LPOFSTRUCT)&OfStruct, OF_WRITE |OF_REOPEN);
  if (Fhnd==-1)
    Error(IDS_CANTWRITE,(LPSTR)OfStruct.szPathName);
  else {
    if(_llseek(Fhnd,SeekPos,0)==-1) return 0;
    Result=_lwrite(Fhnd,pBuffer,Size);
    close(Fhnd);
  }
  SeekPos +=Result;
  if (SeekPos>FileSize) FileSize=SeekPos;
  return Result;
}
```

Next, the assignment operator **=** is redefined to copy the contents of files:

```
File& File::operator=(File& File2)
{
  DWORD BufSize=GlobalCompact(0);
  if (BufSize>0x4000) BufSize=0x4000;
  GlobalMem Mem(BufSize);
  DWORD BytesRead=1;
  while (BytesRead) {
    BytesRead=File2.Read(&Mem,BufSize);
    BytesRead=Write(&Mem,BytesRead);
  }
```

```
    return File2;
}
```

When copying files, it is helpful to use a large buffer, but there may be insufficient memory. The API function **GlobalCompact(0)** returns the amount of memory that can be found by compacting global memory and discarding discardable blocks. If the parameter is zero, the function only reports how much memory can be made available; it does not actually discard anything. Using all of the memory is unnecessary, so the member function limits the buffer to around 16K.

Finally, the member function **Size** returns the size that the file was when it was last opened:

```
DWORD File::Size()
{
    return FileSize;
}
```

The value returned by **Size** should be considered an indication; other users may change the size of a file during the existence of an instance of the **File** class.

Using the File Class

When reading and writing to a file using the **File** class, stop the operations whenever the **Read** or **Write** member functions return zero. Here is an example that reads a file into a block of global memory:

```
File MyFile("MYFILE.TXT");
GlobalMem Buffer(MyFile.Size()+1);
if (!MyFile.Read(Buffer, MyFile.Size())) {
    // Error
}
```

The sample MDI program in Chapter 10 provides an example of the **File** class.

An application will not normally need to derive from the **File** class, but there are two possibilities for deriving from **File**. These are a class that supports the Lempel-Ziv data compression algorithm, and a class that supports multimedia file I/O.

The Data Compression File I/O Functions

Microsoft provides a number of functions for reading files that have been compressed using the Lempel-Ziv data compression algorithm. The functions reside in a Dynamic Link Library (DLL) called LZEXPAND.DLL, which is distributed with Windows version 3.1. Windows version 3.0 users can also run applications that use these routines, provided that they copy LZEXPAND.DLL to the Windows directory. If your application uses the library, you may distribute it to Windows version 3.0 users.

The functions provided in the API only open, close, and read compressed files. The functions will not write to a compressed file. To create the file, you must run the Microsoft COMPRESS utility, included with the SDK. Compressed files are useful for applications that have a large amount of read-only data, and they are especially useful for installation programs where the application data is packed on diskettes.

To create a class that reads compressed files, you only need do the following:

☐   Include the header file LZEXPAND.H.

☐   Replace the call to **OpenFile** with a call to **LZOpenFile**.

☐   Replace the call to **close** with a call to **LZClose**.

☐   Replace the call to **_lread** with a call to **LZRead**.

☐   Replace the call to **_llseek** with a call to **LZSeek**.

These functions work on a virtual expanded image of the file, so if you ask to read 100 bytes, the **LZRead** function returns 100 uncompressed bytes. Similarly, if you seek to position 1000 bytes in the file, the **LZSeek** function positions the file pointer at a position corresponding to 1000 bytes on the uncompressed image. If the file is not compressed at all, these functions work as normal file I/O routines.

There are some extra API functions that are useful with compressed files. The **GetExpandedName** function returns the original expanded name of the compressed file, and takes two parameters. The first parameter points to the name of the compressed file, and the second points to a buffer that is to contain the expanded name.

For uncompressing entire files, use the **LZCopy** function. This function copies a compressed file to the destination file, uncompressing it as it does so. An application that wants to uncompress several files can use **LZCopy** for each file, but it is quicker to use the **CopyLZFile** function. To use this function, first call **LZStart** to allocate the buffers, call **CopyLZFile** for each file, and then call **LZDone** to deallocate the buffers.

The Multimedia File I/O Services

Microsoft also provides a comprehensive set of facilities for writing multimedia applications. There are functions for playing waveform and MIDI sound files, functions for getting input from a joystick, and many other functions useful to developers of multimedia applications.

Included in the multimedia services are a set of basic file I/O functions. While these functions are useful to multimedia applications, they are also useful to developers of applications that do not claim to be multimedia (monomedia applications!). The multimedia file I/O functions provide two advantages to monomedia developers over the conventional file I/O routines:

☐ They read and write more than 64K using huge pointers.

☐ They can use an intermediate buffer.

Other facilities are applicable to multimedia files, but these two are useful in many general applications.

The ability to read and write more than 64K is an obvious advantage for applications that cannot control the size of objects in a file. An intermediate buffer is also useful for applications that read and write small blocks of data from the file. Although SmartDrive buffers disk access so that the application does not actually go to the disk every time it needs some data, the application is still be quicker if it keeps a local buffer and avoids going through SmartDrive. In addition, SmartDrive does not work with the floppy or CD-ROM drives.

To use the multimedia routines, do the following:

☐   Include the header file MMSYSTEM.H.

☐   Replace the call to **OpenFile** with a call to **mmioOpen.**

☐   Replace the call to **close** with a call to **mmioClose.**

☐   Replace the call to **_lread** with a call to **mmioRead.**

☐   Replace the call to **_lwrite** with a call to **mmioWrite**.

☐   Replace the call to **_llseek** with a call to **mmioSeek.**

The **mmioOpen** function takes three parameters: the filename, a pointer to an information block, and some flags. The pointer to the information block should be **NULL** for basic I/O. The flags can be a combination of the following:

MMIO_READ	Opens a file for reading.
MMIO_WRITE	Opens a file for writing.
MMIO_READWRITE	Opens a file for both reading and writing.
MMIO_CREATE	Creates a file or truncates it to zero length.
MMIO_DELETE	Deletes a file.
MMIO_ALLOCBUF	Allocates an 8K buffer for use with the file.
MMIO_EXIST	Checks whether the file exists. Returns TRUE if it does.

The other functions are similar to their general Windows counterparts, except that **mmioRead** and **mmioWrite** take a **huge** pointer instead of a **far** pointer.

This discussion on unformatted file I/O is digressing from object-oriented C++ programming, so let us take another last look at the **iostream** library.

Using the Iostream Classes for Screen Output

The **iostream** library is undeniably useful for formatted text file I/O, but on its own it does not provide any Windows screen I/O. The library does support console I/O, assuming that an application has just one window that serves as a "glass Teletype," where output is written to the bottom and scrolls off the top. Windows applications usually have more sophisticated user interfaces than that, but occasionally the need arises for an application that just displays some output in a window as if that window were a glass Teletype machine.

This can be done by writing to a memory block and then displaying that block in a window. Edit controls are very suitable for this. Here is a short program that uses iostream to display some text:

streams.cpp

```
#include "about.hpp"
#include "editwin.hpp"
#include <strstrea.h>

class SimpleBox : public About{

public:
void InitDialog();
};
```

The **SimpleBox** class displays a simple dialog box, similar to an **About** box. **WinMain** displays the box and returns when the user closes the box:

```
HANDLE hInst;

int PASCAL WinMain(HANDLE hInstance, HANDLE hPrevInstance,
   LPSTR lpszCmdLine, int nCmdShow)
{
    hInst=hInstance;
    SimpleBox aBox;
    aBox.OpenBox(NULL,"Streams");
    return 0;
}
```

The initialized box copies some text into an edit control. To do this, it creates an instance of **ostrstream**.

```
void SimpleBox::InitDialog()
{
  About::InitDialog();
  char * pBuf = new char[200];
  ostrstream EditBuf(pBuf,200);
  EditBuf << "Here is some text\r\n";
  EditBuf << 3.2 << " times " << 2 <<" is " << 3.2*2 << "\r\n";
```

```
EditBuf << 255 << " in hex is 0x" << hex << 255 << dec;
SetDlgItemText(hWnd,100,pBuf);
}
```

Ostrstream is a class which is derived from **ostream**, but which writes to a memory buffer instead of to a file. **SimpleBox** provides a buffer when it creates **EditBuf,** the instance of **ostrstream.** Having done so, it can output to **EditBuf** using the **ostream** operators as if **EditBuf** were a file. When **SimpleBox** has written the buffer, it sends the buffer to the edit control with **SetDlgItemText**, as shown in Figure 8-3.

Summary

Paradoxically, the powerful object-oriented **iostream** class library for formatted text is not as useful under Windows as it is for designing simple DOS applications. Windows applications tend to make their data visible in a more graphical manner than files or windows filled with plain text, and so they have less need for the **iostream** library. Not only that, but Windows applications frequently write their data structures directly to files as unformatted binary data, in which case the facilities are not object-oriented at all. The **File** class described in this chapter simplifies unformatted file I/O as much as possible. If you need formatted I/O, either to files or to Windows controls, the standard **iostream** library is the perfect C++ solution.

Streaming to an edit control

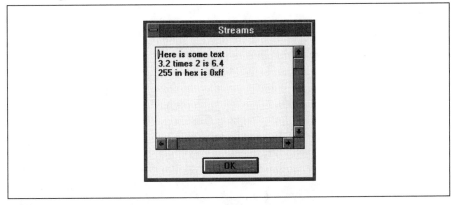

CHAPTER

The Clipboard

A ll Windows users are familiar with the clipboard. We all cut and paste data with our favorite word processor or spreadsheet. If you are developing a new word processor or editor of any sort, you are probably thinking of adding clipboard support. On the other hand, if you are developing some other application, you may think that you can dispense with the clipboard. That might be a pity. Users may wish to be able to copy data from your application and paste it into another, or they may wish to cut and paste within your application in ways that you thought unnecessary.

If you have developed an application for dentists, for example, there probably is a dialog box or a form where the dentist can enter information about a new patient. It may be that records for new patients have details in common with those for existing patients. Perhaps whole families register when they move to the area. In that case, the dentist might like to copy details about an existing patient into the form for a new patient. It would be helpful if the application offered at least limited clipboard support.

An easy way to provide clipboard support is to use an edit control. Edit controls have clipboard support built in. If you have a database application that retrieves and displays a lot of text when a user makes a query, you can simply send the text to an edit control so that the user can cut parts of the text and paste it into another application. You still must implement an *Edit* menu, but when the user chooses an edit menu item, you only need to send a **WM_CUT, WM_COPY**, or **WM_PASTE** message to the control, and it does the rest. Chapter 10, on the Multiple Document Interface (MDI), describes an extended edit control class that implements clipboard support.

If your application generates much numerical data, you should at least make the data available to the clipboard in text format as a string of numbers separated by TAB characters. That lets users paste the data into a spreadsheet and analyze it further, or perhaps make a chart of the data. You might also support a spreadsheet format such as Data Interchange Format (DIF), or formatted text. If your application generates images, you should support bitmaps or the Tag Image File Format (TIFF). Word processors ought to support the Rich Text Format (RTF).

In many applications, such as the hypothetical dentist's application, users frequently cut and paste within the application, but rarely to or from other applications. In that case, you can define your own special clipboard format. You could have a **CF_PATIENT** format where each item of data is tagged with the name of the field. It would then be a simple matter to paste the information into a new record. If someone ever wants to paste the data into another application, you can convert it into a simple text format, perhaps with each record item on a separate line of text.

As you may have guessed by now, this chapter is going to introduce a **Clipboard** class that makes using the clipboard a simple affair. If there is a difficulty, it is in converting the application data into different formats. In the end, of course, you must do that anyway. Under DOS, applications tend to be large integrated systems that do a little bit of everything. With Windows, and most other operating systems for that matter, applications are more specific and off-load functions to other applications where possible.

Suppose your application for dentists can automatically generate letters to order more amalgam. It would be more useful if it simply invoked the user's favorite Windows word processor, rather than offering a crude word-processing facility itself. A hypothetical accounting package would be more useful if it could export data in spreadsheet formats than if it offered a couple of built-in financial functions.

If you write a conversion routine for your data, you can use the same routine to write files in another format, to support Dynamic Data Exchange (DDE) and to support the clipboard. In that case it will not be too difficult to support the clipboard in addition to DDE and files.

Design Issues

Placing data in the clipboard is not very difficult. You simply supply a block of global memory containing the data, and specify which format it is in. You can choose from several predefined formats, or you can invent your own. To retrieve data, you ask for any data in a specified format. There are no problems implementing a class that supports cutting and pasting of data in a certain format.

If your application supports several different formats, as it probably should, you can convert the data to all the different formats and paste them all into the clipboard. If any other application needs one of these formats, it will be available. Of course, that would be a terrible waste of time and memory, since it is unlikely that more than one format will ever be used. The format that will be used most often will be your own private format, which did not need converting in any case.

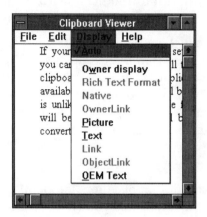

Windows offers a solution. You can put **NULL** blocks of memory of a specified format into the clipboard. If an application ever decides to retrieve this data, Windows sends the original owner of the data a message, **WM_RENDERFORMAT**, specifying the required format. The owner should then render the data in the required format and put it in the clipboard. If the owner is being destroyed and unrendered formats still remain in the clipboard, Windows sends a **WM_RENDERALLFORMATS** message to the owner before destroying it, so that it can convert all unrendered formats while it has a chance.

Does this mean that it's necessary to add **RenderFormat** and **RenderAllFormats** member functions to the **Window** class and redefine them in the application's main window? That would be a nuisance, which can be avoided by making the **Clipboard** class a descendant of the **Window** class. The **Clipboard** class can then intercept all clipboard-specific messages and call related member functions. An instance of **Clipboard** creates an invisible window, specifically to receive clipboard messages. An application defines a subclass of **Clipboard** to render formats on request.

Clipboard Viewers

It is possible to write a clipboard viewer for application-specific data. Many applications do not have such a viewer, because users do not often look at the clipboard. You can avoid writing a clipboard viewer if your application supports some displayable format, such as plain text (the **CF_TEXT** clipboard format). The clipboard displays that instead of the private format. In addition, you can support a special display clipboard format, such as **CF_DSPTEXT**, which the clipboard will display instead of the plain **CF_TEXT** format. If you support a display format, you can add extra information that might not be appropriate if the data were pasted into another application, such as commentary or labels. The Microsoft Write application supports a clipboard viewer (Figure 9.1) that displays the clipboard text as it would appear in a document, with the correct font and formatting.

If you wish to support the Microsoft Object Linking and Embedding (OLE) standard and you make your application an OLE server, applications other than Clipboard can ask your application to display your data in another display context. Consider structuring your application so that

The Write Clipboard Viewer

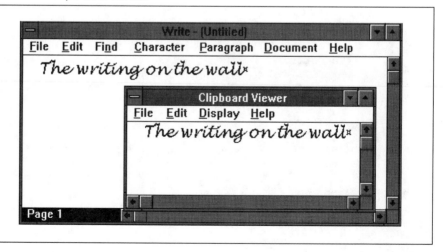

it can display data in any context, not just the application's main window. If you can display your data in any window or display context, it will not be difficult to add a clipboard viewer, since the viewer is just another display context.

The only design issue here concerns the clipboard viewer scroll bars. A class derived from **Clipboard** would like to define instances of **ScrollBar** that act on the clipboard viewer window scroll bars. The subclass cannot do this directly, since the Clipboard application window is not in the class system and does not support the **ScrollBar** class. The **Clipboard** class represents an application's clipboard data, and not the Windows clipboard viewer itself.

Instead, the subclass defines **ScrollBar** instances for its own invisible window, and the **Clipboard** class maps these instances onto the scroll bars in the Clipboard application. The **Clipboard** class tries to make its own invisible window act as the clipboard viewer.

Implementation

The **Clipboard** class described here will support format rendering and clipboard viewers. Format rendering is the real reason for using the **Clipboard** class; the clipboard viewer is more of a curiosity.

clipbrd.hpp

```
#ifndef CLIPBOARD_INC
#define CLIPBOARD_INC

#include "window.hpp"
#include "memory.hpp"

class Clipboard : public Window {
public:
  static Clipboard * Instance;    // Pointer to
                                  // current clipboard
  Clipboard(
    HWND PhWnd);                  // Parent window handle

  ~Clipboard();

  virtual void Put(              // Put data in clipboard
    GlobalMem * pData,           // The data
    WORD Format=CF_TEXT,         // Its format
```

```
      BOOL bEmpty=TRUE);           // Empty clipboard first

   virtual GlobalMem * Get(        // Returns contents of
   WORD Format=CF_TEXT);           // clipboard in specified
                                   // format

   virtual BOOL Available(         // Returns TRUE if specified
      WORD Format=CF_TEXT);        // format is available
```

Clipboard defines **public** member functions to put data into the clipboard in a certain format, to get data in a certain format, and to check whether data is available in the clipboard. The **Put** member function has an extra parameter **bEmpty** that specifies whether the clipboard should first be emptied. If you are putting new data into the clipboard, empty it first. If you are simply adding an alternative format, do not empty the clipboard.

Both **Put** and **Get** specify **GlobalMem** memory instances explicitly. The clipboard does not accept local memory.

```
protected:
   GlobalMem * LastData;
   LONG MessageProc(HWND hWnd, unsigned msg, Event& evt);
   LPSTR Register(WNDCLASS& wc);
   virtual void RenderFormat(     // Render data in the
      WORD Format){};             // format requested

   virtual void RenderAllFormats(){};
   virtual void ClipboardEmptied(){};
   virtual void PaintClipboard(   // Paint the clipboard
      HWND hWnd,                  // viewer window
      PAINTSTRUCT FAR * pPs){};

   virtual void SizeClipboard(    // The size of the clipboard
      HWND hWnd,                  // viewer has changed
      RECT FAR * pRC){};

   virtual LPSTR AskCBFormatName(){return "";};

}; // class Clipboard

#endif // CLIPBOARD_INC
```

The virtual member functions correspond to the format rendering messages and the messages for the clipboard viewer.

```
#include "clipbrd.hpp"
#include "control.hpp"

Clipboard * Clipboard::Instance=NULL;

Clipboard::Clipboard(HWND PhWnd)
{
  Create("",WS_CHILD,0,0,0,0,PhWnd,NULL); //invisible window
  Instance=this;
  LastData=NULL;
}
```

The constructor creates an invisible window simply by omitting the **WS_VISIBLE** style. The class contains a static item **Instance** that other classes can use to get a pointer to the application **Clipboard** instance. The syntax

Clipboard::Instance

is a pointer to the last **Clipboard** instance created.

```
Clipboard::~Clipboard()
{
  Instance=NULL;
  if (LastData){
    LastData->Handle=NULL;
    delete LastData;
  }
  if (HorzScrollBar) HorzScrollBar->hWnd=hWnd;
  if (VertScrollBar) VertScrollBar->hWnd=hWnd;
}
```

Clipboard keeps a pointer to the last **Memory** instance stored, since this is the memory block that will be rendered if necessary. When the **Clipboard** instance is destroyed, this **Memory** instance is also deleted. However, when an instance of **Memory** is deleted, its destructor frees the associated memory block. In this case, the block must not be freed, since the Windows clipboard now owns the memory. To prevent the memory from being freed, the destructor sets the memory handle to **NULL.**

Any window scroll bars that exist have probably been remapped onto the Clipboard application scroll bars by changing the value in their **hWnd** item. The destructor must reset the value of **hWnd** before destroying the **ScrollBar** instances.

```
LPSTR Clipboard::Register(WNDCLASS& wc)
{
  wc.style=0;
  wc.lpszClassName="ClipboardClass";
  RegisterClass(&wc);
  return "ClipboardClass";
}
```

Since the window is invisible, the **Register** member function only has to specify the name. The other items—the window menu, the default background color, and the icon—do not have any significance in an invisible window.

```
void Clipboard::Put(GlobalMem * Data,WORD Format, BOOL bEmpty)
{
  BOOL bOpened=OpenClipboard(hWnd);
  if (bOpened && bEmpty) EmptyClipboard();
  SetClipboardData(Format,Data?Data->Handle:NULL);
  if (Data) {
    if (bEmpty) {
      if (LastData){
        LastData->Handle=NULL;
        delete LastData;
      }
      LastData=Data;
    }
    else {
      Data->Handle=NULL;
      delete Data;
    }
  }
  if (bOpened) CloseClipboard();
}
```

The **Put** member function sends the data to the clipboard. If **BEmpty** is **TRUE,** indicating that the clipboard should first be emptied, **Clipboard** considers the new data to be the primary format that will be rendered to other formats on request. The **Memory** instance for the primary format is saved in **LastData.**

If **Put** cannot open the clipboard, another application has probably opened it and is trying to extract data that needs rendering by this application. If **Put** cannot open the clipboard, it allows data to be added to the clipboard. **Put** does not allow the clipboard to be emptied if another application has opened it.

Put acts as a sink for the **Memory** instances, so an application must not free any memory that it has passed to **Put.**

```
GlobalMem * Clipboard::Get(WORD Format)
{
  HANDLE hRes=NULL;

  if (OpenClipboard(hWnd)) {
    hRes=GetClipboardData(Format);
    CloseClipboard();
  }
  GlobalMem * pMem=new GlobalMem(0);
  if (hRes) pMem->SetHandle(hRes,FALSE);
  return pMem;
}
```

The **Get** member function retrieves data from the clipboard and wraps it up in a **GlobalMem** instance. To do that, **Get** creates an instance of **GlobalMem** of zero size. That prevents the **GlobalMem** constructor from actually allocating any memory. **Get** can then replace the instance handle with the handle that the clipboard returns. All clipboard data belongs to the clipboard, and neither the application that sets the data nor the application that gets it may delete the memory block. **SetHandle** specifies **FALSE** to indicate that this is public data and the **GlobalMem** destructor must not free it. **Get** is a source of **GlobalMem** instances and the application should delete them after use.

```
BOOL Clipboard::Available(WORD Format)
{
  BOOL Result=FALSE;
  if (OpenClipboard(hWnd)) {
    if (Format==CF_TEXT || Format==CF_OEMTEXT)
      Result=( IsClipboardFormatAvailable(CF_TEXT)
          || IsClipboardFormatAvailable(CF_OEMTEXT));
    else Result=IsClipboardFormatAvailable(Format);
    CloseClipboard();
  }
  return Result;
}
```

Available checks whether a specified format is present in the clipboard, without actually retrieving the format. The clipboard automatically converts between **CF_TEXT** format and the **CF_OEMTEXT** format, so if either format is present, and if either format is requested, **Available**

Working with 32 Bits

Windows NT supports Unicode as well as the DOS character set and the Windows ANSI character set. Unicode is the 16-bit character set that supports virtually all characters that exist. The 8-bit ANSI character set is not yet obsolete, so applications can choose whether to use ANSI or Unicode. Windows NT provides an extra clipboard format for text, called **CF_UNICODETEXT**. As with **CF_OEMTEXT,** Windows NT automatically converts all three text formats as far as possible.

Similarly, Windows NT supports enhanced metafiles. A metafile is a recording of Graphics Device Interface (GDI) operations that can be played back into a device context. A metafile is a compact way to represent diagrams and figures made up of many separate GDI operations. An enhanced metafile supports the extra Windows NT facilities. Most importantly, an enhanced metafile is truly device-independent. Windows NT applications should use enhanced metafiles, but some applications may wish to use ordinary metafiles to maintain compatibility with Windows version 3.1. The format for enhanced metafiles is **CF_ENHMETAFILE**. As with text, the clipboard automatically converts graphics between the two formats.

---

returns **TRUE. CF_OEMTEXT** is text using the DOS character set instead of the Windows ANSI character set. Windows applications do not use the DOS character set very much, but **CF_OEMTEXT** data will be in the clipboard if the user has selected some text in a DOS application window.

MessageProc translates clipboard window messages into event member functions. It passes any other messages on to the **MessageProc** in the **Window** class.

```
LONG Clipboard::MessageProc(HWND hWnd, unsigned msg, Event& evt)
{
  switch (msg) {
  case WM_RENDERFORMAT:
```

```
      RenderFormat(evt.wParam);
      break;

    case WM_RENDERALLFORMATS:
      RenderAllFormats();
      break;

    case WM_DESTROYCLIPBOARD:
      ClipboardEmptied();
      break;

    case WM_PAINTCLIPBOARD:
    {
      PAINTSTRUCT FAR * Ps =
        (PAINTSTRUCT FAR *)GlobalLock((HGLOBAL)evt.lParam);
      PaintClipboard((HWND)evt.wParam, Ps);
      GlobalUnlock((HGLOBAL)evt.lParam);
      break;
    }
```

The **WM_PAINTCLIPBOARD** message is different from the normal **WM_PAINT** message. The **wParam** contains the handle of the window in the Clipboard application and **lParam** contains a handle to a block of global memory containing the **PAINTSTRUCT** data. This is the same structure that the ordinary **WM_PAINT** message uses. The class must lock this block to obtain the memory address, and release it after use.

```
    case WM_SIZECLIPBOARD:
    {
      if (VertScrollBar) VertScrollBar->hWnd=(HWND)evt.wParam;
      if (HorzScrollBar) HorzScrollBar->hWnd=(HWND)evt.wParam;
      RECT FAR * pRC =
        (RECT FAR *)GlobalLock((HGLOBAL)evt.lParam);
      SizeClipboard((HWND)evt.wParam, pRC);
      GlobalUnlock((HGLOBAL)evt.lParam);
      break;
    }
```

Windows always sends a **WM_SIZECLIPBOARD** message before any **WM_PAINTCLIPBOARD** messages. Here again the **lParam** contains a memory handle that the class must lock to find the address of the **RECT** data. **Clipboard** remaps the **ScrollBar** instances onto the Clipboard application scroll bars by changing the **hWnd** items of the two instances. When the user moves the scrollbars in the Clipboard viewer application, the **ScrollBar** instances in the **Clipboard** class instance will be notified.

```
case WM_VSCROLLCLIPBOARD:
  if (VertScrollBar)
      ((Control *)VertScrollBar)->CodeHandler
      (LOWORD(evt.lParam),HIWORD(evt.lParam));
  break;

case WM_HSCROLLCLIPBOARD:
  if (HorzScrollBar)
      ((Control *)HorzScrollBar)->CodeHandler
      (LOWORD(evt.lParam),HIWORD(evt.lParam));
  break;
```

The clipboard scroll messages are also different from the normal **WM_VSCROLL** and **WM_HSCROLL** messages. The event type is now in the low-order word of **lParam** and the thumb position is in the high-order word.

```
case WM_ASKCBFORMATNAME:
  LPSTR pStr=AskCBFormatName();
  LPSTR pClip=(LPSTR)evt.lParam;
  while (evt.wParam- && *pStr) *pClip++=*pStr++;
  *pClip=0;
  break;
```

The **AskCBFormatName** member function simply returns a pointer to a string. **Clipboard** must copy this string into the data area pointed to by **lParam.** The **wParam** parameter specifies the maximum number of characters to copy.

```
default:
  return Window::MessageProc(hWnd,msg,evt);
}
return TRUE;
}
```

Clipboard passes the other messages back up to the message handler in the **Window** class.

Using the Clipboard Class

The **Clipboard** class, as it stands, will support text in CF_TEXT format; this is the most common format. Unless your application is relatively trivial, you will need to derive a subclass of **Clipboard** to support the additional clipboard formats, and perhaps to support a clipboard viewer.

In your application, you should add an *Edit* menu containing items for the clipboard operations. A standard *Edit* menu contains these items in this order:

, <u>U</u>ndo (last operation)
. <u>R</u>epeat (last operation
. Cu<u>t</u> (to clipboard)
. <u>C</u>opy (to clipboard)
. <u>P</u>aste (from clipboard)
. <u>D</u>elete (selection, leaving the clipboard intact)

The underlined letters indicate the menu accelerator keys. If your application does not support *Undo* or *Repeat*, you can omit those items. Your application should disable the *Cut, Copy*, and *Delete* options when nothing is selected, and it should disable the *Paste* item when the clipboard does not contain suitable data. In Chapter 10 is a section that explains how to implement an *Edit* menu and how to disable items using the **InitMenu** member function in the **Window** class.

You should also define accelerator keys for the menu items, so that users can perform operations without having to pull down a menu. In the past, Microsoft has always insisted that applications conform to the IBM Common User Access (CUA) recommendations. To help program-mers comply with this requirement, Microsoft included a copy of the IBM CUA document with the Windows 3.0 SDK. The CUA recommends:

❏   ALT-BACKSPACE for Undo

❏   SHIFT-DELETE for Cut

❏   CTRL-INSERT for Copy

❏   SHIFT-INSERT for Paste

Microsoft has recently stopped recommending the IBM CUA, and new versions of Microsoft applications use a different set of accelerators. These are:

☐   CTRL-Z for Undo

☐   CTRL-X for Cut

☐   CTRL-C for Copy

☐   CTRL-V for Paste

In fact, the Microsoft applications still respond to the IBM CUA accelerators, but the Microsoft accelerators are the ones that are described in the documents. It is true that the new accelerators are slightly easier to use than the IBM accelerators, but it is a pity that the interface standards change with the wind in this fashion. For the moment, we will need to support both sets of accelerators in our applications.

Your first step should be deciding which clipboard formats your application will support.

Formats Available

The following formats are predefined for use with the clipboard:

CF_TEXT	ANSI text
CF_OEMTEXT	Text in the OEM character set (usually the PC DOS character set)
CF_METAFILEPICT	A metafile picture structure
CF_BITMAP	A device-dependent bitmap
CF_DIB	A device-independent bitmap
CF_SYLK	Data in the Microsoft Symbolic Link (SYLK) data exchange format
CF_DIF	Data in the Lotus DIF format
CF_TIFF	An image in TIFF format
CF_DSPTEXT	Text suitable for displaying in the clipboard viewer

CF_DSPBITMAP	A bitmap suitable for displaying in the viewer
CF_DSPMETAFILEPICT	A metafile suitable for displaying in the viewer
CF_OWNERDISPLAY	Data for which the application provides a clipboard viewer

Applications can also register additional, private formats using the API **RegisterClipboardFormat** function. The parameter is the name of a private format, and the function returns a unique format code that the application can then use with the **Put**, **Get**, and **Available** member functions.

Text-Only Applications

If your application only supports the **CF_TEXT** format, there is no need to derive a subclass from **Clipboard,** since you can use the **Clipboard** class directly. Just use **Put** to place data in the clipboard and **Get** to take it out.

Clipboard data is public data and the application must not modify it or free it. Normally, you should copy data into a new instance of **GlobalMem** before calling **Put**, and you should copy the data returned by **Get** and then delete the **GlobalMem** instance. Your code should look something like this:

```
case IDM_COPY:  // Copy chosen from menu
{
  GlobalMem * pClip= new GlobalMem(SelectionSize+1);
  pClip->Load(pData, SelectionSize);
  Clipboard::Instance->Put(pClip);
  break;
}
```

When you allocate the memory for a text string, you must not forget to add an extra byte for the zero character that terminates the string. If you do not have a pointer to the **Clipboard** instance, you can use the **Instance** item in **Clipboard** itself.

```
case IDM_PASTE:  // Paste chosen from menu
{
  GlobalMem * pClip=Clipboard::Instance->Get();
```

```
    Mydata->Load(pClip, Position);
    delete pClip;
    break;
}
```

The data returned by **Get** is also null-terminated. If you are pasting the data into a text, remember not to include the terminator. You cannot use the size of the memory block to determine the length of the string, since the block size will be rounded up to the next 16 bytes. You must use the API function **lstrlen** or copy the string byte by byte until you encounter the **NULL** terminator.

When **pClip** is deleted, only the instance of **GlobalMem** will be deleted. The memory block itself will not be freed, since **Clipboard** has marked it as public data.

Using Multiple Formats

If you want to support multiple formats, you will usually want to place data in the clipboard in the format that your application uses, and render the other formats on request. Usually, your data will be in a private format, so you will have to register that as well.

You should derive a subclass of **Clipboard** to register the format and render the formats when needed. It is usually convenient to have this subclass redefine **Put** and **Get**, so that your application only needs to concern itself with data in the primary format. The redefined **Put** and **Get** can take care of alternative formats.

 Remember   Your application may be able to render its data into many other formats, but it will not necessarily be able to render those formats back into its own data. To take an extreme example, you can render text as a bitmap, but you cannot very easily convert bitmaps back to text.

You must define the **RenderFormat** member function to render the formats on request. The **wParam** item in the **Event** class specifies the format required. The member function must render the primary format data and add the new data to the clipboard using the **Put** member function.

You must also define the **RenderAllFormats** member function. The system calls the member function when the application is being destroyed, and it must render all the formats that you have placed in the clipboard.

An Example of Multiple Formats

The code of a typical class that supports a private format and **CF_TEXT** looks something like this:

```
MyClipboard::MyClipboard(HWND PhWnd):Clipboard(PhWnd)
{
  MyFormat=RegisterClipboardFormat("CF_MYFORMAT");
}
```

The constructor registers the private format.

```
void MyClipboard::Put(GlobalMem * pData, WORD Format)
{
  Clipboard::Put(pData,MyFormat);
  Clipboard::Put(NULL,CF_TEXT,FALSE);
}
```

The redefinition of **Put** ignores the **Format** parameter. It places the private data in the clipboard, destroying the previous clipboard contents. It also places the text format in the clipboard, but without any data, and without emptying it first. That signifies that the application can render the data to the **CF_TEXT** format on request.

```
GlobalMem * MyClipboard::Get(WORD Format)
{
  GlobalMem * pMem;
  if (Available(MyFormat))
    pMem=Clipboard::Get(MyFormat);
  else pMem=new GlobalMem(0);
  return pMem;
}
```

Get tries to retrieve data in the private format, but if there is none, it returns an empty instance. Applications should prevent users from pasting from the clipboard when there is no suitable data, by shading the *Paste* item in the menu. If this application can convert other formats into the private format, it can try asking for those formats, starting with the most suitable, and converting the data when it finds a format.

```
void MyClipboard::RenderFormat(WORD Format)
{
  if (Format==CF_TEXT && LastData){
    GlobalMem* TextMem= new GlobalMem(LastData->Size());
    TextMem->Load(LastData);

    // render the data in TextMem to text

    Clipboard::Put(TextMem,CF_TEXT,FALSE);
  }
}

void MyClipboard::RenderAllFormats()
{
  RenderFormat(CF_TEXT);
}
```

The **RenderFormat** member function renders the data to text and places it in the clipboard. The sample program in Chapter 10 on the MDI uses a subclass of **Clipboard**.

Writing a Viewer for the Windows Clipboard

If you write a clipboard viewer, it is because your data is in a private format that only your application can display accurately. The Windows Clipboard application will then call your viewer to display the data. You should first derive a subclass of **Clipboard** to handle the private format and any other formats that your application can render.

Normally, if the clipboard is open while your application data is in it, it chooses one of the standard formats, such as **CF_DSPTEXT** or **CF_TEXT** and asks your application to render the data in that format. The clipboard then displays the data itself.

If, on the other hand your application adds the **CF_OWNERDISPLAY** format to the clipboard, it ignores the other formats and asks your application to display the data. Your **Clipboard** subclass should redefine the clipboard viewer member functions. Each member function should handle the following areas.

PaintClipboard   The member function should paint the Clipboard application window. The parameters are:

hWnd   The Clipboard application window handle.

pPs   A pointer to a **PAINTSTRUCT** data structure. The structure contains (amongst other things) **hdc**, the display context, and **rcpaint**, the rectangle within the window that needs painting.

SizeClipboard   This member function indicates the size of the Clipboard application window. The viewer needs the size either to set the scroll bar range and position, or to set the image scaling if it uses the GDI **MM_ISOTROPIC** or **MM_ANISOTROPIC** mapping modes. With these two mapping modes, an image can be scaled to fit a window. The parameters are:

hWnd   The Clipboard application window handle.

pRC   A pointer to a **RECT** data structure. The structure contains the size of the window. **pRC–>top** and **pRC–>left** are both zero.

AskCBFormatName   This member function simply returns a pointer to a string containing the format name.

An Example of a Clipboard Viewer

This example extends the multiple formats example to support a clipboard viewer as well.

```
EditClip::EditClip(HWND PhWnd):Clipboard(PhWnd)
{
  MyFormat=RegisterClipboardFormat("CF_MYFORMAT");
  VScroll = new ScrollBar(hWnd,SB_VERT);
  HScroll = new ScrollBar(hWnd,SB_HORZ);
  VScroll->Position(this,
    (SCROLLBARCALLBACK)&EditClip::VScrolled);
}
```

The constructor creates the scroll bars and specifies a callback **VScrolled** for the vertical scroll bar.

```
void EditClip::Put(GlobalMem * pData,
                WORD Format, BOOL bEmpty)
{
  Clipboard::Put(pData,MyFormat);
  Clipboard::Put(NULL,CF_TEXT,FALSE);
  Clipboard::Put(NULL,CF_OWNERDISPLAY,FALSE);
}
```

The **Put** member function adds the extra **CF_OWNERDISPLAY** format that will cause Clipboard to invoke the viewer. The **Get** member function is the same as before.

```
void EditClip::SizeClipboard(HWND hWnd, RECT FAR * pRC)
{
  rClip=*pRC;
  Lock Text(LastData);
  HDC hDC=GetDC(hWnd);
  rClip.bottom=
    DrawText(hDC,Text.Buffer,-1, &rClip,
      DT_EXPANDTABS | DT_LEFT |
      DT_WORDBREAK | DT_NOPREFIX | DT_CALCRECT);
  ReleaseDC(hWnd,hDC);
  HScroll->SetRange(0,0);
  VScroll->SetRange(0,max(0,rClip.bottom-pRC->bottom));
}
```

The viewer will use the API function **DrawText** to format the text so that it is word-wrapped in the Clipboard window. If **DrawText** is called with the **DT_CALCRECT** flag, it does not draw the text, but does return the height of the text. The viewer uses this value to set the lower edge of the **rClip** rectangle. **rClip** has the same width as the Clipboard window, but it has the height of the displayed text, and this height may be more than the height of the window.

The viewer sets the range of the horizontal scroll bar to zero, causing it to disappear. If the height of the text is greater than the height of the window, it sets the range of the vertical scroll bar to the difference in height.

```
void EditClip::VScrolled(ScrollBar& Bar, int Pos)
{
```

```
UpdateWindow(Bar.hWnd);
ScrollWindow(Bar.hWnd,0,-rClip.top-Pos,NULL,NULL);
rClip.top=-Pos;
}
```

When the user moves the vertical scroll bar, the viewer scrolls the contents of the window and offsets the rectangle **rClip** by the value of the scroll bar.

```
void EditClip::PaintClipboard(HWND hWnd,
              PAINTSTRUCT FAR * pPs)
{
  Lock Text(LastData);
  DrawText(pPs->hdc,Text.Buffer,-1, &rClip,
    DT_EXPANDTABS | DT_LEFT |
    DT_WORDBREAK | DT_NOPREFIX);
}
```

The **PaintClipboard** member function needs only to draw the text at the position specified by **rClip**.

```
LPSTR EditClip::AskCBFormatName()
{
  return "MyFormat";
}
```

The **AskCBFormatName** member function returns the name of the format.

This clipboard viewer example is included in the application in Chapter 10 that demonstrates the MDI interface. To do a proper job, the viewer should have defined scroll bar callbacks for **Line** and **Page** as well as **Position**. The **Line** member function would scroll the text by one line, and the **Page** member function would scroll by one line less than a full window.

Summary

Although controls such as the edit control have clipboard support built in, many applications can benefit by supporting private clipboard formats and allowing the user to move complex data within the application.

In addition, it is far more useful to make application data available to other Windows applications than to add extra functions to process the data within the application. Any application that handles data should support a spreadsheet format. If you do not want to use a particular spreadsheet format, you can use formatted text, with TAB characters between fields and new lines between rows. All spreadsheets support formatted text.

Once you have written a conversion function for the data, it is easy to use the **Clipboard** class for supporting multiple clipboard formats. Chapter 11 shows how to use the same routines to support DDE links.

CHAPTER

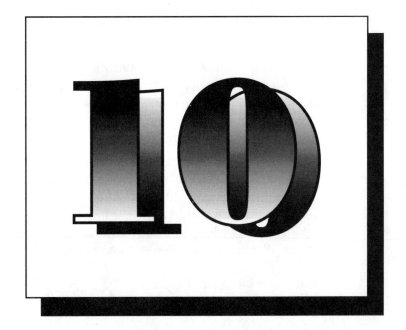

The Multiple Document Interface

337

*T*he Multiple Document Interface (MDI) is a standard way of displaying multiple windows within an application's main window. The windows may contain documents or worksheets; the MDI is useful with almost any type of window. Many major Windows applications, including File Manager and Program Manager, use the MDI. Most applications can benefit from using the MDI, but it is especially useful for applications that display and process files or database records. Users of such applications like being able to browse between files or records without having to open and close them all the time. Some novice users complain about *all these windows cluttering up the screen,* but they warm to the interface when they realize that they can use it with the windows maximized. The *Window* menu or the CTRL-F6 key will switch between windows.

Microsoft has provided MDI facilities in the API since Windows 3.0. The MDI API provides facilities for arranging the windows and icons, scrolling the windows within the application's main window, and adding window names to the *Window* menu. With all these facilities available, it should be simple for an application to make use of them.

Even so, many Windows applications do not use the MDI even though they ought to. Why is that? What is the problem? Before MDI, applications usually had just one main window that displayed some data, perhaps a file. If the user wanted to see another file, the application would discard the first data and read in the new data from the other file.

An application programmed in C would have stored a lot of parameters concerning the window, and perhaps the data itself in ordinary **static** or **extern** data. Even if the application kept the data itself in a memory block, it probably would store the handle to the block in **static** data. The application's code would contain declarations for all the variables that the application would use, perhaps something like this:

```
UINT    WinWidth;
UINT    WinHeight;
HWND    hWnd;
HGLOBAL hMem;
char    FileName[120];
UINT    CursorPos;
BOOL    bFloggleToggle;
UINT    nItems;
```

These items would probably be used throughout the application. The problem here is that **static** data is unique. If the application has multiple windows, it needs multiple copies of all these data items.

If you are programming in C, the solution is to put all this data in a structure and allocate space for it in a memory block. You can then store the handle to the block in a data area associated with the window itself. The API functions **SetWindowWord** and **GetWindowWord** can do this if you allocate storage space when the window class is registered. If you set the **cbWndExtra** item in the **WNDCLASS** to two, Windows reserves two bytes of storage for the application's data. That amount of storage is enough for a memory handle.

Working with 32 Bits

Two bytes is not enough storage for a memory handle in the 32-bit versions of Windows. In these versions, a handle is also 32 bits, so you must use **SetWindowLong** and **GetWindowLong** instead. You must also reserve four bytes instead of two.

Whenever the data is needed, the programmer can retrieve the memory handle and lock it to get its address. The memory block address is cast to a pointer to the new structure, and the data can be accessed, like this:

```
// Retrieve memory from window
pMyData= (MYSTRUCT *)
         LocalLock(GetWindowWord(hCurWin,GWW_MYDATA));
// ...
// Access data via pMyData
if (pMyData->bFloggleToggle) {
  pMyData->CursorPos=pMyData->WinWidth/pMyData->nItems;
//...
```

The application must get the address from the window whenever it processes a message. Simply getting the address when a window becomes active does not work, since non-active windows in the background can also receive messages. Although the problem of needing multiple copies of data has a solution, applications using **static** and **extern** data need rewriting to use a window memory block instead, if they are to support the MDI. This has made many developers decide against MDI support.

C++ makes things much easier. Window-specific items can, indeed should, be declared in a class and accessed by the class member functions. The application only has to declare a new class instance for each new window. Each window then has its own copy of the data. If you are programming in C++, there is little reason not to use the MDI, once you have a set of classes for MDI applications.

Design Issues

MDI applications consist of three elements:

☐   The MDI *Frame* is the main application window. The Frame has a menu bar and a client area.

☐   The MDI *Client* is a plain gray window that will contain the documents. The Client window has automatic scroll bars that appear if the user positions part of a document outside the Client window. The MDI Client is in the Frame client area, but does not necessarily fill it. As Figure 10-1 shows, the Frame client area may also contain button bars, status ribbons, and other facilities that are provided by the application, not by the MDI.

☐   Several MDI *Child* windows. These may all be instances of the same class, but an application can have more than one class of MDI Child window.

The Client is a child of the Frame, and the Children are child windows of the Client. Typically, the children have just a plain client area that displays the data. The Frame may have a status ribbon, a button bar, or some other facility that all the children share. Whenever a Child window becomes active, the application updates the facility to correspond to that particular instance of the Child.

Typically, the Frame handles any operation that affects the entire application. The most important operations are to open new Child windows and to quit the application. Other operations that the Frame

Components of an MDI application

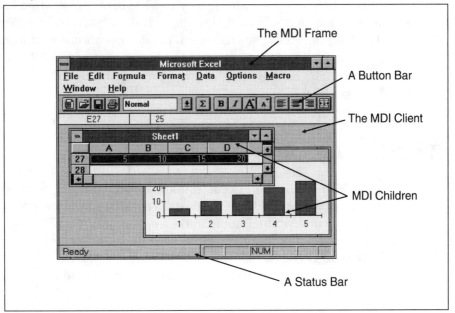

might perform are setting application options and displaying the *About* box. If the application has any components outside of the client area, such as buttons or status bars, the Frame also handles those. The Frame window has a menu, but it passes most menu commands directly to the active Child.

The Client can arrange the Child windows within its client area in various ways, but does nothing more. Applications can send the Client messages asking it to arrange the Children; an application might do this in response to a menu selection. The Client can tile the windows, cascade the windows, and arrange iconized windows along the bottom of its display area. The Client also displays scroll bars if the child windows overlap its display area, and scrolls the windows when the user operates the scroll bars. The application does not have to intervene in this scrolling.

The MDI Child windows provide the main functionality of the application. Although an application may have several Child windows open, only one is active at a time, and this window receives all the input to the application. Although MDI Child windows do not have their own menus within their window frames, they use the main application menu in the MDI Frame as if it belonged to them. If the Children are different types, the MDI Frame changes the menu to one appropriate to the active Child. The Frame also passes most of the menu commands (**WM_COMMAND** messages) on to the active Child. Figure 10-2 shows the hierarchy of the MDI windows.

Window Messages

An MDI application needs to handle some messages differently than it would handle ordinary windows. The MDI Frame works in a similar way to a conventional application window, but it must pass all unprocessed messages to the API function **DefFrameProc** instead of **DefWindowProc**. Similarly, MDI Children must pass all unprocessed messages to the API function **DefMDIChildProc**. In addition, the Child must pass the following messages to **DefMDIChildProc**, even if it processes them:

 The window hierarchy of a typical MDI application

FIGURE 10-2

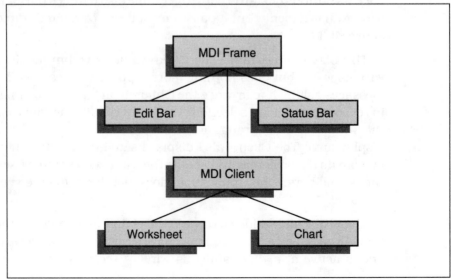

WM_CHILDACTIVATE	Sent when a Child is activated or deactivated.
WM_GETMINMAXINFO	Sent when a window is resized.
WM_MENUCHAR	Needed when a menu contains bitmaps.
WM_MOVE	Sent after the Child has been moved.
WM_SETFOCUS	Sent when the Child gains the input focus.
WM_SIZE	Sent after a Child has been resized.
WM_SYSCOMMAND	Sent when an item in the system menu is selected.

The Client window itself has its own message procedure, and the application should not handle its messages. There are, however, a number of messages that an application can send to the Client. Typically, the MDI Frame sends one of the following messages in response to the user clicking a menu item:

WM_MDIACTIVATE	Activates a Child. **wParam** contains the Child's window handle.
WM_MDICASCADE	Arranges the Children in a cascade fashion.
WM_MDICREATE	Creates a Child. (**lParam** points to a **MDICREATESTRUCT** data structure.)
WM_MDIDESTROY	Destroys the Child specified in **wParam**.
WM_MDIGETACTIVE	Returns the currently active Child.
WM_MDIICONARRANGE	Arranges iconized Children.
WM_MDIMAXIMIZE	Maximizes the Child specified in **wParam**.
WM_MDINEXT	Activates the next Child.
WM_MDIRESTORE	Restores the Child specified in **wParam** from the maximized state.
WM_MDISETMENU	Changes the menu in the Frame.
WM_MDITILE	Arranges the Children in a tile fashion.

When one of these messages is available, the application must use it. For example, an application must destroy Children by sending **WM_MDIDESTROY** to the Client. They may not be destroyed directly. The MDI classes must redefine the **MessageProc** member function in order to handle these messages and to call the MDI default procedures **DefFrameProc** and **DefMDIChildProc**.

The Message Loop

The message loop for an MDI application is similar to the message loop for a normal application, but the loop should call the API function **TranslateMDISysAccel** to translate child window accelerators. MDI Children use CTRL accelerators instead of ALT accelerators, for example, users enter CTRL-F4 to close a Child window, but enter ALT-F4 to close an ordinary window.

Menus

MDI Child windows do not have their own menus; they use the Frame menu. If more than one type of Child exists, each type probably needs a different menu. In that case, instances of the Children must replace the Frame menu with the menu appropriate to that type, whenever the Child is activated. Not only that, if no Children are visible, the Frame menu ought to be replaced by a very simple menu, containing little else besides a *New* item and an *Open* item to open a new Child.

Microsoft Excel changes the menu depending on whether a spreadsheet (Figure 10-3) or a chart (Figure 10-4) is active. If no Child windows are active, Excel displays a simple menu (Figure 10-5), containing only the items that are appropriate when there are no Children.

When the user selects a menu item, Windows sends the Frame the **WM_COMMAND** message to the Frame. If the menu item is an object derived from **Window,** its **Command** member function is called. The Frame will process certain menu items, such as *Open* or *About.* If the Frame does not handle the menu item, it calls the **Command** member function of the currently active Child. The Child can then handle the selection in its own **Command** member function as if it had its own menu.

The same process applies to the **InitMenu** member function. This function is called just before Windows displays a pull-down menu, giving the application a chance to gray or check individual menu items. The Frame **InitMenu** member function should call the **InitMenu** member function in the currently active Child. The Client window does not intervene in these transactions. The Client's only purpose is to arrange the windows when necessary.

FIGURE
10-3
Excel displaying a worksheet as the active document

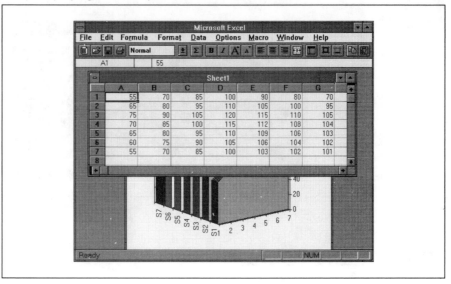

FIGURE
10-4
Excel displaying a chart as the active document

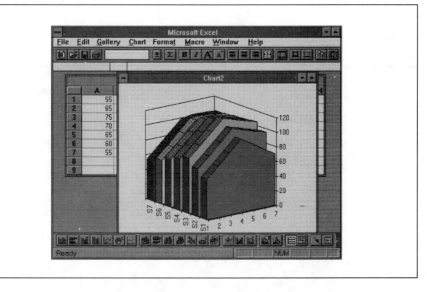

The minimal menu in Excel

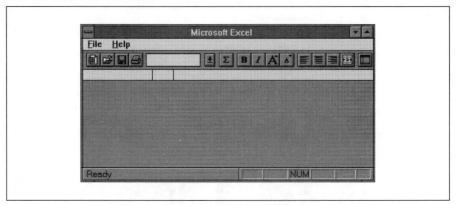

The Window Menu

Generally, an MDI application has a pop-up menu called *Window*, as shown in Figure 10-6. This menu contains options to tile and cascade the windows, and it also contains a list of the Child windows available. The application specifies the menu items that arrange the windows explicitly (*Tile, Cascade,* and so on), but the Client maintains the numbered list of Children. The application merely has to inform the Client

A Window menu

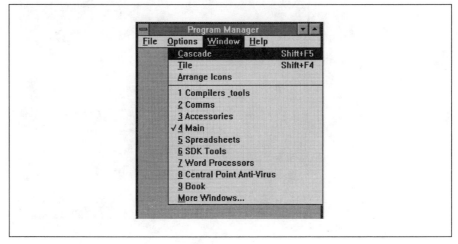

which pop-up menu is the *Window* menu. That can be done either when creating the Client or, if the menu changes, by sending the Client a **WM_MDISETMENU** message. You can specify any pull-down menu as the *Window* list menu. The first menu on the left a zero index. Whenever your application creates a new Child window, the Client adds the child's name to the end of that menu. It is an accepted convention that the second menu from the right be called *Window* and that it contain items for arranging the Child windows, plus a list of the actual Child windows. To avoid confusing users, it's a good idea to follow this convention. In addition, the menu on the far right is usually the *Help* menu. If your application does not support Help, then the *Window* menu is the rightmost menu.

If a Child class is going to replace the Frame menu, it must be able to inform the Client which pull-down menu is now the *Window* menu, since the new menu may be longer or shorter than the previous menu.

Implementation

In this implementation there are three MDI classes: **MDIFrame**, **MDIClient**, and **MDIChild**. The class hierarchy is shown in Figure 10-7. Note that all three classes are derived from the **Window** class, not from each other. The class and window hierarchies differ. A Frame window is the parent of the Client window, which is the parent of the Child windows. There is no need to derive the **MDIClient** and **MDIChild** classes from **MDIFrame**, since they serve no common function other than that of the base **Window** class.

An application normally derives a subclass of **MDIFrame**, and one or more subclasses of **MDIChild**. There is no need to derive a subclass of **MDIClient**, however. The Client should always be the same, whatever the application.

The MDIFrame Class

The **MDIFrame** class is derived from the **Window** class. Here is its definition:

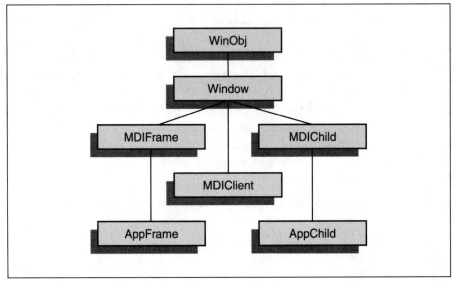

FIGURE 10-7   The MDI class hierarchy

mdiframe.hpp

```
#ifndef, MDIFRAME_INC
#define, MDIFRAME_INC

#include "window.hpp"
#include "mdiclien.hpp"
#include "mdichild.hpp"

class MDIFrame : public Window {
protected:
  MDIClient * Client;
  WORD WindowId;
  LPSTR pMenu;
  WORD WindowMenu;

public:
  static MDIFrame * Frame;       // pointer to application
                                 // frame instance

  virtual void CreateFrame(
    LPSTR pName=NULL,            // Window name
    LPSTR pMenu=NULL,            // Menu resource name
    WORD WindowMenu=0,           // Position of window list
    WORD WindowId=0,             // Window menu id
    int x= CW_USEDEFAULT,        // Position
```

```
        int y= CW_USEDEFAULT,
        int width= CW_USEDEFAULT,   // Size
        int height= CW_USEDEFAULT);

    ~MDIFrame();
    int MessageLoop();
    LONG MessageProc( HWND hWnd, unsigned msg, Event& evt);

    void CloseAllChildren();      // Closes all MDI children
    BOOL QueryClose();

    BOOL ChildIterator(           // Iterates through children
      WinObj * Inst,              // invoking callback
      BOOL(WinObj::*pCallback)(MDIChild *, LPSTR),
      LPSTR Param);

    BOOL CloseChild(              // Closes an MDI child
      MDIChild * pWin,
      LPSTR pNull);

    BOOL QueryChild(
      MDIChild * pWin,
      LPSTR pNull);

    void RestoreMenu();           // Restores default menu
                  // If no children

    BOOL NoChild(MDIChild * pWin, LPSTR pNull);
}; // class MDIFrame

typedef BOOL(WinObj::*MDICHILDCALLBACK)(MDIChild *, LPSTR);

#endif // MDIFRAME_INC
```

The functions are explained in the next section. An application almost invariably has just one instance of a **MDIFrame**, and so it is convenient to keep a **static** pointer to that instance within the class. That allows the Child instances to access it.

mdiframe.cpp

```
#include "mdiframe.hpp"
#include "mdichild.hpp"
#include "mdiframe.h"

MDIFrame * MDIFrame::Frame=NULL;

void MDIFrame::CreateFrame(LPSTR pName,
```

```
LPSTR pMenu, WORD WindowMenu,WORD WindowId,
int x, int y,
int width, int height)
{
    CLIENTCREATESTRUCT ccs;

    /* Create the frame */
    Create(pName,WS_OVERLAPPEDWINDOW | WS_CLIPCHILDREN,
      x,y,width,height,NULL,NULL);
    DefaultHandler=NULL;
    HMENU hMenu = LoadMenu (hInst, pMenu);
    HMENU hWindowMenu = GetSubMenu (hMenu, WindowMenu);
    MDIFrame::WindowId=WindowId;
    MDIFrame::pMenu=pMenu;
    MDIFrame::WindowMenu=WindowMenu;
    ccs.hWindowMenu = hWindowMenu;
    ccs.idFirstChild = WindowId+100;
    Frame=this;
    Client =new MDIClient(hWnd, &ccs);
    RestoreMenu();
}
```

Instead of using **CreateWindow**, an application uses **CreateFrame** to create an MDI Frame. **CreateFrame** is usually called from the constructor of the class derived from **MDIFrame**. **CreateFrame** takes the application name (**pName**) and the intial size of the window, along with three other parameters specifying the menu. These are the parameters:

pMenu	The name of the menu as specified in the resource file.
WindowMenu	The offset within the menu of the drop-down menu that will contain the list of child windows. Usually this is the menu called *Window*. The first menu has offset zero. The Frame menu may not have a *Window* menu, since initially there are no child windows. In that case **WindowMenu** should be zero.
WindowId	This is the menu ID of the first item in the *Window* menu. All the menus supplied by the Children should also use this ID for the *Window* menu.

CreateFrame first creates an application window using the **Create** member function from the **Window** class. After setting the Frame menu, **CreateFrame** creates an instance of **MDIClient**. **MDIClient** will need the

CLIENTCREATESTRUCT containing the *Window* menu and the menu ID of the first Child.

```
MDIFrame::~MDIFrame()
{
  CloseAllChildren();
}
```

Before destroying the Frame, the destructor must destroy all the **MDIChild** instances.

```
LONG MDIFrame::MessageProc( HWND hWnd, unsigned msg,
                            Event& evt)
{
    switch(msg) {

    case WM_INITMENU:
    {
      WORD status;
      HMENU hmenu = (HMENU) evt.wParam;
      if (MDIChild::ActiveChild) {
            status = MF_ENABLED;
      }
      else status = MF_GRAYED;
      // The following menu items are enabled
      // if there is an active window */
      EnableMenuItem (hmenu,
          WindowId+IDM_WINDOWTILE, status);
      EnableMenuItem (hmenu,
          WindowId+IDM_WINDOWCASCADE, status);
      EnableMenuItem (hmenu,
          WindowId+IDM_WINDOWICONS, status);
      EnableMenuItem (hmenu,
          WindowId+IDM_WINDOWCLOSEALL, status);
      InitMenu((HMENU)evt.wParam);
    }
    break;
```

MessageProc redefines some messages. The **WM_INITMENU** event occurs when the user has pulled down a menu, but before the menu appears. If there are no active children, **MessageProc** can disable the menu items for arranging the children. The **MDIChild** class maintains **ActiveChild** to point to the currently active child. If there are any children at all, one of them will be active.

```
case WM_COMMAND:
   if (!(HWND)evt.lParam ){
      switch ((WORD)evt.wParam-WindowId){
      case IDM_WINDOWTILE:
         /* Tile MDI windows */
         SendMessage (Client->hWnd,
                        WM_MDITILE,0,0);
         break;

      case IDM_WINDOWCASCADE:
         /* Cascade MDI windows */
         SendMessage (Client->hWnd,
                        WM_MDICASCADE,0,0);
         break;

      case IDM_WINDOWICONS:
         /* Auto - arrange MDI icons */
         SendMessage (Client->hWnd,
                        WM_MDIICONARRANGE,0,0);
         break;

      case IDM_WINDOWCLOSEALL:
         if (QueryClose())
            CloseAllChildren();
         break;
      }
   }
   if (Window::MessageProc(hWnd,msg,evt)) return TRUE;
   return DefFrameProc(hWnd, Client->hWnd, msg,
                        evt.wParam, evt.lParam);
```

If the user selects any of the menu items for arranging child windows or icons, the Frame sends a corresponding message to the Client. For the **IDM_WINDOWCLOSEALL** item, **QueryClose** calls **QueryClose** in each child in turn, giving the child a chance to either save files or to veto the operation. Only if all the children agree to the close will **CloseAllChildren** be called. **CloseAllChildren** closes all the windows without further ado.

```
case WM_QUERYENDSESSION:
   // OK to end Windows session?
   return QueryClose();
```

The **WM_QUERYENDSESSION** message is exceptional, because the application can return **FALSE** when it has processed it. The default case calls **DefFrameProc** if **MessageProc** in the **Window** class returns

FALSE, but we do not want to call **DefFrameProc** if **QueryClose** returns **FALSE.** If we do, **DefFrameProc** returns **TRUE** and the Windows session terminates, even though the application has vetoed the operation. To avoid that, **MessageProc** handles the message here.

```
  default:
   LONG Res=Window::MessageProc(hWnd,msg,evt);
   if (Res) return Res;
   else return DefFrameProc(hWnd, Client->hWnd, msg,
                              evt.wParam, evt.lParam);

  }
  return TRUE;
}
```

For any other events, the member function calls **MessageProc** in the **Window** class. **MessageProc** in the **Window** class normally calls **DefaultHandler** if it does not handle a message, but since **DefaultHandler** is **NULL**, it just returns **FALSE** without calling anything. In this case, the member function can call **DefFrameProc**, the default function for handling MDI Frame messages.

```
WORD MDIFrame::MessageLoop()
{
  MSG msg;
  while (GetMessage(&msg, NULL, 0, 0)) {
    if(   msg.message >=WM_KEYFIRST
        && msg.message <=WM_KEYLAST) {
       Window * pWin=GetWin(GetParent(msg.hwnd));
        if (pWin && pWin->DialogMessage(msg)) continue;
    }
    if ( !TranslateMDISysAccel (Client->hWnd, &msg) &&
      (!hAccel ||
      !TranslateAccelerator (hWnd, hAccel, &msg))){
      TranslateMessage (&msg);
      DispatchMessage (&msg);
    }
  }
  return msg.wParam;
}
```

MDI applications must modify the message loop to call the API function **TranslateMDISysAccel** before calling **TranslateAccelerator**. The **MDIFrame** class redefines **MessageLoop** to include the extra call.

```
BOOL MDIFrame::ChildIterator(WinObj * Inst,
  BOOL(WinObj::*pCallback)(MDIChild *, LPSTR),
  LPSTR Param)
{
  HWND hCwnd= GetWindow (Client->hWnd, GW_CHILD);
  while ( hCwnd ){
    MDIChild * pWin=(MDIChild*) GetWin(hCwnd);
    do {
     hCwnd=GetWindow(hCwnd,GW_HWNDNEXT);
     } while (hCwnd  && GetParent(hCwnd)!=Client->hWnd);
    if (!pWin) continue;
    if (!(Inst->*pCallback)(pWin,Param)) return FALSE;
  }
  return TRUE;
}
```

ChildIterator is a useful function for any operation that involves all of the Child windows. The function that closes all the Child windows will use this function. The function invokes the callback function for each existing Child. The operation continues until either there are no more children, or the callback returns **FALSE**.

```
VOID MDIFrame::CloseAllChildren ()
{
  Client->Show(SW_HIDE);
  ChildIterator(this,
      (MDICHILDCALLBACK)&MDIFrame::CloseChild,NULL);
  Client->Show();
}
```

CloseAllChildren is an example of how to use **ChildIterator**. It calls **ChildIterator** with the **CloseChild** callback. **ChildIterator** can take an optional parameter, which will be supplied to the callback, but here the parameter is not used. The member function hides the Client during this operation to avoid having the client area repainted each time it closes a Child.

```
BOOL MDIFrame::CloseChild(MDIChild * pWin, LPSTR pNull)
{
 delete pWin;
 return TRUE;
}
```

The callback function itself simply deletes the instance of the Child. The **MDIChild** destructor takes care of closing the window.

```
BOOL MDIFrame::QueryClose()
{
  return ChildIterator(this,
        (MDICHILDCALLBACK)&MDIFrame::QueryChild,NULL);
}

BOOL MDIFrame::QueryChild(MDIChild * pWin, LPSTR pNull)
{
  return pWin->QueryClose();
}
```

QueryClose and **QueryChild** make use of **ChildIterator** to call the **QueryClose** member function for each Child.

```
void MDIFrame::RestoreMenu()
{
  if (ChildIterator(this,
     (MDICHILDCALLBACK)&MDIFrame::NoChild,NULL)) {
    HMENU hMenu = LoadMenu (hInst, pMenu);
    HMENU hWindowMenu = GetSubMenu (hMenu, WindowMenu);
#ifdef WIN32
    HMENU hOldMenu  =
       (HMENU)SendMessage (Client->hWnd, WM_MDISETMENU,
      (UINT)hMenu,(DWORD)hWindowMenu);
#else
    HMENU hOldMenu  =
       (HMENU)SendMessage (Client->hWnd, WM_MDISETMENU,
       0,MAKELONG(hMenu,hWindowMenu));
#endif
    if (hOldMenu) DestroyMenu(hOldMenu);
    DrawMenuBar (hWnd);
  }
}

BOOL MDIFrame::NoChild(MDIChild * pWin, LPSTR pNull)
{
  return FALSE;
}
```

As the user activates a Child, it resets the Frame menu to something appropriate to that class of Child. Although Child windows do not have menus in their own window frames, they still have their own menu in the application's main Frame. As long as Children exist there is no problem, but when the user has closed all the Children, the Frame should restore its own menu. This menu is simple, containing only the items that are valid when there are no Children.

The destructor in **MDIChild** calls **RestoreMenu**. If there are no other Children, **RestoreMenu** restores the original Frame menu. **RestoreMenu** cannot rely on the contents of **ActiveChild** to know whether they are other Children. When a Child is being closed, one of the other Children may not yet have activated. Instead, **RestoreMenu** calls the **ChildIterator** with the **NoChild** callback. If **NoChild** returns **FALSE**, there is still another Child window and so there is no need to restore the default menu.

Working with 32 Bits

The **WM_MDISETMENU** message has the two menu handles in **wParam** and **lParam** in the 32-bit version, while the two handles are packed into **lParam** in the 16-bit version. The only other difference in packing among the MDI messages concerns the **WM_MDIACTIVATE** message, and then only when it is received by a Child window. The **MDIChild** class, described later, will use the **WM_MDIACTIVATE** message.

The MDIClient Class

The **MDIClient** class is a relatively simple class. The **MDIFrame** class creates an instance of **MDIClient** and sends it messages when the Child windows need arranging, but other than that neither the Frame nor the Children need to use it. Classes derived from **MDIFrame** and **MDIChild** do not need to know about the **MDIClient** instance.

mdiclien.hpp

```
#ifndef  MDICLIENT_INC
#define  MDICLIENT_INC

#include "window.hpp"
```

```
class MDIClient : public Window{
public:
  static HWND hWnd;
  MDIClient(
    HANDLE PhWnd,                  // Parent window handle
    CLIENTCREATESTRUCT * ccs,  // Create structure
    int Id=0xCAC,
    int x= CW_USEDEFAULT,        // Position
    int y= CW_USEDEFAULT,
    int width= CW_USEDEFAULT,  // Size
    int height= CW_USEDEFAULT);

  ~MDIClient();
}; // class MDIClient

#endif // MDICLIENT_INC
```

Again, since there will only be one instance of **MDIClient**, it keeps its window handle as **static** data. The **MDIFrame** class used this handle for sending messages to the Client. The **MDIChild** class will also send the Client messages.

```
#include "mdiclien.hpp"

HWND MDIClient::hWnd=NULL;

MDIClient::MDIClient(HWND PhWnd,
            CLIENTCREATESTRUCT * ccs,int Id,
            int x, int y,int width, int height)
{
  hWnd =Window::hWnd= CreateWindow("mdiclient",NULL,
        WS_CHILD | WS_CLIPCHILDREN |
        WS_VSCROLL | WS_HSCROLL | WS_VISIBLE,
            x,y,width,height,
        PhWnd,(HMENU)Id,hInst, (LPSTR)ccs);
}

MDIClient::~MDIClient()
{   hWnd=Window::hWnd=0;
}
```

mdiclien.cpp

The constructor simply calls **CreateWindow** to create a window with the API preregistered class **mdiclient**. **CreateWindow** takes the

CLIENTCREATESTRUCT data structure as a parameter. There is no need to provide a window function for **MDIClient**; it has its own.

```
MDIClient::~MDIClient()
{
  hWnd=Window::hWnd=0;
}
```

Nothing special needs to be done when the Client is destroyed; it has no resources of its own. The destructor sets the **hWnd** item to **NULL** in order to disable the **Window** class destructor.

The MDIChild Class

The main difference between the **MDIChild** class and the **Window** class from which it is derived is in the **MessageProc** function. For certain messages **MDIChild** must call **DefMDIChildProc**, even if it processes the message itself.

mdichild.hpp

```
#ifndef   MDICHILD_INC
#define   MDICHILD_INC

#include "window.hpp"
#include "mdiclien.hpp"

class MDIChild : public Window{
public:
  static MDIChild * ActiveChild;
  void CreateChild(
    LPSTR pName=NULL,         // Window name
    LPSTR pMenu=NULL,         // Menu name
    WORD WindowMenu=0,        // Position of window list
    LONG Style=-1,
    int x= CW_USEDEFAULT,     // Position
    int y= CW_USEDEFAULT,
    int width= CW_USEDEFAULT, // Size
    int height= CW_USEDEFAULT);

  ~MDIChild();
  LONG MessageProc( HWND hWnd, unsigned msg, Event& evt);
```

```
    virtual void Activate(          // Child has been activated
      BOOL bActive){};

    void Restore(){                 // Restores child from icon
      SendMessage (MDIClient::hWnd,
                  WM_MDIRESTORE,(UINT)hWnd,0);}

    void Maximize(){                // Maximizes child
      SendMessage (MDIClient::hWnd,
                  WM_MDIMAXIMIZE,(UINT)hWnd,0);}

protected:
  LPSTR MenuName;
  WORD WindowMenu;
}; // class MDIChild

#endif // MDICHILD_INC
```

The two functions **Restore** and **Maximize** are so simple that they are defined here in the class definition. They send a message to the client, asking it either to restore the window from the iconized or maximized state, or to maximize the window.

Restore   Restores the Child window from the maximized or iconic state to a normal Framed window in the Client area.

Maximize   Maximizes the Child window.

mdichild.cpp

```
#include "mdichild.hpp"
#include "mdiclien.hpp"
#include "mdiframe.hpp"

MDIChild * MDIChild::ActiveChild=NULL;

void MDIChild::CreateChild(LPSTR pName,LPSTR pMenu,
                          WORD WindowMenu,LONG Style,
int x, int y,
int width, int height)
{
    MDICREATESTRUCT mcs;

    WNDCLASS wc;
    wc.style          = 0;
    wc.lpfnWndProc    = (WNDPROC) DefMDIChildProc;
```

```
wc.cbClsExtra     = 0;
wc.cbWndExtra     = 0;
wc.hInstance      = hInst;
wc.hIcon          = LoadIcon(NULL,IDI_APPLICATION);
wc.hCursor        = LoadCursor(NULL,IDC_ARROW);
wc.hbrBackground  = (HBRUSH)(COLOR_WINDOW+1);
wc.lpszMenuName   = 0;

if (pName==NULL) pName="";
MenuName=pMenu;
MDIChild::WindowMenu=WindowMenu;
mcs.szTitle = pName;

mcs.szClass = Register(wc);
mcs.hOwner = hInst;

mcs.x = x;
mcs.cx = width;

mcs.y = y;
mcs.cy = height;
LONG ActiveWin=
  SendMessage(MDIClient::hWnd,WM_MDIGETACTIVE,0,0);
if (Style !=-1) mcs.style=Style;
else if (!LOWORD(ActiveWin) || HIWORD(ActiveWin))
  mcs.style=WS_MAXIMIZE;
else mcs.style = 0;

/* tell the MDI Client to create the child */
hWnd = (HWND)SendMessage (MDIClient::hWnd,
                WM_MDICREATE,
                0,
                (LONG)(LPMDICREATESTRUCT)&mcs);

if (!hWnd)
  Error(IDS_APPLERROR,(LPSTR)"Creating MDI Child");
SetHandler();
ActiveChild = this;
PostMessage(hWnd,WM_MDIACTIVATE,(UINT)hWnd,(DWORD)hWnd);
}
```

The class does not create MDI Children by calling **CreateWindow** directly. Instead, it sends a **WM_MDICREATE** message to the Client, and the Client will create the window. The message contains the address of an **MDICREATESTRUCT** data structure that the **MDIChild** constructor must initialize.

The data structure contains most of the items that are normally supplied to the **CreateWindow** function. The exception is the handle of the parent window, since the Client will be the parent.

As with the **Window** class, the **MDIChild** class initializes the **WNDCLASS** structure with reasonable default values. For MDI Child windows, the default message function is **DefMDIChildProc**. MDI Children may not specify a menu when they register the class, but they should specify an icon.

It is useful to have the Child window initially maximized if it is the first window, or if the currently active window is also maximized. The **WM_MDIGETACTIVE** message returns the currently active window in the low-order word and a flag indicating whether the window is maximized in the high-order word.

After having created the Child window, the constructor posts a message to itself to inform the window that it is active. The reason for posting the message, rather than calling **Activate** directly, is to give the constructor in the derived class a chance to initialize the derived class. Child windows usually redefine **Activate** to do some action when the window is activated. The Client window will send **WM_ACTIVATE** messages when the user changes from one window to another, but not when the window first becomes active after its creation. By sending the message to itself in the constructor, the MDI Child ensures that its **Activate** function is invoked on its first activation.

Working with 32 Bits

When sent to a Child, the **MDI_ACTIVATE** message is the other MDI message whose parameter packing differs in the 16- and 32-bit versions of Windows. Unfortunately, in the 32-bit version, a parameter is lost. The 16-bit message contains a Boolean flag in the **wParam**, indicating whether the Child is being activated or deactivated, and the handles of the window being deactivated and the window being activated in the **lParam**. Most 16-bit applications ignore the window handles and just look at the flag. Under 32-bit Windows, the flag disappears. The **wParam** contains the handle of the window being deactivated, and the **lParam** contains the handle of the window being activated. This means that if a 32-bit application Child just wants to know whether it is being activated or not, it must compare the value in **lParam** with its own window handle. If the values are equal, it is being activated.

```
MDIChild::~MDIChild()
{
  if (ActiveChild==this) {
    ActiveChild=NULL;
  }
  if (hWnd) {
    DelWin(hWnd);
    SetWindowLong(hWnd,GWL_WNDPROC,
               (LONG) DefaultHandler);
    SendMessage(GetParent(hWnd),
               WM_MDIDESTROY,(UINT)hWnd, 0L);
    hWnd=NULL;
  }
  MDIFrame::Frame->RestoreMenu();
}
```

The destructor is similar to the **Window** class destructor but rather than calling **DestroyWindow,** it must send a **WM_MDIDESTROY** message to the Client. After the window has been destroyed, the destructor calls the **RestoreMenu** member function in **MDIFrame**, giving the Frame a chance to restore the default menu when there are no other Children.

```
LONG MDIChild::MessageProc( HWND hWnd, unsigned msg,
                            Event& evt)
{
  switch (msg){

    case WM_MDIACTIVATE:
      if ((HWND)evt.lParam == hWnd){
          ActiveChild    = this;
          if (MenuName) {
            HMENU hMenu = LoadMenu (hInst, MenuName);
            HMENU hWindowMenu =
              GetSubMenu (hMenu, WindowMenu);
            /* Set the new menu */
#ifdef WIN32
            HMENU hOldMenu  =
              (HMENU)SendMessage (MDIClient::hWnd,
              WM_MDISETMENU,
              (UINT)hMenu,(UINT)hWindowMenu);
#else
            HMENU hOldMenu  =
              (HMENU)SendMessage (MDIClient::hWnd,
              WM_MDISETMENU,
              0,MAKELONG(hMenu,hWindowMenu));
#endif
            if (hOldMenu) DestroyMenu(hOldMenu);
            DrawMenuBar (GetParent(MDIClient::hWnd));
          }
          Activate(TRUE);
      }
      else{
          ActiveChild = NULL;
          Activate(FALSE);
      }
      break;
```

Whenever the user activates the Child, it replaces the Frame menu with its own particular menu. The previous menu is discarded. **Activate** is a virtual member function that subclasses can redefine. The parameter indicates **TRUE** or **FALSE**.

```
    case WM_SIZE:
      Size(LOWORD(evt.lParam),
           HIWORD(evt.lParam),
           evt.wParam);
      return DefMDIChildProc (hWnd, msg,
```

```
                                    evt.wParam, evt.lParam);

      case WM_SETFOCUS:
        SetFocus((HWND)evt.wParam);
        return DefMDIChildProc (hWnd, msg,
                                    evt.wParam, evt.lParam);
```

For the **WM_SIZE** and **WM_SETFOCUS** events, **MessageProc** must call **DefMDIChildProc** whether or not the application will handle the message.

```
      default:
        return Window::MessageProc(hWnd, msg, evt);
    }
    return TRUE;
}
```

The member function passes all the other messages on to the **Window** class **MessageProc** member function.

Using the MDI Classes

Now that the MDI classes are in place, it is easy to write MDI applications by deriving subclasses of **MDIFrame** and **MDIChild**. Applications will not need to concern themselves with the **MDIClient** class unless they want to add extra facilities for arranging Child windows.

Deriving MDIFrame Subclasses

The Frame of an MDI application deals with opening and closing Child windows. If the application has any other ancillary windows that are not part of the MDI, the Frame usually handles these as well. These windows could be button bars or status ribbons, for example. A typical **MDIFrame** subclass should do the following:

☐ The constructor should call **CreateFrame**, specifying a default minimal menu, and it may create the other ancillary windows.

☐ The **Register** member function should provide a window class name and an icon. You may set the window background to **NULL**, since the MDI Client and the other ancillary windows should always fill the Frame's client area.

☐ If there are ancillary windows such as button bars, you must provide a **Size** member function to tile them to fit the Frame's client area. You must also resize the MDI Client window. If there are no ancillary windows then there is no need to provide a **Size** member function, since the Client will resize itself automatically to fill the Frame's client area.

   Be careful, because **Size** will be called before **CreateFrame** returns and before the ancillary windows have been created. Watch out for uninitialized items. You may find that things are easier if you create the ancillary windows in some arbitrary size and then invoke **Size** explicitly after creating them.

☐ The **MDIFrame** subclass should provide **InitMenu** and **Command** member functions to handle the menu items that are relevant to the Frame, but the subclass should pass other events on to the currently active Child, if any.

Deriving MDIChild Subclasses

Your application will need a subclass for each type of Child that it supports. **MDIChild** subclasses are very similar to the **Window** subclasses in non-MDI applications. These are the differences:

☐ The constructor calls **CreateChild** instead of **CreateWindow**.

☐ The constructor usually opens the file or data record associated with the window.

❑ The **Register** member function should not specify a menu; you pass the name of the menu to **CreateChild** in the constructor.

❑ The **InitMenu** and **Command** member functions do not need to handle menu events that the Frame intercepts.

Managing Local Memory

Whenever you create an instance of a class with the **new** operator, you allocate some local memory for it. Local memory is a limited resource, and if not enough is available, **new** will fail. If that happens, **new** displays an out-of-memory message and returns a **NULL** pointer.

A non-MDI application usually has an upper limit to the amount of local memory required. Provided that there is at least that amount of memory available, **new** will always succeed. There is no need to take specific precautions to ensure that instances have indeed been allocated.

With an MDI application, on the other hand, there is no limit to the number of Children that a user may open, and sooner or later **new** will fail. If **new** fails and returns a **NULL** pointer, the application must cancel the current operation. If the application carries on as though nothing has happened, there will be a memory protection fault when it accesses that instance.

Of course, it is all very well to say that you should check the result of every call to **new**, but that task is quite tedious. It is not always obvious how to recover from an operation when **new** suddenly fails.

One solution to this problem is to try to allocate a reasonable amount of working storage in the local heap, say 500 bytes, when entering the Child constructor. If that fails, the constructor can delete the Child immediately. The memory is released at the end of the constructor, thus ensuring that there is always a reserve of local memory available for creating further instances.

MDI applications should use global memory rather than local memory where possible, especially in Child windows.

Converting Old C Applications to the MDI

The MDI classes may be useful for converting ordinary C Windows applications to MDI applications. C applications usually use **static** data, which is unique. It is possible to derive a subclass of **MDIChild** and to copy all this **static** data into the class definition. If you convert the old C functions to class member functions, all the old code that previously referred to the **static** data will refer to class data.

The application's window function will become a **MessageProc** member function. You will still have to handle certain menu options in the Frame subclass.

Of course, it will be more elegant to rewrite the old application entirely in C++, but that might not be cost effective. A conversion might only take a day or so, and since there is no need to touch the contents of most of the original functions, you can expect the converted application to be reasonably reliable.

MultNote—an Example MDI Application

The example program MultNote is an MDI version of the Windows Notepad application. The program also illustrates the use of the **Clipboard** class, including the clipboard viewer.

MultNote introduces three new general-purpose classes:

EditWin   Derived from the **Edit** class and adds facilities that an editor window will need.

ButtonBar   A button bar providing quick access to selected menu items. The user can click on a button rather than pulling down a menu and selecting an item in it.

Timer   A class to invoke a callback when a certain time has elapsed.

Although it is convenient to use the edit control in this example program, there is a disadvantage. The edit control uses local memory for its text. Since local memory is limited to 64K less the size of the stack, it is impossible to use MultNote on large files, such as the WINDOWS.H file. The application also runs out of local memory after opening a number of smaller files. Still, MultNote is a useful alternative to Notepad, especially if you wish to cut and paste between files.

Before going ahead with MultNote, let us examine the three new classes.

The EditWin Class

The **Edit** class is fine for entering little bits of information in dialog boxes, but the **Edit** class does not implement all of the features of the edit control. **EditWin** is derived from **Edit** and adds three extra facilities:

☐   Clipboard support.

☐   The *Undo* facility. The edit control can undo the last modification.

☐   Editing local memory blocks directly. Instead of sending text to the control and retrieving it afterwards, the control can work directly with a memory block supplied by the application.

Since these facilities are built in to the edit control in any case, **EditWin** needs to do little more than sending appropriate messages to the control. Here is the definition of **EditWin**:

editwin.hpp

```
#ifndef   EDITWIN_INC
#define   EDITWIN_INC

#include "edit.hpp"
#include "memory.hpp"

class EditWin : public Edit{
protected:
  LocalMem * CurrentBuffer;
```

CurrentBuffer is a pointer to the memory block that the control may be using.

```
public:
  EditWin(
    HWND PhWnd,              // Parent window handle
    int Id,                 // Identifier for control
```

```
    DWORD Style=0,              // control style
    int x= CW_USEDEFAULT,      // Position
    int y= CW_USEDEFAULT,
    int width= CW_USEDEFAULT,  // Size
    int height= CW_USEDEFAULT)
    :Edit(PhWnd,Id,"",
     Style?Style:(ES_MULTILINE|ES_AUTOHSCROLL|
       ES_AUTOVSCROLL|WS_HSCROLL|WS_VSCROLL),
     x,y,width,height){CurrentBuffer=0;};
```

The constructor creates an instance of **Edit** with automatic scroll bars.

```
    void Buffer(                // Set edit buffer
      LocalMem * Buf);

    LocalMem * Buffer();        // Return edit buffer

    int Size() ;                // Return size of text

    BOOL Modified();            // TRUE if text modified

    void Modified(BOOL bFlag);  // Sets modified flag

    BOOL Undo(){                // Undos changes
      return SendMessage(hWnd,EM_UNDO,0,0);};

    BOOL CanUndo(){             // TRUE if can undo changes
      return SendMessage(hWnd,EM_CANUNDO,0,0);};

    GlobalMem * Selection();    // Returns current selection

    BOOL Selected();            // TRUE if text selected

    void Paste(                 // Pastes data into buffer
      GlobalMem * pMem);

    void Paste()                // Pastes clipboard into buffer
      {SendMessage(hWnd,WM_PASTE,0,0);};

    void Copy()                 // Copies selection to clipboard
    {SendMessage(hWnd,WM_COPY,0,0);};

    void Cut()                  // Cuts selection to clipboard
    {SendMessage(hWnd,WM_CUT,0,0);};
}; // class EditWin

#endif // EDITWIN_INC
```

The three member functions **Paste()**, **Copy()**, and **Cut()** cause the control to cut and paste directly to or from the clipboard in **CF_TEXT** format. **Paste(GlobalMem * pMem)** replaces the current selection with the contents of the memory. **Selection** returns the current selection in a global memory block.

The remaining member functions are implemented like this:

editwin.cpp

```
#include "editwin.hpp"

void EditWin::Buffer(LocalMem * Mem)
{
    if (!CurrentBuffer){
      HLOCAL hOld=
        (HLOCAL)SendMessage(hWnd, EM_GETHANDLE,0,0);
      if (hOld) LocalFree(hOld);
    }
    CurrentBuffer = Mem;
    SendMessage(hWnd, EM_SETHANDLE,
                (DWORD)Mem->Handle, 0L);
}
```

The **EM_GETHANDLE** and **EM_SETHANDLE** messages get and set the control's internal buffer. When the class resets the edit buffer, it should free the old buffer. It only does this when the old buffer does not come from another **LocalMem** object.

If the edit control is in a dialog box, you can only set its buffer if the dialog box has been created with the **DS_LOCALEDIT** style. You can specify this style with your dialog editor when you are drawing the dialog box template. If the style is not set, the edit controls have their buffers in another data segment.

```
LocalMem * EditWin::Buffer()
{
    return CurrentBuffer;
}
```

If the class providing the **LocalMem** instance keeps a pointer to it, it does not need to call **Buffer()**. The instance of **LocalMem** and the memory handle do not change; only the text within the memory changes. The edit control may reallocate memory in the block as the text shrinks or grows.

```
int EditWin::Size()
{
  return GetWindowTextLength(hWnd);
}
```

Size returns the actual length of the text. The size of the memory block used by the edit control will usually be somewhat larger than this. The text will not always be null-terminated either, so using **lstrlen** on the buffer is not a good idea.

```
BOOL EditWin::Modified()
{
  return SendMessage(hWnd,EM_GETMODIFY,0,0);
}

void EditWin::Modified(BOOL bFlag)
{
  SendMessage(hWnd,EM_SETMODIFY,bFlag,0);
}

GlobalMem * EditWin::Selection()
{
  DWORD CharPos=SendMessage(hWnd,EM_GETSEL,0,0);
  WORD First= LOWORD(CharPos);
  WORD Last= HIWORD(CharPos);
  GlobalMem* pMem=new GlobalMem(Last-First+1);
  if (pMem && pMem->Handle) {
   Lock BufSource(CurrentBuffer);
   pMem->Load((LPSTR)BufSource.Buffer+First, Last-First);
  }
  return pMem;
}
```

Selection creates an instance of **GlobalMem** and copies the currently selected text into it. The application should delete the instance after use.

```
BOOL EditWin::Selected()
{
  DWORD CharPos=SendMessage(hWnd,EM_GETSEL,0,0);
  return !!(HIWORD(CharPos)-LOWORD(CharPos));
}
```

The **EM_GETSEL** message returns the position of the beginning and the end of the selection in the high- and low-order words. If these are different, then something is selected. The double **!!** operator converts this value into **TRUE** or **FALSE**. It returns **TRUE** if the difference is non-zero and **FALSE** if the difference is zero and nothing is selected. This happens just in case someone writes a line such as

if (MyEdit->Selected( )==TRUE)

```
void EditWin::Paste(GlobalMem * pMem)
{
  LPSTR pStr="";
  if (pMem && pMem->Handle) {
    Lock BufSource(pMem);
    pStr=BufSource.Buffer;
    delete pMem;
  }
  SendMessage(hWnd,EM_REPLACESEL,0,(DWORD)pStr);
}
```

The **GlobalMem** instance is deleted after use.

The ButtonBar Class

The **ButtonBar** class provides a window containing icon buttons. Each button corresponds to an item in the current menu. When specifying buttons, the application only needs to provide an icon and the menu item identifier. The **ButtonBar** class labels the buttons using the text of the menu item, and discards anything that appears after a TAB in this text.

If the menu item has an underlined letter, indicating an accelerator, this letter is also underlined on the button. The application should provide accelerators so that the user can invoke a menu item by simply keying in the underlined letter with the ALT key depressed. For example, it should define ALT-O as an accelerator for the *Open* item. Be careful not to specify duplicates! You should assign an appropriate letter to each item on your menu, even if the letter falls in the middle of the item name. If you do not, the user will not be able to select all the menu items with the keyboard. Many menu items have standard accelerators in any case; for example, SHIFT-INSERT for *Paste*.

The MultNote application uses large buttons, but you could use small buttons instead. If the buttons are smaller than 32 pixels square, the text will not be visible, but you will have space for a multitude of buttons.

The **ButtonBar** class is derived from **ListBox**, and the buttons are owner-draw list items. The application can declare a callback that will be invoked when the user clicks on any of the buttons. The button bar is shown here:

Here is the definition of **ButtonBar**:

butnbar.hpp

```
#ifndef   BUTTONBAR_INC
#define   BUTTONBAR_INC

#include "iconbutn.hpp"
#include "listbox.hpp"

// Specification of a button
class ButtonSpec {
public:
   LPSTR Icon;              // Name of Icon
   WORD MenuCommand;        // Corresponding menu Id
   BOOL bEnabled;           // TRUE if enabled
}; // class ButtonSpec
```

The **ButtonSpec** class defines a single button. To define a row of buttons, create a null terminated array of **ButtonSpec** items. Here are the elements of **ButtonSpec**:

LPSTR Icon	A pointer to the name of an icon, as defined in the resource file
WORD MenuCommand	The corresponding menu item identifier
BOOL bEnabled	Whether the item is initially enabled

```
class ButtonBar :  public ItemMeasurement,
                   public ListBox,
                   private IconButton {
```

```
public:
  ButtonBar(
    HWND PhWnd,                  // Parent window handle
    int Id,                      // Child Id
    WORD bx,WORD by,             // Button size
    int x= CW_USEDEFAULT,        // Position
    int y= CW_USEDEFAULT,
    int width= CW_USEDEFAULT,    // size of bar
    int height= CW_USEDEFAULT);

  ~ButtonBar();

  void Buttons(                  // Define buttons
    ButtonSpec * pSpec);
  WORD Command();                // returns menu id of
                                 // selected button
  WORD HeightOfWidth(            // returns  minimum height
    WORD Width){                 // of bar given a certain width
    return by*(Count()*bx/Width +1);};

  void Enable(                   // Enables or disables a button
    WORD Id,                     // Menu Id
    BOOL bEnable);               // TRUE or FALSE
```

The two extra parameters in the constructor, **bx** and **by**, specify the width and height of the individual buttons. **ButtonBar** must define the member function **Click** to use **Click** in the **ListBox** class rather than **Click** in **IconButton**. Listed here are the purposes of the other public member functions:

Buttons   Sets the contents of the bar. **pSpec** points to an array of **ButtonSpec** items. The last item must be **NULL**.

Command   Returns the menu identification of the button being clicked.

HeightOfWidth   Given a value for **Width**, in pixels, returns the optimum height for the button bar, based on the number of items it contains, and their size.

Enable   Enables or disables a button. If a button is disabled, it is grayed. **Id** specifies the menu identification of the button.

```
protected:
  ButtonSpec * pSpec;
  HBRUSH Brush;
  HFONT hFont;
  WORD bx,by;
  void DrawItem(DRAWITEMSTRUCT FAR* pDs);
  HBRUSH CtlColor(HDC hDC);
  LONG CodeHandler(int NotifyCode, int Extra=0){
    return ListBox::CodeHandler(NotifyCode,Extra);};
}; // class ButtonBar

#endif
```

The class needs the usual member functions required by owner-draw
list boxes.

butnbar.cpp

```
#include "butnbar.hpp"
```

```
ButtonBar::ButtonBar(HWND PhWnd, int Id,WORD bx, WORD by,
    int x, int y, int width, int height)
    :ItemMeasurement(by),
     ListBox(PhWnd,Id,
       LBS_MULTICOLUMN|LBS_OWNERDRAWFIXED|LBS_HASSTRINGS,
       x,y,width,height),
       IconButton(PhWnd,Id,NULL)
{
  Brush=CreateSolidBrush(GetSysColor(COLOR_BTNSHADOW));
  hFont=CreateFont(15,0,0,0,0,0,0,0,ANSI_CHARSET,
                   0,0,0,FF_SWISS,NULL);
  ListBox::SetFont(hFont);
  bRecessed=FALSE;
  ColumnWidth(bx);
  ButtonBar::bx=bx;
  ButtonBar::by=by;
}
```

The constructor creates a multi-column owner-draw list box, with the
buttons appearing side by side. The column width is set to the width of
the buttons. The button labels have a sans-serif font, and the bar
background is dark gray.

```
ButtonBar::~ButtonBar()
{
```

```
DeleteObject(Brush);
DeleteObject(hFont);
IconButton::hWnd=0;
RECT rc;
GetClientRect(GetParent(ListBox::hWnd),&rc);
PostMessage(GetParent(ListBox::hWnd),WM_SIZE,0,
          MAKELONG(rc.right,rc.bottom));
}
```

When the bar is destroyed, it posts a **WM_SIZE** message to the parent. That gives the parent the chance to rearrange the other windows to fill the space left by the button bar.

```
void ButtonBar::Enable(WORD Id, BOOL bEnable)
{
  ButtonSpec * pTmp=pSpec;
  int i=0;
  while (pTmp->Icon && pTmp->MenuCommand!=Id) {
    pTmp++;
    i++;
  }
  if (pTmp->Icon
    && (bEnable && !pTmp->bEnabled
        || !bEnable && pTmp->bEnabled)){
    if (bEnable) {
      Select(i);
    }
    pTmp->bEnabled=bEnable;
    if (!bEnable) {
      Select(i);
    }
      Select(-1);
  }
}
```

Enable searches the button specification to find the button having the correct menu identification. If **bEnable** is different from the current setting, it changes the flag and redraws the button.

Windows sends **WM_DRAWITEM** messages to request the button bar to draw itself when buttons are clicked or selected, but the **Enable** function needs to provoke Windows into sending the message so that **DrawItem** can draw the button in the new state. The simplest way to have an individual button redrawn is to select it and then deselect it. The routine takes care to select the button while it is the disabled state. If the button is already disabled, **Enable** first selects it, **Enable** activates it, and then releases it. If the button is already enabled, **Enable** first disables it, and then selects it before releasing it. Windows requests that the button be drawn twice, but **DrawItem** ignores the request if the button is selected and disabled. **DrawItem** always draws the button if it is deselected, enabled or not.

Since **DrawItem** only draws the button in the deselected state, it will not appear to click in and out graphically.

```
void ButtonBar::Buttons(ButtonSpec * pSpec)
{
  ListBox::SetRedraw(FALSE);    // defer updates
  WORD OldCount=Count();        // actual nr of buttons
  Reset();                      // empty it
  ButtonBar::pSpec=pSpec;
  while (pSpec->Icon) {
    char sz[48];
    sz[0]=0;
    // get the menu string for this spec
    GetMenuString(GetMenu(GetParent(ListBox::hWnd)),
      pSpec->MenuCommand,sz,sizeof sz, MF_BYCOMMAND);
    char * psz=sz;
    // search for a tab char and replace it with 0
    while (*psz) {
      if (*psz=='\t') *psz=0;
      else psz++;
    }
    Add(sz);                    // add the string to the list
    pSpec++;
  }

  // if the number of buttons has changed, get parent to
  // check size
  if (OldCount!=Count()) {
   RECT rc;
   GetClientRect(GetParent(ListBox::hWnd),&rc);
   SendMessage(GetParent(ListBox::hWnd),WM_SIZE,0,
            MAKELONG(rc.right,rc.bottom));
  }
  ListBox::SetRedraw(TRUE);
}
```

The **Buttons** member function fills the list with buttons. This is the member function that fills the list with the buttons. To avoid having the bar redrawn every time a single button is added, **Buttons** turns the redraw flag off until after it has added all the buttons and resized the bar. The function takes the text of each button from the current menu and adds it to the list. A menu item often contains the name of an accelerator as well as the item label, and the accelerator name is then separated from the label by a TAB character, like this:

Paste<Tab>Shift-Insert

The **Buttons** member function truncates any item containing a TAB by replacing the TAB character with a zero terminator.

If the number of buttons changes, the class sends a **WM_SIZE** message to the parent since the button bar may need resizing. If there are too many buttons for the current width, the parent should increase the height of the bar to allow an additional row of buttons.

```
WORD ButtonBar::Command()
{
  if (Count()>0 && pSpec[Selection()].bEnabled){
    WORD Val=pSpec[Selection()].MenuCommand;
    return Val;
  }
  else return 0;
}
```

Command returns the menu identifier of the currently selected item. The application calls this function when the user clicks the bar, and calls the function associated with the menu item.

```
HBRUSH ButtonBar::CtlColor(HDC hDC){ return Brush;};
```

CtlColor returns the brush whenever the background needs updating. Windows uses this brush to paint the area of the bar that is not occupied by buttons.

```
void ButtonBar::DrawItem(DRAWITEMSTRUCT FAR* pDs)
{
  hIcon=LoadIcon(hInst,pSpec[pDs->itemID].Icon);

  // mask off the focus state
  pDs->itemState &= ~ODS_FOCUS;
  pDs->itemAction &= ~ODA_FOCUS;
```

```
      // if this button is disabled then if it
      // selected do nothing, otherwise set
      // the disabled flag.
      if (!pSpec[pDs->itemID].bEnabled){
        if (pDs->itemState & ODS_SELECTED) return;
        pDs->itemState |= ODS_DISABLED;
      }

      // always draw the entire button on selection
      if (pDs->itemAction & ODA_SELECT)
        pDs->itemAction=ODA_DRAWENTIRE;
      SetTextColor(pDs->hDC, GetSysColor(COLOR_WINDOWTEXT));
      char sz[48];
      Text(pDs->itemID,sz);
      DrawButton(pDs,sz,hIcon);
  }
```

The **DrawItem** member function modifies some of the items in the **DRAWITEMSTRUCT** to suit the button bar. These flags are the same flags that were described in Chapter 5 on owner-draw controls. **DrawItem** removes the **ODS_FOCUS** and **ODA_FOCUS** flags, since the focus rectangle looks inappropriate in a button bar. If the button is disabled, **DrawItem** sets the **ODS_DISABLED** flag. However, if a disabled button is selected, the member function returns without doing anything. When the selection status changes, **DrawItem** always redraws the button, since its enabled status may have changed as well. Finally, **DrawItem** calls the **DrawButton** function from the **IconButton** class to actually draw the button.

The Timer Class

When an instance of the **Timer** class is created, it invokes a callback function whenever a specified time has elapsed. This class uses the Windows timer facility. The Windows timer is a system service that generates events whenever a certain amount of time has elapsed since the last event. Using the API, there are two ways of having a timer notify the application:

☐ You can specify a Windows callback function, provided it is a C function, not a C++ member function.

☐ If you do not specify a callback, Windows sends a **WM_TIMER** message to a specified window.

Although Windows callback functions must be C functions, many callback functions can be supplied an application-specific 32-bit value as an extra parameter. If this parameter is a class instance, the C callback can, in turn, call a member function in a certain class instance, using the value supplied as a parameter. Unfortunately the callback for system timers does not receive an application-supplied value, and so it is difficult to use the timer callback function in a C++ system.

The **Timer** class creates its own invisible window specifically to handle the **WM_TIMER** message. There will be a separate window for each instance of **Timer**. Whenever the window receives the **WM_TIMER** message, it call a member function, in the same way that the control classes did, in Chapter 4.

An instance of **Timer** invokes the callback repeatedly until the callback returns **FALSE,** or the instance is destroyed.

Keep in mind that there is a system limit on the number of timers, so you cannot guarantee that you will be allocated a timer.

timer.hpp

```
#ifndef TIMER_INC
#define TIMER_INC

#include "window.hpp"

class Timer :  public Window {
public:
  Timer(                        // Set Timer
    HWND PhWnd,
    WORD Elapse);               // Elapsed time

  void Tick(                    // Set callback
    WinObj * Instance,
    BOOL (WinObj::*pCallback)());
  ~Timer();

protected:
  LPSTR Register(WNDCLASS& wc);
  WinObj * TimerInstance;
  BOOL (WinObj::*TimerCallback)(void);
  LONG MessageProc(HWND hWnd,
```

```
        unsigned msg, Event& evt);

}; // class Timer

typedef BOOL (WinObj::*TIMERCALLBACK)(void);
#endif // TIMER_INC
```

The constructor specifies the parent window and the value of the timer in milliseconds.

Tick specifies the member function that will be called when the specified time has elapsed.

timer.cpp

```
#include "timer.hpp"

Timer::Timer(HWND PhWnd, WORD Elapse)
{
  Create("",WS_CHILD,0,0,0,0,PhWnd,NULL); //invisible window
  if (!SetTimer(hWnd,1,Elapse,NULL)) delete this;
}
```

The constructor creates an invisible window and sets a timer for it using the API **SetTimer** function. The timer identification number is always 1, since there will never be more than one timer per window.

```
void Timer::Tick(WinObj * Instance,
            BOOL (WinObj::*pCallback)(void))
{
  TimerInstance=Instance;
  TimerCallback=pCallback;
}
```

Tick stores the callback instance and address in class data items.

```
Timer::~Timer()
{
  KillTimer(hWnd,1);
}
```

The destructor kills the timer using the API **KillTimer** function.

```
LPSTR Timer::Register(WNDCLASS& wc)
{
  wc.style=0;
  wc.lpszClassName="TimerClass";
```

```
RegisterClass(&wc);
return "TimerClass";
}
```

Since the window is invisible and does not need an icon or a brush, **Register** only needs to supply a class name.

```
LONG Timer::MessageProc(HWND hWnd, unsigned msg, Event& evt)
{
switch (msg) {
case WM_TIMER:
if (!TimerInstance
    || (TimerInstance->*TimerCallback)()) delete this;
break;

default:
return Window::MessageProc(hWnd,msg,evt);
}
return TRUE;
}
```

When the **WM_TIMER** event arrives, **MessageProc** invokes the callback. If the callback returns **FALSE,** it deletes the instance. All other messages are passed on to the **MessageProc** member function in the **Window** class.

Note that the standard Windows timer is rather coarse. It only guarantees that the event will arrive after the time has elapsed, thus the event may well arrive late. For most applications, that is good enough, but multimedia applications require more precision. Those applications, and any others that require a high-precision timer, can use the timer services in the Windows multimedia extensions.

The NoteFrame Class

Now to get back to the MultNote application. The **NoteFrame** class derives from **MDIFrame** and implements the application Frame. **NoteFrame** takes care of opening new Child windows and displaying the *About* box. It also maintains a button bar for some of the menu items, as shown in Figure 10-8.

**FIGURE
10-8**   The MultNote application

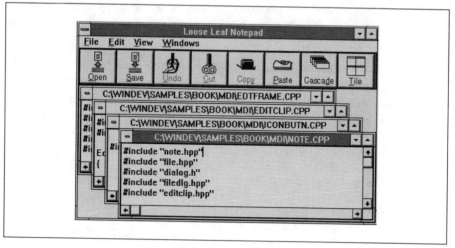

The button bar will contain buttons for opening and saving files, editing text, and arranging the windows. These buttons should be disabled and grayed when appropriate. The Edit *Cut* and *Copy* buttons should be disabled when no text is selected, and the *Paste* button should be disabled when the clipboard is empty. The *Undo* button should be grayed when there is nothing to undo.

When the menu does this, the **InitMenu** member function can update the menu items just before the user pulls the menu down. There is no need to keep the menu up to date while it is not visible.

Although the button bar ought to be kept constantly up-to-date, this is impractical. Every keystroke could change the button bar status. The constant redrawing could slow down data entry on slow machines. In practice, it is sufficient to update the button bar every second or so. This is the time it takes for a user to stop typing and to reach for the mouse to click on the button bar. With an update time of 1,500 milliseconds, the button bar appears to be updated in real time, but the changes are sparse enough not to affect the overall performance of the application.

NoteFrame uses the **Timer** class to update the button bar. A menu option turns the button bar on or off. On small screens, many users find that the button bar takes up too much space. Some users prefer to use the keyboard as much as possible and don't like to take time to click on buttons.

If there are no Child windows, only the *Open* button has any significance. When the program starts, or whenever there are no windows, we replace the full button bar by a bar containing just the *Open* button, as shown in Figure 10-9.

NoteFrame also creates an instance of **EditClip**, a class derived from **Clipboard**. For the sake of example, the application will pretend that the contents of the edit window are in some private format that it must render into text. The **EditClip** also implements a clipboard viewer.

nteframe.hpp

```
#ifndef   NOTEFRAME_INC

#define   NOTEFRAME_INC

#include "mdiframe.hpp"
#include "butnbar.hpp"
#include "timer.hpp"

class NoteFrame : public  MDIFrame{
public:
  NoteFrame(LPSTR pName=NULL,
     int x= CW_USEDEFAULT, int y= CW_USEDEFAULT,
     int width= CW_USEDEFAULT, int height= CW_USEDEFAULT);

protected:
  BOOL  Command( UINT Id, UINT Code, HWND hControl);
  BOOL  Size( UINT Width, UINT Height, UINT Type);
  LPSTR Register(WNDCLASS& wc);
  BOOL  InitMenu(HMENU hMenu);
  BOOL AlreadyOpen(MDIChild * pWin, LPSTR pName);
  void BarClicked(ListBox& bbar);
  BOOL EnableBar();
  void MakeBar();

  ButtonBar* pBar;
  Timer * pTimer;
};
#endif
```

The definition of **NoteFrame** simply defines the member functions and contains pointers to the button bar and the timer. It does not need a pointer to the **EditClip** instance. The **Clipboard** class from which **EditClip** is defined contains a **static** pointer to the last instance of **Clipboard** that was created.

FIGURE 10-9 MultNote displaying a single button

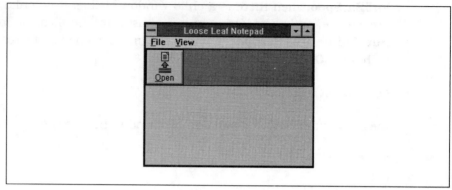

Applications usually only need one instance of the **Clipboard** class, although it is conceivable that a complex application would need more than one. Such an application might want to implement two different types of clipboard viewer, for instance.

nteframe.cpp

```cpp
#include  "nteframe.hpp"
#include "mdichild.hpp"
#include "note.hpp"
#include "dialog.h"
#include "about.hpp"
#include "filedlg.hpp"
#include "editclip.hpp"
#include "mdiframe.h"

ButtonSpec FullBarSpec[9] ={
{"Open",IDM_OPEN,TRUE},
{"Save",IDM_SAVE,TRUE},
{"Undo",  IDM_UNDO,FALSE},
{"Cut",IDM_CUT,FALSE},
{"Copy",IDM_COPY,FALSE},
{"Paste",IDM_PASTE,FALSE},
{"Cascade",4000+IDM_WINDOWCASCADE,TRUE},
{"Tile",4000+IDM_WINDOWTILE,TRUE},
{NULL,0,0}};

ButtonSpec BarSpec[2] ={
{"Open",IDM_OPEN,TRUE},
{NULL,0,0}};
```

There are two alternative button specifications. **NoteFrame** uses **FullBarSpec** when there is a child window visible. If no child windows are visible, only the *Open* button has any significance, and then **NoteFrame** uses **BarSpec**. Each icon name is defined in the resource file with an **ICON** statement like this:

Open ICON icon.ico

meaning that the icon **Open** can be found in the file OPEN.ICO.

```
NoteFrame::NoteFrame(LPSTR pName,
int x, int y,
int width, int height)
{
  pBar=NULL;
  CreateFrame(pName,"FrameMenu",0,4000,x,y,width,height);
  hAccel=LoadAccelerators(hInst, "NoteAccel");
  new EditClip(hWnd);
  MakeBar();
}
```

The constructor creates the Frame and the instance of the **EditClip** class described in Chapter 9 that supports communication with the Windows clipboard and the clipboard viewer. The **MakeBar** member function creates the button bar. This application uses some keyboard accelerators that have been defined in the resource file with the name NoteAccel. The accelerators must be loaded into **hAccel,** since the message loop uses **hAccel** to translate keystrokes. **LoadAccelerators** is an API function. The string **FrameMenu** is the name of the default Frame menu, again defined in the resource file. The position of the windows menu will have to be either 0 or 1, since this menu only has two pull-down menus.

```
LPSTR NoteFrame::Register(WNDCLASS& wc)
{
  wc.lpszClassName = (LPSTR) "NoteFrame";
  wc.hIcon = LoadIcon(hInst, "MultNote");
  wc.hbrBackground=NULL;
  RegisterClass(&wc);
  return "NoteFrame";
}
```

When **NoteFrame** registers the class, it should define an application icon. The client area of the Frame is never seen, so **Register** sets it to **NULL**. It is not strictly necessary to set it to **NULL**; **Register** could have left it defined as the default brush.

```
BOOL NoteFrame::Size(UINT Width, UINT Height, UINT Type)
{
  RECT rc;
  SetRect(&rc,0,0,Width,Height);
  RECT rBar=rc;
  if (pBar) rBar.bottom=pBar->HeightOfWidth(rc.right);
  RECT rClient=rc;
  if (pBar) rClient.top=rBar.bottom+2;
  Client->Move(&rClient);
  if (pBar) pBar->ListBox::Move(&rBar);
  return TRUE;
}
```

When the user resizes the Frame, the Frame must resize the button bar and the Client window to fit the new client area. **pBar** points to the instance of **ButtonBar**, but if there is no button bar, **pBar** will be **NULL**. **HeightOfWidth** returns the optimum height of a button bar that extends right across the Frame's client area. The height depends on the number of buttons, since the button bar displays buttons in more than one row if necessary. **Move** is a member function defined in the **Window** class that moves a window to fit a given rectangle. Notice that when this function moves the bar, it must precede **Move** with the **ListBox::** tag. That is because **ButtonBar** is derived from both the **ListBox** and the **IconButton** class, and **Move** is defined in both of those classes. Remember that the compiler requires you to specify which of the two **Move** functions you wish to use.

```
void NoteFrame::MakeBar()
{
  pBar=new ButtonBar(hWnd,2,60,55,0,0,0,0);
  pBar->ListBox::Click(this,
        (LISTBOXCALLBACK)&NoteFrame::BarClicked);
  pBar->Buttons(BarSpec);

  pTimer=new Timer(hWnd,1500);
  pTimer->Tick(this,
        (TIMERCALLBACK)&NoteFrame::EnableBar);
}
```

MakeBar creates an instance of **ButtonBar** and **Timer**. The individual buttons will be 60 pixels wide and 55 pixels high. The **MakeBar** function fills the button bar with the initial single *Open* button defined in **BarSpec**, and sets the timer to 1,500 milliseconds. The new instances are given the callbacks **BarClicked** and **EnableBar**.

```
LONG NoteFrame::InitMenu( HMENU hMenu )
{
  CheckMenuItem(hMenu,IDM_BAR,pBar?MF_CHECKED:MF_UNCHECKED);
  if (MDIChild::ActiveChild)
      return MDIChild::ActiveChild->InitMenu(hMenu);
}
```

The **InitMenu** function gives the application a chance to check or gray menu items just before they are displayed. The only menu item that **NoteFrame** needs to administer is the **IDM_BAR** item, which switches the button bar on and off. **NoteFrame** sets a check on it if there is a button bar. **NoteFrame** passes the event to the active Child if there is one, and the Child sets the *Edit* menu items acording to the state of the clipboard and the edit control. The **Note** class, discussed in the next section, shows how this is done. **InitMenu** uses the static item **ActiveChild**, defined in the **MDIChild** class, to get the instance of the currently active MDI window.

```
void NoteFrame::BarClicked(ListBox& lb)
{
  SendMessage(hWnd,WM_COMMAND,pBar->Command(),0);
  pBar->Select(-1);
  ::SetFocus(hWnd);
}
```

When the bar is clicked, this member function sends the Frame a **WM_COMMAND** message to simulate a menu item being chosen. After the event has been processed, the button is deselected and the focus is given back to the main window. **Select(-1)** deselects all the buttons that are currently selected. **BarClicked** could have called the **Command** member function directly, but that would have bypassed the code in the **MDIFrame** class that handles the MDI items to cascade and tile the windows.

```
BOOL NoteFrame::EnableBar()
{
  if (!pBar) return TRUE;
  if (Note::pCurrent) {
    if (pBar->Count()==1)
      pBar->Buttons(FullBarSpec);
    Note::pCurrent->EnableBar(pBar);
  }
  else if (pBar->Count()>1)
      pBar->Buttons(BarSpec);
  return FALSE;
}
```

The timer calls **EnableBar** on expiring. **EnableBar** enables or disables individual buttons, but it may first need to change the button bar depending on whether or not there are any Child windows. If there is a Child and there is only one button, **EnableBar** will replace it by the full row of buttons defined in **FullBarSpec**. If there are no Child windows but the full row of buttons is being displayed, they will be replaced by the single *Open* button defined in **BarSpec**. If there is an active Child window, **NoteFrame** passes it the event so that the Child can enable or disable the edit buttons.

```
BOOL NoteFrame::Command(UINT Id, UINT Code, HWND hControl)
{
    switch (Id){
  case IDM_ABOUT:
  {
    About AboutBox;
    AboutBox.OpenBox(hWnd,"ABOUT");
    break;
  }
```

NoteFrame uses the generic **About** class described in Chapter 6. A new *About* box template (shown here) was drawn using the dialog editor.

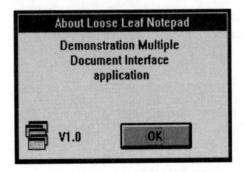

```
case IDM_NEW:
  new Note();
  break;
```

Note is the class that will be derived from **MDIChild**. If no filename is supplied to its constructor, it creates an empty edit control in an MDI window.

```
case IDM_OPEN:
{
  FileDlg Open(".\\*.cpp");
  if (Open.OpenBox(hWnd,"OPEN_FILE")) {
    if (ChildIterator(this,
        (MDICHILDCALLBACK)&NoteFrame::AlreadyOpen,
        Open.FilePath()))
    new Note(Open.FilePath());
  }
  break;
}
```

Here again, **Note** uses the **FileDlg** class described in Chapter 6, which reviewed dialog boxes. **MultNote** assumes that nobody would ever want to look at anything other than .CPP files, so that is the default suffix.

It is possible that there is already a window open on the specified file. To find out, the member function calls the **ChildIterator** function that was defined in the **MDIFrame** class to scan all the current Children. **AlreadyOpen** sets the focus and returns **FALSE** if it finds a window with the specified file path.

If the file is not already open, **Note** opens a new Child on it.

```
case IDM_BAR:
  if (pBar){
    delete pBar;
    pBar=NULL;
  }
  else MakeBar();
  break;
```

IDM_BAR toggles the button bar on and off. If the bar exists, it is deleted, otherwise the **case** statement creates a bar. When deleting the bar, it must set **pBar** to **NULL**, since this is the only way (other than by counting child windows) that the application can tell whether the bar is there or not.

```
default:
    if (MDIChild::ActiveChild)
        return MDIChild::ActiveChild->
          Command(Id, Code,hControl);
    return FALSE;
    }
    return TRUE;
}
```

Note passes all other **Command** events on to the active Child, if there is one.

```
BOOL NoteFrame::AlreadyOpen(MDIChild * pWin, LPSTR pName)
{
  char Title[120] ;
  pWin->GetText(Title,120);
  if ( !lstrcmp(pName,Title)) {
    pWin->Restore();
    ::SetFocus(pWin->hWnd);
    return FALSE;
  }
  return TRUE;
}
```

NoteFrame calls **ChildIterator** with the **AlreadyOpen** member function when a file is about to be opened in the **IDM_OPEN** case, as shown in the example above. **ChildIterator** calls **AlreadyOpen** for each Child window. If the title of the window matches the filename, the function returns **FALSE** to indicate that the search has finished. It also restores the window in case it has been iconized, and gives it the focus.

The Note Class

Note is derived from **MDIChild**. Each instance of **Note** will have an edit control that completely fills its client area, and the edit control will be handled by the **EditWin** class.

In a normal application, if the user chooses one of the menu items *Cut*, *Copy*, or *Paste*, **Note** only has to call one of the **EditWin** member functions **Cut**, **Copy**, or **Paste**, and the edit control copies data to or from the clipboard in the **CF_TEXT** format. **MultNote**, however, pretends that the data in the edit control is in a private format that must be converted and rendered when necessary. The rendering is done by the **EditClip** class, derived from **Clipboard**. The instance of **NoteFrame** would have already created an instance of **EditClip**.

Again, a normal application would define the keyboard accelerators SHIFT-DEL, CTRL-INS and SHIFT-INS for *Cut, Copy,* and *Paste.* These accelerators would also be mentioned in the menu, for the benefit of those who are unfamiliar with Windows. **MultNote** just lets the edit control handle these key sequences. As a result, if the user types an accelerator, the clipboard transfers the data in the **CF_TEXT** format, but if the user chooses a menu item, data is transferred in the private format. This is so that you can check whether the data is really being rendered from one format to the other. If you type SHIFT-DEL and then select *Paste*, data is rendered from **CF_TEXT** to the private format, and if you select *Cut* and then type SHIFT-INSERT, data is rendered from the private format to **CF_TEXT**. Try doing this with the Windows Clipboard application window open and you will see the clipboard viewer from this application in action.

note.hpp

```
#ifndef NOTE_INC
#define NOTE_INC

#include "mdichild.hpp"
#include "editwin.hpp"
#include "butnbar.hpp"

class Note: public MDIChild {
public:
  static Note * pCurrent;
  Note(LPSTR pName=NULL,
          int x= CW_USEDEFAULT,
          int y= CW_USEDEFAULT,
          int width= CW_USEDEFAULT,
```

```
                int height= CW_USEDEFAULT);
    BOOL QueryClose() ;
    BOOL InitMenu(HMENU hMenu );
    BOOL Command(UINT Id, UINT Code, HWND hControl);
    void EnableBar(ButtonBar * pBar);

protected:
    EditWin * pEdit;
    LocalMem * pBuffer;

    void Activate(BOOL bActivate){
      pCurrent=bActivate?this:NULL;}
    LPSTR Register(WNDCLASS& wc);
    ~Note();
    BOOL Save(LPSTR Path, BOOL bOverWrite);
    BOOL SaveAs();
    BOOL SetFocus(HWND hPrev){
        ::SetFocus(pEdit->hWnd);return TRUE;};
    BOOL Size( UINT Width, UINT Height, UINT Type);
};
#endif
```

Two member functions are defined in the class definition. **Activate**
maintains the **pCurrent** item to point to the currently active instance of
Note. **SetFocus** passes the focus on to the edit control.

note.cpp

```
#include "note.hpp"
#include "file.hpp"
#include "dialog.h"
#include "filedlg.hpp"
#include "editclip.hpp"

Note * Note::pCurrent=NULL;

Note::Note(LPSTR pName,
int x, int y,
int width, int height)
{
  LocalMem Reserve(500);
  if (!Reserve.Handle) {
    delete this;
    return;
  }

  // create the MDI child
  char Untitled[20];
```

```
if (!pName) LoadString(hInst,IDS_UNTITLED, Untitled, 20);
CreateChild(pName?pName:Untitled,"NoteMenu",3,0);

// create the edit control
RECT rc;
GetClientRect(hWnd,&rc);
pEdit =new EditWin(hWnd,1,0,0,0,rc.right,rc.bottom);

// open a file if a path was specified
File * pEditFile;
if (pName){
  pEditFile = new File(pName);
  pBuffer = new LocalMem(pEditFile->Size()+1);
}
else pBuffer = new LocalMem(512);

// delete the instance if the resources are not available
if ( !pEdit || !pBuffer || !pBuffer->Handle) {
  delete this;
  return;
}

// read the file into the buffer
if (pName){
  pEditFile->Read(pBuffer,pEditFile->Size());
  delete pEditFile;
}

// put the buffer into the edit control
pEdit->Buffer(pBuffer);
::SetFocus(pEdit->hWnd);
}
```

The constructor continues only if there is a 500-byte working area available in local memory. If the memory cannot be allocated, it deletes the instance.

If it can allocate the working area, the constructor creates the Child window. The file specification will be the title of the window. If there is no specification, the title will be *Untitled*. The menu associated with the window is called **NoteMenu** in the resource file. The fourth pull-down menu of **NoteMenu** is the *Window* menu. **CreateChild** specifies 3 for the *Window* menu, since the fourth menu has the index 3.

As soon as it has created the Child window, the constructor places an edit control in the client area. The **EditWin** class creates an edit control with extended facilities.

The constructor creates an instance of the **File** class based on the file specification and allocates a memory buffer big enough to hold the file. If there is no file specification, it allocates a buffer of 512 bytes instead. If there is insufficient memory for any of these items, the constructor deletes the Child; otherwise it reads the file into the memory buffer and sends the buffer to the edit control. Finally it gives the edit control the focus.

Notice that there is no need to lock the memory in **pBuffer.** The **Read** member function in **File** handles the locking. The constructor will release the 500 bytes of working storage when it returns.

```
Note::~Note()
{
  if (pEdit) delete pEdit;
  if (pBuffer) delete pBuffer;
  if (pCurrent==this) pCurrent=NULL;
}
```

The destructor deletes the instances that the constructor created. **pCurrent** is a pointer that is maintained to point to the active instance of **Note**.

```
LPSTR Note::Register(WNDCLASS& wc)
{
  wc.hIcon = LoadIcon(hInst, "Note");
  wc.lpszClassName = (LPSTR) "Note";
  RegisterClass(&wc);
  return "Note";
}
```

Register should give the Child an icon since the user can minimize MDI Children within the Client window.

```
BOOL Note::QueryClose()
{
  char Path[120];
  GetText(Path,120);
  if (pEdit->Modified()) {
   WORD Reply=Message(MB_ICONEXCLAMATION|MB_YESNOCANCEL,
     IDS_SAVECHANGES,(LPSTR)Path);
   if (Reply==IDCANCEL) return FALSE;
   if (Reply==IDYES) return Save(Path,TRUE);
  }
```

```
  return TRUE;
}
```

The **QueryClose** member function is called just before the window is closed. If the member function returns **FALSE**, the close is vetoed and the window remains open. This version of **QueryClose** displays a message box (shown here) if the contents of the edit control have been modified since the last time the file was accessed. The user has the option of saving the changes, ignoring the changes (which will then be lost), or cancelling the close operation.

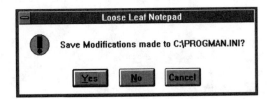

This member function will also be called when the user chooses to close the complete application. If any window vetoes the close, then no windows are closed at all.

```
BOOL Note::Save(LPSTR Path, BOOL bOverWrite)
{
  if (!Path || Path[1]!=':') return SaveAs();
  {
    File TryFile(Path,OF_EXIST);
    if (TryFile.Size() && !bOverWrite)
      if (Message(MB_ICONEXCLAMATION|MB_YESNOCANCEL,
        IDS_OVERWRITE,(LPSTR)Path)!=IDYES) return FALSE;
  }
  File EditFile(Path,OF_CREATE);
  WORD FileSize=pEdit->Size();
  if (EditFile.Write(pBuffer,FileSize)==FileSize){
    pEdit->Modified(FALSE);
    return TRUE;
  }
  return FALSE;
}
```

The **Save** member function writes the contents of the edit control to the file specified by **Path.** If **Path** is not a valid file specification, **Save** calls the **SaveAs** member function instead. **Save** assumes that the specification is invalid if the second character is not a colon. Of course, that is not an exhaustive test, but the path will always be either a full specification, or something like *Untitled*.

If the file already exists and the **bOverWrite** flag is **FALSE, Save** displays a message box (shown here) asking the user whether the existing file should really be overwritten. The **bOverWrite** flag will be **TRUE** when saving to the file specified in the window title.

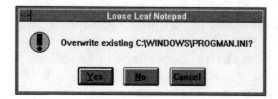

If all is well, **Save** writes the edit control memory to the file and clears the edit modify flag. Notice that **Save** creates two instances of **File**. It first creates **TryFile**, and then uses the **OF_EXIST** flag to see whether the file exists. Next, it discards **TryFile** and creates **EditFile** to write the file. **OF_CREATE** creates the file if it does not exist; otherwise, it truncates the file to zero length. **OF_WRITE** is only used for writing into an existing file, and fails if the file does not exist.

```
BOOL Note::SaveAs()
{
  char Path[120];
  LPSTR pExt;
  GetText(Path,120);
  if (Path[1]!=':') {
   lstrcpy(Path,".\\");
   pExt="*.TXT";
  }
  else {
    pExt=Path+lstrlen(Path);
    while (*(pExt-1)!='\\') pExt--;
    *pExt=0;
    while (*pExt!='.') pExt++;
  }
  FileDlg SaveAs(Path,pExt);
  if (!SaveAs.OpenBox(hWnd,"SAVE_FILE")) return FALSE;
  if ( Save(SaveAs.FilePath(),FALSE)) {
    SetText(SaveAs.FilePath());
    return TRUE;
  }
```

```
       return FALSE;
}
```

SaveAs displays a dialog box prompting the user for a filename. If the current window has a file specification as its title, the default directory and suffix will be extracted from that. If the current window is untitled, the default directory is the current directory, and the default suffix is .TXT.

If the dialog box returns **TRUE**, indicating that the user has clicked on *OK*, **SaveAs** passes the file specification to the **Save** member function. The **bOverWrite** flag in **Save** is **FALSE**, so **Save** asks if the file exists already. After saving the file, it updates the window title to the new specification.

As a matter of interest, if a Child window is maximized, Windows replaces the Frame title by the application name, or whatever the original title was, followed by the title of the Child. This does not affect **GetText** and **SetText** for the window itself. **GetText** still returns the file specification alone, even if the Child is maximized.

```
BOOL Note::Size( UINT Width, UINT Height, UINT Type)
{
  RECT rc;
  SetRect(&rc,0,0,Width,Height);
  pEdit->Move(&rc);
  return TRUE;
}
```

If the size of the Child changes, the edit control must be resized to fit in the new client area.

```
LONG Note::InitMenu( HMENU hMenu )
{
  EnableMenuItem(hMenu, IDM_PASTE,
    EditClip::Instance->Available()?MF_ENABLED:MF_GRAYED);
  EnableMenuItem(hMenu, IDM_COPY,
    pEdit->Selected()?MF_ENABLED:MF_GRAYED);
  EnableMenuItem(hMenu, IDM_CUT,
    pEdit->Selected()?MF_ENABLED:MF_GRAYED);
  EnableMenuItem(hMenu, IDM_UNDO,
    pEdit->CanUndo()?MF_ENABLED:MF_GRAYED);
  return TRUE;
}
```

Note enables items in the *Edit* menu. If anything is available in the clipboard, *Paste* is enabled. If any text is selected in the edit control, *Cut* and *Copy* are enabled, and if the edit control has anything in its undo buffer, *Undo* is enabled.

```
void Note::EnableBar(ButtonBar * pBar)
{
  pBar->Enable(IDM_PASTE,EditClip::Instance->Available());
  pBar->Enable(IDM_COPY,pEdit->Selected());
  pBar->Enable(IDM_CUT,pEdit->Selected());
  pBar->Enable(IDM_UNDO,pEdit->CanUndo());
}
```

The same thing happens for the button bar, with the exception that the button bar is updated every 1,500 milliseconds, on the timer event, while the menu is only updated just as the user pulls it down.

```
BOOL Note::Command( UINT Id, UINT Code, HWND hControl)
{
  switch (Id) {
  case IDM_UNDO:
    pEdit->Undo();
    break;
```

Note handles the menu events passed on from the Frame. **IDM_UNDO** just invokes the **EditWin** class **Undo** member function.

```
  case IDM_PASTE:
    {
      GlobalMem * pMem;
      pMem=EditClip::Instance->Get();
      pEdit->Paste(pMem);
      break;
    }
```

IDM_PASTE could have just called the **EditWin Paste** member function to copy data directly from the clipboard to the edit control. The more roundabout manner used here demonstrates what a more complex application will do if the display window is not an edit control. **EditClip** returns data from the clipboard and the code just pastes it into the edit control. **Get** is a **Memory** instance source and **Paste** is a sink. There is no need to create or delete the memory instance explicitly.

```
case IDM_COPY:
  {
    GlobalMem * pMem=pEdit->Selection();
    EditClip::Instance->Put(pMem);
    break;
  }

case IDM_CUT:
  {
    GlobalMem * pMem=pEdit->Selection();
    EditClip::Instance->Put(pMem);
    pEdit->Paste(NULL);
    break;
  }
```

IDM_COPY and **IDM_CUT** do the same thing in the other direction. To delete a selection in the **IDM_CUT** case, **Note** replaces it by an empty string.

```
case IDM_SAVE:
  {
    char * pName = new char[150];
    GetText(pName,150);
    Save(pName,TRUE);
    delete pName;
    break;
  }
```

IDM_SAVE saves to the file to the specification in the window title. If the title contains the string *Untitled*, **Save** automatically calls **SaveAs**.

```
case IDM_SAVEAS:
    SaveAs();
    break;

default:
    return FALSE;
  }
return TRUE;
}
```

The **WinMain** function is similar to that of other applications.

ntemain.cpp

```
#include "nteframe.hpp"
#include "note.hpp"

HANDLE hInst;
HANDLE hPrevInst;
LPSTR  CmdLine;

int PASCAL WinMain(HANDLE hInstance, HANDLE hPrevInstance,
    LPSTR lpszCmdLine, int nCmdShow)
{

    hInst = hInstance;
    char * pName = new char[80];
    LoadString(hInst,IDS_APPNAME, pName, 80);

    NoteFrame Win(pName);

    delete pName;

    // if there is a parameter, open a window on the file
    if (lpszCmdLine && lpszCmdLine[0]) new Note(lpszCmdLine);
    Win.Show(nCmdShow);
    return Win.MessageLoop();
}
```

If Windows calls the application with a command line parameter, **WinMain** can open a window on that file. There are various ways in which a user can specify a parameter, a parameter can be specified directly with the File Manager *Run* option. The user may specify a parameter in the command line associated with the icon for a Program Manager item.

The Resource File

A glance at the resource file will show how the menus and other items are defined.

multnote.rc

```
#include "windows.h"
#include "messages.hpp"
#include "dialog.h"
#include "filedlg.h"
#include "mdiframe.h"
#include "dialog.dlg"
#include "filedlg.dlg"
```

```
MultNote ICON multnote.ico
Note ICON note.ico
GreenTick ICON gntick.ico
RedXCross ICON redcross.ico
Exit ICON exit.ico
Checked ICON check.ico
Unchecked ICON uncheck.ico
Save ICON save.ico
Open ICON open.ico
Undo ICON undo.ico
Cut ICON cut.ico
Copy ICON copy.ico
Paste ICON paste.ico
Cascade ICON cascade.ico
Tile ICON tile.ico
```

The application icon should appear first in the list, since this is the icon that is taken by Program Manager and similar applications.

```
STRINGTABLE
BEGIN
IDS_APPNAME      "Loose Leaf Notepad"
IDS_OVERWRITE    "Overwrite existing %s?"
IDS_SAVECHANGES "Save Modifications made to %s?"
IDS_UNTITLED     "Untitled"

#include "strings.rc"
END
```

The strings used by the application are defined here, ready for translation into other languages. Strings.rc is a list of messages used by the general classes.

```
NoteMenu MENU
BEGIN
  POPUP "&File"
  BEGIN
    MENUITEM "&New",                 IDM_NEW
    MENUITEM "&Open",                IDM_OPEN
    MENUITEM "&Save",                IDM_SAVE
    MENUITEM "Save &As",             IDM_SAVEAS
    MENUITEM SEPARATOR
    MENUITEM "&About MultNote...", IDM_ABOUT
  END
```

```
  POPUP "&Edit"
  BEGIN
    MENUITEM "&Undo\tAlt+BkSp",   IDM_UNDO
    MENUITEM "&Cut",          IDM_CUT
    MENUITEM "Cop&y",         IDM_COPY
    MENUITEM "&Paste",            IDM_PASTE
  END

  POPUP "&View"
  BEGIN
    MENUITEM "&Button Bar",       IDM_BAR
  END

  POPUP "&Windows"
  BEGIN
    MENUITEM "&Tile\tShift+F4",    4000+IDM_WINDOWTILE
    MENUITEM "Casca&de\tShift+F5",4000+IDM_WINDOWCASCADE
    MENUITEM "Arrange &Icons",     4000+IDM_WINDOWICONS
    MENUITEM "Close &All",         4000+IDM_WINDOWCLOSEALL
  END
END
```

NoteMenu is the full menu, used when there is a Child window visible.

```
FrameMenu MENU
BEGIN
  POPUP "&File"
  BEGIN
    MENUITEM "&New",   IDM_NEW
    MENUITEM "&Open",  IDM_OPEN
    MENUITEM SEPARATOR
    MENUITEM "&About MultNote...", IDM_ABOUT
  END

  POPUP "&View"
  BEGIN
    MENUITEM "&Button Bar", IDM_BAR
  END
END
```

FrameMenu contains only those items that are valid when there are no Child windows visible. If any of the menus share common items, as they do here, they should have the same menu identifiers.

```
NoteAccel ACCELERATORS
BEGIN
```

```
"o",    IDM_OPEN,ALT
"s",    IDM_SAVE,ALT
"u",    IDM_UNDO,ALT
"c",    IDM_CUT,ALT
"y",    IDM_COPY,ALT
"p",    IDM_PASTE,ALT
"t",    4000+IDM_WINDOWTILE,ALT
"d",    4000+IDM_WINDOWCASCADE,ALT
VK_F4,  4000+IDM_WINDOWTILE,SHIFT,VIRTKEY
VK_F5,  4000+IDM_WINDOWCASCADE,SHIFT,VIRTKEY
VK_BACK,  IDM_UNDO,ALT,VIRTKEY
END
```

The first eight accelerators correspond to the underlined letters in the button bar labels. Although the buttons are not activated when the user types one of these accelerators, the equivalent menu item is invoked, and so the effect is the same.

Drag-and-Drop

Windows 3.1 allows users to drag files from the Windows File Manager and drop them onto an application. Under Windows 3.0, users could drop files onto Program Manager, but not other applications. At the time of this writing, Microsoft has released the specifications for drag-and-drop clients, but not for servers.

 Note If your users will be using Windows version 3.1 or later, you should make each of your MDI applications a drag-and-drop client. Drag-and-drop is especially useful with MDI applications, since the user can drop a collection of files and have the application open them all.

It is quite simple to implement drag-and-drop. An application must first register a window as being "droppable." If a window is registered, and the user drags a file onto it, Windows sends it a **WM_DROPFILES** message. The system cursor changes to something that looks like a tombstone when it is over a droppable window. Windows also provides functions that return the names of the files that the user is dragging. The drag-and-drop mechanism is in SHELL.DLL and the functions are defined in SHELLAPI.H. Link your application with the import library

SHELL.LIB. You may distribute SHELL.DLL to those users who only have Windows 3.0, so they will be able to run your application as well, although they will not be able to drop files onto it.

It is possible to derive a class from **Window** that implements drag-and-drop. The class can arrange things so that it calls a virtual member function whenever the user drops a file on the window.

dragdrop.hpp

```
#ifndef DRAGDROP_INC
#define DRAGDROP_INC

#include "window.hpp"

class DragDrop : public Window {
protected:
  ~DragDrop();
  void AcceptDrag(BOOL bAccept);
  LONG MessageProc(HWND, unsigned, Event& evt);
  virtual BOOL Dropped(LPSTR pFileName){return TRUE;};
};

#endif
```

Any class derived from **DragDrop** need only call **AcceptDrag(TRUE)** in its constructor, and define the **Dropped** member function. If the user drags several files onto the window, **DragDrop** will call **Dropped** repeatedly for each file, so long as Dropped returns **TRUE**. **Dropped** should return **FALSE** if the application cannot accept any more files.

In **Dropped**, you can do what you want with the filename: open it, delete it, and so on. If you have ever wanted a Trashcan utility, you now know how to make one. (Nobody will make one for you, for fear of being sued.)

dragdrop.cpp

```
#include "dragdrop.hpp"

extern "C" {
#include "shellapi.h"
}



DragDrop::~DragDrop()
{
 DragAcceptFiles(hWnd, FALSE);
```

```
}

void DragDrop::AcceptDrag(BOOL bAccept)
{
  DragAcceptFiles(hWnd,bAccept);
}

LONG DragDrop::MessageProc( HWND hWnd, unsigned msg,
                               Event& evt)
{
    switch(msg) {

    case WM_DROPFILES:
    {
      char File[120];

      WORD cFiles = DragQueryFile((HANDLE) evt.wParam,
                                OxFFFF, (LPSTR) NULL, 0);
      for(int i = 0; i < cFiles; i++) {
      DragQueryFile((HANDLE) evt.wParam, i,
                    File, sizeof(File));
      if (!Dropped(File)) break;
      }

      DragFinish((HANDLE) evt.wParam);
      return 0;
    }

    default:
      return Window::MessageProc(hWnd,msg,evt);
    }
}
```

The class calls the API function **DragAcceptFiles** to enable or disable drag-and-drop. When files are dropped on the window, and it receives a **WM_DROPFILES** message, it can call **DragQueryFile** to get the file specifications. Calling **DragQueryFile** with the parameter **OxFFFF** makes it return the number of files that are being dropped.

Adding Drag-and-Drop to an MDI Application

For an MDI application, it would be nice to have the Frame window accept drag-and-drop files. The problem there is that the application

Frame window is derived from **MDIFrame**. How can it be derived from **DragDrop** as well?

Multiple inheritance might be an answer. It ought to be possible to derive the Frame window from both **MDIFrame** and **DragDrop**. The problem is that both classes have a **MessageProc** member function, and the **CPPWinProc** function will just call one of them, and not the other. You could try redefining **MessageProc** in the application Frame class, to call the two member functions, but then some messages will be processed twice.

A simpler solution is to derive **MDIFrame** from **DragDrop** instead of **Window**. The application only accepts dragged files if it calls **AcceptDrag**. so if you have an MDI application that is not file-based, you can just omit the call to **AcceptDrag**.

To support drag-and-drop, make these changes to **MDIFrame**:

```
#include "dragdrop.hpp"

class MDIFrame : public DragDrop{
```

Derive **MDIFrame** from **DragDrop** instead of **Window**.

```
LONG MDIFrame::MessageProc( HWND hWnd, unsigned msg, Event& evt)
{
    switch(msg) {
    . . .
    default:
     LONG Res=DragDrop::MessageProc(hWnd,msg,evt);
    . . .
```

In **MessageProc,** pass unprocessed messages back up to **DragDrop** instead of **Window**.

To support drag-and-drop, call **AcceptDrag** and provide a **Dropped** member function. Here is the code for the **MultNote** application that would do so:

```
NoteFrame::NoteFrame(LPSTR pName,
int x, int y,
int width, int height)
{
  pBar=NULL;
  CreateFrame(pName,"FrameMenu",0,4000,x,y,width,height);
```

```
hAccel=LoadAccelerators(hInst, "NoteAccel");
new EditClip(hWnd);
MakeBar();
AcceptDrag(TRUE);
}
```

The constructor calls **AcceptDrag(TRUE)**.

```
BOOL NoteFrame::Dropped(LPSTR pFile)
{
   Note * pNote;
   if (ChildIterator(this,
       (MDICHILDMETHOD)&NoteFrame::AlreadyOpen,pFile)){
   pNote=new Note(pFile);
   return !!pNote->hWnd;
   }
   return TRUE;
}
```

Dropped creates a new MDI Child for each file. If there is already a Child for a file, **Dropped** does nothing.

Summary

C++ lends itself very well to MDI applications. MDI classes handle the messages and peculiarities of the MDI. The application designer has do to little more than distribute functions among the different types of Children and the Frame. The designer must take care not to use too much local memory in an MDI application, but otherwise an MDI application is no more difficult to write than a conventional application with a single window.

Any application that can display more than one type of window, or which can display data from a number of sources, should use the MDI.

If you have an existing application that has been written in ANSI C, but which does not support MDI, you may be able to convert it to MDI using these classes. You will need to split your window function into a Frame function and a Child function, and you will need to turn most of the global **static** data into **MDIChild** class data. Other than that, you can leave most of the C code as it is.

Unfortunately, it seems that only a minority of C programmers use ANSI C, and many do not yet use function prototypes. You may have some cleaning up to do before you can compile the C code with a C++ compiler. Utilities such as PC-Lint generate function prototypes for old C code.

This chapter introduced a **ButtonBar** class, a **Timer** class, and a **DragDrop** class, along with an extended **EditWin** class that offers more facilities then the plain **Edit** class. These new classes can be used in any application, not just MDI applications.

The classes I have described up until now provide the fundamental building blocks for constructing stand-alone Windows applications. Chapter 11 will show how DDE classes can help you build applications that can communicate and cooperate with other Windows applications.

CHAPTER

Dynamic Data Exchange

*D*ynamic Data Exchange (DDE) is a Microsoft protocol for exchanging data between applications by means of messages. Under Windows, any application can send messages to another application, provided that it knows the other application's window handle. If you write two applications and you want them to communicate, you can just invent some new messages and have the two applications send them to each other. Your two applications will be able to communicate with each other, but not with any other application. However, if you use DDE messages, your applications will also be able to communicate with any other application that supports the same DDE protocol.

The DDE protocol lets applications send each other unsolicited data and commands, and it also lets applications set up a link whereby an application informs another whenever a specific data item changes. An application can be a DDE server, when it makes data available to other applications, or it can be a DDE client, when it uses the data provided by a server. It is also possible for an application to be both a client and a server at the same time.

Many programmers consider DDE to be one of the more difficult areas of Windows application development. If time and budget resources are a bit tight, many developers are tempted to use them for adding a feature or two, not for DDE support.

If you are developing a major Windows application, market forces virtually oblige you to support DDE, but most applications are aimed at vertical markets or are designed for in-house use. Some users in these limited markets have tended to think of Windows as a novelty, and perhaps even now do not realize how DDE can help them. MS-DOS does not have DDE, and most other major operating systems do not have anything equivalent, so most users do not know what they are missing. This is likely to change now that Windows is becoming a standard operating system for personal computers.

 Remember Users are becoming more sophisticated, and are starting to demand that new software provide the advanced facilities they have seen in other applications.

Under MS-DOS, a typical application tries to do everything. A user might have only one major application. If it were a system for managing rabbit farms, the farmer might have that application, a few utilities, and maybe a word processor and a couple of games. The main application would generate business reports and letters. It might also analyze figures and display charts and graphs.

With Windows, applications can work together and leave many tasks, such as formatting reports and analyzing data, to word processors or spreadsheets. If your application has a limited market, it usually saves everybody money if the application can share data with other applications, rather than doing everything itself. Not only that, third-party applications such as word processors are far more powerful than anything similar you might add to your own application. Even if your customers only start by using the applications with stock templates and macros that you provide, sooner or later they will appreciate the flexibility that these applications give them.

You can share data between applications using the clipboard, and your application should support the clipboard. The clipboard is fine for manual data transfer; however, to provide your users with automatic or real-time data transfer, you need DDE.

What to Do with DDE

Let's review some of the uses of DDE. DDE does not always get the attention it deserves, and many training courses and books only mention it in passing. Perhaps this is understandable, given that most users still only use one major application. DDE is also a hidden protocol, so users should not need to know that they are using it. The user term for a DDE connection is a *link*.

Analyzing Data in a Spreadsheet

The classic DDE server application generates a lot of data that other applications would like to have. If the data is continually changing, it is impractical for a user to cut and paste it using the clipboard, so DDE is the ideal transfer mechanism. The literature usually quotes a stock price feed as an example. The application retrieves stock prices from a real-time stock exchange feed and displays them as they come in. It acts as a graphical user interface ticker tape machine. If the application supports

DDE, the user can employ a Windows spreadsheet to analyze the data. Thus, the user can arrange for the application to update the spreadsheet whenever a new price for a certain stock comes in. Most spreadsheet users, even if they are not programmers, can write macros to analyze data and create graphs and charts.

In many applications, a relatively simple Windows program gathers data and makes it available to a spreadsheet by DDE. The data is often collected from an industrial data logger or laboratory measuring equipment. Other applications retrieve data from remote databases. In all these cases, the spreadsheet user can analyze the data in the same way, after selecting *Paste Link* from a menu to link the data to the spreadsheet.

It is not necessary to have a real-time feed before DDE becomes useful. Many Windows applications are bookkeeping packages of one sort or another. Here again, if the data is available by DDE, the user can write worksheets to analyze the data in ways not covered by the bookkeeping application. MS-DOS applications provide this facility through text files. The user opens the application, which writes the data to a disk file in a formatted text form. The user then closes the application, starts the spreadsheet application, and reads in the data. DDE is much faster. Once a worksheet containing DDE links has been prepared, the user simply opens it and the spreadsheet application fetches the latest data directly from the other application.

Generating Pro Forma Reports

Reports and stock letters can be laid out with a spreadsheet or a word processor and stored as a template or worksheet with DDE links embedded. When anyone needs a report, the application supplies the latest values through DDE and the word processor or spreadsheet can print out the complete document.

This is a useful technique for applications that have a limited market, since it is rarely worthwhile adding sophisticated report-generating facilities to these applications. With DDE, the users can have all the power they will ever need for the price of a word processor or spreadsheet package. If you supply some templates for these packages to get your users started, they can set up your application without needing to know how the other applications work.

Sending Commands to an Application

Many major applications have a DDE command set, so that other applications can control them remotely. By convention, if the application has a macro language, the macros can also be executed by DDE. Your application can send DDE commands directly from the program code, or indirectly from its own macro language, if it has one.

If you know that a certain application is installed, this feature is a useful facility. If your application uses the Excel spreadsheet for generating reports, it can automate the entire procedure. Your application can start Excel, send a DDE command to open the report worksheet, supply the data by DDE, and send DDE commands to print the report and close the worksheet.

Today, different applications use different DDE commands, so if your users do not have Excel, this trick will not work. The best you can do is to make the command strings available so that you or your users can easily adapt them to suit different applications. Microsoft is planning to publish a macro language standard. One it is available, if all vendors stick to the standard, your applications will be able to send general DDE commands to any Windows application, or at least to any application of a similar type.

Receiving Commands in Your Application

In the same way, your application can accept commands from other applications. You may think that your application can do without such a luxury, since in any case other applications can send keystrokes to any Windows application, including your own. Users can write macros that send keystrokes, using Excel or a similar application. If your application has a standard *File Open* dialog box, a macro can send your application the key sequence ALT-F, O, <*filename*>, ENTER to make it open a file. Even so, there are several disadvantages to using keystrokes:

❑   The keystrokes are language-dependent. If you make your application available in different languages, the keystrokes will be different for each language. In Europe, it is quite common for organizations to have copies of an application in different languages. In a German version of an application, the *File* menu might be called *Datei* and would need the ALT-D sequence to pull it down.

☐   Between one version of the application and another, the keystrokes may change. If you add some extra facilities and rearrange a dialog box, users may find that their old macros no longer work.

☐   Using keystrokes is slow. Dialog boxes must be initialized, and they sometimes pop up and disappear. The windows keep flashing from the active to the inactive state. All this activity is distracting when the program is being controlled automatically.

☐   It is difficult to handle error conditions, such as missing or locked files. An interactive application would typically display a message box when an error occured, but this would interrupt a keystroke sequence.

If your application supports DDE commands, these problems can be avoided. You might insist that the command syntax use keywords in a certain language, such as English, even if the user interface is in another language. That would be reasonable, since the commands are normally invisible to the user. Alternatively, your application could accept command keywords in alternative languages, regardless of the language used in that version of the application.

With DDE commands, all unnecessary activity can be suppressed. If your application supports an *Open (<filename>)* command, for example, it can simply open the file without any further ado. There is no need to initialize the *Open File* dialog box.

DDE servers return an error code if a client sends them a command that cannot be executed. The client can then take appropriate action and avoid sending the server further out-of-context commands. For example: If the client sends the server a command to open a file and the server cannot find the file and returns an error code, then the client can refrain from sending the server commands to edit and process the file.

The macro language of most major applications allows sending DDE commands to other applications, so users can use Excel or something equivalent to write macros that control your application through DDE. Your application only needs to provide a set of DDE commands and not a macro language. That is an important difference since writing a macro processor is not a trivial task.

Design Issues

Two main issues arise when programming DDE: handling the DDE protocol itself, and handling the links and conversations in the applications. Many programmers focus mainly on the protocol, but the real concern, in any but the simplest application, is handling the links and conversations.

The DDE Protocol

The DDE protocol is based on messages. Applications send each other messages offering or requesting data. The data is transferred in global memory blocks and the name of the data is passed as a global atom. An *atom* is a Windows handle onto a text string. It is more efficient to transfer atoms rather than the strings themselves. Messages must be acknowledged in the correct manner. As well as specifying the messages, the DDE protocol states which of the two partners has the responsibility for deleting the atoms and global memory blocks.

If the protocol is not implemented correctly, applications may be blocked, or atoms and memory blocks may be left orphaned. It is important to get the protocol right. The Microsoft DDE Management Library (DDEML) is available in the Windows version 3.1 SDK. This library simplifies DDE by wrapping up the message protocol in a higher-level layer using Windows function callbacks. DDEML is easier to use than the basic DDE message protocol, especially for C programs. Paradoxically, it is easier to implement a DDE class around the messages than around the DDEML. This is because an application should only have one instance of a DDEML, which handles all of the DDE conversations. With the DDE messages, it is quite easy to have an instance of a class for each DDE conversation, a conversation being an exchange of messages between applications. You can use DDEML if you want to, but the message protocol is still valid. The classes described in this chapter will use DDE messages.

It is straightforward to implement the DDE protocol according to the specification. Unfortunately, some "Well-Known" applications do not implement the protocol correctly on their side. To deal with these rogue applications, the protocol must be able to recover from the cases where the corresponding application does not respond correctly, or where an application terminates unexpectedly.

Obviously, the DDE protocol can easily be wrapped in a C++ class.

Dealing with Multiple Conversations

An exchange of DDE messages between a client and a server is known as a *DDE conversation*. A conversation is always one-to-one and always concerns a DDE topic. The server defines the topics, but most servers support a general *System* topic. If the server processes files, then the currently open files will also be topics. An application can have several DDE conversations going on at the same time. The conversations may be with different applications, or with different topics within an application. It is difficult for an application to handle all these different messages itself, so the solution is to set up an invisible window for each conversation. This is the same technique that the **Clipboard** and **Timer** classes used.

If the DDE conversations are represented by child windows, the conversation can be terminated automatically when the parent window is destroyed. The parent does not need to keep track of all the current conversations.

Handling Links

Once a DDE conversation has been established, a DDE client can do one of the following things:

- ☐ It can terminate the conversation.

- ☐ It can request some data and wait for the reply.

- ☐ It can send the server some unsolicited data.

- ☐ It can send the server a command.

- ☐ It can ask the server to update some data whenever the data changes. By doing this it is establishing a link.

The first four services can be handled synchronously. That means the client can send the request and wait for the acknowledgment. If these services are implemented by a class member function, the member function only needs to return control to the client when it has received a reply.

The last service, the link, is asynchronous. Although the server acknowledges the request directly, the client never knows when the data might arrive, and, of course, the client cannot remain blocked until then. The solution is for the client to specify a callback member function that can be called when the data arrives. This is analogous to the **Button** class callback that is called when the user clicks on a button.

A link always concerns an item within a topic. Again, it is the server that defines what an item might be. In Excel, an item is a cell or a range of cells in the worksheet. A single DDE conversation may have several links open, and they must be cancelled explicitly when the conversation ends. To handle the links, the client must maintain a list of them.

Links may be *hot* or *warm*. For a hot link, the server sends the data whenever it is available. For a warm link, the server simply advises when the data changes, but does not send the data. The client must request the actual data. A warm link is more efficient if the client does not always need the data immediately. For example, a document may have several links embedded in it, but the data corresponding to a link may be scrolled outside the document window. The data may change several times before it is scrolled back. It would be more efficient to establish a warm link. The client could just mark the data as changed, and only request it when it is scrolled back into view.

Hot and warm links do not affect the design of the class very much. The same callback can be used for both types of links. If the client requests a warm link, the callback will be passed a **NULL** memory block.

Clients and Servers

An application may be a DDE client, a DDE server, or both at the same time. Client conversations are easier to keep track of. An application can decide that it needs some data from another application, create a conversation, get the data, and close the conversation. If the client conversations are made children of an application window, they will be terminated properly when the window closes.

For a server application, more thought is needed. In the first place, the application must decide which topics to support. It ought to support the general *System* topic. The other topics depend on the application type. In a file-based application, the other topics are usually file paths. In an MDI application with several document windows open, the application may support several file topics.

A DDE server must have a top-level window that watches for **WM_DDE_INITIATE** messages. A top-level window is one that does not have a parent. When a client wishes to start a conversation, it sends **WM_DDE_INITIATE** messages to all top-level windows in the system. Sending the message to all windows would be inefficient, since that would include all the minor windows and controls visible on the screen. The message will contain atoms representing an application and topic. If another application supports the name and topic of the requested application, it acknowledges the message, a conversation is established, and the other top-level windows simply ignore the message.

This top-level window need not be the main application window. The application can create a separate top-level window to handle DDE **WM_DDE_INITIATE** messages, and this window can then create child windows to handle each conversation, as shown in Figure 11-1.

If the application is also a DDE client, it may start additional DDE conversations independently of the server window. The window representing a DDE client conversation usually belongs to the main application window, or to one of its children.

Callbacks are convenient for clients, but they are awkward for servers. An application could specify a callback that the server window could call when it received a **WM_DDE_INITIATE** message, but then the server would need additional callbacks for the new conversation. The result would be a double layer of callbacks. To complicate matters further, most DDE operations are asynchronous with the server. The server must be ready to accept any request or command from the client at any time, so callbacks are needed to handle everything.

It is simpler for an application to create a subclass of a generic DDE server class. The subclass can then define virtual member functions to handle all the different events in the same way that an application derives

FIGURE
11-1

Window hierarchy of a DDE server

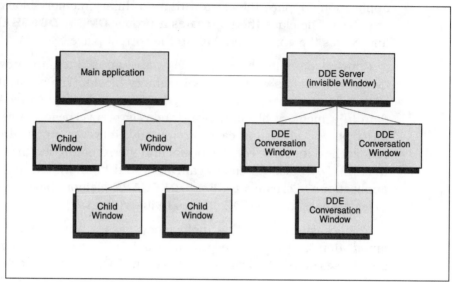

a class from the **Window** class to handle keyboard and mouse events. This is quite simple conceptually, but it does require that the server class be able to access the other classes in the application. This may mean making the derived DDE server class a **friend** of the main application classes so that it can access the protected and private data in those classes.

In the DDE classes presented in this chapter, the **DDEClient** class can be used directly with callbacks. The **DDEServer** class is a virtual base class, and you should derive a subclass for each application.

DDE Memory Blocks

When a program allocates a global memory block with a view to using it for DDE, the allocation must specify the **GMEM_DDESHARE** flag. Global memory blocks allocated with this flag may be shared between applications.

The first few bytes of a DDE memory block contain flags that are used by the DDE protocol, and the actual data appears after these bytes. In the **DDEClient** and **DDEServer** classes described in this chapter, the application supplies the class with an ordinary memory block, without any flags. The class then allocates a proper **GMEM_DDESHARE** block and copies the application data to the correct place.

Copying data in this way allows the application to provide local memory blocks as well as global memory blocks. The application does not need to concern itself with the DDE flags. If the application keeps the data in a memory block anyway, there is no overhead, since the data must be copied in any case. Frequently, however, applications must render the data in the correct format and then create a new memory block that the DDE classes copy again. It would be more efficient for such applications to create a **GMEM_DDESHARE** memory block directly and to leave space for the DDE classes to insert flags.

For occasional use, this inefficiency passes unnoticed, but if your application is going to be primarily a DDE server, consider deriving subclasses of the DDE classes that accept DDE memory blocks directly.

The Clipboard

If you were to put a DDE server in the rabbit farm application referred to earlier in this chapter, a user could access the data from another application by specifying the application name, the topic name, and the

Working with 32 Bits

In Windows NT, each application has its own address space, so although an application can send another application a message containing the address of a memory block, the other application cannot access the memory. Windows NT actually intercepts DDE messages and copies the contents of the memory blocks into the other application's address space so that it can access them. It only does this, however, if the memory has been allocated with the **GMEM_DDESHARE** flag.

item. For example, an Excel user might access your data by entering a formula looking something like this:

='RABBIT' | 'c:\rabbit\1990\qtr2\wk3.rbt'!RabbitPopulation

This would be cumbersome. If the item were a range of figures, perhaps between certain dates, it might be difficult to identify the item exactly. The usual way of creating a DDE link is to copy the data to the clipboard from the server application and then to do a *Paste Link* in the client, as shown in Figure 11-2. This is an easy concept for the user to understand, since it just an extension of the familiar clipboard. The word *Link* implies that the data is linked to the original application.

To support the clipboard link concept, the DDE server only has to support an extra clipboard format, **link**. Clipboard data in **link** format just specifies the DDE application, topic, and item of the clipboard data. Whenever the user copies data to the clipboard in the server application, the server should add the **link** format. In the same way, a client can use the contents of the **link** clipboard format to get the DDE specification of the item in the clipboard.

Since most DDE applications will want to use this facility, it will be useful to provide a subclass of the **Clipboard** class to handle it.

The Paste Link menu item in Excel

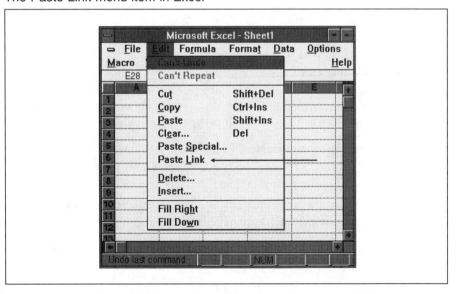

Implementation

Three classes are described in this chapter:

☐ The **DDEClient** class

☐ The **DDEServer** class

☐ The **DDEClip** class, a subclass of **Clipboard** for handling the *Paste Link* operation

The **DDEClient** and **DDEServer** classes require a simple list class to maintain the links, so that must come first. List classes are quite often supplied with C++ compilers, but they are not always Windows-oriented.

The SList Class

The **SList** class implements a single linked list in which element points to the next element. To find an element in the list, an application must scan it from the beginning. Doubly linked lists can be scanned in either direction at the expense of an additional pointer, but for all the classes described here, a single linked list will do fine.

The list usually contains pointers to instances of some class. The generic **SList** class handles lists of **void** pointers, but to preserve type checking, you will want to derive subclasses to handle lists of pointers to instances of a particular class. The subclass of **SList** will cast **void** pointers to class or structure pointers. If your application needed a list of complex numbers, it would derive a class **ComplexList** from **SList** and in that class it would cast **void*** to **Complex***.

It is tiresome having to define a subclass whenever you want to use **SList**, but there are two mechanisms that make the job easier:

☐ The first mechanism is a set of **define** statements supplied in the standard GENERIC.HPP file.

☐ The other mechanism, which is not yet universally available, is *Templates*.

A single-linked list

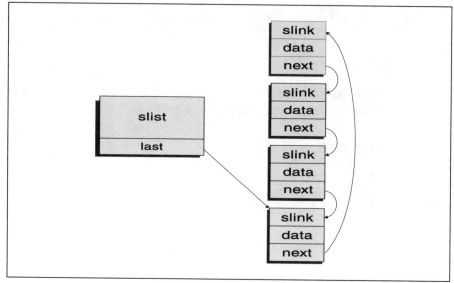

Not all compilers support both of these facilities. If templates are supported, the GENERIC.HPP file may not be supplied. Since the code here tries to be compiler independent, it will implement both these mechanisms.

The first task is to define the **SList** class. A list will be composed of a number of links (not DDE links, but links in a chain). Each link will contain a pointer to the actual data and a pointer to the next link in the chain, as shown in Figure 11-3. The last link will point back to the head of the chain. The **SList** class will maintain a pointer to the last link.

The source code here is adapted from Bjarne Stroustrup's book, *The C++ Programming Language* (1986, Addison-Wesley).

slist.hpp

```
#ifndef SLIST_INC
#define SLIST_INC

#include "winobj.hpp"

class SLink {
  friend class SList;
  friend class SListIterator;
```

```
  SLink(void *a) {e = a; next = 0; };
  ~SLink() {if (e) delete e;};
  SLink* next;
  void *e;
}; // class SLink
```

The **SLink** constructor takes a pointer to the data and the destructor deletes the data when the link is deleted.

```
class SList {
  friend class SListIterator;
public:
  SList();
  SList(void *a);
  void clear();

  int insert(void *);
  int append(void *);
  int unlink(void *);
  void *get();
  ~SList() { clear(); }
private:
  SLink* last;
}; // class SList
```

The **SList** class contains member functions for inserting an item at the head of the list and appending an item at the end of the list. The **get** member function returns the item at the head of the list. The **unlink** member function removes an item from the list. Not all implementations of **SList** include **unlink**, although it is often included in implementations of double-linked lists.

```
class SListIterator {
public:
  SListIterator(SList* s) { cs = s; ce = cs->last; }
  void *operator()(void);
private:
  SLink* ce;
  SList* cs;
}; // class SListIterator

#endif //  SLIST_INC
```

The iterator will be used to search through the list. To use it, a program first declares an iterator on a list. Each time the iterator's **( )** operator is used, the iterator returns the next item in the list. Once the iterator reaches the end of the list, it returns **NULL**. It cannot be reset, and after use it is discarded.

slist.cpp

```
#include "slist.hpp"

SList::SList()
{
    last = 0;
}

SList::SList(void *a)
{
  if ((last = new SLink(a))!=0)
  last->next = last;
}
```

The **SList** constructor will either initialize an empty list or create a list with an initial element.

```
int SList::insert(void *a)
{
  SLink* t = new SLink(a);
  if (!t) return(-1);
  if (last) {
    t->next = last->next;
    last->next = t;
  }
  else {
    last = t;
    last->next = last;
  }
  return(0);
}
```

To insert a link at the head of the list, **last->next** is moved to point to the new link. The new link itself will point to the old list head. If the list is empty, the pointer **last** is simply set to point to the new link.

```
int SList::append(void *a)
{
  SLink* t = new SLink(a);
  if (!t) return(-1);
```

```
     if (last) {
        t->next = last->next;
        last = last->next = t;
     }
     else {
        last = t;
        last->next = last;
     }
     return(0);
}
```

To append a link, the procedure is similar, but **last** is also moved to point to the new link, making it the head instead of the tail.

```
void *SList::get()
{
  if (last == 0) return 0;
  SLink* f = last->next;
  void *r = f->e;
  f->e=0;
  if (f == last) last = 0;
  else last->next = f->next;
  delete f;
  return r;
}
```

The **get** member function returns the item at the head of the list and removes the link. Before deleting the link, **last->next** is set to the link that follows the old head. If the head was also the last link, **last** is set to zero to indicate that the list is now empty.

```
int SList::unlink(void *a)
{
  if (last == 0) return 0;
  SLink* prev=last;
  SLink* f = last->next;
  do {
     if (f->e==a) {
        if (f->next==f) last=0;
        else if(last==f) last=prev;
        prev->next=f->next;
        delete f;
        return 0;
     }
     prev=f;
```

```
    f=f->next;
  } while (f!=last->next);
  return -1;
}
```

The **unlink** function searches the list for an item, beginning at the head of the list. As it searches, it maintains a pointer **prev** to the previous link. When a link is removed, **prev** can be set to point at the link that follows the one being unlinked.

```
void SList::clear()
{
  SLink* l = last;
  if (l==0) return;
  do {
    SLink* ll = l;
    l = l->next;
    delete ll;
  } while (l != last);
  last = 0;
}
```

The **clear** function goes through the list and deletes all the links.

```
void *SListIterator::operator()()
{
  void * ret = ce?(ce=ce->next)->e:0;
  if (ce==cs->last) ce=0;
  return ret;
}
```

The **SlistIterator ( )** operator function returns the current item and moves the cursor **ce** on to the next link. When the cursor reaches the end of the list, the **( )** function disables it by setting it to zero.

The **GSList** and **GSListIterator** classes are generic classes that an application uses to create linked lists of a particular type.

gslist.hpp

```
#ifndef GSLIST_INC
#define GSLIST_INC

#include "slist.hpp"

#ifdef __TEMPLATES__
  template <class type> class GSList : public SList {
```

```
      public:
      GSList():SList(){};
      GSList(type *a):SList(a){};
      int insert(type *a) { return SList::insert(a); };
      int append(type *a) { return SList::append(a); };
      int unlink(type *a) { return SList::unlink(a); };
      type *get() { return (type *) SList::get(); };
}; // class GSList

template <class type> class GSListIterator
                      : SListIterator {
      public:
      GSListIterator(GSList<type>& s)
        :SListIterator ((SList*) &s) {};
      type *operator()()
      { return (type *) SListIterator::operator()(); };
}; // class GSListIterator
```

If templates are available, defining a template class is relatively straightforward. A template class is a parameterized class definition. Within the template you can give items a type, but you only need specify that type when you declare an instance of the template class. In the preceding definition of **GSList**, the key word **template** indicates that this is a template class, and the specification **<class type>** indicates that type is a placeholder for a class that will be supplied when an instance of **GSList** is declared.

The **GSList** template class acts as a wrapper around **SList** and casts the **void*** pointers to class pointers. For example, to declare a list of complex numbers a programmer would write:

GSList<Complex> ComplexList;

and the compiler would ensure that the parameters to **append**, **insert**, and the other functions were all of the type, **Complex**.

If templates are not available, then a generic class can be defined using the macros defined in GENERIC.H.

```
#else
  #include <generic.hpp>
  #define GSList(type) name2(GSList,type)
  #define GSListIterator(type) name2(GSListIterator,type)
```

The **name2** is a name concatenation macro defined in GENERIC.HPP. It is used to generate identifiers, so **GSList(Complex)** would become **GSListComplex**.

```
#include "generic.hpp"
#define GSList(type) name2(GSList,type)
#define GSListIterator(type) name2(GSListIterator,type)

#define GSListdeclare(type)\
class GSList(type): public SList {\
  public:\
    int insert(type *a) { return SList::insert(a); }\
    int append(type *a) { return SList::append(a); }\
    int unlink(type *a) { return SList::unlink(a); }\
    type *get() { return (type *) SList::get(); }\
    GSList(type)():SList(){}\
    GSList(type)(type *a) :SList((void *) a){};\
    ~GSList(type)(){clear();}\
};\
\
class GSListIterator(type) : public SListIterator {\
  public:\
    GSListIterator(type)(GSList(type)& s) :\
    SListIterator((SList *) &s) {}\
    type *operator()()\
    { return (type *) SListIterator::operator()(); }\
};
#endif // __TEMPLATES__

#endif // GSLIST_INC
```

This is similar to the template code, but the entire definition is now a **define** statement. A **define** statement is terminated by the end of a line, unless the last character on the line is a backslash, so each line of the definition must end with the backslash.

The **GSListdeclare(type)** definition will define a wrapper class, so **GSListdeclare (Complex)** will declare a **GSList(Complex)** class and a **GSListIterator(Complex)** class. Since these are also the subject of a **define** statement, they are equivalent to a **GSListComplex** class and a **GSListIteratorComplex** class. Another macro in GENERIC.HPP, **declare**, can be used to define the wrapper, so that **declare (GSList, Complex)** will be replaced by **GSListdeclare(Complex)**. To define a list of complex numbers, a programmer must first define the class and later declare the list, like this:

```
declare(GSList,Complex);      //declare class GSListComplex
GSList(Complex) ComplexList;  //declare an instance
                              // of GSListComplex
```

Templates are easier to work with, but the end result is the same.

The DDEClient Class

Now that it is possible to define lists of class instances, it is possible to create the **DDEClient** class. Keep in mind that an application will use **DDEClient** when it wishes to use the facilities of another DDE server, such as Excel.

ddeclien.hpp

```
#ifndef DDELINK_INC
#define DDELINK_INC

#include "window.hpp"
#include "memory.hpp"
#include "gslist.hpp"

class LinkItem {
public:
    char Name[32];                    // Data for link
    WORD Format;
    WinObj * Inst;
    void (WinObj::*pCallback)(LPSTR, WORD, GlobalMem*);

    LinkItem(
      LPSTR pName,                    // Link name
      WORD Format,                    // data format
      WinObj * Inst,                  // callback function
      void (WinObj::*pCallback)(LPSTR, WORD, GlobalMem*)){
        lstrcpy(Name,pName);
        LinkItem::Format=Format;
        LinkItem::Inst=Inst;
        LinkItem::pCallback=pCallback;
    };
}; // class LinkItem
```

The **LinkItem** class contains the item name, the clipboard format and the callback for a particular link. Since a conversation may have many links, the **DDEClient** class will maintain a list of **LinkItem** instances.

```
#ifndef __TEMPLATES__
declare(GSList,LinkItem);
#endif
```

If the compiler does not support templates, the list class has to be declared here.

```
class DDEClient : public Window {
public:
  DDEClient(
    HWND PhWnd);            // Parent window handle

  ~DDEClient();

  BOOL Initialize(         // Start a link with a Server
    LPSTR Server,          // for a certain Topic
    LPSTR Topic);

  BOOL Execute(            // Execute a command
    LPSTR ComString);      // on the Server;

  GlobalMem * Request(     // Get the value of a
    LPSTR Item,            // certain Item
    WORD Format);          // in the specified
                           // Clipboard format

  BOOL Link(               // Start a link with an Item
    LPSTR Item,            // in the specified format
    WORD Format,           // with the callback
    WinObj * Inst,         // Link is hot by default
    void (WinObj::*pCallback)(LPSTR, WORD,GlobalMem*),
    BOOL bDeferred=FALSE);

  BOOL Unlink(             // Cancel a link
    LPSTR Item,
    WORD Format=NULL);

  BOOL Poke(               // Send the Server some data
    LPSTR Item,            // in a specified format
    WORD Format,
    Memory * Data);
```

There are public member functions for the six operations a client can perform:

```
protected:
  HWND ServerWnd;
  BOOL bTerminated;
```

The client needs to remember the server's window handle. Generally, the handle will be **NULL** after the conversation has been ended. The **bTerminated** flag is needed to deal with servers that terminate a conversation in a non-standard way.

```
    LPSTR Register(WNDCLASS& wc);
    void Terminate();
    BOOL PostDDEMessage(UINT msg, UINT uiLo, UINT uiHi);
    void UnpackDDEMessage(UINT msg, DWORD lParam,
               UINT* puiLi, UINT* puiHi);
    GlobalMem * CopyDDEMem(HANDLE hMem, LPSTR Item,
                        WORD&  Format, BOOL& bRelease);
    WORD WaitForAck(LPSTR Item);
    HGLOBAL WaitForData(LPSTR Item);
    void WaitForTerminate();
    WORD WaitForExecute(HANDLE hMem);
    LONG MessageProc(HWND hWnd, unsigned Msg, Event& evt);

#ifdef __TEMPLATES__
  GSList<LinkItem> LinkItems;
#else
  GSList(LinkItem) LinkItems;
#endif
}; //class DDEClient
```

The list is declared with either **<>** or **( )** brackets, depending on whether templates or generic macros are used.

```
typedef void (WinObj::*LINKCALLBACK)(LPSTR, WORD,GlobalMem*);

#endif // DDELINK_INC
```

The **LINKCALLBACK typedef** can be used to cast member functions for a link callback.

```
#include "ddeclien.hpp"
extern "C" {
#include <dde.h>
}
```

ddeclien.cpp

```
DDEClient::DDEClient(HWND PhWnd)
{
  ServerWnd=0;
  Create("",WS_CHILD,0,0,0,0,PhWnd,NULL);
}
```

The constructor creates an invisible window to handle the DDE conversation, but it does not start the conversation. The application starts the conversation with the **Initialize** function. DDE conversations quite often skip from topic to topic, and it is useful to be able to initiate conversations without having to delete the **DDEClient** instance and create a new one.

```
LPSTR DDEClient::Register(WNDCLASS& wc)
{
  wc.style=0;
  wc.lpszClassName="DDELink";
  RegisterClass(&wc);
  return "DDELink";
}
```

The **Register** member function is just as Spartan as the one used for the **Timer** and **Clipboard** invisible windows.

```
DDEClient::~DDEClient()
{
  Terminate();
}
```

When the instance is destroyed, if there is a conversation in progress, it must be terminated.

```
BOOL DDEClient::PostDDEMessage(UINT msg,
                               UINT uiLo, UINT uiHi)
{
#ifdef WIN32
  return PostMessage(ServerWnd, msg, (UINT)hWnd,
                     PackDDElParam(msg, uiLo,uiHi));
#else
  return PostMessage(ServerWnd, msg, (UINT)hWnd,
```

```
                    MAKELONG(uiLo, uiHi));
#endif
}

void DDEClient::UnpackDDEMessage(UINT msg, DWORD lParam,
                                 UINT* puiLo, UINT* puiHi)
{
#ifdef WIN32
  UnpackDDElParam(msg, lParam, puiLo, puiHi);
#else
  *puiLo = LOWORD(lParam);
  *puiHi = HIWORD(lParam);
#endif
}
```

A DDE message always gives the window handle of the sender in the **wParam** parameter. The message provides two pieces of additional

Working with 32 Bits

PostDDEMessage and **UnpackDDEMessage** are useful functions, but the main reason for using them is to ensure portability between 16-bit and 32-bit versions of Windows. The information sent is often a handle to global memory, and these handles are 32-bits long in 32-bit Windows. This means that it is impossible to pack two such items into the 32-bit **lParam**. In 32-bit Windows, certain DDE messages have been redefined so that the **lParam** contains the handle of a small global memory block which can hold the two pieces of information. The 32-bit API provides the **PackDDElParam** and **UnpackDDElParam** functions to simplify the allocation, packing, and unpacking. These functions work with all the DDE messages except the **WM_INITIATE** and **WM_TERMINATE** messages. They even work with the messages that take only 16-bit values, and are identical in the two versions of Windows.

The application that receives the message should call **FreeDDElParam** to free the small memory block used to hold the information.

information as well. The type of information depends on the message, but the two pieces are always packed into the **lParam**. **PostDDEMessage** and **UnpackDDEMessage** pack and unpack the information.

```
void DDEClient::Terminate()
{
  if (ServerWnd) {
    LinkItem* pLink;
    while ((pLink=LinkItems.get())!=0){
      ATOM atomItem=GlobalAddAtom(pLink->Name);
      PostDDEMessage(WM_DDE_UNADVISE,
                     pLink->Format, atomItem);
      WaitForAck(pLink->Name);
    }
    HWND hTemp=ServerWnd;
    ServerWnd=NULL;
    PostMessage(hTemp,WM_DDE_TERMINATE,(UINT)hWnd,0);
    ServerWnd=NULL;
    WaitForTerminate();
  }
}
```

The **Terminate** member function closes down the current conversation. If **ServerWnd** is **NULL**, no conversation is in progress; otherwise, **Terminate** performs the following steps:

☐ Cancel all the links by sending an **WM_DDE_UNADVISE** message to the server. The server must acknowledge each cancel. The information for each link is pulled off the head of the list using **get**.

☐ Post the server a **WM_DDE_TERMINATE** message.

☐ Wait until the server has replied with a **WM_DDE_TERMINATE** message.

```
BOOL DDEClient::Initialize(LPSTR Server, LPSTR Topic)
{
  Terminate();
  bTerminated=FALSE;
  ATOM atomApp=GlobalAddAtom(Server);
  ATOM atomTopic=GlobalAddAtom(Topic);
  SendMessage((HWND)-1,WM_DDE_INITIATE,
              (UINT)hWnd,MAKELONG(atomApp,atomTopic));
  GlobalDeleteAtom(atomApp);
  GlobalDeleteAtom(atomTopic);
```

```
    return !!ServerWnd;
}
```

Before a new conversation can begin, the current conversation must be terminated; the instance can only handle one conversation at a time. If the application wants to have multiple conversations, it must create multiple instances of **DDEClient**. To start a conversation, **Initialize** creates atoms containing the target server name and topic and sends them to all the top-level windows in the system. The **–1** parameter signifies to Windows that all the top-level windows should receive the message.

SendMessage acts immediately. The message is not queued. Since the server will also reply with a **SendMessage**, the reply would have been received by the **DDEClient** message procedure before **SendMessage** returns! This means that the **ServerWnd** item would have been set when **SendMessage** returns, provided of course, that there is an application that can support the required server and topic.

The client has the responsibility of deleting the atoms. The double **!!** converts **ServerWnd** into a Boolean value—**TRUE** if the handle is valid and **FALSE** if it is **NULL**.

```
BOOL DDEClient::Execute(LPSTR ComString)
{
  if (!ServerWnd) return FALSE;
  GlobalMem ComdMem(lstrlen(ComString)+1,
            GMEM_MOVEABLE | GMEM_DDESHARE);
  ComdMem.Load(ComString,lstrlen(ComString)+1);
  if (PostDDEMessage(WM_DDE_EXECUTE,0,(UINT)ComdMem.Handle))
    return WaitForExecute(ComdMem.Handle);
  return FALSE;
}
```

To request the server to execute a command, this is the procedure:

- ❑   Create a DDE global memory block large enough for the command.

- ❑   Load the command into it.

- ❑   Post the memory handle to the server in a **WM_DDE_EXECUTE** message.

- ❑   Wait for the acknowledgment.

The member function **WaitForReply** deletes the global memory block
when the acknowledgment arrives.

```
GlobalMem * DDEClient::Request(LPSTR Item,WORD Format)
{
  if (!ServerWnd) return NULL;
  ATOM atomItem=GlobalAddAtom(Item);
  if (PostDDEMessage(WM_DDE_REQUEST, Format,atomItem)){
    HGLOBAL hData=WaitForData(Item);
    if (hData) {
      BOOL bRelease;
      GlobalMem * pReturn =
          CopyDDEMem(hData,Item, Format, bRelease);
      if (bRelease){
    GlobalFree(hData);
      }
      return pReturn;
    }
  }
  else GlobalDeleteAtom(atomItem);
  return NULL;
}
```

To request the contents of an specific item, the client:

☐　Creates an atom containing the name of the item.

☐　Posts the server a **WM_DDE_REQUEST** message containing the
item atom and the required format.

☐　Waits for a reply.

If the reply is positive, **CopyDDEMem** copies it into a new memory
block.

```
GlobalMem * DDEClient::CopyDDEMem(HANDLE hMem, LPSTR Item,
                      ORD& Format, BOOL& bRelease)
{
  Format=0;
  bRelease=FALSE;
  if (!hMem)  return NULL;
  GlobalMem * DDEMem=
    new GlobalMem(GlobalSize(hMem)-sizeof(DDEDATA));
  DDEDATA FAR* DDEData=(DDEDATA FAR*)GlobalLock(hMem);
  DDEMem->Load((LPSTR)&(DDEData->Value),
```

```
                GlobalSize(hMem)-sizeof(DDEDATA));
    Format=DDEData->cfFormat;
    if (DDEData->fAckReq){
      ATOM atomItem=GlobalAddAtom(Item);
      PostDDEMessage(WM_DDE_ACK,0x8000,atomItem);
    }
    bRelease=DDEData->fRelease;
    if (!DDEMem->Handle) {
      delete DDEMem;
      DDEMem=NULL;
    }
    return DDEMem;
}
```

CopyDDEMem will create a new global memory object and copy the DDE data into it. The application can treat the memory as its own and delete it when it is no longer required. The first few bytes of the DDE data contain flags that are not copied, but **CopyDDEMem** examines the flags and acts on them.

If the server has set the **fAckReq** flag, the client must acknowledge reception of the data by posting back a **WM_DDE_ACK** message with **0x8000** as parameter. This is useful for links, since it prevents the client from being flooded by data. The server waits for acknowledgment before sending another update.

If the server has set the **bRelease** flag, the client has responsibility for deleting the DDE memory block. If the flag is set, **CopyDDEMem** deletes the memory after copying it.

Although it is convenient to copy the data into a DDE block, as the last section pointed out, if your application uses DDE intensively, you might prefer to use the DDE memory block directly. In that case, be careful if the **bRelease** flag is not set, since then the memory belongs to the server. The server may well delete the memory as soon as the transfer has been acknowledged. If you will need the data for any length of time, you will have to copy it anyway when the **bRelease** flag is not set.

```
BOOL DDEClient::Link(LPSTR Item, WORD Format,WinObj * Inst,
      void (WinObj::*pCallback)(LPSTR, WORD, GlobalMem*),
      BOOL bDeferred)
{
  if (!ServerWnd || !Inst || pCallback==NULL)return FALSE;
  BOOL Result=FALSE;
  GlobalMem  DDEMem(sizeof(DDEADVISE),
```

```
                     GMEM_DDESHARE);
  if (!DDEMem.Handle) return FALSE;
  DDEADVISE FAR* pAdvise=
    (DDEADVISE FAR*) Lock(&DDEMem).Buffer;
  pAdvise->fAckReq=TRUE;
  pAdvise->fDeferUpd=bDeferred;
  pAdvise->cfFormat=Format;
  ATOM atomItem=GlobalAddAtom(Item);
  if (PostDDEMessage(WM_DDE_ADVISE,
                       (UINT)DDEMem.Handle,atomItem))
    Result=WaitForAck(Item);
  else GlobalDeleteAtom(atomItem);
  if (Result) {
    DDEMem.Handle=NULL;
    LinkItems.insert(new LinkItem(Item,Format,
                                   Inst,pCallback));
  }
  return Result;
}
```

The **Link** member function asks the server to start a link on a certain topic. The member function sends the server a **WM_DDE_ADVISE** message containing the item name in an atom, and a small DDE memory block containing some flags and the clipboard format required. **Link** sets the **fAckReq** flag to indicate that the server should wait for an acknowledgment after advising of a data update. The **fDeferUpd** and **bDeferred** flags indicate whether the link is hot or warm. If **fDeferUpd** is set, the server signals when the item changes, but does not send the new value. The client should request it separately. That is a warm link.

The **cfFormat** specifies the clipboard format in which the data should be sent. For example, **CF_TEXT** specifies a formatted text format. Chapter 9 on the **Clipboard** class discusses clipboard formats in more detail. It is possible that the server cannot support the format. If not, it returns a negative acknowledgment and **Link** returns **FALSE** to the application. An application may wish to try several formats, beginning with the most appropriate format, and then trying successively simpler formats until it finds one that the server supports.

If the server acknowledges the request, **Link** puts a new item in the link list containing the callback for that item and format. When the server advises that the item has changed, **DDEClient** can look up the item in the list and call the callback. **DDEClient** needs the format in the list since an application can set up different links on the same item in different formats and with different callbacks.

When a client starts a link, the server does not send any data until it changes. Usually, an application wants to request the current value of the data after establishing a link.

```
BOOL DDEClient::Unlink(LPSTR Item, WORD Format)
{
  BOOL Result=FALSE;
#ifdef __TEMPLATES__
    GSListIterator< LinkItem> LinkIterator=LinkItems;
#else
    GSListIterator( LinkItem) LinkIterator=LinkItems;
#endif
  LinkItem* pLink;
  while ((pLink=LinkIterator())!=0){
    if (!lstrcmp(Item,pLink->Name) && Format==pLink->Format) {
      ATOM atomItem=GlobalAddAtom(Item);
      PostDDEMessage(WM_DDE_UNADVISE, Format,atomItem);
      if (WaitForAck(Item)) Result=TRUE;
      LinkItems.unlink(pLink);
      break;
    }
  }
  return Result;
}
```

Unlink will cancel a link, but only if it can find the link in the list of current links. To search the list, **Unlink** creates an iterator **LinkIterator** on the list. **LinkIterator( )** returns successive links until the end of the list is encountered.

If the link is found, **Unlink** sends the server a **WM_DDE_UNADVISE** message to cancel it. If the server acknowledges, **Unlink** removes the link from the list.

```
BOOL DDEClient::Poke(LPSTR Item, WORD Format, Memory * Data)
{
  if (!ServerWnd || !Data || !Data->Handle) return FALSE;
  BOOL Result=FALSE;
  GlobalMem  DDEMem(Data->Size()+sizeof(DDEPOKE),
                GMEM_DDESHARE);
  if (!DDEMem.Handle) return FALSE;
  DDEPOKE FAR* pPoke=
    (DDEPOKE FAR*) Lock(&DDEMem).Buffer;
```

```
    pPoke->fRelease=TRUE;
    pPoke->cfFormat=Format;
    DDEMem.Load(Data,(LPSTR)&(pPoke->Value)
                      -(LPSTR)pPoke);
    ATOM atomItem=GlobalAddAtom(Item);
    if (PostDDEMessage(WM_DDE_POKE,
                      (UINT)DDEMem.Handle, atomItem))
      Result=WaitForAck(Item);
    else GlobalDeleteAtom(atomItem);
    if (Result) {
      DDEMem.Handle=NULL;
    }
    return Result;
}
```

The **Poke** member function sends the server some unsolicited data in a specified format. An application uses **Poke** when it wants to change the value of an item in the server. **Poke** sends the server a **WM_DDE_POKE** message containing a handle to the data and an atom containing the name. The data is a DDE memory block, and here again, the block contains some flags, followed by the actual data. **Poke** creates a DDE memory block and copies the application data into it. **Poke** sets the **fRelease** flag to indicate to the server that it should delete the block after use.

The server may refuse the data and send a negative acknowledgment. The server refuses the data if it cannot handle the format, so the client application may have to try several formats before finding one that is acceptable to the server.

```
WORD DDEClient::WaitForAck(LPSTR Item) {
   if (bTerminated) return FALSE;
   SetTimer(hWnd,1,3000,NULL);
   MSG msg;
   msg.message=0;
   while (msg.message!=WM_DDE_TERMINATE
        && msg.message!=WM_TIMER){
     GetMessage(&msg,hWnd,0,0);
     if ( msg.message==WM_DDE_ACK) {
       ATOM atomItem;
       WORD wStatus;
       char ItemName[32];
       ItemName[0]=0;
       UnpackDDEMessage(WM_DDE_ACK, msg.lParam,
                   (UINT*)&wStatus,
```

```
                        (UINT*)&atomItem);
        GlobalGetAtomName(atomItem,ItemName,32);
        if (!lstrcmp(Item,ItemName)){
        GlobalDeleteAtom(atomItem);
        KillTimer(hWnd,1);
        return !!(wStatus & 0x8000);
        }
    }
    DispatchMessage(&msg);
    }
    KillTimer(hWnd,1);
    return FALSE;
}
```

WaitForAck waits for the server to acknowledge a request to start a link or poke some data.

In a perfect world, the client can expect the server application to acknowledge all DDE messages, even if the acknowledgment is negative. In practice, a server might at times fail to acknowledge a message. The server might not implement the DDE protocol correctly. It may fail to return a negative acknowledgment if it cannot handle a request. More commonly, the server might fail unexpectedly with the DDE conversation still open.

To handle these breaches of protocol, DDE applications should have a timer so that they can cancel the current request if there is no reply. **WaitForAck** could have used the **Timer** class, but since **DDEClient** has a message procedure in any case, it is just as simple to use the API routines directly.

WaitForAck contains a **GetMessage** loop that listens for messages intended for the window associated with this conversation. It will not retrieve messages intended for the rest of the application. When the function receives a **WM_DDE_ACK** message, **WaitForAck** deletes the atom, kills the timer, and returns the acknowledgment flag. If a **WM_TIMER** or **WM_DDE_TERMINATE** message arrives, the transaction is cancelled.

```
HGLOBAL DDEClient::WaitForData(LPSTR Item) {
    if (bTerminated) return FALSE;
    SetTimer(hWnd,1,3000,NULL);
    MSG msg;
    msg.message=0;
    while (msg.message!=WM_DDE_TERMINATE
```

```
        && msg.message!=WM_TIMER){
     GetMessage(&msg,hWnd,0,0);
     if ( msg.message==WM_DDE_DATA) {
       char ItemName[32];
       ItemName[0]=0;
       ATOM aItem;
       HGLOBAL hReply;
       UnpackDDEMessage(WM_DDE_DATA,msg.lParam,
                       (UINT*)&hReply, (UINT*)&aItem);
          GlobalGetAtomName(aItem, ItemName,32);
       if (!lstrcmp(Item,ItemName)){
     GlobalDeleteAtom(aItem);
#ifdef WIN32
        FreeDDElParam(WM_DDE_DATA, msg.lParam);
#endif
        KillTimer(hWnd,1);
        return hReply;
      }
     }
     DispatchMessage(&msg);
   }
   KillTimer(hWnd,1);
   return FALSE;
}
```

The **WaitForData** function waits for the server to send some data in reply to the **WM_DDE_REQUEST** message. It works in a similar way to **WaitForAck** and it returns a handle to the data.

```
void DDEClient::WaitForTerminate() {
   if (bTerminated) return;
   SetTimer(hWnd,1,3000,NULL);
   MSG msg;
   msg.message=0;
   while (msg.message!=WM_DDE_TERMINATE
       && msg.message!=WM_TIMER){
     GetMessage(&msg,hWnd,0,0);
     if ( msg.message==WM_DDE_TERMINATE) {
     bTerminated=TRUE;
     }
     DispatchMessage(&msg);
   }
   KillTimer(hWnd,1);
}
```

```
WORD DDEClient::WaitForExecute(HANDLE hMem) {
    SetTimer(hWnd,1,60000,NULL);
    MSG msg;
    msg.message=0;
    while (msg.message!=WM_DDE_TERMINATE
        && msg.message!=WM_TIMER){
      GetMessage(&msg,hWnd,0,0);
      if (msg.message==WM_DDE_ACK){
        WORD wStatus;
        HGLOBAL hCommand;
        UnpackDDEMessage(WM_DDE_ACK,msg.lParam,
                        (UINT*)&wStatus, (UINT*)&hCommand);
        if (hCommand==hMem) {
#ifdef WIN32
          FreeDDElParam(WM_DDE_ACK, msg.lParam);
#endif
          KillTimer(hWnd,1);
          return !!(wStatus &0x8000);
        }
      }
      DispatchMessage(&msg);
    }
    KillTimer(hWnd,1);
    return FALSE;
}
```

WaitForTerminate and **WaitForExecute** wait for an acknowledgment to the **WM_DDE_TERMINATE** and **WM_DDE_EXECUTE** message. When the server replies to a **WM_DDE_EXECUTE** message, the **WM_DDE_ACK** message will contain the original memory handle instead of an atom. A command may take some time to execute, so the time-out is set to 60 seconds instead of 3 seconds. For some applications that might do a lot of processing, even 60 seconds may be too short. You might want to set the timer to several minutes, or remove it altogether. The timer is only needed to release the client if the server should fail unexpectedly while executing the command. If the user closes down the server properly, it sends a **WM_DDE_TERMINATE** message to cancel the transaction.

```
LONG DDEClient::MessageProc(HWND hWnd,
                            unsigned Msg, Event& evt)
{

  switch (Msg) {
  case WM_DDE_ACK: // Reply to Initiate
  {
```

```
      GlobalDeleteAtom(LOWORD(evt.lParam));
      GlobalDeleteAtom(HIWORD(evt.lParam));
      if (!ServerWnd) ServerWnd=(HWND)evt.wParam;
    break;
  }
```

MessageProc will handle any messages that arrive asynchronously. The **WM_DDE_INITIATE** message is sent directly to the window procedure, instead of being posted to its message queue. If the server supports the topic, it will send an **WM_DDE_ACK** message back directly to **MessageProc**. The message will arrive here. All other **WM_DDE_ACK** messages are retrieved by the **WaitForReply** member function, so a message arriving here must be a reply to **WM_DDE_INITIATE**. The code deletes the atoms and sets **ServerWnd**. When **SendMessage** in the **Initiate** member function returns, **ServerWnd** will have been set.

```
    case WM_DDE_DATA:
    {
      char Item[32];
      ATOM aItem;
      HGLOBAL hData;
      UnpackDDEMessage(WM_DDE_DATA,evt.lParam,
                    (UINT*)&hData, (UINT*) &aItem);
#ifdef WIN32
      FreeDDElParam(WM_DDE_DATA, evt.lParam);
#endif
      GlobalGetAtomName(aItem,Item,32);
      GlobalDeleteAtom(aItem);
      WORD Format;
      BOOL bRelease;
      GlobalMem * AdviseData
        =CopyDDEMem(hData, Item, Format, bRelease);
      if (bRelease) {
        GlobalFree(hData);
      }
#ifdef __TEMPLATES__
      GSListIterator< LinkItem> LinkIterator=LinkItems;
#else
      GSListIterator( LinkItem) LinkIterator=LinkItems;
#endif
      LinkItem* pLink;
      while ((pLink=LinkIterator())!=0){
        if (!lstrcmp(Item,pLink->Name)
          && (Format==pLink->Format || !AdviseData)) {
        ((pLink->Inst)->*(pLink->pCallback))
```

```
      (pLink->Name,pLink->Format,AdviseData);
        break;
      }
    }
  break;
  }
```

The server will send a **WM_DDE_DATA** message whenever the data in a link changes. **DDEClient** copies the data to a new global memory block and passes it to the application callback. **DDEClient** uses the list iterator again to find the callback in the list. **CopyDDEMem** acknowledges the data if necessary.

```
case WM_DDE_TERMINATE:
{
  if ((HWND)evt.wParam==ServerWnd){
    HWND hTemp=ServerWnd;
    ServerWnd=NULL;
    LinkItems.clear();
    PostMessage(hTemp,WM_DDE_TERMINATE,(UINT)hWnd,0);
  }
  if (!bTerminated) {
    bTerminated=TRUE;
    PostMessage(hWnd,Msg,evt.wParam,evt.lParam);
  }
  break;
}
```

The server may terminate the conversation at any time, and it should do so when the user closes it down. If **DDEClient** receives a **WM_DDE_TERMINATE** message, it deletes the list and acknowledges the message. **ServerWnd** is set to **NULL** when the conversation is cancelled.

When **DDEClient** cancels the link, the server should post a **WM_DDE_TERMINATE** message in return. **DDEClient** waits for this acknowledgment in **WaitForReply**. Unfortunately, certain applications, such as early versions of the Microsoft Program Manager, send the acknowledgment instead of posting it. If the acknowledgment is sent, it arrives here in the message procedure, bypassing **WaitForReply**. To handle these rogue servers, **MessageProc** posts **WM_DDE_TERMINATE** back to the client's message queue, so that **WaitForReply** can receive it. The **bTerminated** flag ensures that **DDEClient** will not get stuck in a loop in this case.

```
case WM_DESTROY:
{
  Terminate();
  if (DelWin(hWnd) && DefaultHandler)
    SetWindowLong(hWnd,GWL_WNDPROC,(LONG) DefaultHandler);
  Window::hWnd=0;
  delete this;
  break;
}
```

Since the conversation is represented by a window, the window will be destroyed when the parent application is destroyed. **DDEClient** will terminate the link correctly before destroying the window.

```
default:
  return Window::MessageProc(hWnd, Msg, evt);
}
return FALSE;
}
```

The DDEClip Class

The **DDEClient** class is usually used in conjunction with the clipboard. The application would add a *Paste Link* item to its *Edit* menu. When this item is selected the application can retrieve an application, topic, and item from the clipboard and start a link with them.

The **DDEClip** class is a subclass of the **Clipboard** class designed to handle DDE links.

ddeclip.hpp

```
#ifndef DDECLIP_INC
#define DDECLIP_INC

#include "clipbrd.hpp"

class DDEClip : public Clipboard {
public:
  DDEClip(
    HWND PhWnd);                // Parent window handle

  void PutLink(                 // Put a link in the clipboard
    LPSTR pApp,
    LPSTR pTopic,
    LPSTR pItem,
```

```
        BOOL bEmpty);          // if TRUE empty clipboard first

     BOOL GetLink(              // Get a link from the clipboard
       LPSTR pApp,
       LPSTR pTopic,
       LPSTR pItem);

     BOOL LinkAvailable()       // Is a link available?
       {return Available(cfLink);};

protected:
    WORD cfLink;
}; // class DDEClip

#endif //  DDECLIP_INC
```

DDEClip adds three new member functions to the **Clipboard** class. **PutLink** is used by DDE servers to place the address of a link in the clipboard when an item is copied to the clipboard. **Getlink** is used by clients to determine the DDE address of whatever is in the clipboard. **LinkAvailable** returns **TRUE** if a link address is present and can be used to enable or gray the *Paste Link* menu item.

ddeclip.cpp

```
#include "ddeclip.hpp"
#include "memory.hpp"

DDEClip::DDEClip(HWND PhWnd):Clipboard(PhWnd)
{
    cfLink=RegisterClipboardFormat("Link");
}
```

The constructor registers the standard clipboard format Link.

```
void DDEClip::PutLink(LPSTR pApp, LPSTR pTopic,
                      LPSTR pItem, BOOL bEmpty)
{
   int AppSize=lstrlen(pApp)+1;
   int TopicSize=lstrlen(pTopic)+1;
   int ItemSize=lstrlen(pItem)+1;
   GlobalMem * LinkMem
     =new GlobalMem(AppSize+TopicSize+ItemSize+1);
   LinkMem->Load(pApp,AppSize,0);
   LinkMem->Load(pTopic,TopicSize,AppSize);
   LinkMem->Load(pItem,ItemSize,AppSize+TopicSize);
   Clipboard::Put(LinkMem,cfLink,bEmpty);
}
```

PutLink must place a global memory block in the clipboard. The block contains the three strings separated by null characters. The entire string is terminated by a second null character, like this:

Application/0Topic/0Item/0/0

```
BOOL DDEClip::GetLink(LPSTR pApp, LPSTR pTopic, LPSTR pItem)
{
  GlobalMem * pMem;
  if (Available(cfLink)){
    pMem=Clipboard::Get(cfLink);
    Lock TmpBuf(pMem);
    LPSTR pTmp=(LPSTR)TmpBuf.Buffer;
    while (*pTmp) *pApp++=*pTmp++;
    *pApp=*pTmp++;
    while (*pTmp) *pTopic++=*pTmp++;
    *pTopic=*pTmp++;
    while (*pTmp) *pItem++=*pTmp++;
    *pItem=*pTmp++;
    delete pMem;
    return TRUE;
  }
  return FALSE;
}
```

GetLink retrieves the address from the clipboard and breaks the string up into the three components. The construction

while (*pTmp) *pApp++=*pTmp++;

is often used in C and C++ programming. It copies characters from one string to another, advancing both pointers until a null character is encountered.

An Example DDE Client Application

This application starts up Microsoft Excel and uses it as a server. If you do not have Excel, you may be able to adapt it to make it work with another application. If not, refer to other examples later in the chapter that do not use Excel.

The application is a dialog box created directly from **WinMain**. Dialog boxes do not need to have a parent window. A dialog box is convenient since the controls can be laid out with a dialog editor. When the application is started, it opens a link to Excel using the general-purpose *System* topic and sends Excel commands to open a new blank worksheet.

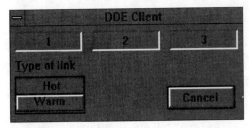

The client wants to set up a link to this new worksheet, but does not know what the topic is. If Excel has just been started, the worksheet might be labelled *Sheet2*, but this will be different if Excel is already running with some worksheets loaded, or if it is not an English version of Excel.

To find the topic, the client sends Excel commands to select a cell in the worksheet and to copy it into the clipboard. Now the client can use the **DDEClip** class to get the topic name and start the link.

The application can change the link from hot to warm to make sure that both these modes work. If the link is warm the application will only update the display every five seconds.

Once the link has been set up, you can change the values in the three Excel cells, as shown in Figure 11-4, and the three windows in the client will be updated automatically.

Here is the code of the client dialog box:

excelbx.cpp

```
#include "excelbx.hpp"
#include "staticfm.hpp"
#include "dialog.h"

void ExcelBox::InitDialog()
{
  new StaticFrame(hWnd, ID_VAL1);
  new StaticFrame(hWnd, ID_VAL2);
  new StaticFrame(hWnd, ID_VAL3);
  pTimer=NULL;
  pList= new IconList(hWnd, ID_LIST);
```

```
pList->Add("Hot");
pList->Add("Warm");
pList->Select(0);
pList->Click(this,(LISTBOXCALLBACK)&ExcelBox::ListClick);

Button * Cancel=new Button(hWnd,IDCANCEL);
Cancel->Click(this,
              (BUTTONCALLBACK)&ExcelBox::CancelClicked);
```

InitDialog first creates instances for the controls. It adds *Hot* and *Warm* to the list box and selects *Hot*.

```
DDELink = new DDEClient(hWnd);
if (!DDELink->Initialize("Excel","System")) {
  if (WinExec("Excel",SW_SHOW)>32)
    DDELink->Initialize("Excel","System");
  else {
    Error(IDS_NOT_FOUND,"");
    CloseBox();
  }
}
```

Then it creates an instance of **DDEClient** and tries to start a conversation with Excel on the *System* topic. If that fails, it is probably because Excel is not running, so it tries to start Excel using the Microsoft SDK **WinExec** function. If **WinExec** returns anything greater than 32, Excel

FIGURE 11-4

The Excel worksheet linked to the client

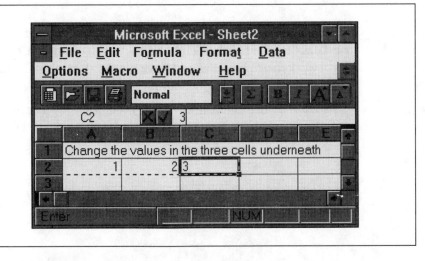

has been started and the application can try starting the conversation again. If Excel is not installed, or is not in the **PATH** environment variable, the application closes itself.

```
DDELink->Execute("[New(1)]");
DDELink->Execute("[Select(\"R2C1:R2C3\")]");
DDELink->Execute("[Copy()]");
```

The application sends Excel commands to perform the following steps:

- ☐ Open a new worksheet.

- ☐ Select the first three columns on row 2.

- ☐ Copy the contents to the clipboard.

The commands could have been sent as one combined string, like this:

[New(1)][Select("R2C1:R2C3")][Copy()]

The commands are standard Excel macro commands, but each command must be enclosed in square brackets, following the DDE standard.

```
char App[12];
char Topic[120];
char Item[12];
DDEClip Clip(hWnd);
Clip.GetLink(App,Topic,Item);
DDELink->Initialize(App,Topic);
```

This tiny application does not have a *Paste Link* menu item, but it uses the **DDEClip GetLink** member function to find the topic name of the Excel worksheet. Excel would have placed the link name in the clipboard when it received the **Copy** command.

As soon as the client knows the topic, it starts a conversation directly with that worksheet. The conversation with the *System* topic is automatically closed.

```
LPSTR pMess=
"Change the values in the three cells underneath\n0\t0\t0";
GlobalMem Data(lstrlen(pMess));
Data.Load(pMess,lstrlen(pMess));
```

```
DDELink->Poke("R1C1:R2C3",CF_TEXT,&Data);
DDELink->Execute("[Formula.GoTo(\"R2C1\")]");
```

A client can set Excel cells with unformatted text. Each cell is
separated by a tab character, and a new line character starts a new row.
The string here writes the text to one row and sets three cells in the next
row to the value zero. The client puts the message in a memory block,
and pokes it into the Excel worksheet. It then sends Excel a command
to move the cursor to the first column of the second row.

```
DDELink->Link("R2C1",CF_TEXT,this,
        (LINKCALLBACK)&ExcelBox::Update);
DDELink->Link("R2C2",CF_TEXT,this,
        (LINKCALLBACK)&ExcelBox::Update);
DDELink->Link("R2C3",CF_TEXT,this,
        (LINKCALLBACK)&ExcelBox::Update);
}
```

Finally, the client sets up three links to each of the three cells. The
data is required in text format and the **Update** member function is the
callback. The client could have set up one link to all three cells like this:

DDELink->Link("R2C1:R2C3",CF_TEXT,this,
            (LINKCALLBACK)&ExcelBox::Update);

Excel would then return all three values separated by tabs.

```
void ExcelBox::CancelClicked(Button& b)
{
  CloseLink();
  CloseBox();
}
```

When the user closes the dialog box, it closes the link in an orderly
manner.

```
void ExcelBox::CloseLink()
{
  DDELink->Initialize("Excel","System"); // Cancel Link
  DDELink->Execute("[File.Close(FALSE)]");
  delete DDELink;
}
```

To close the conversation, the client need only destroy the instance of **DDEClient**, **DDELink**. It will be destroyed automatically in any case when the window is destroyed. This client takes the opportunity to close the worksheet that has been opened.

```
void ExcelBox::ListClick(ListBox& List)
{
  DDELink->Unlink("R2C1",CF_TEXT);
  DDELink->Link("R2C1",CF_TEXT,
    this,(LINKCALLBACK)&ExcelBox::Update,List.Selection());
  DDELink->Unlink("R2C2",CF_TEXT);
  DDELink->Link("R2C2",CF_TEXT,
    this,(LINKCALLBACK)&ExcelBox::Update,List.Selection());
  DDELink->Unlink("R2C3",CF_TEXT);
  DDELink->Link("R2C3",CF_TEXT,
    this,(LINKCALLBACK)&ExcelBox::Update,List.Selection());
  bOldValues=FALSE;
  if (List.Selection() && !pTimer){
    pTimer=new Timer(hWnd,5000);
    pTimer->Tick(this,(TIMERCALLBACK)&ExcelBox::Ticked);
  }
}
```

When the user selects *Hot* or *Warm*, the client cancels the links and starts new links with the selected "temperature." If the link is warm, the client starts a 5-second timer and updates the display when the timer expires.

```
BOOL ExcelBox::Ticked()
{
  if (bOldValues) {
    GlobalMem* pMem;
    pMem=DDELink->Request("R2C1",CF_TEXT);
    Update("R2C1", CF_TEXT,pMem);
    pMem=DDELink->Request("R2C2",CF_TEXT);
    Update("R2C2", CF_TEXT,pMem);
    pMem=DDELink->Request("R2C3",CF_TEXT);
    Update("R2C3", CF_TEXT,pMem);
    ListClick(*pList);
  }
  return FALSE;
}
```

The timer will call **Ticked** every 5 seconds when the link is warm. If **bOldValues** is set, indicating that the values have changed, the function requests the data from Excel and displays it.

```
void ExcelBox::Update(LPSTR pItem, WORD Format,
                      GlobalMem * pMem)
{
  if (!pMem) {
    bOldValues=TRUE;
    return;
  }
  Lock Text(pMem);
  LPSTR pStr=(LPSTR)Text.Buffer;
  while (*pStr && *pStr!='\t' && *pStr!='\r') pStr++;
  *pStr=0;
  int Column=pItem[3]-'1';
  SetDlgItemText(hWnd, ID_VAL1+Column, (LPSTR)Text.Buffer);
  delete pMem;
}
```

When Excel reports an update, the data may be **NULL**. If it is, the link is warm, so the client sets the **bOldValues** flag to indicate that the data is out of date. The **pItem** will point to a string containing the row and column like this: *R2C3*. **Update** can extract the column number and use it to set the dialog item text. Another possibility would have been to use three different callbacks.

That is all there is for the dialog box. The definition simply declares the member functions used.

excelbx.hpp

```
#ifndef EXCELBOX_INC
#define EXCELBOX_INC

#include "graydial.hpp"
#include "ddeclien.hpp"
#include "button.hpp"
#include "ddeclip.hpp"
#include "iconlist.hpp"
#include "timer.hpp"

class ExcelBox : public GrayDialog {
```

```
public:
  ExcelBox():GrayDialog(TRUE){};

protected:
  void InitDialog();
  void CloseLink();
  void CancelClicked(Button& b);
  void Update(LPSTR pItem, WORD Format, GlobalMem * pMem);
  void ListClick(ListBox& pList);
  BOOL Ticked();
  DDEClient * DDELink;
  BOOL bOldValues;
  Timer* pTimer;
  ListBox* pList;
};

#endif
```

The **WinMain** function creates the dialog box.

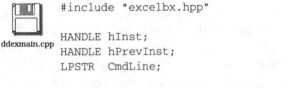

ddexmain.cpp

```
#include "excelbx.hpp"

HANDLE hInst;
HANDLE hPrevInst;
LPSTR  CmdLine;

int PASCAL WinMain(HANDLE hInstance, HANDLE hPrevInstance,
    LPSTR lpszCmdLine, int nCmdShow)
{
    hInst = hInstance;

    ExcelBox Box;
    Box.OpenBox(NULL,"DDEEXCEL");
    return 0;
}
```

Since the dialog box is modal, the application does not need a message loop, not even for the DDE messages. **DDEClient** handles DDE messages in its own message loop.

These dialog box applications are quick to write and are useful for simple utilities, even if you do not use DDE. If you are not fussy, you can put the complete application in one source file.

The DDEServer Class

The **DDEServer** class is designed as a virtual class from which application DDE servers can be derived. A DDE server calls a virtual member function when a request arrives from a client, and an application can derive a class from **DDEServer** with these member functions defined. The **DDEServer** class has a dual role to play, because it is used to detect clients wishing to start a conversation, as well as the conversations themselves.

Note When a class must process many different events, as the **Window** and **DDEServer** classes must do, it is simpler to use virtual member functions and derive a subclass to handle the events. When a class only handles one or two events, as the **DDEClient** class and the **Control** classes do, it is simpler to use callback functions.

ddeserv.hpp

```
#ifndef DDESERVER_INC
#define DDESERVER_INC

#include "window.hpp"
#include "memory.hpp"
#include "gslist.hpp"

extern "C"{
  #include <dde.h>
}

class ServerLinkItem {
public:
  char Name[32];
  BOOL bAck;
  WORD Format;
  ServerLinkItem(LPSTR pName,BOOL bAck,WORD Format){
    lstrcpy(Name,pName);
    ServerLinkItem::bAck=bAck;
    ServerLinkItem::Format=Format;
  };
}; // class ServerLinkItem
```

The server also needs to keep track of links. There are no callbacks, but the **bAck** flag indicates whether the server should ask the client to acknowledge link data messages.

```
#ifndef __TEMPLATES__
  declare(GSList,ServerLinkItem);
#endif

class DDEServer : public Window {

public:
  DDEServer(                      // Create a server
   LPSTR pApplication);           // for an application

  DDEServer(                      // Create a conversation
    HWND PhWnd,                   // Top-level server
    LPSTR pTopic,                 // topic
    HWND hClient);                // Client's handle

  BOOL Advise(                    // Advise client
    LPSTR pItem,                  // that an item has changed
    WORD Format,
    Memory * Data);
```

There are two constructors. **DDEServer(LPSTR pApplication)** sets up a server to watch for requests to initiate a conversation. **DDEServer(HWND PhWnd, LPSTR pTopic, HWND hClient)** is used to start a conversation. The only other public member function is **Advise**, which the application uses whenever some linked data changes.

```
protected:
#ifdef __TEMPLATES__
  GSList<ServerLinkItem> LinkItems;
#else
  GSList(ServerLinkItem) LinkItems;
#endif
  static char Application[32];
  HWND hClientWnd;
  HWND hServerWnd;

  virtual void Initiate(          // Client has requested
    LPSTR pTopic,                 // a conversation
    HWND hClient){};

  virtual Memory* Request(        // Return the item requested
    LPSTR pItem,
    WORD Format)
    {return NULL;};

  virtual BOOL Poke(              //  Client has poked an item
```

```
      LPSTR pItem,
      WORD Format,
      GlobalMem * pData){
      return FALSE;};

   virtual BOOL Link(           // Client has requested a link
      LPSTR pItem,
      WORD Format,
      BOOL bDeferred){
      return FALSE;};

   virtual void Unlink(         // Close the link
      LPSTR pItem,
      WORD Format){};

   virtual BOOL Execute(        // Execute the command string
      LPSTR pComd)
      {return FALSE;};
```

All the other requests are handled by these virtual member functions.

```
   ~DDEServer();
   void Terminate();
   LPSTR Register(WNDCLASS& wc);
   BOOL PostDDEMessage(UINT msg, UINT uiLo, UINT uiHi);
   void UnpackDDEMessage(UINT msg, DWORD lParam,
                UINT* puiLi, UINT* puiHi);
   LONG MessageProc(HWND hWnd, unsigned Msg, Event& evt);
   WORD WaitForReply(LPSTR Item);
   void InitiateEvent(Event& evt);
   void RequestEvent(Event& evt);
   void AdviseEvent(Event& evt);
   void UnadviseEvent(Event& evt);
   void PokeEvent(Event& evt);
   void ExecuteEvent(Event& evt);
}; // class DDEServer


#endif // DDESERVER_INC
```

The other protected functions are explained in the following section:

ddeserv.cpp

```
#include "ddeserv.hpp"

char DDEServer::Application[32]=;
```

```
DDEServer::DDEServer(LPSTR pApplication)
{
  Create("",WS_POPUP,0,0,0,0,0,NULL);  //invisible window
  lstrcpy(Application,pApplication);
  hClientWnd=NULL;
  hServerWnd=hWnd;
}
```

The initial DDE window must have the **WS_POPUP** style, since the **WM_DDE_INITIATE** message will not be sent to child windows. The application name used by DDE should normally be the same as the application filename, without the .EXE extension. Some applications rely on the names being the same to launch an application and start a DDE conversation in one operation.

```
LPSTR DDEServer::Register(WNDCLASS& wc)
{
  wc.style=0;
  wc.lpszClassName="DDEServer";
  RegisterClass(&wc);
  return "DDEServer";
}
```

The **Register** member function is implemented as for the other invisible windows.

```
BOOL DDEServer::PostDDEMessage(UINT msg, UINT uiLo, UINT uiHi)
{
#ifdef WIN32
  return PostMessage(hClientWnd, msg, (UINT)hWnd,
                     PackDDElParam(msg, uiLo,uiHi));
#else
  return PostMessage(hClientWnd, msg, (UINT)hWnd,
                     MAKELONG(uiLo, uiHi));
#endif
}

void DDEServer::UnpackDDEMessage(UINT msg, DWORD lParam,
                                 UINT* puiLo, UINT* puiHi)
{
#ifdef WIN32
  UnpackDDElParam(msg, lParam, puiLo, puiHi);
  FreeDDElParam(msg, lParam);
#else
  *puiLo = LOWORD(lParam);
```

```
  *puiHi = HIWORD(lParam);
#endif
}
```

The **PostDDEMessage** and **UnpackDDEMessage** functions pack and unpack the DDE information from a message, according to whether the system is 16- or 32-bit Windows.

```
DDEServer::DDEServer(HWND PhWnd,LPSTR pTopic, HWND hClient)
{
  Create("",WS_CHILD,0,0,0,0,PhWnd,NULL);    //invisible window
  hClientWnd=hClient;
  hServerWnd=hWnd;
  SendMessage(hClientWnd,WM_DDE_ACK,
       (UINT)hServerWnd,
       MAKELONG(GlobalAddAtom(Application),
       GlobalAddAtom(pTopic)));
}
```

If the server agrees to a conversation, it acknowledges the **WM_DDE_INITIATE** message with a **WM_DDE_ACK** message, returning its window handle and the application and topic strings in atoms.

```
DDEServer::~DDEServer()
{
  Terminate();
  if (hWnd) {
    if (DelWin(hWnd) && DefaultHandler)
      SetWindowLong(hWnd,GWL_WNDPROC,(LONG) DefaultHandler);
    DestroyWindow(hWnd);
    hWnd=0;
  }
}
```

The destructor terminates the conversation before destroying the window.

```
void DDEServer::Terminate()
{
  ServerLinkItem* pLink;
  while ((pLink=LinkItems.get())!=0) {
    Unlink(pLink->Name,pLink->Format);
    delete pLink;
  }
  if (hClientWnd) {
```

```
    HWND hTemp=hClientWnd;
    hClientWnd=NULL;
    PostMessage(hTemp,WM_DDE_TERMINATE,(UINT)hServerWnd,0);
    DWORD lTimeOut=GetTickCount()+10000;
    MSG msg;
    while (GetTickCount()<lTimeOut) {
     if (!PeekMessage(&msg,hServerWnd,
       WM_DDE_FIRST,WM_DDE_LAST,PM_REMOVE)) continue;
     if (msg.message==WM_DDE_TERMINATE) break;
     DispatchMessage(&msg);
    }
  }
}
```

To terminate the conversation, the server cancels all the links on the list and sends the client a **WM_DDE_TERMINATE** message. The client should post a **WM_DDE_TERMINATE** message back. An instance of **DDEServer** can only be engaged in one conversation. Separate instances handle other conversations. When the conversation is terminated, the instance can be deleted.

```
BOOL DDEServer::Advise(LPSTR pItem, WORD Format, Memory * Data)
{
  if (!hClientWnd) return FALSE;
  if (!hClientWnd ) return FALSE;
#ifdef __TEMPLATES__
    GSListIterator<ServerLinkItem> LinkIterator=LinkItems;
#else
    GSListIterator(ServerLinkItem) LinkIterator=LinkItems;
#endif
  ServerLinkItem* pLink;
  while ((pLink=LinkIterator())!=0)
    if (!lstrcmp(pItem,pLink->Name)) break;
  if (!pLink) return FALSE;
  BOOL Result=FALSE;
  GlobalMem  DDEMem(Data->Size()+sizeof(DDEDATA),
      GMEM_ZEROINIT | GMEM_DDESHARE);
  if (!DDEMem.Handle) return FALSE;
  DDEDATA FAR * pData=(DDEDATA FAR *) Lock(&DDEMem).Buffer;
  pData->fRelease=TRUE;
  pData->cfFormat=Format;
  pData->fResponse=0;
  pData->fAckReq=pLink->bAck;
  DDEMem.Load(Data,(LPSTR)&(pData->Value)-(LPSTR)pData);
  ATOM atomItem=GlobalAddAtom(pItem);
  if ( PostDDEMessage(WM_DDE_DATA,
```

```
                         (UINT)DDEMem.Handle, atomItem))
    if (pLink->bAck)
      Result=WaitForReply(pItem);
    else Result=TRUE;
  else GlobalDeleteAtom(atomItem);
  if (Result){
    DDEMem.Handle=NULL;
  }
  return Result;

}
```

The application uses **Advise** to inform the server that a link has
changed. The application supplies the item name, the clipboard format
of the data, and the data itself. The data can be in either a local or a global
memory block.

Advise copies the data into a DDE memory block and sets the flags.
The **fAckReq** flag is set from the **bAck** value in the list. **Advise** sends the
data in a **WM_DDE_DATA** message. If **bAck** is set, the client is expected
to acknowledge. In fact, it is the client that originally set the **bAck** flag
when it set up the link. If the server is obliged to wait for an acknowledgment, it will not send further data until the client has processed the first
data. Without the acknowledgment, the client might become overrun with
data.

```
WORD DDEServer::WaitForReply(LPSTR pItem) {
    SetTimer(hServerWnd,1,3000,NULL);
    MSG msg;
    msg.message=0;
    while (msg.message!=WM_DDE_TERMINATE
        && msg.message!=WM_TIMER){
      GetMessage(&msg,hServerWnd,0,0);
      if ( msg.message==WM_DDE_ACK) {
        ATOM atomItem;
        WORD wStatus;
        char ItemName[32];
        ItemName[0]=0;
        UnpackDDEMessage(WM_DDE_ACK, msg.lParam,
                        (UINT*)&wStatus, (UINT*)&atomItem);
        GlobalGetAtomName(atomItem,ItemName,32);
        if (!lstrcmp(pItem,ItemName)){
          GlobalDeleteAtom(atomItem);
          KillTimer(hWnd,1);
          return !!(wStatus & 0x8000);
```

```
      }
    }
    DispatchMessage(&msg);
  }
  KillTimer(hServerWnd,1);
  return FALSE;
}
```

WaitForReply is similar to the **WaitForAck** member function used in **DDEClient**. The server uses a three-second time-out.

```
LONG DDEServer::MessageProc(HWND hWnd, unsigned Msg,
                            Event& evt)
{
  switch (Msg) {
  case WM_DDE_INITIATE:
    InitiateEvent(evt);
    break;

  case WM_DDE_REQUEST:
    RequestEvent(evt);
    break;

  case WM_DDE_ADVISE:
    AdviseEvent(evt);
    break;

  case WM_DDE_UNADVISE:
    UnadviseEvent(evt);
    break;

  case WM_DDE_POKE:
    PokeEvent(evt);
    break;

  case WM_DDE_EXECUTE:
    ExecuteEvent(evt);
    break;


  case WM_DDE_TERMINATE:
    if (hClientWnd){
      PostMessage(hClientWnd,WM_DDE_TERMINATE,
                  (UINT)hServerWnd,0);
      hClientWnd=NULL;
    }
```

```
        PostMessage(GetParent(hWnd),WM_USER_DELETE,
                              0,(DWORD)this);
        break;

    case WM_DESTROY:
      Terminate();
      if (DelWin(hWnd) && DefaultHandler)
        SetWindowLong(hWnd,GWL_WNDPROC,
                      (LONG)DefaultHandler);
      Window::hWnd=0;
      delete this;
      break;

    default:
      return Window::MessageProc(hWnd, Msg, evt);
    }
    return FALSE;
}
```

For most DDE messages, **DDEServer** calls a virtual member function to handle them. The exceptions are **WM_DDE_TERMINATE** and **WM_DE-STROY**.

When a **WM_DDE_TERMINATE** message arrives, **DDEServer** acknowledges it and deletes the instance. When **WM_DESTROY** arrives, **DDEServer** terminates the current conversation before deleting the instance. The application only has to delete the top-level **DDEServer** window. Windows then deletes all the conversation windows, and the conversations will be terminated correctly.

```
void DDEServer::InitiateEvent(Event& evt)
{
  char App[32]="";
  char Topic[120]="";
  GlobalGetAtomName(LOWORD(evt.lParam),App,32);
  GlobalGetAtomName(HIWORD(evt.lParam),Topic,120);
  if (!App[0] || !lstrcmp(App,Application))
    Initiate(Topic,(HWND)evt.wParam);
}
```

Only the top-level **DDEServer** instance receives **WM_DDE_INITIATE** messages. If the application names match, **DDEServer** passes the event to the virtual member function **Initiate**. If **Initiate** agrees with the topic, it creates another instance of DDEServer to set up a conversation with the client.

```
void DDEServer::RequestEvent(Event& evt)
{
  ATOM atomItem;
  WORD cfFormat;
  UnpackDDEMessage(WM_DDE_REQUEST,evt.lParam,
                  (UINT*)&cfFormat, (UINT*)&atomItem);
  char Item[32];
  if (!hClientWnd){
    GlobalDeleteAtom(atomItem);
    return;
  }
  GlobalGetAtomName(atomItem,Item,32);
  Memory * MemReq=Request(Item,LOWORD(evt.lParam));
  if (MemReq && MemReq->Handle) {
    GlobalMem DDEMem(MemReq->Size()+sizeof(DDEDATA),
      GMEM_MOVEABLE | GMEM_DDESHARE);
    if (DDEMem.Handle) {
      DDEDATA FAR * pData=
          (DDEDATA FAR *)Lock(&DDEMem).Buffer;
      pData->fRelease=TRUE;
      pData->cfFormat=cfFormat;
      pData->fResponse=TRUE;
      pData->fAckReq=FALSE;
      DDEMem.Load(MemReq,
              (LPSTR)&(pData->Value)-(LPSTR)pData);
      PostDDEMessage(WM_DDE_DATA, (UINT)DDEMem.Handle,
                  atomItem);
      DDEMem.Handle=NULL;
      delete MemReq;
      return;
    }
  }
  PostDDEMessage(WM_DDE_ACK, 0, atomItem);
}
```

RequestEvent is called when the client needs some data. Whenever any of these events arrive, the server may have already started to terminate the conversation. In that case, **hClientWnd** will be **NULL**, and any requests should be ignored and the atoms deleted.

The virtual member function **Request** should return the data in the specified format. **RequestEvent** copies the data into a DDE memory block and sends it back to the client. The client does not acknowledge the data, since **fAckReq** is **FALSE**. The **fRelease** is **TRUE** to indicate that the client should release the data.

```
void DDEServer::AdviseEvent(Event& evt)
{
  ATOM atomItem;
  HGLOBAL hOptions;
  UnpackDDEMessage(WM_DDE_ADVISE,evt.lParam,
                   (UINT*)&hOptions, (UINT*)&atomItem);
  if (!hClientWnd){
    GlobalDeleteAtom(atomItem);
    GlobalFree(hOptions);
    return;
  }
  char Item[32];
  GlobalGetAtomName(atomItem,Item,32);
  DDEADVISE FAR * DDEData=
    (DDEADVISE FAR * )GlobalLock(hOptions);
  BOOL bAckLink=DDEData->fAckReq;
  WORD Format=DDEData->cfFormat;
  ServerLinkItem * pLink=
    new ServerLinkItem(Item,bAckLink,Format);
  LinkItems.insert(pLink);
  BOOL bAck=Link(Item, Format, DDEData->fDeferUpd);
  if (bAck)  {
    GlobalFree(hOptions);
  }
  else delete LinkItems.get();
  PostDDEMessage(WM_DDE_ACK, bAck?0x8000:0, atomItem);
}
```

The **AdviseEvent** member function is called when the client wishes to establish a link with a data item. The client sends a DDE memory block containing the **fAckReq** flag and the required format. **AdviseEvent** adds a new item to the list of links and calls the virtual member function **Link**. **Link** should mark the data so that the application can call **Advise** whenever the data changes. The application will need to know the instance of **DDEServer** that created the link, the format required, and whether the link is hot or warm. If **Link** refuses to establish the link, perhaps because the application does not support the item or the format, **AdviseEvent** removes the link from the list.

AdviseEvent always acknowledges the request, returning either a positive acknowledgment (**0x8000**) or a negative acknowledgment (**0x0000**).

```
void DDEServer::UnadviseEvent(Event& evt)
{
  ATOM atomItem;
  WORD cfFormat;
  UnpackDDEMessage(WM_DDE_UNADVISE, evt.lParam,
                  (UINT*)&cfFormat, (UINT*)&atomItem);

  if (!hClientWnd){
    GlobalDeleteAtom(atomItem);
    return;
  }
  char Item[32];
  GlobalGetAtomName(atomItem,Item,32);
#ifdef __TEMPLATES__
    GSListIterator<ServerLinkItem> LinkIterator=LinkItems;
#else
    GSListIterator(ServerLinkItem) LinkIterator=LinkItems;
#endif
  ServerLinkItem* pLink;
  while ((pLink=LinkIterator())!=0)
    if (!lstrcmp(Item,pLink->Name)
        && cfFormat==pLink->Format) break;
  if (pLink) {
    Unlink(pLink->Name,cfFormat);
    LinkItems.unlink(pLink);
  }
  PostDDEMessage(WM_DDE_ACK, pLink?0x8000:0, atomItem);
}
```

When the client wishes to cancel a link, **UnadviseEvent** looks for the link in the list and calls the virtual member function **Unlink**. **UnadviseEvent** always acknowledges the request, but if the link cannot be found in the list, the acknowledgment is negative.

```
void DDEServer::PokeEvent(Event& evt)
{
  char Item[32];
  ATOM atomItem;
  HGLOBAL hData;
  UnpackDDEMessage(WM_DDE_POKE,evt.lParam,
                  (UINT*)&hData, (UINT*)&atomItem);
  if (!hClientWnd){
    GlobalDeleteAtom(atomItem);
    GlobalFree(hData);
    return;
  }
  GlobalGetAtomName(atomItem,Item,32);
```

```
DDEPOKE FAR * DDEData=(DDEPOKE FAR * )GlobalLock(hData);
GlobalMem * DDEMem=
  new GlobalMem(GlobalSize(hData)-sizeof(DDEPOKE));
DDEMem->Load((LPSTR)&(DDEData->Value),
             GlobalSize(hData)-sizeof(DDEPOKE));
BOOL bAck=Poke(Item,DDEData->cfFormat,DDEMem);
BOOL bRelease=DDEData->fRelease;
if (bAck && bRelease) {
  GlobalFree(hData);
}
PostDDEMessage(WM_DDE_ACK, bAck?0x8000:0, atomItem);
}
```

If the server receives a **Poke** message, the client is trying to send unsolicited data. The first few bytes of the DDE memory block contain the data format and the **bRelease** flag. If **bRelease** is **TRUE**, the server should delete the DDE memory block after use. The virtual member function **Poke** handles the data, but **PokeEvent** first copies it into an ordinary global memory block. PokeEvent always acknowledges the request.

```
void DDEServer::ExecuteEvent(Event& evt)
{
  HGLOBAL hMem;
  WORD wStatus;
  UnpackDDEMessage(WM_DDE_EXECUTE,evt.lParam,
                  (UINT*)&wStatus, (UINT*)&hMem);
  if (!hClientWnd){
    GlobalFree(hMem);
    return;
  }
  LPSTR pStart=(LPSTR)GlobalLock(hMem);
  LPSTR pEndBlock=pStart+GlobalSize(hMem);
  BOOL bAck=FALSE;
  while (pStart<pEndBlock && *pStart=='['){
    LPSTR pEnd=pStart;
    while (*pEnd!=']') pEnd++;
    *pEnd=0;
    bAck=Execute(pStart+1);
    *pEnd=']';
    if (!bAck) break;
    pStart=pEnd+1;
  }
  GlobalUnlock(hMem);
 PostDDEMessage(WM_DDE_ACK, bAck?0x8000:0, (UINT)hMem);
}
```

ExecuteEvent is called when the client wishes to have the server execute a command. The virtual member function **Execute** handles the command. To simplify matters a little, **ExecuteEvent** breaks up the command sting into individual commands and removes the square brackets that surround the commands. **ExecuteEvent** can then call **Execute** for each separate command.

An Example DDE Server Application

The **DDEServer** class by itself does nothing. A DDE server application must derive a specific instance of **DDEServer**, defining the virtual member functions. The following example helps illustrate how that might be done.

DDEServe is a simple window containing three colored scroll bars as shown in Figure 11-5. The bars have a range of 1 to 100, and the user is free to move them. Each scroll bar is supported as a DDE item, so other applications can link to DDEServe to get the current value of a scroll bar. If a client application pokes a value to one of the three scroll bars, DDEServe sets the scroll bar thumb to correspond to the new value. Clients can send DDEServe command strings, and DDEServe simply displays these in the window without processing them further.

The DDEServe application

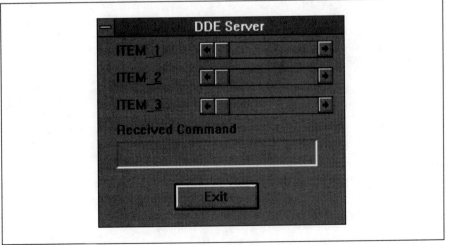

DDEServe is implemented as a dialog box in a manner similar to that of the previous example client application that linked with Excel. Here is the dialog box code:

serverbx.hpp

```
#ifndef SERVERBOX_INC
#define SERVERBOX_INC

#include "graydial.hpp"
#include "colscrll.hpp"
#include "servtest.hpp"
#include "button.hpp"
#include "staticfm.hpp"
#include "gslist.hpp"

class DDELink {
public:
  char Name[32];
  BOOL bDeferred;
  WORD Format;
  DDEServer* Server;
  DDELink(LPSTR pName,WORD Format,
          BOOL bDeferred,DDEServer* Server){
    lstrcpy(Name,pName);
    DDELink::bDeferred=bDeferred;
    DDELink::Format=Format;
    DDELink::Server=Server;
  };
};
```

The application will need to maintain a list of links so that it can advise all the clients when a scroll bar moves. For each link, DDEServe needs to know the item name, whether the link is hot or warm, the required format, and the instance of **DDEServer** that started the link. The application will only support the **CF_TEXT** format.

```
#ifndef __TEMPLATES__
  declare(GSList,DDELink);
#endif

class ServerBox : public GrayDialog {
friend class DDEServerTest;
public:
  ServerBox():GrayDialog(TRUE){pInstance=this;};
```

The **DDEServerTest** class will be derived from **DDEServer**. It must be a **friend** class in order to access the protected data items in **ServerBox**. The constructor creates a gray modal dialog box and puts the **this** instance pointer in a static data item so that **DDEServerTest** can find it.

```
protected:
  void InitDialog();
  void CancelClicked(Button& b);
  BOOL AddLink(LPSTR pItem, WORD Format,
              BOOL bDeferred, DDEServer& Server);
  BOOL RemoveLink(LPSTR pItem, WORD Format,
              DDEServer& Server);
  void ScrollMoved(ColorScrollBar& Bar, int Position);
  DDEServerTest * pDDEServer;
  static ServerBox * pInstance;
#ifdef __TEMPLATES__
    GSList<DDELink> DDELinks;
#else
    GSList(DDELink) DDELinks;
#endif
  ColorScrollBar * pItem1;
  ColorScrollBar * pItem2;
  ColorScrollBar * pItem3;
  StaticFrame * pCommand;
};

#endif
```

serverbx.cpp

```
#include "serverbx.hpp"
#include "dialog.h"

ServerBox * ServerBox::pInstance=NULL;

void ServerBox::InitDialog()
{
  pItem1=new ColorScrollBar(hWnd,ID_ITEM1);
  pItem1->SetRange(0,100);
  pItem1->Color(RGB(0,0,0),RGB(255,0,0));
  pItem1->SetText("ITEM_1");
  pItem1->Position(this,
          (SCROLLBARCALLBACK)&ServerBox::ScrollMoved);

  pItem2=new ColorScrollBar(hWnd,ID_ITEM2);
  pItem2->SetRange(0,100);
  pItem2->Color(RGB(0,0,0),RGB(0,255,0));
  pItem2->SetText("ITEM_2");
```

```
  pItem2->Position(this,
          (SCROLLBARCALLBACK)&ServerBox::ScrollMoved);

  pItem3=new ColorScrollBar(hWnd,ID_ITEM3);
  pItem3->SetRange(0,100);
  pItem3->Color(RGB(0,0,0),RGB(0,0,255));
  pItem3->SetText("ITEM_3");
  pItem3->Position(this,
          (SCROLLBARCALLBACK)&ServerBox::ScrollMoved);

  Button * Cancel=new Button(hWnd,IDCANCEL);
  Cancel->Click(this,
          (BUTTONCALLBACK)&ServerBox::CancelClicked);

  pCommand=new StaticFrame(hWnd,ID_COMMAND);
  pDDEServer = new DDEServerTest();
}
```

InitDialog sets up instances of the controls and creates an instance of **DDEServerTest**. This instance waits for requests to initiate a conversation. The application will create a separate instance for each actual conversation.

The scroll bars are colored black at the minimum value, and red green and blue at the maximum value.

```
void ServerBox::CancelClicked(Button& b)
{
  delete pDDEServer;
  CloseBox();
}
```

The root instance of **DDEServerTest** must be deleted when the window is closed. The root instance takes care of deleting all of the conversation instances.

```
BOOL ServerBox::AddLink(LPSTR pItem, WORD Format,
                        BOOL bDeferred, DDEServer& Server)
{
  if (Format==CF_TEXT && (!lstrcmpi(pItem,"ITEM_1")
      || !lstrcmpi(pItem,"ITEM_2")
      || !lstrcmpi(pItem,"ITEM_3"))){
    DDELinks.append(
      new DDELink(pItem,Format,bDeferred,&Server));
    return TRUE;
```

```
    }
    else return FALSE;
}
```

DDEServe will accept any link to one of the items *ITEM_1*, *ITEM_2* or *ITEM_3*, provided the request is for the **CF_TEXT** format. If the link is acceptable, DDEServe add it to its list of links.

```
BOOL ServerBox::RemoveLink(LPSTR pItem, WORD Format,
                           DDEServer& Server)
{
#ifdef __TEMPLATES__
    GSListIterator<DDELink> LinkIterator=DDELinks;
#else
  GSListIterator(DDELink) LinkIterator=DDELinks;
#endif
  DDELink* pLink;
  while ((pLink=LinkIterator())!=0)
    if (!lstrcmp(pItem,pLink->Name)
    && Format==pLink->Format
    && &Server==pLink->Server) break;
  if (pLink) {
    DDELinks.unlink(pLink);
    return TRUE;
  }
  return FALSE;
}
```

RemoveLink removes an item from the list of links. Both **AddLink** and **RemoveLink** will be called from an instance of **DDEServerTest**. Callbacks are not needed, since **DDEServerTest** has been written specifically for this application.

```
void ServerBox::ScrollMoved(ColorScrollBar& Bar, int Position)
{
  char Item[32];
  Bar.GetText(Item,32);
#ifdef __TEMPLATES__
    GSListIterator<DDELink> LinkIterator=DDELinks;
#else
  GSListIterator(DDELink) LinkIterator=DDELinks;
#endif
  DDELink* pLink;
  while ((pLink=LinkIterator())!=0){
    if (!lstrcmp(Item,pLink->Name)
```

```
            && pLink->Format==CF_TEXT){
          LocalMem* pMem;
          if (!pLink->bDeferred){
            pMem=new LocalMem(4);
            Lock Buf(pMem);
      wsprintf((LPSTR)Buf.Buffer,"%d",Position);
          }
          pLink->Server->Advise(pLink->Name,CF_TEXT,pMem);
          if (pMem) delete pMem;
        }
      }
    }
```

Whenever a scroll bar is moved, **ScrollMoved** searches the list of links. If there is a link for that scroll bar, **ScrollMoved** calls **Advise** in the instance of **DDEServerTest** that handles the link. **ScrollMoved** creates a small local memory block and copies the value of the scroll position into it in text form.

The only DDE-specific operation that **ServerBox** does is to create the root instance of **DDEServerTest** and to advise of data changes. Everything else is handled by **DDEServerTest**.

servtest.hpp

```
#ifndef SERVERTEST_INC
#define SERVERTEST_INC

#include "ddeserv.hpp"
#include "memory.hpp"

class DDEServerTest : public DDEServer {
public:
  DDEServerTest():DDEServer("DDEServe"){};
  DDEServerTest(HWND PhWnd, LPSTR pTopic, HWND hClient):
    DDEServer(PhWnd, pTopic, hClient){};
protected:
  Memory * Request(LPSTR pItem, WORD Format);
  BOOL Poke(LPSTR pItem, WORD Format, GlobalMem * pData);
  void Initiate(LPSTR pTopic, HWND hClient);
  BOOL Link(LPSTR pItem, WORD Format, BOOL bDeferred);
  void Unlink(LPSTR pItem, WORD Format);
  BOOL Execute(LPSTR pString);
};

#endif
```

DDEServerTest will define the virtual member functions of **DDEServer**. The application name is DDEServe.

servtest.cpp

```
#include "servtest.hpp"
#include "Serverbx.hpp"
#include <stdlib.h>

void DDEServerTest::Initiate(LPSTR pTopic, HWND hClient)
{
  if (!lstrcmpi(pTopic,"System"))
    new DDEServerTest(hWnd, pTopic,hClient);
}
```

DDEServerTest only accepts conversations on the *System* topic. If a request arrives, **Initiate** creates a separate instance of **DDEServerTest** to handle the conversation.

```
Memory * DDEServerTest::Request(LPSTR pItem, WORD Format)
{
  if (Format!=CF_TEXT) return NULL;
  LocalMem * ResMem=new LocalMem(4);
  Lock ResBuf(ResMem);
  if (!lstrcmp(pItem,"ITEM_1")){
    wsprintf((LPSTR)ResBuf.Buffer,"%d",
      ServerBox::pInstance->pItem1->GetPosition());
    return ResMem;
  }
  if (!lstrcmp(pItem,"ITEM_2")){
    wsprintf((LPSTR)ResBuf.Buffer,"%d",
      ServerBox::pInstance->pItem2->GetPosition());
    return ResMem;
  }
  if (!lstrcmp(pItem,"ITEM_3")){
    wsprintf((LPSTR)ResBuf.Buffer,"%d",
      ServerBox::pInstance->pItem3->GetPosition());
    return ResMem;
  }
  delete ResMem;
  return NULL;
}
```

When a request for data arrives, **Request** handles it if the format is **CF_TEXT** and if the request is for one of the three items supported. **Request** creates a local memory block and puts the data into it as text.

Request can use the **static** data item **pInstance** to get a handle on the dialog box.

```
BOOL DDEServerTest::Poke(LPSTR pItem, WORD Format,
                        GlobalMem * pData)
{
  if (Format!=CF_TEXT) return FALSE;
  Lock Buf(pData);
  char szValue[32];
  lstrcpy(szValue,(LPSTR)Buf.Buffer);
  int Value = atoi(szValue);
  ColorScrollBar* pScroll=NULL;
  if (!lstrcmp(pItem,"ITEM_1"))
    pScroll=ServerBox::pInstance->pItem1;
  else if (!lstrcmp(pItem,"ITEM_2"))
    pScroll=ServerBox::pInstance->pItem2;
  else if (!lstrcmp(pItem,"ITEM_3"))
    pScroll=ServerBox::pInstance->pItem3;
  if (pScroll){
    pScroll->SetPosition(Value);
    ServerBox::pInstance->ScrollMoved(*pScroll,Value);
    return TRUE;
  }
  return FALSE;
}
```

If a client pokes some data, **Poke** sets the position of the corresponding scroll bar. The data must be in **CF_TEXT** format, and it will contain the scroll bar position as text. **Poke** must also call **ScrollMoved** so that **ServerBox** is aware that the scroll bar position has changed. **ServerBox** then informs any other clients linked to that scroll bar that the value has changed.

```
BOOL DDEServerTest::Link(LPSTR pItem, WORD Format,
                         BOOL bDeferred){
  return ServerBox::pInstance->AddLink(pItem, Format,
                            bDeferred, *this);
}

void DDEServerTest::Unlink(LPSTR pItem, WORD Format){
  ServerBox::pInstance->RemoveLink(pItem, Format, *this);
}
```

The **Link** and **Unlink** member functions call **AddLink** and **RemoveLink** in **ServerBox**.

```
BOOL DDEServerTest::Execute(LPSTR pString)
{
   ServerBox::pInstance->pCommand->SetText(pString);
   return TRUE;
}
```

Execute places the string in the command control of the dialog box.

ddesmain.cpp

```
#include "Serverbx.hpp"

HANDLE hInst;
HANDLE hPrevInst;
LPSTR  CmdLine;

int PASCAL WinMain(HANDLE hInstance, HANDLE hPrevInstance,
    LPSTR lpszCmdLine, int nCmdShow)
{
    hInst = hInstance;

    ServerBox Box;
    Box.OpenBox(NULL, "DDEServer");
    return 0;
}
```

Again, **WinMain** creates the dialog box and returns.

FIGURE 11-6   A Word for Windows document linked to DDEServe

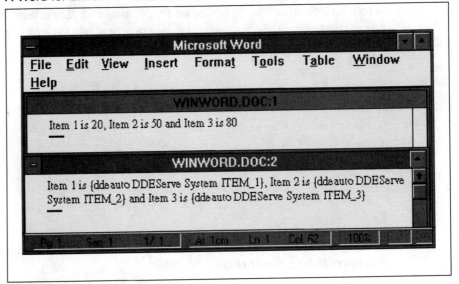

A DDE Client that Links with DDEServe

The server application above can be used by any application that supports DDE. It is possible to link the scroll bars with an Excel chart so that the chart changes as the scroll bars are moved. It is also possible to link the scroll bars to text in a Word for Windows document, as shown in Figure 11-6.

If you do not have an application that supports DDE, the following example client can be used with DDEServe directly. The DDEClien application is another dialog box with three scroll bars as shown here. The scroll bars are linked to DDEServe. As the bars in DDEServe are moved, the scroll bars in DDEClien move in sympathy. If the scroll bars in DDEClien are moved, the new values are poked into DDEServe.

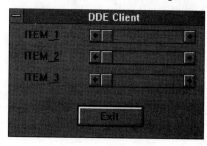

The two applications would appear to be more or less identical, but other DDE clients cannot link with DDEClien, since it is not a server.

clientbx.hpp

```
#ifndef CLIENTBOX_INC
#define CLIENTBOX_INC

#include "graydial.hpp"
#include "colscrll.hpp"
#include "ddelink.hpp"
#include "button.hpp"
#include "gslist.hpp"

class ClientBox : public GrayDialog {
public:
  ClientBox():GrayDialog(TRUE){};

protected:
  void InitDialog();
  void CancelClicked(Button& b);
  void ScrollMoved(ColorScrollBar& Bar, int Position);
```

```
  void Update(LPSTR pItem, WORD Format, GlobalMem * pMem);
  DDEClient * pDDEClient;
  ColorScrollBar * pItem1;
  ColorScrollBar * pItem2;
  ColorScrollBar * pItem3;
};

#endif
```

clientbx.cpp

```
#include "clientbx.hpp"
#include "dialog.h"
#include <stdlib.h>

void ClientBox::InitDialog()
{
  pItem1=new ColorScrollBar(hWnd,ID_ITEM1);
  pItem1->SetRange(0,100);
  pItem1->Color(RGB(0,0,0),RGB(255,0,0));
  pItem1->SetText("ITEM_1");
  pItem1->Position(this,
    (SCROLLBARCALLBACK)&ClientBox::ScrollMoved);

  pItem2=new ColorScrollBar(hWnd,ID_ITEM2);
  pItem2->SetRange(0,100);
  pItem2->Color(RGB(0,0,0),RGB(0,255,0));
  pItem2->SetText("ITEM_2");
  pItem2->Position(this,
    (SCROLLBARCALLBACK)&ClientBox::ScrollMoved);

  pItem3=new ColorScrollBar(hWnd,ID_ITEM3);
  pItem3->SetRange(0,100);
  pItem3->Color(RGB(0,0,0),RGB(0,0,255));
  pItem3->SetText("ITEM_3");
  pItem3->Position(this,
    (SCROLLBARCALLBACK)&ClientBox::ScrollMoved);

  Button * Cancel=new Button(hWnd,IDCANCEL);
  Cancel->Click(this,
    (BUTTONCALLBACK)&ClientBox::CancelClicked);
```

InitDialog first sets up the controls and then tries to establish a conversation.

```
  pDDEClient = new DDEClient(hWnd);
  if (!pDDEClient->Initialize("DDEServe","System")) {
    if (WinExec("DDEServe",SW_SHOW)>32)
```

```
            pDDEClient->Initialize("DDEServe","System");
}
```

If a conversation with DDEServe cannot be established, DDEClien launches it and tries again.

```
pDDEClient->Link("ITEM_1",CF_TEXT,this,
                (LINKCALLBACK)&ClientBox::Update);
pDDEClient->Link("ITEM_2",CF_TEXT,this,
                (LINKCALLBACK)&ClientBox::Update);
pDDEClient->Link("ITEM_3",CF_TEXT,this,
                (LINKCALLBACK)&ClientBox::Update);
```

The client sets up links with the three scroll bars.

```
Update("ITEM_1",CF_TEXT,NULL);
Update("ITEM_2",CF_TEXT,NULL);
Update("ITEM_3",CF_TEXT,NULL);
}
```

Update is the link callback, but calling it directly with a **NULL** memory block prompts **Update** to request the current value from DDEServe.

```
void ClientBox::CancelClicked(Button& b)
{
  delete pDDEClient;
  CloseBox();
}

void ClientBox::ScrollMoved(ColorScrollBar& Bar, int Position)
{
  char Item[32];
  Bar.GetText(Item,32);
  LocalMem Data(4);
  Lock Buf(&Data);
  wsprintf((LPSTR)Buf.Buffer,"%d",Position);
  pDDEClient->Poke(Item,CF_TEXT,&Data);
}
```

When the client's scroll bars are moved, the client pokes the new values to DDEServe.

```
void ClientBox::Update(LPSTR pItem, WORD Format,
                       GlobalMem * pMem)
{
```

```
if (!pMem) pMem=pDDEClient->Request(pItem,CF_TEXT);
Lock Text(pMem);
char szValue[32];
lstrcpy(szValue,(LPSTR)Text.Buffer);
int Value=atoi(szValue);
if (!lstrcmpi(pItem,"ITEM_1"))
  pItem1->SetPosition(Value);
else if (!lstrcmpi(pItem,"ITEM_2"))
  pItem2->SetPosition(Value);
else if (!lstrcmpi(pItem,"ITEM_3"))
  pItem3->SetPosition(Value);
delete pMem;
}
```

Update, the link callback, is called through DDE when the DDEServe scroll bars are moved. **Update** sets the thumb position of the client scroll bars. Usually in an application, **Update** would call the scroll bar callback, **ScrollMoved**, so that the application is aware that the scroll bar has moved. For this application, **Update** must not call **ScrollMoved**, since **ScrollMoved** would poke the value into DDEServe, which would then call **Update** because there is a link. An endless DDE loop between the two applications would be the result.

An Install Program

Most of the examples have been deliberately contrived to demonstrate as many features as possible, so it would be refreshing to have an example that could be useful in the real world.

If you distribute any program, even to a limited market, it is useful to have a program to install it. Of course, if you are distributing a major application, such as a word processor, you are likely to need a sophisticated installation program to install different options and change several types of files. There are a number of commercial installation programs that you can buy and configure to your product.

More often than not, the application will be fairly simple to install. Quite often, you only need to copy one or two files to the hard disk and install the application in Program Manager. There may be an option or two. Perhaps there are different versions of the application for different versions of Windows, or perhaps the application is available in different languages.

This Install program is intended for the more simple applications. The base **InstallDlg** class lets the user select a directory and a Program Manager group, as shown in Figure 11-7. The class will install the program icon in Program Manager using DDE commands.

You can derive subclasses of **InstallDlg** to handle more complex installations, but the base class will probably do for installing 95 percent of the Windows applications available.

The Profile Class

InstallDlg will use a new class, **Profile**. **Profile** provides a simple way of reading and writing to profile files. These are the .INI files. Most people know of the WIN.INI and SYSTEM.INI files, even if they do not fully understand the contents. Any application can have its own private .INI file, and they are very useful for storing user preferences for an application, or any application-specific parameters that you would like to keep while the application is not running.

FIGURE 11-7   The Install utility

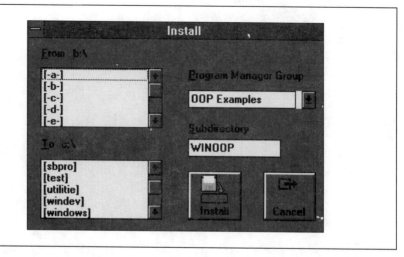

Working with 32 Bits

In Windows NT, the profile files are replaced by a central Registry. All the API profile functions work as they do for DOS Windows, except that they query the Registry instead of scanning an .INI file. Therefore, there is no need to change applications for NT as long as they use the API functions, or a class such as **Profile**, that uses the API functions internally.

The only thing that an application must avoid doing is to write directly to the .INI file. Some installation programs copy a default .INI file into the user's system but that will not work under NT.

There are Microsoft SDK functions **GetPrivateProfileInt** for integers and **GetPrivateProfileString** for strings, but the **Profile** class extends the facilities and makes them easier to use.

profile.hpp

```
#ifndef  PROFILE_INC
#define  PROFILE_INC

#include "winobj.hpp"

class Profile : public WinObj{

protected:
  char AppName[20];
  char FileName[150];

public:
  Profile(
    UINT Name,               // Resource Id of name
    LPSTR pFile=NULL);       // FileSpec

  Profile(
    LPSTR pName,             // Application name
    LPSTR pFile=NULL);

  void StringSet(            // Set a profile string
```

```
        LPSTR pKey,
        LPSTR pData);

    void StringGet(                // Get a profile string
        LPSTR pKey,
        LPSTR pData,
        UINT Size,
        LPSTR pDefault="");

    DWORD HexGet(                  // Get a hex number
        LPSTR pKey,
        DWORD Default=0);

    void HexSet(                   // Set a hex number
        LPSTR pKey,
        DWORD Value);

    int IntGet(                    // Get an Int
        LPSTR pKey,
        int Default=0);

    void IntSet(                   // Set an Int
        LPSTR pKey,
        int Value);
}; // class Profile

#endif   // PROFILE_INC
```

In addition to integers and strings, the **Profile** class provides 32-bit values in hex. A standard profile file integer is only 16 bits in 16-bit Windows and is insufficient for many values, such as colors that are 24 bits wide.

profile.cpp

```
#include "profile.hpp"

Profile::Profile(UINTName, LPSTR pFile)
{
    LoadString (hInst, Name, AppName, sizeof(AppName));
    if (!pFile) {
      lstrcpy(FileName,AppName);
      lstrcat(FileName,".ini");
    }
    else lstrcpy(FileName,pFile);
}

Profile::Profile(LPSTR pName, LPSTR pFile)
```

```
{
    lstrcpy(AppName,pName);
    if (!pFile) {
      lstrcpy(FileName,AppName);
      lstrcat(FileName,".ini");
    }
    else lstrcpy(FileName,pFile);
}
```

An instance of **Profile** can be created in one of two ways: by providing the entry in the string table of the application name, or by providing the application name directly as a string. As a default, the profile file is assumed to be the application name with an .INI suffix, but the full path name of the profile name may also be specified.

```
void Profile::StringSet(LPSTR pKey, LPSTR pData)
{
    WritePrivateProfileString(AppName,pKey,pData,FileName);
}

void Profile::StringGet(LPSTR Key, LPSTR pData,
                        UINT Size, LPSTR pDefault)
{
    GetPrivateProfileString(AppName,pKey,pDefault,
                            pData,Size,FileName);
}
```

The string and integer functions just call the Microsoft SDK routines directly.

```
DWORD Profile::HexGet(LPSTR pKey, DWORD Default)
{
    char sz[12];
    DWORD i=0;

    if (!GetPrivateProfileString(AppName,pKey,"",sz,12,FileName))
      return Default;
    LPSTR sp=sz;
    while (*sp) {
      i <<=4;
      if (*sp<='9') i += *sp-'0';
      else i += (*sp&0x4f) -'A' +10;
      sp++;
    }
    return i;
```

```
}

void Profile::HexSet(LPSTR pKey, DWORD Value)
{
  char sz[12];
  wsprintf(sz,"%lx",Value);
  WritePrivateProfileString(AppName,pKey,sz,FileName);
}
```

HexGet and **HexSet** convert the 32-bit value into a hexadecimal string and write that to the file.

```
int Profile::IntGet(LPSTR pKey, int Default)
{
  return GetPrivateProfileInt(AppName,pKey,Default,FileName);
}

void Profile::IntSet(LPSTR pKey, int Value)
{
  char sz[12];
  wsprintf(sz,"%d",Value);
  WritePrivateProfileString(AppName,pKey,sz,FileName);
}
```

The API does not include a **WritePrivateProfileInt** function, so **IntSet** converts the integer into a string and writes that.

The InstallDlg Class

The **InstallDlg** class is derived from the **Dialog** class:

install.hpp

```
#ifndef INSTALLDLG_INC
#define INSTALLDLG_INC

#include "edit.hpp"
#include "combobox.hpp"
#include "dirlist.hpp"
#include "graydial.hpp"
#include "iconbutn.hpp"


class InstallDlg : public GrayDialog {
public:
```

```
     InstallDlg():GrayDialog(TRUE){};
protected:
  void InitDialog();
  void OkClicked(Button& b);
  void CancelClicked(Button& b){CloseBox();};
  void DoubleClick(ListBox& lb){OkClicked(Button());};
  BOOL Copy(                      // Copy a single file
    LPSTR FromPath,
    LPSTR ToPath,
    LPSTR FName);

  virtual BOOL InstallFiles(     // Install all files
    LPSTR FromPath,
    LPSTR ToPath){};

  virtual LPSTR Command()        // Command to execute
    {return "";};                // the application

  virtual LPSTR Name()           // Name of the application
    {return "";};

  virtual LPSTR SubDir()         // default subdirectory
    {return "";};

  virtual LPSTR Group()          // Default Program
    {return "";};                // Manager group

  virtual BOOL Installed(        // Files have been installed
    LPSTR ToPath)
    {return TRUE;};

  ComboBox * GroupBox;
  DirListBox * LbFrom;
  DirListBox * LbTo;
  Edit* pSubDir;
};
#endif
```

The **InstallDlg** class contains virtual member functions that sub-classes can use to define the fields in the dialog box and the Program Manager group. These are the member functions in the class:

BOOL InstallFiles(LPSTR FromPath, LPSTR ToPath)   This function installs the application files. **FromPath** is the source directory, usually the distribution diskette, and **ToPath** is the directory in which the user wishes to install the application. If the subclass returns **FALSE**, **Install** stops the installation, but the dialog box remains on the screen.

LPSTR Command( )   This function returns the command string that runs the application. Install adds the directory path. The string is usually the application name with the .EXE suffix, but if any command line switches are needed, they can be specified here. **InstallDlg** passes this string to Program Manager.

LPSTR Name( )   This function returns the name of the application as it will appear under the application icon in Program Manager.

LPSTR SubDir( )   This function specifies the "suggested" subdirectory that **InstallDlg** will create for the application.

LPSTR Group( )   This function specifies the "suggested" Program Manager group. This could be an existing group, such as *Accessories* or *StartUp*—but remember, these names are language-dependent.

BOOL Installed(LPSTR ToPath)   This function indicates that the files have been installed, and the item has been added to Program Manager. The subclass can use this member function to display a *Program Installed* message or to run the newly installed program. If the subclass returns **TRUE**, **Install** closes the dialog box.

The combo box in the dialog box will be initialized with a list of current Program Manager groups.

install.cpp

```
#include "install.h"
#include "file.hpp"
#include "profile.hpp"
#include "ddeclien.hpp"
#include "install.hpp"
#include <direct.h>

void InstallDlg::InitDialog()
{
    char Buffer[120];
    Button * Ok=new IconButton(hWnd,IDOK,"AppIcon");
    Ok->Click(this,
        (BUTTONCALLBACK)&InstallDlg::OkClicked);

    Button * Cancel=new IconButton(hWnd,IDCANCEL,"exit");
```

```
Cancel->Click(this,
        (BUTTONCALLBACK)&InstallDlg::CancelClicked);
pSubDir= new Edit(hWnd,ID_SUBDIR);
pSubDir->SetText(SubDir());

LbFrom=new DirListBox(hWnd,ID_LIST_FROM,ID_PATH_FROM,".");
LbFrom->DClick(this,
        (LISTBOXCALLBACK)&InstallDlg::DoubleClick);
if (lstrlen(SubDir())) lstrcpy(Buffer,"C:\\");
else GetWindowsDirectory(Buffer,sizeof Buffer);
LbTo=new DirListBox(hWnd,ID_LIST_TO,ID_PATH_TO,Buffer);
LbTo->DClick(this,
        (LISTBOXCALLBACK)&InstallDlg::DoubleClick);
GroupBox = new ComboBox(hWnd,ID_GROUP);
```

InitDialog sets up the controls. If there is a "suggested" subdirectory, **InstallDlg** offers to install the files in this directory on drive C:. If there is no subdirectory, **InstallDlg** offers to install the application in the Windows directory. This simple installation procedure might be appropriate for a small utility.

```
Profile Groups("Groups","progman.ini");
char GroupName[8];

int GroupNr=0;
while(++GroupNr<99) {
   wsprintf(GroupName,"Group%d",GroupNr);
   Groups.StringGet(GroupName,Buffer,sizeof Buffer);
   if (!Buffer[0]) continue;
   File GrpFile(Buffer);
   GrpFile.Seek(0x16);
   int NamePos;
   GrpFile.Read((LPSTR)&NamePos,2);
   GrpFile.Seek(NamePos); // position of group name
   GrpFile.Read(Buffer, sizeof Buffer);
   GroupBox->Add(Buffer);
   }
   GroupBox->SetText(Group());
}
```

InitDialog uses the PROGMAN.INI profile file, which appears in Figure 11-8, to find the .GRP files in which Program Manager stores details of each group. The 16-bit value at offset 0x16 in these .GRP files contains the offset within the file of the group name. **InitDialog** reads this name and adds it to the combo box.

FIGURE 11-8 Program Manager files

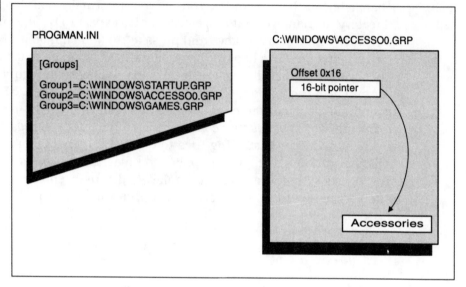

```
void InstallDlg::OkClicked(Button& b)
{
    if (GetFocus()==LbTo->hWnd){
      char DirName[60];
      LbTo->DirSelection(DirName, sizeof DirName);
      LbTo->SetPath(DirName);
          return;
        }
    if (GetFocus()==LbFrom->hWnd){
      char DirName[60];
      LbFrom->DirSelection(DirName, sizeof DirName);
      LbFrom->SetPath(DirName);
          return;
        }
    char Buffer[200];
    HCURSOR hOldCur=SetCursor(LoadCursor(NULL,IDC_WAIT));
    pSubDir->GetText(Buffer,sizeof Buffer);
    LbTo->SetPath(Buffer);
    mkdir(Buffer);
    LbTo->SetPath(Buffer);
    if (!InstallFiles(LbFrom->Path(), LbTo->Path())) return;
```

When the user clicks on the *Install* button, he or she may be trying to change one of the directories. A user would normally double-click on a directory to change it, but a user might also expect to be able to select a directory with the arrow keys and press RETURN to change it. If either of the two directory lists has the focus, **InstallDlg** assumes that the user is just trying to change directories. It extracts the chosen directory from the list and sets the listbox to that directory. Recall that the **DirList** class maintains a current directory for each instance, so there is no problem in having two list boxes that contain different directory listings. If neither list has the focus, **InstallDlg** tries to create the subdirectory and then calls **InstallFiles** to copy the application files. **InstallDlg** is resilient to any liberties that the user may take. If the user enters an existing directory or a path in the directory box, that will be acceptable.

```
char GroupName[60];
GroupBox->GetText(GroupName, sizeof GroupName);
if (GroupName[0]) {
  DDEClient ProgMan(hWnd);
  ProgMan.Initialize("PROGMAN","PROGMAN");
  wsprintf(Buffer,"[CreateGroup(%s)]",(LPSTR)GroupName);
  ProgMan.Execute(Buffer);
  wsprintf(Buffer,"[AddItem(%s\\%s,%s)]",
          LbTo->Path(),Command(),Name());
  ProgMan.Execute(Buffer);
}
SetCursor(hOldCur);
if (Installed(LbTo->Path())) CloseBox();
}
```

InstallDlg uses DDE commands to install the application in Program Manager. Program Manager is the DDE application *PROGMAN* and supports the topic *PROGMAN*. **InstallDlg** sends the commands *CreateGroup* to create a new group and *AddItem* to install the application into it. If the group exists, the *CreateGroup* command simply activates it. Always use *CreateGroup*, even if you are sure that the group exists—the alternative command *ShowGroup* appears not to work correctly with some versions of Program Manager.

When you are using **wsprintf**, remember to cast strings to **LPSTR**. Since **wsprintf** accepts a variable number of parameters, they are not typed, and so pointers are not automatically converted to **far**. If you give **wsprintf** a **near** pointer, the application will fail.

```
BOOL InstallDlg::Copy(LPSTR FromPath, LPSTR ToPath, LPSTR FName)
{
  char From[120];
  char To[120];
  if (FromPath[lstrlen(FromPath)-1]=='\\')
    FromPath[lstrlen(FromPath)-1]=0;
  if (ToPath[lstrlen(ToPath)-1]=='\\')
    ToPath[lstrlen(ToPath)-1]=0;
  wsprintf(From,"%s\\%s",FromPath,FName);
  wsprintf(To,"%s\\%s",ToPath,FName);
  File FromFile(From);
  if (FromFile.Size()) {
    File ToFile(To,OF_CREATE);
    ToFile=FromFile;
    return TRUE;
  }
  return FALSE;
}
```

Copy will copy a file from one path to another. If the path specifications contain a terminating backslash, **Copy** removes it. If the source file cannot be opened, or if it is empty, **Copy** returns **FALSE**.

install.h

```
#define ID_SUBDIR        109
#define ID_EDIT_FROM     102
#define ID_EDIT_TO       106
#define ID_GROUP         111
#define ID_LIST_FROM     104
#define ID_LIST_TO       107
```

If you want to design your own dialog box, or perhaps add options to the existing box, use the values defined in INSTALL.H.

Using InstallDlg

It is a simple matter to derive classes from **InstallDlg**. Now, here is an installation program intended to install itself.

instexpl.cpp

```
#include "install.hpp"

HANDLE hInst;

class InstallExample : public InstallDlg {
```

```
virtual BOOL InstallFiles(LPSTR FromPath, LPSTR ToPath){
  return Copy(FromPath,ToPath,"install.exe");
};
virtual LPSTR Command(){return "install.exe";};
virtual LPSTR Name(){return "Install";};
virtual LPSTR SubDir(){return "WINOOP";};
virtual LPSTR Group(){return "OOP Examples";};
};

int PASCAL WinMain(HANDLE hInstance, HANDLE hPrevInstance,
    LPSTR lpszCmdLine, int nCmdShow)
{

    hInst = hInstance;

    if (hPrevInstance)  return 0;
    InstallExample Id;
    Id.OpenBox(0,"INSTALL");

    return 0;
}
```

The **InstallExample** class defines the virtual member functions, and **WinMain** creates the dialog box. **InstallExample** proposes to copy INSTALL.EXE to a new subdirectory called **WINOOP**, and to create a new Program Manager group called *OOP Examples.*

Keep in mind that the user is not obliged to run Program Manager. There are other shells available. If the user has the Norton Desktop for Windows, for example, **InstallDlg** will not find the list of existing groups to display in the combo box. The Norton Desktop does support the *PROGMAN* DDE topic, however, so if the user accepts the suggested group, or enters the name of an existing group, the application will be properly installed in a Norton Desktop group.

Tips for Implementing DDE Applications

With the DDE classes you can add DDE facilities to your application quite simply. Your *primary* goal, however, should be to make things simple as possible for the user. Users should be able to use the facilities without needing to know what DDE is.

DDE Clients

For the user, the simplest way of linking data is with the *Paste Link* menu command. You should support *Paste Link,* using the **DDEClip** class.

When you close your application, you should store details of the link in a file, together with the last values received. When the file is reopened, you should ask the user whether the links should be reestablished. The user may have a reason for not establishing the link. Perhaps there are not enough system resources to run another application at that moment, or perhaps the user knows that the linked data is on a network node that is temporarily inaccessible.

Your application may use a word processor or spreadsheet for generating reports and documents. Your application might send the other application commands to open an existing template, and then poke data into the template, before sending a command to print the document. You should consider placing the commands in an external file. The user then has a chance of modifying the commands to suit a new or alternative version of the other application. Even if the user is unable to do that, you will find it easier to modify and distribute the changes to users if the changes are in an external file.

DDE Servers

The first problem is to define the topic and item names. You should support the *System* topic. If the application is based on files or documents, the file specification will usually be the topic. The choice of item names will depend on the type of application, but remember that a DDE item may be a range of items.

If your application has a large choice of items and does not expect very many links, it is usually more efficient to place all the links for a topic in one list and to check the list whenever the application data changes. If a topic has a fixed number of items, it may be more efficient to maintain a separate list for each item.

Even if you do not want to support data links, you should consider implementing the DDE *Execute* command facility. If you do that, users who have an application with a macro language supporting DDE can use it to automate your application.

If you want to design your application so that it can support DDE *Execute*, take care that the dialog boxes simply prompt the user for information and do not act on it. Open a dialog box, and, when it returns, use the data in the dialog box instance to execute the command. If you do that, it is a simple matter to execute DDE commands when they arrive. For example, if you open a dialog box and then process the results, as the MultNote application did in Chapter 10, here is what happens:

```
case IDM_OPEN:
  FileDlg Open(".\\*.cpp");
  if (Open.OpenBox(hWnd,"OPEN_FILE")) {
    if (ChildIterator(this,
          (MDICHILDCALLBACK)&NoteFrame::AlreadyOpen,
        Open.FilePath())))
    new Note(Open.FilePath());
  }
  break;
```

Then when you are parsing remote commands, you can implement them without having to display a dialog box, like this:

```
case COMMAND_OPEN:
  if (ChildIterator(this,
      (MDICHILDCALLBACK)&NoteFrame::AlreadyOpen,
      Param1))
  new Note(Param1);
  break;
```

Summary

Any application that generates or accepts raw data, especially numeric data, can benefit from using DDE. If the application supports DDE, users can use the data in other applications that support DDE, especially in spreadsheet programs and word processors.

For other applications, you might consider implementing a DDE command set. Users can then use another application that provides a macro language to automate your application. Both Excel and Word for Windows have an extensive macro language.

There are also other facilities for communication between applications available under Windows. Object Linking and Embedding (OLE) is especially useful for document-based applications. Remote Procedure Calls (RPC) is a mechanism for implementing client-server systems when the server is on a network node. RPC is interesting because it works across operating systems, so the server could be a Windows NT or UNIX machine, and the client a DOS Windows machine.

 Remember Supporting Dynamic Data Exchange is a simple way of greatly increasing the power and flexibility of most applications. Even if your users are not yet accustomed to sharing data between different applications, they will ultimately appreciate the time and labor that they save with this capability.

Epilog

You have probably noticed that in each chapter of this book, the class implementation was fairly difficult to follow, but that once the class was written, it was very easy to use. In fact, there have been three different levels of complexity:

☐ Designing base classes requires in-depth experience with Windows.

☐ Deriving new classes from an existing base class might require some knowledge about a particular area of Windows, but this task is much quicker and easier than writing the base class.

☐ Using a class is quick and easy, and in most cases requires only a minimal knowledge of Windows.

In fact, you have seen that object-oriented programming is a scalable environment suitable for programmers of all levels of experience. OOP offers power and performance to skilled developers, and the simplicity of building-blocks to those grappling with the environment for the first time. This versatility is the primary reason why you or your company should adopt object-oriented programming for your projects.

You should also have noticed the potential for reusing C++ classes, and you may well be thinking of using at least one or two of the classes in this book for your next project. If you go further and develop new classes, then publicize them! Reusable classes are no good if their inventor keeps them secret, so let others know about them. If your company would prefer not to make your work public, then at least let the other people in your company know about it.

I am certain that object orientation is going to be the major software engineering methodology of this decade, and that C++ will be the major computing language (after COBOL, of course). Most major companies in the United States and Europe have adopted C++ and object-oriented program design, so if your company has not, now is the time to start.

APPENDIX

Installing the
Supplemental Diskette

*T*he diskette that accompanies this book contains the source code for the classes, and all the files that you will need for compiling and linking the example programs.

Before installing the diskette, you should have installed both Microsoft Windows itself, and your compiler. Once they are installed, follow these three steps to build the example programs:

☐   Copy the contents of the diskette to your hard disk.

☐   Build the class libraries.

☐   Build the example programs.

There are batch files on the diskette that build the libraries and programs for the most common compilers, but there are so many combinations of compilers and versions of Windows that I cannot guarantee that you will not have to modify something in order to build the system. It is also likely that you will have to modify the batch files or even the class source if there has been a new release of the compiler or Windows since this book was published. You should treat the batch files as templates to get you started.

Copying The Diskette to Your Hard Disk

The files on the disk have been compressed using the PKZIP utility. To install them on your hard disk, follow these steps:

☐   Create a new directory on your hard disk.

☐   Expand the files using the PKUNZIP utility. Be sure to use the -d option.

For example, if the new directory is called C:\PORTER then the command:

PKUNZIP -d b:\porter.zip c:\porter\

will expand the files and place them in a directory tree starting at C:\PORTER.

If you do not have a copy of PKUNZIP, there is a copy on the diskette. If you find PKUNZIP useful, do not forget to register. (You will find a registration coupon at the back of this book.)

When you have copied the files, you should look for a file called CHANGES.TXT, which may contain details of any last-minute changes. You will also find a Help file that provides a ready reference to the class library. The file is PORTER.HLP. To see the Help information, use the Windows Help utility. You might find it easier if you install an item in Program Manager with the command:

WINHELP PORTER.HLP

then you will be able to invoke the Help system by clicking on the Program Manager icon.

While we do everything we can to ensure the quality of this book/disk package, occasional problems may arise. If you find that the disk is physically defective, please call or write:

Osborne McGraw-Hill
2600 Tenth Street
Berkeley, CA 94710
1-800-227-0900
(Monday through Friday, 8:30 – 4:30, Pacific Standard Time)

The store where you purchased this package does not carry replacement diskettes, so please contact Osborne directly. Osborne can only replace defective disks. If you have questions of a technical nature you should contact the Technical Support department for your compiler. Remember that the major compilers are supported on CompuServe, and that you will often find other participants in a CompuServe forum who are prepared to answer any technical questions that you might have.

Building the Libraries.

When you have copied the files onto your hard disk, you will find that they are arranged in a number of directories. Each chapter that contains an example program has a corresponding directory. These directories are called CHAP03, CHAP04 and so on. There are also two directories called SOURCE and INCLUDE, and these contain the header files (.HPP) and the source files (.CPP) for all the reuseable classes.

The next step is to compile the classes in the SOURCE directory, and put them in object libraries in a new LIB directory. You will then be able to use these object libraries with the example programs and your own programs.

The classes should be arranged into these four libraries:

- CPPLIB - Contains all of the general purpose classes.

- CUSTLIB - Contains the owner-draw control classes.

- MDILIB - Contains the MDI-specific classes described in Chapter 10.

- DDELIB - Contains the DDE-specific classes described in Chapter 11.

You will find Make files in the SOURCE directory for building these libraries. Make is a utility that will automatically compile and link a number of separate modules into one application or library. A copy of Make is usually supplied as part of the compiler package, although it may be called something else—the Microsoft version is called either NMAKE or NMK.

If you have the Borland, Microsoft, or Zortech compiler, you will find a batch file in the main directory (the directory you may have called PORTER) . There are five batch files in all:

- BORLND30.BAT - Generates the libraries and the example programs for the Borland command line compiler, version 3.0, and the Windows 3.0 API.

- BORLND31.BAT - Generates the libraries and the example programs for the Borland command line compiler, version 3.1.

- MSC16.BAT - Generates the libraries and the example programs for the Microsoft 16-bit compiler, version 7.0.

- MSC32.BAT - Generates the libraries and the programs for 32-bit Windows, using the Microsoft 32-bit compiler.

❏   ZORTECH.BAT - Generates the libraries and the programs for the Zortech compiler, version 3.0.

If you have one of these compilers you should be able to simply run the batch file and watch as the system is built, but before you do, read the compiler-specific section later in this Appendix.

The Borland compiler is available in both a command line version or as an Integrated Development Environment (IDE) version. The IDE version is useful when you are developing a system interactively, but you need the command line version to build with Make. The more expensive Borland packages come with both versions of the compiler, while the budget packages only provide the IDE. If you only have the IDE, or if you have not installed the command line version, you will not be able to use the batch file, but in the SOURCE directory, you will find four files with the .PRJ suffix, corresponding to the four libraries. If you open one of these .PRJ files with the Borland IDE, you will be able to build the library from within the IDE. You will also find a .PRJ file for each of the example programs. Before you do this, you should create the new LIB directory under the directory where you installed the files. The batch files do this automatically.

If you have another compiler, you will need to adapt the Make files before building. All the Make files except those for the Zortech compiler use a common header file called INCLUDE.MAK, located in the main directory. INCLUDE.MAK contains all of the compiler-dependent commands and switches. You will usually be able to add another section to INCLUDE.MAK for the new compiler, using the existing commands as an example.

As they stand, the Make files will generate debugging information for all the classes. If you do not want debugging information, or if you are short of disk space, you can prevent debugging information from being generated by removing the definition of DEBUG from INCLUDE.MAK.

If you have a newer or older version of either the compiler or the Windows SDK, you may also need to change the switches in the INCLUDE.MAK file. Depending on which compiler you are using, you may see some compiler warnings when you compile the source.

Generating the Programs

Once the libraries have been built you can build the individual example programs. If you have run one of the batch files, it should have built the programs after having built the library. If you are building the programs manually, you will find Make files and .PRJ files in each of the chapter directories. You can use these or modify them as you wish. Notice that the Make files provided for building the example programs use the same INCLUDE.MAK file as the Make files for building the libraries.

If you have any problems, it is probably because the compiler cannot find a system include file or library. You may need to adjust the INCLUDE.MAK file. The next section covers likely problems for the compilers covered by the batch files.

Compiler Specifics

The batch files assume that the compiler has been correctly installed. As we all know, correctly installed software is more of an exception than a rule, so you may need to adapt your Make files or the batch files to suit your installation. You might also have problems with the **define** and **typedef** statements in the WINDOWS.H file. There are many versions of this file and they are all slightly different. This section highlights the most likely problems for specific compilers.

Microsoft 16-bit

There should be two environment variables, INCLUDE and LIB, that point to the Microsoft header files and libraries respectively. These should be set in your AUTOEXEC.BAT file, but if they are not, you can set them explicitly. The easiest way to do this is to insert SET commands at the beginning of the MSC16.BAT file.

The Microsoft compiler requires more memory when compiling C++ files than when it is compiling plain C files. If you have only used the compiler for C programs up until now, or if your machine has less than 4 MB of memory, you might encounter memory-related problems.

Borland Command Line

This compiler does not use environment variables, so you should set the directories for the Borland header files and libraries by modifying INCLUDE.MAK. The standard INCLUDE.MAK file assumes that the Borland system is installed on the same logical drive as the files for this book, in the directory \BORLANDC. If the Borland system is located on another logical drive, or if you have changed the name of the main Borland directory, you must change the directories in the Borland section of INCLUDE.MAK. Version 3.0 of the Borland compiler package provided version 3.0 of the Windows SDK, which did not include the files SHELL.LIB and SHELLAPI.H needed to implement drag-and-drop. The package also provided version 3.0 of the resource compiler, which does not recognize the /30 switch. Version 3.1 of the resource compiler uses this switch to mark executable files as able to be run under Windows 3.0.

The batch file BORLND30.BAT file defines the symbol NOSHELL to indicate that the Windows Shell facilities, which include drag-and-drop, are not available. In version 3.0 of the Borland compiler, there is a benign problem that causes it to output a shower of warning messages when compiling the class library. Just ignore them.

If you actually have version 3.1 of the Windows SDK, you should use BORLND31.BAT, even if you have version 3.0 of the compiler. If you are still using version 3.0 of the Borland compiler, you should consider upgrading. In addition to providing version 3.1 of the Windows SDK, the 3.1 compiler is faster for compiling C++ programs.

Borland IDE

If you are using the Borland IDE, you must open each project file (the .PRJ files) and build the project. Here again, if the Borland system is installed anywhere other than the BORLANDC directory on the same logical drive as the example files, you will need to change the directories using the *Options/Directories* menu item. Do not forget to create the LIB directory.

If you still have version 3.0 of the Windows SDK, you should remove the file DRAGDROP.CPP from the CPPLIB project, and add NOSHELL to the list of compiler definitions.

Zortech

At the time of writing only version 3.0 of the Zortech system was available. By the time you read this, a new version should be available. If you use version 3.0 you should be aware of the following points:

The Zortech Make utility is not compatible with the Microsoft Nmake utility, so there is a separate Make file in each directory called ZORTECH.MAK. You should use these Make files to build the system. The ZORTECH.BAT batch file calls each of these Make files in turn.

There were some problems with the resource compiler that came with Zortech version 3.0; as a result, it will not compile the resources for most of the examples in this book. This problem should have been corrected by now, but if it has not, you will need to use another resource compiler. The Make files use the Microsoft resource compiler, so if you have another resource compiler, such as the Whitewater resource toolkit, you will need to modify the Make files.

Version 3.0 of the Zortech compiler does not yet support the new Windows 3.1 features, and in particular, it does not include the SHELL library that implements drag-and-drop. If you do not have the SHELL.LIB and the SHELLAPI.H files, you will need to remove DRAGDROP.CPP from the ZORTECH.MAK file in the SOURCE directory and compile using the NOSHELL definition.

Microsoft 32-bit

I have tested the system with an early pre-release of Windows NT, so there may be some differences with the NT system that is available now.

Like the 16-bit version of the compiler, the Make file for the 32-bit compiler assumes that the environment variables INCLUDE and LIB are set to point to the correct directories. Under NT, you can set these environment variables using the Control Panel. After setting them, you will need to log in again before they take effect, but you will not need to reboot.

The WIN32 section of the INCLUDE.MAK file can be configured to build for different processors, but I have only tested it with the Intel processor.

If All Else Fails...

If you still cannot get the software installed and the compiler technical support department cannot help you, you can try contacting me on CompuServe 100014,1127. If you do not subscribe to CompuServe, but are on the InterNet, the address is 100014.1127@compuserve.com. Notice that (in the InterNet version, the comma between the two numbers becomes a dot.)

Please feel free to write to me if you have any other comments or ideas regarding this book.

Index

511

Z

PKZIP/PKUNZIP SHAREWARE LICENSE

To register PKZIP/PKUNZIP, please return this form with a CHECK or MONEY ORDER for $47 (U.S.) to:

PKWARE

7545 North Port Washington Road
Glendale, WI 53217

Complete and return this registration card to be granted a single user license. Licensed users will be entitled to a copy of the complete documentation and notification of future updates and new products.

After signing and returning this registration card, you may make copies of PKZIP/PKUNZIP for backup purposes and operate the programs on any computer, providing only one user and one copy of the programs are in use at any one time.

--✂

Single User Registration

I am enclosing my fee of $47 for registration of PKZIP/PKUNZIP. Please send the latest documentation and inform me of future updates.

Name: _____

Company: _____

Street Address: _____

City: _____

State: _____

Zip: _____

Home phone: _____

Business phone: _____

I agree to the terms and conditions of this software license:

Signature: _____ Date: _____